THE NEANDERTALS

THE NEANDERTALS

Of Skeletons, Scientists, and Scandal

Erik Trinkaus **and**
Pat Shipman

VINTAGE BOOKS

A Division of Random House, Inc.

New York

Library of Congress Cataloging-in-Publication Data
Trinkaus, Erik.
The Neandertals: of skeletons, scientists, and scandal/Erik Trinkaus and
Pat Shipman.—1st Vintage Books ed.
p. cm.
Originally published: New York: A. A. Knopf, 1993.
Includes bibliographical references and index.
ISBN 0-679-73299-3 (pbk.)
1. Neanderthals. 2. Fossil man—History. I. Shipman, Pat, 1949– .
II. Title.
[GN285.T73 1994]
573.3—dc20 93-42583
CIP

Display Typography designed by Mia Risberg

Manufactured in the United States of America
10 9 8 7 6 5 4 3

To Kim and Alan,
Zachary and Amelia,
Sable and Chutney:
thanks

Contents

Authors' Note

This is a book about the history of science and the science of history. It is also a book about people, from long-dead Neandertals to living scientists, and the way in which each person's present shapes his or her view of the past. Neither of us is an historian of science, nor is this a scholarly text. It is simply a story—as accurate a tale as we can make it, but one that is shaped by the recognizable imprint of our own prejudices and biases. It is, inevitably, our own peculiar view of a field in which we both grew up.

In writing this work, we have quoted liberally from the written and spoken words of many others. With the exception of occasionally trying to improve clarity (for example, by changing the capitalization of words from uppercase to lowercase or vice versa), we have left each author's words as they were written, complete with archaic or alternative spellings and grammar. Our intent is to transmit the full flavor and ambiance of the originals. For our own words, we have chosen to follow current spellings of names and places—Neander*tal* instead of Neander*thal*, for example, or Beijing instead of Peking. And yet, where these words are incorporated into the name of an institution, we have given that institution's preferred spelling at the time in question. To avoid pedantry, we have ignored the technical distinction between *cranium* (the bones of the upper jaw, face, and braincase) and *skull* (a cranium plus a lower jaw) and have used the terms interchangeably. The notes at the end of the text give full references (and occasional asides) for the reader who wishes to know more.

Throughout this enterprise, many colleagues, friends, and acquaintances have shared their knowledge with us, ferreted out obscure information or photographs, or entertained and educated us with reminiscences about events and persons long gone. We are indebted to those listed below. If we have omitted individuals or institutions, it is not from a lack of gratitude. We owe so much to so many that it is difficult to compile a comprehensive list.

Thanks to Ofer Bar-Yosef, Amilcare Bietti, Lewis R. Binford, Daniel Borzeix,

Mme. Bouyt, C. Loring Brace IV, Günter Bräuer, Gert Brieger, Daniel Cahen, Rachel Caspari, Jean-Jacques Cleyet-Merle, Claudine Cohen, Glen Cole, Silvana Condemi, Yves Coppens, Jean-Marie Cordy, Suzanne Dallemegne, John de Vos, Giacomo Giacobini, Phillip Gingerich, Mrs. Hooijer-Ruben, F. Clark Howell, William W. Howells, Jean-Jacques Hublin, Robert Kruszynski, Steven Kuhn, André Langaney, André Leguebe, D. Loubatières, Giorgio Manzi, Ernst Mayr, Rosine Orban, Jakov Radovčić, Mrs. J. Seebo, B. Holly Smith, Fred H. Smith, Ralph S. Solecki, Frank Spencer, T. Dale Stewart, Mary C. Stiner, Christopher B. Stringer, Anne-Marie Tillier, François Twiesselmann, Bernard Vandermeersch, Randall White, (the late) Allan Wilson, and Milford Wolpoff. And also our special gratitude to Jonathan Segal, our editor at Knopf, for his thoughts, encouragement, and enthusiasm.

We have also been aided and abetted by the staffs of the Musée de l'Homme, the Bibliothèque Nationale, the Natural History Museum (London), the Rheinisches Landesmuseum, the Harvard Peabody Museum, the American Museum of Natural History, the Smithsonian Institution, the Welch Library of the Johns Hopkins University School of Medicine, and the Enoch Pratt Library.

For encouragement and sometimes unwitting but crucial moral support, we also thank Ginny Armstrong, Marla Caplan, (the late) Galina Gorokhoff, John de Montfort, Gail and Roger Lewin, Claire Van Vliet, and Delta Willis. Finally, let us flourish a cliché and thank our spouses, without whom . . .

Important Fossil Discoveries

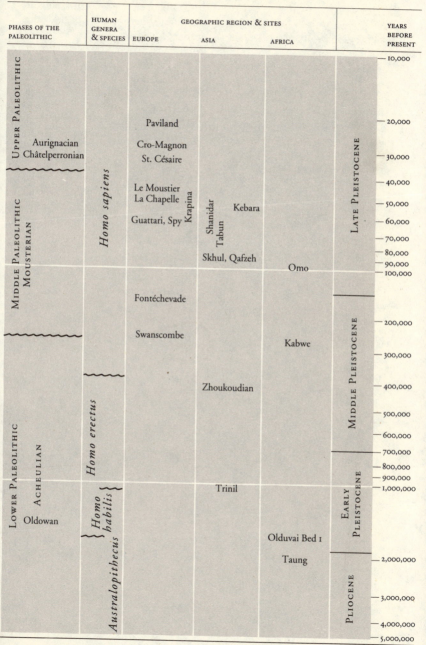

| PHASES OF THE PALEOLITHIC | HUMAN GENERA & SPECIES | GEOGRAPHIC REGION & SITES | | | YEARS BEFORE PRESENT |
		EUROPE	ASIA	AFRICA	
Upper Paleolithic — Aurignacian, Châtelperronian	*Homo sapiens*	Paviland, Cro-Magnon, St. Césaire, Le Moustier, La Chapelle, Krapina, Guattari, Spy	Shanidar, Tabun, Kebara, Skhul, Qafzeh	Omo	— 10,000 — 20,000 — 30,000 — 40,000 — 50,000 — 60,000 — 70,000 — 80,000 — 90,000 — 100,000 (Late Pleistocene)
Middle Paleolithic — Mousterian					
Lower Paleolithic — Acheulian, Oldowan	*Homo erectus*	Fontéchevade, Swanscombe	Zhoukoudian, Trinil	Kabwe	— 200,000 — 300,000 — 400,000 — 500,000 — 600,000 — 700,000 — 800,000 — 900,000 — 1,000,000 (Middle Pleistocene / Early Pleistocene)
	Homo habilis			Olduvai Bed 1, Taung	— 2,000,000
	Australopithecus				— 3,000,000 — 4,000,000 — 5,000,000 (Pliocene)

Cast of Characters

Important figures in the discovery and interpretation of Neandertals

Albert I of Monaco: Scion of the royal family, patron of prehistory and paleoanthropology, and founder of the Anthropological Museum of Monaco and the Institut de Paléontologie Humaine in Paris.

Andrews, Roy Chapman: Leader of the Central Asiatic Expedition to the Gobi Desert to find traces of early humans, who wrote the engaging and influential books *On the Trail of Ancient Man* and *Meet Your Ancestors*.

Arambourg, Camille: Modern French paleontologist, successor to Marcellin Boule at the Muséum National d'Histoire Naturelle, whose studies began dismantling Boule's apish reconstruction of Neandertals.

Arensburg, Baruch: Modern Israeli anatomist, one of the directors of the excavations at Kebara and coauthor of the description of the Kebara Neandertal skeleton, which includes a hyoid bone and a nearly complete pelvis.

Bar-Yosef, Ofer: Modern Israeli archeologist, one of the co-directors of the excavations at Kebara and defender of the idea that anatomically modern humans preceded Neandertals in the Levant.

Black, Davidson: Canadian physician who later studied under Grafton Elliot Smith; generally considered responsible for finding, recognizing, and naming *Sinanthropus pekinensis*, now known as *Homo erectus*, at Zhoukoudian.

Blanc, Alberto Carlo: Italian paleoanthropologist who described the Neandertal cranium from the Grotta Guattari at Monte Circeo and developed a theory that Neandertals had religious beliefs.

Bordes, François: French geologist and archeologist who proposed the standard, typological system for identifying and classifying Lower and Middle Paleolithic tools and tool assemblages, based on the European sequence.

Boucher de Crèvecoeur de Perthes, Jacques: Onetime playwright and favorite of Emperor Napoleon Bonaparte who described early stone tools from Abbeville, France, and was fooled by modern human remains that were planted in association with genuine stone tools at Moulin Quignon.

Boule, Marcellin: Predominant human paleontologist in France in the early twentieth century, director of the Institut de Paléontologie Humaine, professor at the Muséum d'Histoire Naturelle, and author of the classic monograph on the "Old Man" from La Chapelle-aux-Saints that painted Neandertals as apish, brutish, and shuffling.

Bouyssonie, Amédée and Jean (Abbés): French brothers and priests who excavated the Neandertal skeleton at La Chapelle-aux-Saints and turned it over to Marcellin Boule for analysis.

Brace, C. Loring IV: Iconoclastic physical anthropologist whose critical review resurrected the fate of the Neandertals as a major issue in anthropology in the early 1960s.

Bräuer, Günter: Modern German physical anthropologist who developed the "out of Africa" hypothesis, arguing that the earliest modern humans developed from archaic humans in Africa and migrated outward.

Broca, Paul: Nineteenth-century French surgeon, founder of the Ecole d'Anthropologie, and a specialist in the exacting measurement of modern and human fossils.

Brose, David: American archeologist who, with Milford Wolpoff, wrote a seminal paper in 1971 pointing out that different tool types were not soundly linked to different types of hominids.

Buckland, William (the Reverend): Oxford professor of geology who popularized the notion of the Biblical Flood as the most recent of a series of global catastrophes. He studied some of the earliest-known human fossils in England and trained Charles Lyell and Roderick Murchison.

Busk, George: English zoologist involved with the Moulin Quignon remains and with the Gibraltar Neandertal, who collaborated with Hugh Falconer in naming *Homo calpicus*.

Cann, Rebecca: American biochemist whose Ph.D. thesis focused on the implications of evolution in mitochondrial DNA for the origin of modern races; a major proponent of the current Eve hypothesis, with her colleagues Mark Stoneking and the late Allan Wilson.

Cave, A. J. E.: English anatomist from St. Bartholomew's Hospital Medical College in London who worked with William Straus, Jr., to show that Neandertals were more modern anatomically than Boule's work had suggested.

Collignon, René: Alsatian anatomist who proposed that the tibial plateau must be perpendicular to the ground for erect, striding gait, a suggestion that was the basis of the false assertion that Neandertals shuffled along with bent knees.

Coon, Carleton: American physical anthropologist, expert on race and racial differences who proposed that the human races had been separate since *Homo erectus* and had evolved toward *Homo sapiens* in parallel. Coon was castigated as a racist in the early 1960s for his modified version of Franz Weidenreich's theory.

Crelin, Edmund: Modern gross anatomist at Yale Medical School and expert in the anatomy of the newborn who, with Phillip Lieberman, reconstructed the vocal tract of Neandertals based on the La Chapelle-aux-Saints skull and concluded that Neandertals lacked true language.

Cuvier, Georges: Gifted comparative anatomist, premiere mammalian paleontologist at the Muséum d'Histoire Naturelle in Paris in the late eighteenth and early nineteenth centuries, and foremost proponent of catastrophism.

Dart, Raymond A.: Australian anatomist working in South Africa who discovered *Australopithecus africanus*, the controversial Taung baby, then the earliest-known hominid.

Darwin, Charles Robert: Author of *The Origin of Species*, generally considered the father of modern evolutionary theory.

Dawson, Charles: English solicitor and enthusiastic amateur prehistorian who discovered the forged Piltdown remains in 1911.

de Mortillet, Gabriel: Revolutionary nineteenth-century anthropologist who joined Broca's Ecole d'Anthropologie, proposed massive social reforms, and revised Edouard Lartet's classification scheme by incorporating archeological materials.

de Puydt, Marcel: Belgian lawyer and amateur archeologist who, with Max Lohest, discovered the Neandertal skeletons at Spy d'Orneau, in 1886.

Dobzhansky, Theodosius: Fruit-fly geneticist, architect of the new evolutionary synthesis, and severe critic of Carleton Coon's *Origin of Races*.

Dubois, Marie Eugène François Thomas ("Eugène"): Dutch anatomist and physician who discovered *Pithecanthropus erectus* (now known as *Homo erectus*) in Java. Dubois insisted *Pithecanthropus* was a human ancestor in the face of bitter criticism, and pioneered the study of brain-to-body-size ratios.

Dupont, Edouard: Belgian geologist who discovered a fossil Neandertal jaw in the Trou de la Naulette in 1865.

Elliot Smith, Grafton: Australian anatomist and brain expert at the University of Manchester, teacher of Davidson Black and Raymond Dart, and major figure in the debate over the forged Piltdown fossils.

Evans, John: London anatomist who showed that the Moulin Quignon jaw was modern.

Falconer, Hugh: British paleontologist involved in uncovering the Moulin Quignon hoax and in excavations in Gibraltar for Neandertals, which he named *Homo calpicus* (with George Busk).

Fraipont, Charles: Son of Julien Fraipont and author of a 1936 monograph on the Neandertal child's cranium from Engis.

Fraipont, Julien: Anatomist at the University of Liège who described the Neandertal skeletons from Spy and suggested they had a bent-kneed, shuffling gait.

Frere, John: First to recognize and publish on worked stone tools from England in 1797.

Fuhlrott, Johann Karl: Schoolteacher from Elberfeld, Germany, to whom the original Neandertal bones were given and who recognized them as belonging to ancient humans.

Garrod, Dorothy: Archeologist, Fellow at Newnham College and later the first woman professor at Cambridge, and leader of the British School of Archaeology's excavations at Mount Carmel when the fossil human remains were found.

Gaudry, Albert: Professor of paleontology at the Muséum Nationale d'Histoire Naturelle, mentor of Marcellin Boule.

Geoffroy Saint-Hilaire, Etienne: Professor of vertebrate zoology at the Muséum Nationale d'Histoire Naturelle, and strong supporter of Jean-Baptiste Lamarck's ideas on evolution.

Gorjanović-Kramberger, Karl: Croatian paleontologist who discovered and described the Krapina Neandertal fossils at the turn of the century.

Haeckel, Ernst: German anatomist, natural philosopher, chief defender of Darwin in Germany, and bitter adversary of his former professor Rudolf Virchow. Haeckel coined the name *Pithecanthropus alalus* for the hypothetical missing link between apes and humans.

Hauser, Otto: Swiss-German antiquities dealer detested by the French for his discovery of the complete Neandertal skeleton in a burial at Le Moustier; also the discoverer of the Cro-Magnon, or anatomically modern, skeleton at Combe Capelle.

Heim, Jean-Louis: Physical anthropologist at the Musée de l'Homme who recently reassembled the La Chapelle-aux-Saints cranium and who also described the Neandertal skeletons from La Ferrassie.

Henslow, John Stevens: Professor of botany at Cambridge and friend of Charles Darwin.

Heys, Matthew H.: English schoolmaster who removed and described the Galley Hill skeleton.

Hinton, Martin Alistair Campbell: Volunteer at the British Museum (Natural History) in the early twentieth century, often cited as a suspect in the Piltdown forgery.

Hooton, Earnest Albert: First American professor of physical anthropology (at Harvard), teacher of many of the subsequent generation of physical anthropologists, and a witty and acerbic commentator on human evolution.

Howell, F. Clark: Influential American anthropologist who, starting in 1951, used the new understanding of evolutionary processes to explain Neandertal morphology in terms of genetic isolation and adaptation to a glacial regime.

Howells, William W.: Former student of E. A. Hooton's, twentieth-century pioneer in measurement and statistical analysis of skulls, and author of the influential *Mankind in the Making*.

Hrdlička, Aleš: Bohemian-born physician and physical anthropologist who conducted many massive anthropometric studies, stoutly challenged the evidence for early fossil humans in the Americas, criticized the forged

Piltdown fossils, and defended Neandertals as ancestors of modern humans.

Hublin, Jean-Jacques: French anthropologist who recently demonstrated that pre-Neandertal European fossils showed Neandertal-like features, thus supporting the continuity hypothesis and demolishing the pre-Sapiens scheme.

Huxley, Julian: Thomas Henry Huxley's grandson, one of the best-known biologists in wartime Britain, first secretary-general of UNESCO, and author of *Evolution: The Modern Synthesis*, a widely read book on the new evolutionary synthesis.

Huxley, Thomas Henry: Brilliant comparative anatomist and paleontologist, known as Darwin's "bulldog" for his spirited defense of the theory of evolution.

Keith, Arthur: Scottish anatomist, one of the foremost authorities on fossil humans in early-twentieth-century Britain. An avid proponent of the pre-Sapiens hypothesis that excluded Neandertals and *Homo erectus* from any direct role in human ancestry, Keith was prominent in the debates over *Eoanthropus dawsoni*, the Piltdown fossil.

King, William: Professor of anatomy at Queen's College, in Ireland, who proposed the name *Homo neanderthalensis* in 1864.

Klaatsch, Hermann: German anthropologist who initially rejected Darwinism and human evolution, but later, with Otto Hauser, named the Combe Capelle skeleton *Homo aurignacensis* and proposed it as the ancestor of only the Caucasian race.

Lamarck, Jean-Baptiste: Former botanist and professor of invertebrate zoology at the Muséum Nationale d'Histoire Naturelle late in the eighteenth century, who proposed a theory of evolution (transformism) prior to Darwin's.

Lartet, Edouard: French solicitor and great prehistorian who, working with Henry Christy, discovered many important Upper Paleolithic sites and proposed a sequence of ages, during which humans had lived, based on the associated animals.

Lartet, Louis: Edouard Lartet's son, a geologist who discovered the Cro-Magnon site that yielded archeological remains and five or more human skeletons that had been deliberately buried.

Leakey, Louis: Son of English missionaries in East Africa trained in anthropology at Cambridge, who shared Arthur Keith's strong belief in the pre-Sapiens theory and who, with his wife Mary, found many important hominid fossils much older than Neandertals in Olduvai Gorge, Tanzania.

Le Gros Clark, Wilfrid E.: Prominent British anatomist of the mid-twentieth century and professor at Oxford, who reversed the rejection of Raymond Dart's Taung baby as a hominid and collaborated with Joseph Weiner and Kenneth Oakley to expose the Piltdown forgery.

Leroi-Gourhan, Arlette: Modern French palynologist whose studies of pollen showed that one of the Shanidar Neandertal burials included wildflowers.

Lévêque, François: Modern conservator of archeological excavations for the Poitou-Charente region, and coauthor, with Bernard Vandermeersch, of the first reports on the Neandertal from Saint-Césaire, which was associated with Upper Paleolithic tools.

Lieberman, Phillip: Speech analyst at Brown University who, with Edmund Crelin, recently proposed that Neandertals lacked true language, relying on evidence from a flawed reconstruction of the Neandertal vocal tract.

Linnaeus, Carl: Seventeenth-century Swedish scientist who devised the systematic classification of organisms according to their physical likenesses.

Lohest, Marie Joseph Maximin ("Max"): Belgian geologist who, with Marcel de Puydt, found the Neandertal skeletons at Spy d'Orneau in 1886 and described them with Julien Fraipont.

Lubbock, John: Neighbor of Charles and Emma Darwin, influential banker, foremost British archeologist of the age, and author in 1865 of *Pre-Historic Times*, a book that set out the sequence of archeological ages in Europe.

Lyell, Charles: Prominent English geologist, great friend of Charles Darwin, and promulgator of uniformitarianism, the premise that the currently observable geologic processes (not catastrophes) acting over vast amounts of time were responsible for modern geologic features.

MacCurdy, George Grant: American archeologist, director of the American School for Prehistoric Research in Palestine who was involved with the discovery and excavation of human fossils at Mount Carmel.

MacEnery, John (Father): Irish clergyman who, in 1825, found fossil human remains associated with flaked flint tools, and extinct fossil animals in Kent's Cavern, England.

Manouvrier, Léonce-Pierre: Professor of physical anthropology at the Ecole d'Anthropologie at the turn of the century, director of the Laboratory of Anthropology at the Ecole des Hautes Etudes, and assistant director of the physiological research station of the Collège de France; a preeminent anthropometrician.

Marston, Alvin: English dentist who found the Swanscombe skull in Kent in 1935 and who seriously questioned the association of the various Piltdown fossils.

Maška, Karel: Schoolteacher turned prehistorian who discovered the Neandertal mandible at Šipka, and one of the founding fathers of central European Paleolithic archeology.

Mayr, Ernst: Bird taxonomist and highly influential evolutionary theorist. Mayr helped bring together natural history and genetic theory to form the new evolutionary synthesis in the mid-twentieth century.

McCown, Theodore D.: American anthropologist who, as a young man, supervised the digging at Skhul and wrote up the Mount Carmel skeletons with Arthur Keith, pointing out the mixture of modern and Neandertal features.

Mendel, Gregor: Austrian monk generally credited with discovering the laws of genetic inheritance through his breeding of peas.

Miller, Gerrit, Jr.: Paleontologist at the American Museum of Natural History who correctly maintained that the Piltdown skull was a chimera comprised of an ape jaw and a human cranium.

Montagu, M. F. Ashley: Anthropologist who disparaged Carleton Coon's book, *Origin of Races*, at length in the 1960s.

Murchison, Roderick Impey: Important geologist of the nineteenth century, leader in many English scientific societies, and opponent of uniformitarianism. His work led to the organization of the earth's history into a standard succession of epochs and eras, with progressively more complex organisms.

Musgrave, Jonathan: Modern English anatomist who used multivariate statistics to compare the hand anatomy of Neandertals and modern humans.

Neander, Joachim: Name used by Joachim Neumann, seventeenth-century vicar and composer, for his musical works; the Neander Tal (Neander Valley) was named after him.

Neumann, Joachim: See Neander.

Neuville, René: French archeologist and consul in Jerusalem in the 1930s, who first excavated Jebel Qafzeh and found anatomically modern but ancient human remains.

Oakley, Kenneth: Chemist and paleontologist at the British Museum (Natural History) whose application of relative fluorine dating revealed that the Piltdown remains were a forgery.

Osborn, Henry Fairfield: Paleontologist at the American Museum of Natural History who believed that Asia was the birthplace of modern humans and helped sponsor the Central Asiatic Expedition to the Gobi Desert, hoping to find early human fossils.

Osterman, Stjepan: University of Zagreb student, assistant to Karl Gorjanović-Kramberger, and sometime supervisor of excavations at Krapina.

Owen, Richard: Prominent nineteenth-century biologist and archenemy of Thomas Henry Huxley.

Patte, Etienne: Paleontologist at the University of Poitiers, whose meticulous 1955 review of the evidence suggested Marcellin Boule's reconstruction of Neandertals as apish and primitive was incorrect.

Pei, Wenzhong: Well-known Chinese paleoanthropologist and director of the Cenozoic Research Laboratory. As field director of excavations at Zhoukoudian, Pei found the first skull of *Sinanthropus pekinensis* (now called *Homo erectus*) in 1929.

Pengelly, William: Successor to John MacEnery in collecting fossils and stone tools from Kent's Cavern in England.

Peyrony, Denis: Prehistorian who excavated the Neandertal burials at La Ferrassie.

Piveteau, Jean: Modern French paleontologist at the Sorbonne, and former student of Marcellin Boule.

Prestwich, Joseph: Nineteenth-century English geologist who was asked to help determine whether the Moulin Quignon finds were authentic.

Putnam, Carleton: Author of *Race and Reason: A Yankee View*, widely perceived as racist; this work provoked accusations that Carleton Coon had collaborated with him and was also racist.

Pycraft, William Plane: Assistant to Arthur Smith Woodward at the British Museum (Natural History) at the time of Piltdown. An expert on birds, Pycraft wrote in 1928 a monograph on the Broken Hill fossils, which he called *Cyphanthropus rhodesiensis*.

Rak, Yoel: Modern Israeli physical anthropologist and coauthor of the description of the Neandertal skeleton from Kebara that includes a hyoid bone and a nearly complete pelvis.

Rosenberg, Karen: Modern American paleoanthropologist who countered Erik Trinkaus's prolonged-gestation hypothesis by arguing that Neandertal's large birth canal simply reflected the robust, large-headed build of the mothers.

Schaaffhausen, Hermann: Professor of anatomy at the University of Bonn who, with Johann Fuhlrott, described the original Feldhofer Neandertal.

Schmerling, Phillipe-Charles: Belgian doctor and anatomist who, in the 1830s, excavated and described fossil human remains (including Neandertals) from the Belgian caves of Engis and Engihoul.

Schwalbe, Gustav: German anatomist, vehement supporter of Darwinism, founder of *Die Zeitschrift für Morphologie und Anthropologie* (*Journal of Morphology and Anthropology*), and known for his unilineal hypothesis that Eugène Dubois's *Pithecanthropus* and Neandertals (*Homo primigenius*) evolved directly into modern humans.

Sergi, Sergio: Father of modern human paleontology in Italy who studied the Saccopastore Neandertal remains and proposed a pre-Neandertal theory of human evolution. Sergi collaborated with Alberto Blanc, comparing the damage on the Monte Circeo Neandertal cranium to that produced by Melanesian headhunters.

Simpson, George Gaylord: Renowned American paleontologist and one of the prime architects of the new evolutionary synthesis who showed how the fossil record could be interpreted in terms of natural selection and evolutionary trends.

Smith, Fred: Modern American physical anthropologist, former student of Milford Wolpoff, analyst of the Neandertal remains from Vindija and Krapina, and a proponent of the hypothesis that Neandertals evolved into modern humans.

Solecki, Ralph: American archeologist who excavated several intact and partial Neandertal skeletons at Shanidar, Iraq, and in the 1970s developed a theory that Neandertals had religious beliefs.

Sollas, William: Prominent English geologist at Oxford in the early twentieth century who was much involved in the Piltdown discussions.

Spencer, Frank: Modern physical anthropologist and historian of science, author of a comprehensive assessment of Aleš Hrdlička's work and a cogent review of the Piltdown incident.

Stewart, T. Dale: Modern physical anthropologist at the Smithsonian Institution who analyzed most of the Shanidar Neandertal remains and subsequently turned them over to Erik Trinkaus for further study.

Straus, William, Jr.: Anthropologist and anatomist at Johns Hopkins University whose work with A. J. E. Cave revealed numerous inaccuracies in Boule's reconstruction of La Chapelle-aux-Saints; he was thus responsible for helping to "humanize" Neandertals.

Stringer, Christopher: English physical anthropologist who is among the staunchest current advocates of the replacement hypothesis, believing that anatomically modern humans arose in Africa and spread outward, replacing Neandertals.

Teilhard de Chardin, Pierre (Père): French Jesuit priest and paleontologist who was involved with finding the canine of the Piltdown skull; he later became an adviser to the Geological Survey of China and was involved with the Zhoukoudian *Homo erectus* fossils, originally known as *Sinanthropus pekinensis*.

Thorne, Alan: Modern Australian paleoanthropologist who, with Milford Wolpoff, formulated and defended the multiregionalism (or regional continuity) hypothesis.

Tillier, Anne-Marie: Modern French paleoanthropologist, trained by Bernard Vandermeersch, who studied and compared the juvenile material of Neandertals and early modern humans in order to understand their development.

Topinard, Paul: Former student of Paul Broca, his successor at the Ecole d'Anthropologie, and an analyst of Neandertals.

Trinkaus, Erik: American author of a monograph on the Shanidar remains and coauthor of this book. Trinkaus emphasizes the importance of deducing behavior from the fossil record.

Twiesselmann, François: Belgian medical doctor and current physical anthropologist at the Institut royal des Sciences naturelles de Belgique (the Belgian Royal Institute of Natural Sciences), and one of the first to apply statistical analyses to the study of fossil humans.

Vallois, Henri: Professor at the Institut de Paléontologie Humaine, director of the Musée de l'Homme, and former student of Marcellin Boule who continued to defend the pre-Sapiens theory after Boule's death.

Vandermeersch, Bernard: Modern French paleoanthropologist who reexcavated Jebel Qafzeh and described the anatomically modern human skeletons found there, and coauthor, with François Lévêque, of the paper announcing the "last Neandertal" found at Saint-Césaire associated with Châtelperronian tools.

Virchow, Rudolf: German physician, teacher, father of modern pathology, and foremost German physical anthropologist in the last half of the nineteenth century. Virchow was deeply opposed to the idea of human evolution and largely responsible for the rejection of Neandertal remains as pathological.

von Koenigswald, G. H. R.: German-Dutch paleontologist who worked in Java with W. F. F. Oppenoorth and discovered the *Homo erectus* fossil humans at Sangiran.

Wallace, Alfred Russel: Self-taught natural historian who independently developed the ideas of survival of the fittest and natural selection, which are more usually identified with Darwin.

Washburn, Sherwood L.: Prominent American physical anthropologist, former student of E. A. Hooton's, and architect in the 1950s of the "New Physical Anthropology," which was based on detailed treatment of functional anatomical units. Washburn accused Carleton Coon of being racist in the early 1960s.

Weidenreich, Franz: German Jewish anatomist, successor to Davidson Black in Beijing, who wrote the monograph on the Zhoukoudian *Homo erectus* (then, *Sinanthropus pekinensis*) remains, and created the regional continuity hypothesis.

Weiner, Joseph: South African anthropologist, trained by Raymond Dart, who worked with Kenneth Oakley and Wilfrid E. Le Gros Clark to show that the Piltdown remains were deliberately forged.

Wilberforce, Samuel (Archbishop): Huxley's antagonist and unsuccessssful leader of the attack on Darwinism at the British Association meeting in Oxford in 1860.

Wilson, Allan: American biochemist who, with Vincent Sarich, pioneered the use of biochemical techniques to measure evolutionary distances and rates. He was a major advocate of the Eve hypothesis, and a proponent of the idea that the evolutionary distinction between Neandertals and modern humans was that only the latter had articulate speech.

Woodward, Arthur Smith: Keeper of Geology at the British Musuem (Natural History) and fish expert who, with Charles Dawson, described the forged Piltdown remains.

Wolpoff, Milford: Modern American physical anthropologist who, with Alan Thorne, updated the multiregionalism hypothesis, which states that different regional groups of *Homo erectus* evolved locally into the different living races of mankind.

THE NEANDERTALS

Prologue

Serendipity played the joker that August day in 1856.

No one would have suspected that anything transpiring in the Neander Valley, near Düsseldorf, would change the course of human history. The valley, though used for years as a site for quarrying limestone, was lovely and green, overlooking the Düssel River; no farms or dwellings interrupted the solitude, ideal for outings or picnics. There was no hint that the place was anything more, or less, than a simple pastoral locale.

The name of the valley harked back to a now-obscure seventeenth-century composer, once the organist at Düsseldorf and vicar of St. Martin's. His actual name, Joachim Neumann, must have seemed too common for church records. Perhaps he was a trifle pompous, inclined to put on airs. Perhaps his vanity outweighed his musical judgment, and he expected his hymns and airs to be better remembered. Did he hope, fondly, that "Praise the Lord, the mighty King of Glory" would go down in history among the great church music of the century? Would his compositions be honored with those of Bach and Buxtehude? Unlikely; and yet, like many composers of the time, he translated his surname into a classical language, coupling Neander, the Greek for "New Man," with his Christian name for posterity's sake.

His flock liked his music, or perhaps his sermons. In any case, they honored his memory by calling the valley the Neander Thal. It was many years later that the *h* was dropped from *thal*, when an attempt was made to modernize German spelling so that it reflected the pronunciation.

Though no contemporary of Neumann, Alexander Pope had epitomized in words a view of our place in nature that would have seemed familiar. Indeed, Pope's words are so elegantly cadenced they might have served as the text for a hymn, the hymn of the New Man:

> *Know then thyself, presume not God to scan;*
> *The proper study of mankind is man. . . .*
> *He hangs between; in doubt to act or rest;*
> *In doubt to deem himself a god, or beast;*
> *In doubt his mind or body to prefer.*

For it was here, in the picturesque New Man Valley, that the greatest human quest began—the quest to reconcile the god and the beast, to understand the essence of human nature.

The small limestone caves and overhangs that dotted the steep slopes had been dissolved out of the solid rock by eons of trickling water. In 1856, only the two Feldhofer grottos remained untouched by quarrymen's picks and blasting powder. The entrance of the grottos lay sixty feet above the Düssel River. The opening was narrow, too small to admit a human easily, and it was impossible to see clearly what lay within, even if the entrance could be reached. The grottos could not be approached from below, for the sheer, rocky cliff face rose nearly vertically from the river to a small plateau at the mouth of the caves. Indeed, this narrow shelf was difficult enough to approach from above, which was why these grottos were the last to be quarried. But the time had come that August day for the caves to be emptied and their contents exposed.

The foreman clambered carefully down to the narrow plateau and laid a charge to open up the caves. After the blast, he assigned two laborers to shovel out the rubble and dirt. As they heaved layers of mud, rocks, and flint out of the Feldhofer grottos, their tools struck bone, and they stopped. What emerged from the soil near the entrance was, first, a skull: long and low with glowering, bestial browridges. Then, on the same level and farther from the opening, lay the strongly built, curved thigh bones of an individual more muscular than any normal human, part of a pelvis, a few ribs, some of the bones of the arm and shoulder.

The foreman thought them bones of a cave bear. Still, he had the workers put the larger bones aside for the schoolteacher from Elberfeld, Johann Karl Fuhlrott, who was a keen natural historian. Maybe Dr. Fuhlrott would want them for his collection; perhaps he could use them to teach the children something new.

Like so many other educated Europeans in 1856, Fuhlrott was thor-

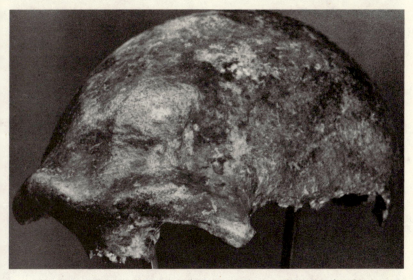

1. The skullcap from the Feldhofer grotto in the Neander Valley, found in 1856. As the first fossil of an extinct, archaic human to be recognized, this specimen opened many decades of controversy over human origins and antiquity.

oughly infected with the natural-history virus. He was a contented collector and happy observer of every plant, animal, and geologic outcrop he encountered. He combed the hilly countryside between Wupper, Düsselbach, and the Rhine, spending many blissful days hiking, collecting, and industriously taking detailed notes on what he found. He was immensely proud to have written, in his younger days, a small book about the classification of plants.

Looking for specimens of ferns or fossils, collecting wildflowers or birds' eggs, were unimpeachable Victorian pursuits, combining healthy outdoor activities with moral lessons. Study of these curiosities invariably illustrated the wisdom and ingenuity of the Creator, who so cunningly adapted His creatures to their allotted lives and who made His creations so appealing to the eye. Natural history afforded ample opportunity for invigorating walks with a young lady or gentleman of one's fancy, with the thoroughly honorable intent of painting pretty watercolors of sea anemones or collecting a new species of moss for the terrarium that graced the parlor. The soon-to-be-famous Dr. Fuhlrott was a true enthusiast of such endeavors.

A few weeks after the excavation was finished, the quarryman from the Feldhofer grotto asked if Dr. Fuhlrott would like to come and take the bones; the schoolteacher responded eagerly that he would. He was delighted at the prospect of crowning his collection with a partial skeleton of a cave bear.

Into Fuhlrott's hands were delivered the bones from the Neander Tal, bones like none ever seen before. And Fuhlrott, to his everlasting credit, knew what they were. No cave bear, no lesser creature however rare and wonderful had been salvaged from that rudely emptied cave. Fuhlrott knew, as he turned the specimens over and over in astonishment, that here was evidence of a new man. Not only seemingly ancient, these bones were unimaginably primitive: a skull of "extraordinary form," it was "a natural conformation hitherto not known to exist."

So many and such varied bones were present that Fuhlrott could see that the skeleton had surely been complete when first uncovered. He questioned the laborers and marched them back to show him the exact spot of the discoveries. How were the bones distributed? The men told him the skull lay nearest the cave entrance, and the other bones on the same horizontal plane. Were there bones of extinct animals, or stone tools? There had been lots of rocks; they couldn't say if they were tools. And how could they know what animals the bones came from?

Fuhlrott gnashed his teeth in frustration. How careless and negligent their collecting had been. Hoping for additional bones or fragments, he searched the remains of the rubble in vain. The details of the laborers' story were recorded in a letter that is now the only roughly contemporary account.

Fuhlrott knew he had made an important discovery, but he could not have foreseen its consequences. He held in his hands the remains of a man who would drag Fuhlrott and his scientific colleagues, present and future, stumbling down a dimly lit path into the past. Along that uneven, twisting road, they would come face-to-face with specters of themselves, monsters of their own making. The fossils were mirrors that reflected, in all their awfulness and awesomeness, the nature and humanity of those who touched them. The new man, in his glowering silence and mystery, would show Fuhlrott and others—however much they squirmed and argued—the unthinkable: that humans were animals, too.

Over the century and a half since the laborers offhandedly shoveled out the bones of the man from the Neander Tal, scholars have sought to understand him and people like him. This striving has led them to reshape, even to re-create, their notion of the world. It has been a restless quest for a reality that can accommodate both these ancestors and their descendants, the humans who study them. Through the years, the shifting paradigms have drawn as much on the scientists and scholars themselves, and the times and social climates in which they lived, as they have on the ancient bones.

The attempt to discern the truth, to read the cryptically encoded message of the past, has proved a keen struggle. Resistance sprang up like an entangling, thorn-studded vine, firmly rooted in the very human dislike of change. The path to new ideas was blocked by obstacles: impassioned denials of facts, poisonous criticisms of analyses, and deadly suppression of theories. Yet the journey toward knowledge, with its El Dorado of new understanding, has proved a potent attracter that outweighed the dangers in the end. From this painful effort—proceeding in fits and starts, traveling direct roads and detours—has been born an image both of ourselves and of those long-since-dead people we call Neandertals.

On that sunny August day in a remote valley in western Germany, a man already dead for forty thousand years began a revolution that would change the world.

I

God or Beast?

The original Neandertal fossils burst onto an unsuspecting world. Almost no fossils from the human lineage had ever been recognized, and none had ever looked significantly different from modern humans, though the handful of scientific publications made much of minor differences. Indeed, the scientific term *hominid*—meaning all members of our evolutionary lineage, from the point of initial divergence from the apes up to and including modern humans—had yet to be coined. No one had figured out how such fossil material should be studied, because no one dreamed that hominid fossils unlike living humans would be found.

If no one expected fossils different from modern humans to be found, there was nonetheless tremendous interest in the skulls of different living human races. These were presented proudly to fledgling anthropological societies by explorers, missionaries, traders, and soldiers, and were examined with care, if utterly unsystematically, to determine their evident qualities. The point of interest was tracing the ancestry of the races, but the term was used differently in the nineteenth century than it is today. Whereas today the races of humans are large groups of people who have been sufficiently isolated from one another reproductively to develop recognizable clusters of biological characteristics—such as the mildly pigmented skin, straight dark hair, and brown eyes with epicanthic folds of the Mongoloids—*race* was then more often used to indicate national rather than strictly biological categories. Attempts to trace the origins of the Welsh as opposed to the English, or the Germans as opposed to the Austrians or French, were common.

Part of this concern with origins had to do explicitly with defining typical characteristics of various races—not only biological ones, but also such traits as honesty, intelligence, moral fiber, artistic nature. While this practice would now be seen as stereotyping and blatantly racist, it was not so then. Indeed, it was widely accepted that the races differed in their abilities and characters and thus in their "natural" place in the world. Inevitably, of course, in any such pronouncement the racial type of the writer came out at the pinnacle of the hierarchy, an attitude that was to cause increasing trouble during the early part of the twentieth century.

Once the skull of "the Australian" or "the Sikh" was in hand, the problems began. What measurements were to be taken? What differences were meaningful? How much variability in skull shape or size was expected, was normal? No one knew, though opinions were abundant.

Part of the interest was also in tracing one's own past, which led to a vibrant concern with the potsherds, ruins, and whatever implements and objects of prehistoric peoples could be found in the immediate area. Amateur archeologists, or antiquarians, as they were more often called, developed elaborate if largely fanciful schemes. One popular approach was to consult early writings, such as Roman or Biblical accounts, for their comments on the qualities, dress, habits, and homeland of various peoples they encountered. Descriptions, even obvious metaphors such as comments about wild or piercing eyes, were taken literally and were linked up with physical features wherever possible. Virtually everything thought to be very old was classified as either Celtic (meaning pre-Roman) or antediluvian (meaning predating the Biblical Flood). For most of the nineteenth century, no one believed in or anticipated discoveries that would demonstrate a history of humans and their ancestors stretching back over more than a few thousand years; the human past was different from the present only in the primitiveness of ancient peoples, not in their very essence and being.

Part of the problem was that in 1856 there was no generally accepted belief in evolution, although scientists had been struggling with evolutionary ideas for years. For centuries, evolution hovered on the verge of blossoming in writings on natural history or travelogues like a will-o'-the-wisp: intangible, unclear, seen only fleetingly and out of the corner of the eye, disintegrating into nothingness when one tried to grasp it. With the acuity of hindsight, it is tempting to see the mid-nineteenth century as ripe for the idea of evolution. It seems now an irresistible notion, like a

great ocean liner plowing calmly and powerfully through the waves—
and dragging with it, as inevitably as seaweed on an anchor, the fact of
the evolution of humans.

To some few, perhaps, evolutionary ideas were inevitable. Indeed,
upon reading Charles Darwin's *The Origin of Species*, Thomas Henry
Huxley exclaimed, "How extremely stupid not to have thought of that!"
It is a generous remark for the man more brilliant than Darwin, the man
who many have said should have, *must* have, discovered evolution—the
man who, in the end, forced the acceptance of Darwin's theory by his
own eloquence and wit. But, while Darwin's evolutionary theory struck
the genius Huxley and resonated like a gong with truth, it was not so
happily received by many others. To most people at the time, evolution—and most particularly human evolution—did not seem likely or
expected at all. When the flower of evolution finally opened in the sun,
nearly all were amazed at the form and color it took.

Still, much of the groundwork had been laid for acceptance of evolutionary ideas. The first step had been the clear recognition of species, a
step that can be laid at the feet of a Swedish scientist, Carl Linnaeus.

Born in 1707 to a clergyman father, Linnaeus had shown an early and
consuming interest in botany, with disastrous consequences for his
schoolwork. While his industrious younger brother did well in school
and went off to the seminary, following in his proud father's footsteps,
Carl Linnaeus was so hopeless as a scholar that his father apprenticed
him to a cobbler. Only the intervention of the family doctor, Rothman,
saved Linnaeus from a life of replacing run-down heels and sewing soles.
Rothman was fascinated with natural science, as were many physicians
of the time. In 1728, with Rothman's persuasion, Linnaeus's father agreed
to allow him to leave the apprenticeship and go to Holland, to enroll
in medical school—virtually the only route to studying science then
available.

In medical school Linnaeus found his niche—and his ticket to immor-
tality—under the guidance of his botany professor. He flourished. In
1737, Linnaeus introduced his astonishing new method of classifying and
naming organisms in a work called *Systema Naturae*. His approach was
elegant. He examined individual organisms, and, based on their observed
traits (color of fur, number of toes, shape of leaf, number of pistils, and
so on), he grouped them into categories, or taxa, that reflected ordered
relationships. Individuals so highly similar to one another that they
produced fertile offspring constituted a species. So that there could be no

confusion about what was meant by a species, each was represented by a type individual that best expressed the characteristics and essence of that species. Species were then grouped together into genera, genera into families, and so on. It was an admirable method that relied implicitly upon the notion that the relationships among species could be worked out by careful studies of their physical features, in the same way that human families trace their resemblances through generations bearing the family nose or dimpled chin.

The beauty of this scheme was its simplicity; anyone could learn to do it and, in the nineteenth century when the passion for natural history ran high, many did. The virtue of Linnaeus's system lay in its specificity. The type individual, and no other, carries a two-part Latin name and a detailed, exacting description that belongs to whatever species it is put into. If relationships are reassessed, as they often are in fossils or other instances where few individuals are known, then the species name goes with the type. Where there are similar species, the description must include a diagnosis, a point-by-point comparison of the similar species coupled with an explanation of what separates them. Gone was the confusion of using long strings of adjectives to differentiate between two similar organisms or, worse yet, colloquial names whose interpretation relied on local knowledge. Imagine the embarrassment of the intrepid hunter going to shoot a "tiger" in Central America, thinking of the noble, 1,200-pound Bengal species and finding himself taking aim at a spotted creature no larger than a domestic tabby.

Linnaeus's work provided, literally, a system of nature. For the first time, there was a logical way to order the creatures of the world. Not incidentally, for the first time there was a rational way to organize specimens in museums and personal collections.

The world was frankly captivated. With the enthusiastic participation of hundreds of amateurs who thrilled to send him specimens in hopes that a new species lay among them, Linnaeus embarked on an orgy of naming. He was in the heady position of creating order out of the chaos of all of the organisms in the world. He was the hero, the authority, the "new Adam in the world's great garden."

Linnaeus loved it all with the passion of a man who has found precisely the right thing to do in life. Several of his portraits show him in the traditional dress of the Lapps, the reindeer-herding people among whom he spent some months. They also show the burning, intense gaze of this "most systematical genius." Though his posture and somewhat

eccentric costume seem unself-conscious, there is a certain hint of smugness in the slight smile. The man who was single-handedly responsible
for bringing order to the natural world was perhaps entitled to self-
congratulation.

Linnaeus's work let scientists—and everyone else, too—recognize and
identify species with certainty. As he remarked, a trifle pompously:

> The first step of science is to know one thing from another. This
> knowledge consists in their specific distinctions; but in order that
> it may be fixed and permanent, distinct names must be recorded and
> remembered.

Now that everyone could agree on what they were talking about, the
door was open for real progress in biology.

But Linnaeus's work by no means assumed, or even implied, evolution; it was a system of naming that said nothing about process. At the
outset, he believed quite firmly in the fixity of species—how could you
list and compare features if these were subject to change? But though
doubts seemed to creep into the later editions of *Systema Naturae*—and
a good botanist such as Linnaeus could hardly have failed to see "sports"
or different plants arising by what we would now recognize as mutation
from normal ones—he would not or could not acknowledge that the
resemblances among species implied paths of descent or networks of
inheritance.

Nonetheless, Linnaeus's *Systema Naturae* was the first step toward
evolution, in that it provided much needed order in our knowledge of the
biological world. It was also, perhaps, the second. For implicit in Linnaeus's approach—and explicit in its rapid acceptance and revolutionary
effect upon natural-history studies—was the notion that the world was
ordered and knowable. Linnaeus's work tacitly proclaimed that there
were natural laws and that people, by careful study, could discover these
laws. The proof of the discovery lay in its applicability; in other words,
if one correctly deduced a natural law, the evidence lay all around and
was readily observable. This firm belief in rules and order, in cause and
effect, in theory and evidence was an essential prerequisite to Darwinian
evolution. Linnaeus's work contributed, too, a heavy emphasis on meticulous anatomical and morphological studies, on comparison and detailed
observation that are the tools of all scientific work.

What Linnaeus's work also provoked was a public infatuation with
natural-history studies. It started with the desire to participate in Linna-

eus's mastering of the world. Send him a new plant, bird, or sea urchin, and you contributed to the compilation of Knowledge. What's more, Linnaeus might even immortalize you by naming it after you!

The interest soon grew from an esoteric pastime followed by a few educated men to an international craze of tremendous longevity. The availability of cheap microscopes and inexpensive aquaria or terraria (known as "fern-cases") led to a boom in natural history that gained ground steadily from the 1820s to the 1870s. Natural-history societies sprang up in every town and province. Collecting expeditions to capture rare mosses or catch yet another cabbage butterfly were organized. Seaside scenes were cluttered with enthusiasts paddling in tidal pools, seeking sea anemones or snails for decorative displays in the drawing room. Young ladies of good family were instructed in drawing and watercolors, so they might sketch their treasures in all their lovely and intricate detail. Written accounts of natural history were Just So Stories with morals and lessons. In Britain, at least, the charm of natural history was greatly enhanced by its purely amateur status. There were no professional natural historians, no exams, no lessons, no schools, no formality or drudgery to it whatsoever.

Popular though natural history was, it was uncoupled from any idea of evolution. Indeed, many of the great eighteenth- and nineteenth-century natural historians were also clergymen (proponents of what was called natural theology), who would have shuddered at any hint of change in God's creations because such would have been a sign of the imperfection of His plan. Unthinkable—or at least unspeakable.

But, in a peculiar way, Christianity itself was also an important prerequisite to the development of evolutionary ideas. The pivotal idea was that time was *linear*. Unlike most religions, which perceive time as cyclical and repetitive, Christian time has a beginning, a middle and, presumably, an end. Jesus Christ, be he historical figure or the Son of God, came once, lived, and died. In short, Christian, and now Western, time is directional; history progresses and does not recur in eternal repetitions; genuinely new discoveries are made; the world changes.

Though Christianity with its peculiar notion of directional time had long been widespread in Europe, peoples' unconscious assumptions about time were colored and changed by two discoveries in the eighteenth and early nineteenth centuries. The first discovery was breathtaking in its simplicity: extinct species were preserved as fossils.

To be sure, fossils had long been observed and studied as curiosities by naturalists such as the English clergyman John Ray, who at the close of the seventeenth century confessed himself puzzled by how purely geochemical processes could produce objects that so strikingly resembled leaves and shells. But there was only a slow-growing recognition that these were truly remnants of once-living organisms. Naturalists were slower still to understand that fossilized bones and teeth represented animals that no longer walked the earth or swam the seas. The first recorded reference to fossil bones is a report in 1758 by a gentleman named Fothergill who described fossil alligator bones found near Whitby, England.

If religion was important to the development of evolutionary ideas, so was politics. In the late eighteenth century, France—in particular, Paris—was the acknowledged European center of scientific work. German universities were strong in geology and mining, and natural history was barely supported at official levels anywhere in Britain. In 1793–95, the new French Republic, under its soon-to-be-emperor, Napoleon Bonaparte, consolidated its lead. The new France Napoleon envisioned would lead the world in this, as in all else.

Twelve professorships—a staggering number—were created in the newly constituted Muséum d'Histoire Naturelle (Museum of Natural History) in Paris, which later added "National" to its name. Four of these dealt with fossils and related issues, and those who took up those professorships had enormous influence. Two were well-established older men: the professor of the new science of geology was Barthélemy Faujas de Saint-Fond, aged fifty-one; the professor in charge of all invertebrates was the former botanist Jean-Baptiste-Pierre-Antoine de Monet, Chevalier de Lamarck, then forty-nine. There were also two young hotshots: Etienne Geoffroy Saint-Hilaire, who at the age of twenty-one became the professor of vertebrate zoology, and his protégé, Georges Cuvier, who at twenty-five (Napoleon's age) was soon to become professor of anatomy, the first of many promotions and successes. Cuvier's specialty was vertebrates, so his work brought him into close contact with Geoffroy Saint-Hilaire, and for some time they were in full agreement about everything.

Then Cuvier set out to make a comprehensive collection of anatomical specimens, which were dissected, drawn, and studied with zeal. His knowledge and influence grew with amazing rapidity. Early in 1796, it was no longer the fledgling but the master anatomist Cuvier who introduced the French scientific world to both the comparative approach to studying fossil animals and the concept of extinction, in a paper entitled

2. Georges Cuvier, the paleontologist at the Muséum National d'Histoire Naturelle (Natural History Museum) in Paris who maintained that the fossil record could be explained as a series of creations, each destroyed by a catastrophe and replaced by a subsequent creation

Mémoire sur les espèces d'élèphants vivants et fossiles, or *Note on the Species of Living and Fossil Elephants.* Scientific acclaim was not enough for Cuvier. His astonishing ability to transform the piles of disarticulated mammal bones, resembling butcher's refuse, into whole animals by using his profound knowledge of the anatomy of living species quickly earned him the public nickname "Magician of the Charnel House." Ambitious, young, and brilliant, Cuvier saw his job as the study of "animal machines" whose bodies worked by mechanistic, functional principles that could be deduced through exacting studies. He was the destiny of nineteenth-century French science personified.

But fossils as remnants of extinct life-forms took on awkward implications. Because the overwhelmingly dominant Christian beliefs of Europe at the time permitted only one episode of creation, the Biblical Creation, and no changes in species since, what, then, did these fossils represent?

A number of creative solutions had been expounded and reworked throughout the seventeenth and eighteenth centuries, arising anew every time someone began to understand that fossils truly represented remains of once-living organisms. Fossils were taken by some to be the remains of species that were still alive somewhere (else). (Thomas Jefferson, learned though he was, entertained the fond hope that Lewis and Clark would discover mastodons still alive in the midwestern United States.)

As exploration in the remoter regions of the world advanced, this notion became harder and harder to sustain. There was nothing better, to the public's mind, than a juicy, hair-raising account of someone else's travels to somewhere exotic. There was an almost insatiable craving for these often-enchanting and always-entertaining travelogues, full of wonderful tales and marvelous engravings. With few exceptions, such books are replete with betrayal by wily and unscrupulous natives, attacks by ferocious wild beasts averted only by the courage and skill of the writer, and impairment by tropical diseases that weakened the body but never the heart of the author, longing only to return to his beloved and long-suffering family who by now must have given up hope of his return. How else could those safe at home in their cozy armchairs experience such vicarious pleasure? Explorers' books sold thousands of copies, even those of dubious veracity. And yet, as darkest Africa and wildest Borneo became relatively familiar places, it became more apparent that many of the extraordinary creatures preserved as fossils were not still alive.

Another idea was that fossils represented species that were destroyed in the Biblical Flood because they failed to board the Ark. The relentless layers of geologic strata, recording untold combinations of species, made this, too, a difficult proposition to defend.

Eventually, this idea mutated into a third concept, known as catastrophism. Geological layers containing fossil species that overlay other layers holding different species represented a series of creations and world-destroying disasters, of which the Bible recounted only the most recent. In its purest form, catastrophism was little more than an intellectual ploy to reconcile geological evidence with belief in the Biblical account of Creation.

Cuvier soon became the leading proponent of a clever variant of catastrophism: the belief that regions of the earth were devastated by geological upheavals or "revolutions" in which all forms of life were destroyed. Recolonization of such areas by species from surrounding areas, rather than multiple creations, accounted for the succession of fossil faunas preserved in the rocks. Because each animal represented a finely tuned machine, tightly integrated and suited to its job in life, only large-scale revolutions of the earth could possibly wipe out species. The extinction of fossil forms, indeed, the destruction by catastrophes of entire worlds very different from the current one was Cuvier's theme song, and he sang it every chance he got.

In France in the early 1800s, things came to a one-on-one confrontation over the interpretation of fossils, an intellectual duel between the young Cuvier, expert in mammalian paleontology, and the aging Lamarck, the renowned French scholar who originally specialized in botany and later turned to invertebrates. Contemporary portraits could not emphasize their differences more clearly. Cuvier at the time was young, handsome, blue-eyed. He was small and tidy of build, vain and arrogant in the Napoleonic mold. His portrait shows him sporting an exuberant crop of powdered curls and a fashionable, double-breasted jacket—the perfect Napoleonic scientist-dandy. Born on August 23, 1769, he was christened Jean-Léopold-Nicolas-Frédéric Cuvier; but as his elder brother died during that year, the infant Cuvier was henceforth known as Georges in his stead. Though born of a good family, Cuvier did not enjoy wealth and leisure. Cuvier's lack of a family fortune proved unexpectedly useful to him during the violence of the French Revolution. While heads rolled in Paris, Cuvier was safe in the provinces, working as a tutor to a noble family in Normandy and studying natural history in his spare time. Some of his notes on mollusks were sent to Geoffroy Saint-Hilaire who, impressed, brought the young Cuvier to join the Muséum d'Histoire Naturelle, where he quickly rose to be professor of zoology.

3. Jean-Baptiste-Pierre-Antoine de Monet, Chevalier de Lamarck, the early-nineteenth-century French biologist who opposed Cuvier and was the first to argue cogently for evolution and the continuity of life

Lamarck was almost twenty-five years older, a product of an earlier time. His portrait shows him weary and anxious-eyed, with a large nose and a flattened, tightly curled, powdered wig. Born to impoverished aristocracy, Lamarck had spent his youth tutoring the son of the great naturalist, Buffon, from whom Lamarck received his scientific training. His portrait suggests that life often disappointed Lamarck; his hardships seemed greater, his successes much slower to come than Cuvier's. His appointment to the professorship at the museum was the hard-won success in mid-life of a man who had struggled to earn his keep and follow his scientific inclinations. He was conservative and old-fashioned, the type that might be called a fuddy-duddy, and yet given to theorizing freely on the basis of convictions without presenting facts.

Cuvier detested Lamarck and with him, evolutionary ideas. It was the fiercely burning hatred of the young and bold, convinced that their way is rigorously scientific, for their elders who seem hidebound, dithering, even senile. The new scientific establishment led by Cuvier also scorned the work of Buffon—Lamarck's mentor and the dominant figure in prerevolutionary French natural history—as mere "cosmological romances" that "retarded the progress of true knowledge in natural history."

For his part, Lamarck must have felt Cuvier spoiled, arrogant, too young, and too quick to succeed. Lamarck had studied under the great master of natural history; it was outrageous that this young pup thought he could fill Buffon's shoes. Lamarck would proceed, as he had always done, and this fad for revolutionary science would surely pass. He worked on, and published, a new revision of the classification of lower animals, which had been left in a state of confusion by the more botanically oriented Linnaeus. It was perhaps a pedestrian work, but a sound and impressive accomplishment.

In 1801, the intellectual duel began. Like Napoleon, then handily defeating Austria, Cuvier was on the rise. Cuvier published his classic work, *Extrait d'une ouvrage sur les espèces de quadrupèdes dont on a trouvé les ossements dans l'intérieur de la terre (On the Species of Quadrupeds of Which the Bones Are Found in the Interior of the Earth)*. In it, he argued that his systematic study of fossils yielded empirical evidence that Earth had undergone one or perhaps many revolutions or cataclysms whose violent effects had overwhelmed and caused the extinction of terrestrial mammals.

There was no evolution, no gradual transformation of species into other species, for this would deny the existence of Cuvier's pet notion: extinction. The notion of change and transmutation of species that Lamarck had mumbled about for years was simply wrong. Besides, Cuvier understood that the tenor of the times was at odds with a view of life that conflicted with church teachings. Napoleon was busily rallying the church to his support, to consolidate his position and secure his ascendancy. Ending the separation of church and state, he had just recognized the Roman Catholic church as the majority religion, while allowing freedom of worship to others. Cuvier, the Napoleonic scientist, was not about to endorse a transformist, anticlerical principle.

Seemingly oblivious to the dramatic political currents swirling about him, Lamarck published his reply to Cuvier in 1801, the year before Napoleon was declared consul for life. Lamarck's great theoretical book, *Système des animaux sans vertèbres* (*System of Invertebrate Animals*), gave the first clear statement of his life's beliefs and showed without doubt his debt to Buffon. In it, Lamarck took the old concept known as the Scala Naturae or the Great Chain of Being and gave it a new, evolutionary twist.

The Scala Naturae was a medieval idea in which all living creatures could be arranged on a continuous scale or chain of ever-greater complexity and perfection, until the entire animal kingdom could be organized one after the other, leading in imperceptible steps from the lowest worm up to God's last creation, humans, and thence upward to angels and archangels. In its original incarnation, the Great Chain of Being was intrinsically a defense of the immutability or fixity of species. Each species had its ordained place in the scheme of things; none could ever change because it had been created perfect for its niche. But Lamarck altered this view in significant ways to make it his own doctrine, transformism.

In simple terms, Lamarck proposed that species wriggled, slithered, crawled, or climbed up the steps of the Scala Naturae over the course of generations. Species thus were not fixed, or immutable; they evolved. Species were therefore not perfect as created but achieved perfection over the course of time. What seems astonishing now is that Lamarck believed this transformation was accomplished through an effort of will or an unconscious longing for destiny. As the animal uses its body parts in new ways, striving to adapt to changed conditions, it changes itself and its progeny. While not evolution in the Darwinian or modern sense, Lamarck's transformism was clearly a form of evolution and just as clearly contradicted the fixity of species.

"One must believe," Lamarck concluded, "that every living thing whatsoever must change insensibly in its organization and in its form. ... One must therefore never expect to find among living species all those which are found in the fossil state, and yet one may not assume that any species has really been lost or rendered extinct."

No extinctions? Cuvier was outraged and leapt to attack, even as Napoleon provoked European war again by expanding the borders of

France to their "natural" positions and by an aggressive colonial policy. By 1804, their parallel victories appeared complete. Napoleon was crowned emperor, the fulfillment of his ten years of increasing power and charismatic leadership. For his part, Cuvier was pointing in triumph to the fruits of a French military expedition to Egypt—a collection of mummified birds and mammals brought back from the pyramids—an expedition which, incidentally, also brought to Europe the famous Rosetta Stone. Although several thousand years old—indeed, almost as old as the Biblical Creation of the Earth (widely supposed by the faithful to have occurred at 9:00 a.m. on Sunday, October 23, 4004 B.C.)—none of the species preserved by the ancient Egyptians was in any way different from the modern ones. No extinctions? Hah! No evolution! Cuvier must have thought to himself, smugly. And what a seemingly perfect test of Lamarck's ideas, as the museum's own report on the expedition observed.

Lamarck was unimpressed; he expected transformations to occur so slowly as to be imperceptible, even over a trivial few thousand years. Unfazed, Lamarck published *Philosophie zoologique* (*Zoological Philosophy*) in 1809, doggedly restating his transformist convictions. Species changed because the world changed and presented new challenges, new conditions. In the famous example, the giraffe stretched his neck ever longer and longer to reach leaves higher and higher on the trees. Over time, the modern giraffe, with its greatly elongated neck, would inevitably evolve from a short-necked type. Lamarck even hinted at an apelike ancestry for humans, without saying what changes might have led an ape to transform itself into a human.

What is now difficult to accept is Lamarck's mechanism of change, known and discredited under the name of the inheritance of acquired traits. He was proposing, in effect, that if you cut the tails off enough mice, some of their offspring would be born tailless. However, because at that time even the most basic apparatus of genetic inheritance was entirely unknown (the use of the word *gene* to refer to the unit of Mendelian inheritance was not to be proposed until 1909), Lamarck's concept of inheritance was as plausible as any other.

It must have been an intense and unpleasant rivalry. Lamarck and Cuvier worked in the same institution, their disagreements and dislike aggravated by almost daily chance meetings or chitchat from colleagues about the other's doings. For years, they traded blows in the form of scientific publications and lectures, the effect of which was only to harden their positions. Their very specialties bespoke their worldviews. The one thought of slow change over eons of time: Lamarck, whose heart lay in myriad, passive, immobile creatures, with thousands upon thousands of offspring—the plants and invertebrates of the world. The other thought of sudden, bold changes, catastrophes, a make-it-or-break-it world: Cuvier, the doyen of lively, agile, scrapping, hissing, running mammals.

In time, Cuvier brushed aside evidence that he himself collected. Invertebrates, he challenged, would show extinctions coincident with changes in geological strata, just as mammals and reptiles did. This was unquestionably poaching on Lamarck's purview, and Lamarck must have grinned to himself and waited for the evidence to come in. When it did, Cuvier's own work on fossil mollusks and other invertebrates contained in adjacent strata showed them surviving apparent catastrophes with aplomb. But Cuvier was not one to capitulate, even when proven wrong. It was simply, he said, recolonization by a few survivors from an adjacent area; the catastrophe had not been as complete as usual.

The dispute spread to their colleagues, among them Geoffroy Saint-Hilaire, who had collected the mummified animals on the Egyptian expedition. Although initially convinced that the Egyptian material confirmed the fixity of species, Geoffroy Saint-Hilaire gradually transformed his views to resemble Lamarck's more closely. Geoffroy Saint-Hilaire prepared to pick up Lamarck's gauntlet.

In the meantime, Cuvier had become a major public figure as well as a leading scientist. While pursuing his academic course with vigor, he had also been appointed Imperial Inspector of Public Instruction, initiating major reforms in public education for which he was knighted, becoming Baron Georges Cuvier, in 1811. In 1814, Cuvier was elected to the Council of State and then managed to survive Napoleon's fall and subsequent exile without relinquishing his own position and considerable influence. Still, the post-Napoleonic period, when a limited monarchy ruled France, was perhaps an atmosphere in which dissension was more readily tolerated. In any case, Geoffroy Saint-Hilaire began publishing open challenges to Cuvier, suggesting that external influences could impact development, that species were thus able to change and evolve. In a book harking back to Lamarck's, called *Philosophie anatomique* (*Anatomical Philosophy*), Geoffroy Saint-Hilaire attempted to establish a continuity between invertebrates and vertebrates—long a major stumbling block to transformists—with cephalopods, the group that includes the nautilus and squid.

"There is, philosophically speaking, only a single animal," he asserted.

In 1825, just a few years before Lamarck's death, Geoffroy Saint-Hilaire boldly brought the fight onto Cuvier's own turf. He had the audacity to offer a new and different interpretation of living and fossil crocodiles from Cuvier's. Using Cuvier's own favorite methods of comparative anatomy, Geoffroy Saint-Hilaire showed that living crocodiles could have evolved from fossil ones under the influence of changing environmental conditions.

Cuvier did not receive this challenge happily. He had continued to grow in power and prestige, and now was appointed director of the museum, a popular public symbol of the scientist. His views, rigid and antievolutionist though they were, were clearly in the ascendancy. He had the power, he had the position, and he had the gift of writing and speaking well. At the time of his death, he was on the verge of being appointed minister of the interior, so irresistible had his influence grown.

Lamarck was now an old man losing his eyesight; his condition symbolized that he represented an older generation and out-of-date ideas. Besides, he had less taste and energy for the fight than Cuvier and, unlike his younger opponent, wrote abysmally boring works. When he died in 1829, blind and impoverished, Lamarck was much the loser of the debate in the eyes of contemporary scientists in France and Britain, yet he was far closer to the truth than Cuvier in any modern assessment.

Not content to end the fight with the death of his lifelong adversary, Cuvier stooped to insulting Lamarck posthumously. In 1832, Cuvier delivered a scathing indictment of Lamarck's theories thinly disguised as an elegy to his old enemy.

> A system resting on such foundations may amuse the imagination of a poet . . . but it cannot for a moment bear the examination of any one who has dissected the hand, the viscera, or even a feather.

In effect, he leveled the worst accusation at Lamarck he could think of: being a romantic, not scientific, natural historian. The thrust was all the more pointed because of the great and rising popularity in Germany of *Naturphilosophie*, a school of avowedly romantic appreciation of the glories of sacred Nature.

Cuvier's ungracious and small-minded vehemence may have been intended as much to bury Lamarck the man as to warn Geoffroy Saint-Hilaire not to resurrect Lamarck's evolutionary position. Cuvier himself died the same year, in a cholera epidemic. One can surmise that whoever gave the elegy was complimentary.

In England in the early nineteenth century, at the same time Cuvier's catastrophism was winning out over evolutionary ideas and Lamarck was struggling unsuccessfully to convince the French of the mutability of species, Erasmus Darwin was proposing a similar, but vague and woolly scheme of evolution in his *Zoonomia; or the Laws of Organic Life*. Darwin's notion gathered relatively few supporters, but it was much discussed, especially in the large and lively Darwin clan in which his famous grandson, Charles, grew up. The trouble was that the elder Darwin was too well known as a bit of a crank, an ideas man with no data to back them up, a spinner of plausible but flimsy theories, to be readily believed. Coleridge, the poet, even coined the term "Darwinizing" to mean constructing wild speculations. Were he not the beloved grandfather of the man who wrote *The Origin of Species,* Erasmus Darwin's contribution to evolutionary thought would be only an esoteric footnote in the history of science. As it is, he may have had a special influence within the Darwin family well beyond that which he enjoyed on the public at large. And, if there was a lesson to be learned from Erasmus Darwin's work, it was to keep your mouth shut about your ideas until you had reams of well-documented evidence to support it. To all appearances, the young Charles took note.

Catastrophism reigned for many years in France, England, and Germany. It was the Englishman William Smith, a practical field geologist with little taste for either theorizing or publishing, and no inclination toward evolutionary ideas, who inadvertently made the observations that eventually undermined catastrophism's hold.

Unperturbed by the theoretical works he had not read, Smith relied on the evidence of his eyes. His education came not in universities, museums, or learned societies through reading and discussion, but on the ground, as he tramped the countryside from one end of England to the other, surveying for coal deposits and laying out canal routes. Though Smith could read and write, he was hardly among the intelligentsia; book-learning and fancy philosophical theories were not for him.

In the late 1700s, Smith observed that the superimposed layers of sedimentary rocks represent time sequences: barring unusual upheavals, the older layers are on the bottom, the younger ones are on the top. In other words, those layers going deeper and deeper into the earth are like rungs on the ladder of time, stretching backward into the past.

For the first time, it began to be widely appreciated that Earth might be very ancient indeed. Time, like geology, seemed to stretch downward and backward into the depths. But so did life. Smith also proposed—and demonstrated irrefutably—that layers of the same age could be recognized and correlated on the basis of the life-forms preserved within them. By 1799, the unassuming Smith had applied this principle to the strata around Bath, though he had only circulated an unpublished manuscript explaining his methods.

No iconoclast, Smith cast his observations in language that was acceptable to the near-universal Christian beliefs of the day. "By use of fossils, we are carried back into a region of supernatural events," said Smith. As for the implicit conflict between layer after layer of extinct life-forms with the Biblical account of Creation, Smith concluded: "Each layer of these fossil organized bodies must be considered as a separate creation or is an undiscovered part of an older creation."

Catastrophism, and successive creations, satisfied Smith. But the principle of trusting to observations, not theory, the sheer depth of geologic time, and the readily apparent changes in organisms that inhabited layer after layer of Earth's crust, were soon to blow up catastrophist theory.

By 1815, Smith had published the first geological map of England, a monumental achievement by anyone's standards. In 1831, this plain man of the out-of-doors, a man by no means well educated or influential, was awarded the first ever Wollaston Medal of the Geological Society of London—a prestigious recognition of his contributions by the premiere scientific society in Smith's field. It was a triumph of common sense and sound observation over class distinctions and received wisdom.

Shortly after the publication of Smith's map of England, the Reverend William Buckland, a professor of geology at Oxford, adopted catastrophism from the French scientists and elaborated and reinforced it. Buckland popularized the identification of the most recent of Cuvier's geologic revolutions with the Biblical Flood, thus providing an authoritative and apparently scientific confirmation of the literal truth of the Biblical account of the Creation.

It was Buckland's style, as much as his substance, that was so influential. Much beloved by his students, Buckland gave some of his geological lectures on horseback so students could learn to read a landscape; even those lectures conducted under more ordinary academic circumstances were regarded as highly entertaining. Without doubt, Buckland—a bald, soft-faced man with kindly eyes and impeccable white collar—inspired or actually trained many of the great English geologists of the nineteenth century in their youth, including Roderick Impey Murchison and Charles Lyell.

In 1821, Buckland believed he had found the perfect proof of his diluvial theory in the form of Kirkdale Cave in Yorkshire. Kirkdale was full of fossil bones that had obviously been gnawed, when fresh, by an extinct species of hyena, whose bones also remained in the cave. *Reliquiae Diluvianae; or, Observations on the Organic Remains contained in Caves, Fissures, and Diluvial Gravels and on Other Geological Phenomena, attesting the action of an Universal Deluge*, published in 1823, was Buckland's pride and joy. This work showed, he believed, that a worldwide flood had swept into the Kirkdale Cave, and the many other similar fossil-bearing caves, killing off both the hyena and its prey. But, as the Bible described, then the floodwaters receded and creation began again.

Buckland remained highly regarded throughout his life, though his critics had some difficulty accepting the notion of an Universal Deluge. Not only did the evidence he cited fail to prove such a flood, but the evidence of one's eyes—the textbook of geology that lay on every hillside in England—suggested otherwise. But Buckland was genial, entertaining, and best of all, he showed that what you had always believed needn't be uncomfortably disturbed by scientific facts.

When, in 1829, a peculiar bequest called for the writing of a series of works "on the Power, Wisdom, and Goodness of God as manifested in the Creation," Buckland—by then Professor of Geology at Oxford *and* Dean of Westminster Abbey—was the obvious choice as one of the authors. The books were known as the Bridgewater Treatises after Francis Henry Egerton, the eighth Earl of Bridgewater, who had left the vast sum of eight thousand pounds for their publication, and they appeared at intervals between 1833 and 1836. The series was to be the last great celebration of the approach known as natural theology, for the accumulating evidence of paleontology and geology posed problem after problem.

As it became apparent that there were striking, even haunting resemblances among forms in successive layers, catastrophism had to be modified—even, so it seems, in France. The next version, known as biological progressionism, suggested that each of these successive creations produced creatures formed along the same general principles because a single Creator was responsible; the unity of design reflects His ideas, not any genetic inheritance. Indeed, the changes in design represent improvements or progress leading toward His grand creation: the human. Biological progressionism thus echoed familiar themes from the much older idea of the Great Chain of Being, once espoused by Lamarck. In effect,

4. Charles Lyell, the founder of modern geology and good friend of Charles Darwin.
Lyell accepted evolution and the Neandertals as human fossils only in the 1860s.

progressionism was a sort of supernatural evolution, except that all the
changes happened between species, not within them. The idea of progress
in the animal world also fitted well with the optimism for the future that
the burgeoning industrial revolution brought with it.

Dispelling catastrophism in all its forms was the last major step that
cleared the way for Darwinian evolutionary thought. This task fell to one
of the giants of nineteenth-century science: Charles Lyell.

Born in 1797, Lyell was the son of a well-to-do Scottish landowner and
a strong-willed woman of good Christian convictions. Shortly after
Charles's birth, his mother insisted that the family move from Scotland
to Hampshire, England, because she believed that wretched drunkenness
was endemic to Scotland. Thus, Lyell was raised in the English countryside with a botanizing, not boozing, father. As a young man at Oxford,
he joined the throngs at Buckland's flamboyant horseback lectures.

His father insisted on Charles's training as a barrister: a good, practical
Scottish profession. In his twenties, Lyell—never as keen on the law as
his father was on his practicing it—joined the British Geological Society
and began devoting nearly all his time to it. His "weak eyes" made it hard
for him to keep up his legal work, but not, apparently, difficult for him
to study, read, and write in years to come.

The Geolog. Soc., as members' letters and notebooks chattily called it,
was one of a host of scientific societies comprised largely of educated
gentlemen who met in London to present papers and discuss ideas.
Unlike France, which had experienced a tumultuous series of political
and social upheavals, England was calm and prosperous. While the overt

official support and institutionalization of science was the pride of Paris, no such circumstance pertained in England. Indeed, British tradition tended to idealize the plucky amateur who succeeded (or failed) spectacularly (such as the explorer Samuel Baker, who with his paramour blithely sailed up the Nile seeking its origin, or Edward Whymper, an artist who decided one day to be the first to climb the Matterhorn) through determination, intelligence, and moral character. English scientific work, now coming to rival that in France, was carried out largely through these less official bodies. This happenstance proved critical to the development of new ideas, which was less painful in a decentralized system where no single authority's view could dominate with such force as Cuvier's did in France.

By 1828, Lyell was the secretary of the Geolog. Soc., a post that probably spoke more for his popularity among his fellows than, necessarily, of his scientific acumen. Lyell had given up his law practice entirely now and happily departed on a geologic tour of the Continent with Roderick Murchison, a well-to-do Scot five years his senior. The two were a motley pair. Lyell was young, already losing his curly, reddish hair, with neat, attractive features and in one portrait, wearing a wonderfully lively plaid waistcoat. He bears an odd resemblance to the young Charles Darwin, though Darwin was younger still. In contrast, Murchison was in mid-life, a ruddy-faced, dark-haired man with a receding hairline and a challenging look in his eye. He looked like a man who knows what he wants. His approach to geological field trips, in the words of Lyell, was a "keep-moving, go-if-it-kills-you system."

Though Murchison and Lyell were soon to develop deep differences of opinion over geology, in the late 1820s the pair were geologizing together in amity. Murchison's future eminence was rapidly becoming clear, but Lyell was still largely an unknown. As geologists, both had come under the influence of Buckland, the foremost spokesman of diluvianism and a man almost universally loved and revered. But, like William Smith, both Murchison and Lyell had been taught to trust their eyes and observe the geological formations and processes around them. The evidence, to Lyell's eyes as he traveled extensively in England and Europe, was clear.

As he wrote to Murchison in 1829:

> My work is in part written and all planned. . . . All my geology will
> come in as an illustration of my views on those principles, and as
> evidence strengthening the system necessarily arising out of the

admission of such principles, which, as you know, are neither more nor less than that *no causes whatsoever* have from the earliest time to which we can look back to the present, ever acted, but those that are *now acting*, and that they never acted with different degrees of energy from that which they now exert.

This letter, and even more so his ground-breaking book, *Principles of Geology*, show Lyell's conviction that a theory known as uniformitarianism explained both the shape of the land and the distribution of the species upon it.

Uniformitarianism was an idea put forth in the late 1700s by James Hutton to the effect that the modern geological processes of wind, rain, river erosion, periodic local flooding, glacial movements, volcanic eruption, and the like were the only processes that had ever worked to shape the earth. Hutton believed, and Lyell later showed, that the processes themselves were uniform; their marked effects—as in the deep valleys carved out by rivers—were simply due to the immensity of the period over which they had operated. No worldwide deluges, no cataclysms of fire, no catastrophes of any sort were needed.

It was a bold thesis to defend, and Lyell, though not mealymouthed, was not one to stir up trouble without having his defenses carefully prepared. Cautious by nature, Lyell, trained as a barrister, had learned well how to build a convincing and watertight argument. His training, or perhaps his upbringing, had also taught him to avoid controversy and to shun confrontation. The quiet, clear exposition of reams of facts was enough; fire and brimstone and bitter attack on his elders were not Lyell's style. Writing to Murchison and making his beliefs clear well in advance of publication, though a perfectly natural thing to do, was also an excellent way to try to enlist the support of one of the most important geologists in Britain. (It did not work, as Murchison opposed uniformitarianism until his death in 1871.) As further security, Lyell persuaded several other geologists to help him gather and check the myriad facts he wished to present in painstaking support of his thesis.

Ironically, a few days before the first volume of Lyell's *Principles of Geology* was published, Murchison's endless research on a particular type of distorted geological formation known variously by the miner's term *greywacke* began to come to fruition in a way that led him to oppose Lyell's ideas. Murchison's thesis, later fully explicated in a book called *Siluria* (Murchison's name for greywacke), placed the elder geologist in direct conflict with his young protégé. Though even his biographer describes *Siluria* as possessing "a total want of literary attractiveness,"

Murchison's magnum opus went through four editions between 1839 and 1852.

Its popularity may be traced both to its sumptuous presentation and to its import rather than to the elegance of its style. Murchison was able to identify an area, based on a suggestion of Buckland's, where he could observe the stratigraphic position, composition, and entombed fossil fauna (animal community) of a "transitional" series of rocks that bridged the gap between the earliest, completely unfossiliferous strata and the more recent rocks containing abundant vertebrate remains. Not only did this resolve a long-standing problem in English geology, but study of the Silurian fauna showed that there was an Age of Invertebrates as important to Earth's history as the famous Age of Mammals on which Cuvier's reputation had been made.

This was an extraordinary discovery. Murchison proposed, and many scientists including Darwin confirmed, that the Silurian fauna was widespread and reasonably uniform. Most important, Silurian faunas contained no vertebrates whatsoever. Murchison's conclusion was that Siluria thus predated the appearance of terrestrial animals and land plants. Since the overlying geological strata, known in England as the Old Red Sandstone, contained all kinds of curiously armored fish, and above that farther still lay strata containing diverse dinosaurs and other reptiles, a pattern of increasing complexity in the fauna through time seemed to be clear.

There are three points of great significance about Murchison's interpretation of Siluria. First, it seemed to confirm the generally progressive nature of the development of species on Earth. There was first an age without organisms, then the age of invertebrates, followed by the age of fishes, then reptiles, mammals, and finally, humans. Second, Murchison's work was the impetus that eventually led to the organization of the history of Earth into the geologic epochs and eras that are used today. The scheme was proposed in 1841 by John Phillips, who not incidentally was William Smith's nephew, pupil, and biographer. Third, Murchison's studies of Siluria caused him to oppose Lyell's theory of uniformitarianism. Murchison's grounds were that the history of life on Earth did not exhibit the uniformity and stability of conditions that Lyell's ideas would suggest. While the Silurian itself showed great uniformity worldwide, the age of mammals, or Tertiary epoch, showed great diversity. Murchison remained steadfastly opposed to Lyell's ideas throughout his life, not seeing that geological mechanisms could remain stable even if climatic, faunal, or other aspects of Earth's history might change.

Thus, Lyell's attempts to avoid controversy were less than wholly successful, because his inherent tact could not disguise the clarity of his challenge to progressionism, diluvianism, and catastrophism. Buckland, like many a professor whose views are later overturned by a brilliant former pupil, may well have felt he had nurtured a viper in his bosom when *Principles of Geology* first appeared in 1830–33. On his part, Lyell's dislike of diluvianism seems to have been as much because he thought it a perversion to make science subservient to religion as because he thought the conclusions were in error. Yet Lyell was not anticlerical or antireligious. In the 1830s, though he made Lamarck's transformist views known in England, Lyell criticized them roundly. In his own works, he came to the edge of believing in evolution and backed off, time and time again. Through most of the rest of his life, Lyell repeatedly tiptoed around the awkward issue of the evolution of humans, and he long withheld his wholehearted support of Darwin in the brouhaha over *The Origin of Species*. Lyell's religious and scientific beliefs continued to grate uncomfortably against one another through nearly all of his lifetime.

At least in later life, Lyell's caution and desire to give careful consideration to all sides of an argument before deciding led to some interesting habits. Late in his own life, Darwin offered the following character sketch:

> During the early part of our life in London, I was strong enough to go into general society and saw a good deal of several scientific men. . . .
>
> I saw more of Lyell than of any other man both before and after my marriage. His mind was characterised, as it appeared to me, by clearness, caution, sound judgment and a good deal of originality. When I made any remark to him on geology, he never rested until he saw the whole case clearly, and often made me see it more clearly than I had done before. He would advance all possible objections to my suggestion, and even after these were exhausted would long remain dubious. . . . On such occasions, while absorbed in thought, he would throw himself into the strangest attitudes, often resting his head on the seat of a chair, while standing up. . . .
>
> His candour was highly remarkable. He exhibited this by becoming a convert to Descent-theory, though he had gained much fame by opposing Lamarck's views.

Though the young Lyell's work provoked some controversy, the book was sufficiently well regarded to be much talked of and to convince many of the enormous depth of geological time, a crucial foundation to the notion of gradual evolution that Darwin was later to propose. The Reverend Adam Sedgwick, Woodwardian Professor of Geology at Cambridge, was one of the most outspoken critics of Lyell's work. Sedgwick was to become a confirmed hypochondriac, given to wrapping himself during services in a bizarre combination of visor, respirator, and boots, in addition to his clerical robes, to guard his health. But in the 1830s, Sedgwick was a well-known geologist and a formidable opponent to a rising young man.

Fortunately for the future of science, Sedgwick was Darwin's tutor at Cambridge. Under the Cambridge system, a tutor meets with his student or students once a week, leading them in discussions on academic topics, setting them essays to write, and generally guiding their intellectual development. Ever the pedant, Sedgwick sent his former student Darwin a copy of the first volume of Lyell's *Principles of Geology*, hot off the presses in 1831, to take along with him on the voyage of the *Beagle*, warning, "Take Lyell's new book with you and read it by all means, for it is very interesting, but do not pay attention to it, except in regard to facts, for it is altogether wild as far as theory goes." Darwin acted upon the first part of his tutor's injunction and ignored the second. It was to prove a fateful decision.

Darwin read—and saw, as the world unfolded before his eyes—that uniformitarianism did explain the geological formations that shaped the land. Lyell's work quite literally changed the way the young Darwin saw the world. He later wrote:

> The very first place which I examined . . . showed me clearly the wonderful superiority of Lyell's manner of treating geology, compared with that of any other author, whose works I have with me or ever afterwards read.

Darwin came, too, to believe in the great antiquity of the world and of life on Earth, as Lyell did. And, his notebooks suggest, Darwin even began to apply the notion of ordinary events happening over long periods of time, thus causing slow, incremental, almost imperceptible changes to the living species he collected, measured, drew, and preserved with such joy. In other words, the very form of the uniformitarian principle was identical to that of Darwinian evolution. It was only the subject—rocks versus organisms—that differed.

In this, of course, Darwin did not agree with his hero, Lyell, who had vigorously opposed Lamarck's transformism and remained acutely uncomfortable with Darwinian evolution for many years. If Lyell was uneasy about Darwinian evolution, so, too, was Darwin himself. All his notebooks and writings suggest that the vision of natural selection and survival of the fittest as the mechanisms for producing change in organisms over time was clear when the *Beagle* arrived back home in England in 1836, five years after it set out. Yet he dithered over it for two decades, until his hand was forced.

In July 1837, a date he insisted upon repeatedly—it was to prove important in the delicate arrangements over priority with Alfred Russel Wallace—Darwin opened his first notebook on the transmutation of species. This was the notebook in which he began collecting facts and ideas bearing on his thesis. And collect facts he did: by his own observation, by conversation and meeting with other natural historians, and by corresponding with endless numbers of natural historians, breeders of domestic animals, and interested parties throughout England. He had learned his grandfather's lesson well: no premature publication of startling ideas, unsupported by facts, would be Charles Darwin's downfall.

Fortunately for Darwin, in 1839 he married the perfect nurse and helpmate, his cousin Emma Wedgwood. She brought calm and sympathy to the happy household, which rapidly filled with ten little Darwins. She was also one of the Wedgwoods of pottery fame and brought with her a handsome marriage settlement. Together with Darwin's substantial family fortune, they lived in considerable comfort and ease—Darwin's constant letters worrying about money notwithstanding—in Down House, now on the outskirts of London.

Darwin slowly turned from the adventurous young man who had bounded off on the round-the-world voyage of the *Beagle* and who had once been so keen on hunting that he routinely left his boots unlaced by the side of his bed "so as not to lose half-a-minute in putting them on in the morning," to a havering, dithering semi-invalid who feared for twenty years to say what he thought. He was hampered by doubts, troubled by the thought of controversy and argument, anxious over the possible disapproval of his beloved wife and dear family, and debilitated by vague and ofttimes convenient illnesses that sound suspiciously hypochondriacal. Darwin worked away on his notebooks for year after year. In the meantime, he published several books, on, among other things, the voyage of the *Beagle*, coral atolls, the geology of South America, volcanic islands, and fossil and living barnacles.

Soon he was going out less and less, finding the excitement of even a brief visit from a friend such as Charles Lyell, the botanist Joseph Hooker, or the brilliant anatomist Thomas Henry Huxley exhausted him and provoked draining bouts of illness. He limited his contact with other minds more and more to the written word, seemingly less willing to make personal contact with others the clearer his evolutionary ideas became. His daily life became a comfortable round of writing and reading; going for walks (often with a small Darwin along) on the property to collect specimens; maintaining his active correspondence, which often yielded still more specimens; and carefully dissecting, drawing, and thinking about his precious specimens.

Often lionized as a great thinker, Darwin plodded along on this subject like an uncertain little man who has gotten hold of an idea too big for him. Perhaps the aptest description of Darwin is that given by his lifelong friend, Thomas Huxley:

> Exposition is not Darwin's forte. But there is a marvelous dumb sagacity about him like that of a sort of miraculous dog, and he gets to the truth by ways as dark as those of the Heathen Chinee.

To this must be added two other views. Quite another side of Darwin is shown by his description of himself shortly before his marriage: "What can a man have to say, who works all morning in describing hawks and owls, and then rushes out and walks in a bewildered manner up one street and down another, looking for the words, 'To let.' "

And more revealing yet was the remark one of his sons was overheard to make upon visiting a friend's house: "But where does Mr. ——— do his barnacles?" So thoroughly did his father's natural-history studies color life at Down House that any child of Darwin's would have thought it only usual to "do barnacles" or beetles, or birds, or butterflies, or myriad other creatures, living or fossil.

What he did not "do," for there was no opportunity, were fossil humans. Yet Darwin cannot have been entirely unaware that claims for human antiquity were beginning to crop up. As early as 1797, when Erasmus Darwin was struggling with evolutionary ideas, a gentleman farmer named John Frere had reported worked-stone tools of a type now known as hand axes or bifaces, found in association with extinct animals in a gravel pit near Hoxne, in England. This clearly implied that humans had been contemporaneous with the extinct species, and Frere knew it. He published excellent drawings of the hand axes and described them as evidently weapons of war, fabricated and used by a people who had not the use of metals. They lay in great numbers at a depth of about twelve feet, in a stratified soil that was dug for the purpose of raising clay for bricks. The situation in which these remains were found may tempt us to refer them to a very remote period indeed, even beyond that of the present world.

Frere's was truly a voice crying in the wilderness. Further publication of his claims in 1800 produced no general recognition, and it was not until many years later that anyone read and believed them.

In Germany, what should have been more convincing evidence was found some years later. Baron Ernst Friedrich von Schlotheim, a paleontologist working in Thuringia, was regularly discovering bones of mammoths, cave bears, and woolly rhinoceroses—all widely recognized as extinct species—in gypsum quarries. In 1820, he announced he had found human teeth mixed in among the extinct animals. Because no form of absolute dating was known until much later, relative dating of fossils, relying on the association of different species into a succession of faunas, was widely used. The presence of human teeth in the same strata with mammoths almost certainly indicated that the two were contemporaneous, and the implication was obvious to anyone learned in fossils.

But Cuvier, the acknowledged authority on fossil mammals, simply suggested that the teeth were from a recent burial that had been dug into the older sediments; the find was, in short, intrusive, as Schlotheim would have noticed if he had observed the sediments carefully. In fact, it was most unlikely that Schlotheim or any other natural historian of the day actually participated themselves in the manual labor of digging. It was routine to hire workmen, inform them what the desired objects were, and peruse the forthcoming discoveries in comfort and leisure. With skepticism from the establishment so strong, Schlotheim gave way to uncertainty and did not pursue his claims, even when a second discovery in Bilzingsleben also showed the association of human and extinct mammalian remains.

But the same type of discovery was being made over and over by isolated individuals working in different areas. The problem was that the finders, or the paleontologists they called in, rarely understood what they had found and, when they did, were usually disbelieved.

In January 1823, Buckland found a skull-less human skeleton in Goat's Hole in Paviland, Wales. It was no wonder that the skeleton was not discovered earlier, as Buckland's description of the locale shows:

It consists of two large caves facing the sea, in the front of a lofty cliff of limestone, which rises more than 100 feet perpendicularly above the mouth of the caves, and below them slopes at an angle of about 40° to the water's edge, presenting a bluff and rugged shore to the waves, which are very violent along this north coast of the estuary of the Severn. These caves are altogether invisible from the land side, and are accessible only at low water, except by dangerous climbing along the face of a nearly precipitous cliff, composed entirely of compact mountain limestone, which dips north at an angle of about 45°.

In fact, this description underplays the extreme difficulty of the access to the cave, which cannot be entered safely without mountain-climbing gear except during very low tides. Nonetheless, in December 1822, an intrepid local surgeon and curate (whose name is not recorded), clearly not put off by cold weather or raw winds, explored the cave and found teeth and a tusk of an extinct elephant. He buried them, and returned with L. W. Dillwyn, Esq., and Miss Talbot, daughter of the owner of the land. They removed the elephant remains "together with a large part of the skull to which it belonged, and several baskets full of teeth and bones" to Penrice Castle, where they awaited Buckland's arrival. In the best paleontological tradition, he hastened to the site, decided most of the cave sediments were undisturbed, and began collecting.

Buckland himself found the human skeleton, dyed red with ocher and certainly part of a burial. The skeleton was accompanied by two handfuls of small shells by the left thigh and, overlying the rib cage, forty or fifty fragments of small, cylindrical ivory rods and rings that appeared to be unmistakably worked by humans. The impressive feat of carrying a corpse to this uninviting place and maneuvering it along the steep, sharp-edged cliff face into the cave escaped Buckland's attention, perhaps because he thought the skeleton more recent than it actually was.

The find was almost immediately nicknamed the Red Lady of Paviland. There were implications that she was a woman "no better than she should be," in the parlance of the day, who hung around the military encampment on the hill above the cave and who, "whatever may have been her occupation, the vicinity of a camp would afford a motive for residence, as well as a means of subsistence." The camp was confidently assigned by Buckland to the Roman invasion of Britain and was declared to be contemporaneous with the remains found within the cave.

"She"—even though the pelvis that is part of the skeleton is unquestionably male—had almost certainly been deliberately buried. Fauna

5. William Buckland's drawing of the excavations of Goat's Hole, at Paviland in south Wales, where in 1822 he discovered the fossil skeleton of an anatomically modern Upper Paleolithic young man. Buckland dubbed it the Red Lady of Paviland, misunderstanding both the fossil's gender and antiquity.

from the cave included extinct species of rhinoceros, hyena, elephant, deer, and so on, with fragments of charcoal and a small flint. Buckland also identified "a portion of the scapula apparently of a sheep"—a decidedly peculiar cohabitant with mammoths and woolly rhinoceroses—which persuaded him that the cave itself contained recent remains, such as the sheep and the Red Lady, as well as much older, antediluvian ones. Despite the association of extinct fauna with human remains, Buckland was unwilling to attribute any great antiquity to the Red Lady.

In this, as in much else, Buckland was mistaken. Recent studies show that the skeleton was an early, anatomically modern, human *male* that lived about twenty-five thousand years ago and died in his early twenties. Though Buckland was wrong about so much pertaining to this skeleton, his interest led to its preservation. Now, this specimen still has the distinction of being the earliest discovered human fossil that is known to science.

What the Red Lady did was spur a hunt for other ancient human remains. In 1825, an Irish clergyman, Father John MacEnery, found human remains, flaked flint tools, and cave bear, extinct hyena, and other fossil animals in a cave known as Kent's Cavern or Kent's Hole near Torquay, Devonshire.

It was a new look at a well-known site. Comprised of an extensive series of interconnected chambers, the cave had been known to local enthusiasts for many years. A series of painted or scratched graffiti on the walls suggests that visitors began coming to the cave in 1571, when one William Petre left the date and his name on the walls. In 1794, a Dr. Maton describes crawling through the cave using a

> candle stuck in a piece of slitted stick . . . the [entrance] was just large enough to admit us. . . . The chill we received was inconceivable, and our clothes were moistened by the continual dropping of water from the roof. . . . [It] was gloomy . . . and we began to imagine ourselves in the abode of some magician.

Conditions were not much different when MacEnery began excavating the cave years later, knowing full well that lively discussions on the antiquity of humans were taking place in several areas of England and Europe. The human material he and his successor at Kent's Cavern, William Pengelly, found proved to be basically of modern human type, like the Red Lady of Paviland.

Although much of the material he had recovered was clearly associated with extinct animal bones and flaked stone tools, MacEnery had difficulty persuading Buckland that it had been sealed beneath the stalagmitic layer and was not from disturbed soil. For this reason, or perhaps because of the controversial nature of such discoveries, MacEnery wrote up his findings but left them in manuscript form; only after his death did a colleague see to their publication in 1859. Still, word got out. A description of the Kent's Cavern work was read to the Geological Society in 1840 by a Mr. Godwin-Austen, who asserted, somewhat testily:

> I must therefore state that my own researches were constantly conducted in parts of the cave which had never been disturbed, and in every instance the bones were procured from beneath a thick covering of stalagmite; so far, then, the bones and works of man must have been introduced into the cave before the flooring of stalagmite.

It was to no avail. John Lubbock, shortly to become one of Britain's foremost archeologists and later to become Lord Avebury, remarked in his book *Pre-historic Times, as Illustrated by Ancient Remains, and the Manners and Customs of Modern Savages,* in 1872,

> Notwithstanding the high authority of Mr. Godwin-Austen, these statements attracted little attention [at the time]; and the very similar assertions made by Mr. Vivian, in a paper read before the Geological Society, were considered so improbable that the memoir containing them was not published.

The slow accretion of human fossils continued. In 1833–34, Phillipe-Charles Schmerling, a Belgian physician and anatomist, published a two-volume account of his investigations of the caves along the Meuse River, near Liège. Many were entirely undisturbed, and some boasted a thick stalagmitic layer that sealed the bones into a layer of real antiquity, similar to that found at Kent's Cavern.

The most famous remains described by Schmerling—fossils that had

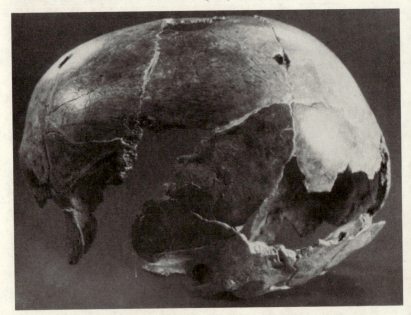

6. The braincase of a two- or three-year-old Neandertal child, found in 1830 by Phillipe-Charles Schmerling in the Engis Cave in Belgium. Not recognized as a Neandertal until a century later, it was the first fossil of its kind to be discovered.

actually been found in late 1829 or early 1830—came from the cave known as Engis. Engis yielded the cranial remains of at least three individuals associated with extinct animals. One skull deteriorated and is thus unknown today. A second partial cranium is now recognized as being a Neandertal child who was about two and a half years old at death. The third is a large, robust male cranium that recent work has shown to be only eight thousand years old and therefore modern, if unusually strongly built. Excavation in the nearby cave of Engihoul led to the discovery of limb bones of humans, again associated with extinct fauna. Though Schmerling understood what he had found and what it meant, the scientific community was entirely unimpressed.

Lyell, who was beginning to develop a pointed interest in human antiquity, visited Belgium in 1833 and was shown the remains by Schmerling himself. As Lyell himself recounts, with some embarrassment, he was as skeptical as most at the time.

> . . . when I expressed some incredulity respecting the alleged antiquity of the fossil human bones, he pointedly remarked, that if I doubted their having been contemporaneous with the bear or rhinoceros, on the ground of Man being a species of more modern date, I ought equally to doubt the coexistence of all the other living species such as the red deer, roe, wild cat, wild boar, wolf, fox, weasel, beaver, hare, rabbit, hedgehog, mole, dormouse, field-mouse, water-rat, shrew and others, the bones of which he had found scattered everywhere indiscriminately through the same mud.

Schmerling's arguments notwithstanding, Lyell failed to be convinced: "I can only plead that a discovery which seems to contradict the general tenor of previous investigations is naturally received with much hesitation." These must rank among the truest words Lyell ever wrote, for they summarize the story of the discovery of Neandertals perfectly. No one was then prepared to hear of human antiquity.

A similar but more extreme fate awaited Jacques Boucher de Crèvecoeur de Perthes. Unlike Schmerling, whose work focused on the physical evidence of human ancestors in the form of skeletal remains, Boucher de Perthes's claim to fame—or notoriety—was his recognition of the primitive stone tools our ancestors had made, like those Frere had found at Hoxne, though no one remembered Frere's work at the time.

Born in 1788 to a well-to-do family that boasted a botanizing father, young Jacques had moved with the rest of his family to Abbeville in 1792,

7. Jacques Boucher de Crèvecoeur de Perthes as a young man during the Napole-onic era. In his later life as a customs agent in Abbeville, in the 1840s, he combined his romantic view of human origins with discoveries of early tools and argued for the existence of pre-Celtic, or Pleistocene, humans. No portraits of him as an older man exist, apparently due to his vanity.

during the Reign of Terror in Paris when the Revolution claimed at least twelve hundred victims. Boucher de Perthes senior became the local correspondent, or representative, of the Académie des Sciences and was eventually to rise to the position of Director of Customs at Abbeville.

Like Cuvier, Boucher de Perthes was one of the many bright young men of the bourgeoisie (lesser aristocracy) who were promoted to high position. In the early 1800s, as Napoleon was rising to power and Cuvier was growing in influence at the Muséum National d'Histoire Naturelle, young Boucher de Perthes was becoming a witty, politically minded author at the court of Napoleon who specialized in writing plays, poems, and songs that turned on the fashion and manners of the day. He was a prolific and charming writer. It was even rumored that he had an affair with Napoleon's lovely sister, the princess Pauline Borghese. It was certainly true that Napoleon himself sent Boucher de Perthes on confidential missions that took him over much of Europe.

Napoleon had made the position of *douanier* or customs officer far more important, and more military, than it is today. He placed special importance on the customs officials in places at the frontiers of his empire—such as Abbeville, situated strategically on the river Somme, facing England. Posted first to Abbeville, Boucher de Perthes was moved to Marseilles, various towns in what is now Italy, and back to Paris with the customs service, where in 1812 he was named to the Central Administration of the Department of Customs, in Paris.

Boucher de Perthes's glittering triumph at this important post was relatively short-lived, because 1812 was also the year of Napoleon's doomed Russian campaign. Unlike Cuvier, who was careful to consolidate his position at the museum and to distance himself from any particular government while keeping in favor with whoever ruled, Boucher de Perthes was clearly perceived as Napoleon's man. By 1815, he was in disgrace, exiled from Paris to La Ciotât on the Mediterranean coast. He was back in the customs service by 1816, but was sent to Morlaix in Brittany. Gradually, with the rapid replacement of one monarch by another, he started on the slow climb to prominence again. In 1825, in middle age, he at last succeeded his father as Director of Customs at Abbeville, where he was to spend the rest of his career.

In Abbeville, Boucher de Perthes met the man who was to change his life and the history of the study of human antiquity. In France at the turn of the eighteenth century, virtually any town of any size had a *société d'emulation,* and Abbeville was no exception. These societies were organizations to promote local pride, or a sort of learned "booster" clubs. These societies were designed to keep intellectual life alive in the provinces and equally, to foster self-improvement and perhaps even a bit of self-aggrandizement. At meetings, the members—who were almost without exception the local men of influence, wealth, and education—would gather to present or listen to papers on diverse topics of interest, including art, natural history, archeology, and curiosities of various types. It went without saying that the Director of Customs would be a stalwart member of the *société.*

In 1829, a physician who had recently moved to Abbeville, Casimir Picard, joined the *société,* of which Boucher de Perthes was then the vice president. Picard's passion was archeology, especially prehistoric stone tools. His particular interest was what were then known as Celtic axes: substantial, polished stone tools now known to be from the Neolithic age only a few thousand years ago. In a paper read to the *société* in 1835, Picard argued that these axes had actually been hafted onto handles of wood, bone, or antler rather than being held in the hand.

Picard was one of the first to use an experimental approach to archeology. He attempted to make and use stone tools such as were being found in excavations. These experiments showed him what techniques of flaking or grinding had been used to manufacture the tools and, also, sometimes, in what tasks they could be usefully employed. He was also an innovator in using more systematic excavation techniques that included the use of stratigraphic data. Though little of Picard's scientific work is now remembered as being of great value, his importance was perhaps in his emphasis on systematic work and his influence on Boucher de Perthes.

The time was perfect for Boucher de Perthes to take up a new interest. The provinces and administrative work for the customs service soon palled to such an extent that his satirical vein was reawakened. He could not resist poking fun at the bureaucrats who surrounded him. In 1835, Boucher de Perthes published an immensely amusing, but also scandalous book called *La Petit Glossaire, traduction de quelques mots financiers, équisse de moeurs administratives (The Little Dictionary, a Translation of Some Financial Terms and Administrative Ways)*. It included such pungent gibes as:

> IMBECILE: You may ask if it is better to be administered by imbeciles or by outright thieves. The answer is by thieves, without question. . . . IMBECILE, see also MUNICIPAL COUNCIL. . . .
> MUNICIPAL COUNCIL: A group comprised of citizens and countryfolk who, patriotically, with a good conscience and good intent, for about six years do all the harm they can to their city, their town, or their village, and who, when their term expires, are either reelected, or go to rest, calling themselves for the rest of their lives: former member of the municipal council.

While the book was a raging public success, to the extent of being either excerpted or plagiarized in many of the magazines of the day, it did not endear Boucher de Perthes to his superiors in the government. His outspokenness, his criticisms of various governmental policies, and his fight for women's emancipation, education for the masses, and other revolutionary ideas ensured that he would not resume a prominent career in Paris.

Boucher de Perthes was obviously growing bored with life in Abbeville as a customs official. Fortunately, Picard's presentations at the *société* meetings were fascinating enough to turn Boucher de Perthes's interests in a new direction: prehistory. The two men became fast friends and collaborated in their archeological pursuits until Picard's death in 1841. In that same year, Boucher de Perthes came into the possession of a flaked, flint hand axe that he said had been associated with remains of extinct mammals at Menchecourt, near Abbeville. He immediately claimed that he had proved the existence of antediluvian man. Unfortunately, because he was apparently not present when the tool was uncovered, and the existence of such a creature as an antediluvian man was not readily acceptable, Boucher de Perthes's ideas were simply scoffed at. It may not have helped his credibility that he was known for writing frivolous plays and satires.

He persisted and persevered, despite the fact that he was becoming widely known as a crank on the subject of prehistoric man. In 1844, after years of inspecting excavations usually made for other purposes and of collecting stone tools, he started the process of publishing a summary of his work as a book entitled *Antiquités Celtiques et Antédiluviennes* (generally known in English as *Celtic Antiquities*). In an attempt to ease its reception, Boucher de Perthes sent a prepublication copy to the Académie des Sciences in Paris in 1846, asking for comments but, in fact, seeking official approval or endorsement.

The first response of the Académie was to try to avoid dealing with Boucher de Perthes's work. When he persisted, they appointed a committee to evaluate it. While they did not feel secure in completely blocking release of the book, they used all the subtle weapons at their disposal to oppose it. In the best bureaucratic style, the committee delayed producing its opinion for at least two years, undoubtedly hoping he would give up. But if Boucher de Perthes had any virtues at all, perseverance was the foremost, and the book was finally distributed in 1849, even though it carried a publication date of 1847.

Part of the difficulty was the novelty of Boucher de Perthes's point of view and part, more apparent in retrospect, was his lack of scientific judgment. The book is a large work, full of poor illustrations of the objects he identified as stone tools and weapons. Intermingled with figures of readily recognizable prehistoric tools, such as the classic teardrop-shaped Acheulian hand axe, are pages and pages of illustrations of eoliths (possible stone tools so minimally altered by humans as to be indistinguishable from natural objects) and entirely unworked pieces fancied by Boucher de Perthes to be images of extinct animals. In fact, of the eighty plates, forty-eight are dedicated to bizarre rocks and only thirty-two to what would now be recognized as authentic tools. His cavalier treatment of stratigraphy and his poor documentation of the excavations as they were carried out by workmen dismayed many who visited his localities in an attempt to discern the truth.

The extent of his disregard is thinly veiled by politeness in the 1840s and 1850s and praise in later years, once his ideas were more widely accepted. For example, in 1864 *The Anthropological Review* in Britain published an item rather snidely entitled "The Fossil Man of Abbeville Again." It is a report summarized from a French publication, *L'Abbevillois*, of some of Boucher de Perthes's work. The disbelief is subtly but clearly conveyed. The article closes with a note from the editor that explicitly denies any endorsement of Boucher de Perthes's findings: "We abstain at present from offering any comment on the above."

In fact, Boucher de Perthes was so notorious that even a later believer in his claims, the British archeologist John Lubbock, remarked in his book:

> For seven years [from 1846 to 1853], M. Boucher de Perthes made few converts; he was looked upon as an enthusiast, almost as a madman. . . . Prophets are proverbially without honour in their own country, and M. Boucher de Perthes was no exception to the rule.

8. The Neandertal skull unearthed in Forbes' Quarry on Gibraltar in 1848. It aroused brief interest in the 1860s when it arrived in London, but was forgotten until the early twentieth century. Although one of the more complete Neandertal skulls ever discovered, it made its debut at a time when few were able, and fewer willing, to recognize its significance to human evolution.

Ironically, the acceptance of the hand axes as genuine tools and Boucher de Perthes's vindication came not because of his own work but because of the work of one of his heretofore harshest critics, Dr. Rigollot, president of the Société des Antiquaires de Picardie (Antiquarian Society of Picardy). In 1853, Dr. Rigollot examined the "drifts" or Pleistocene gravel beds at St. Acheul and himself discovered hand axes in association with extinct mammal bones. Rigollot's previously skeptical stance, the care with which he examined and reported the position of the remains, and the better quality of his illustrations lent credibility to his claims. Indeed, the objects recognized as tools by Frere and later by Boucher de Perthes are now known as Acheulian hand axes or bifaces, so instrumental was Rigollot's work at St. Acheul.

Even after Rigollot's conversion to Boucher de Perthes's cause, it was never officially endorsed. The final acceptance of the antiquity and genuineness of the hand axes came after visits in 1858–59 from several eminent English geologists, among them Charles Lyell, Joseph Prestwich, John Evans, J. W. Flower, and Hugh Falconer. Not tied to the highly centralized French scientific establishment, which had so thoroughly rejected Boucher de Perthes, this group visited the Somme Valley, inspected many of his localities, and even excavated hand axes for themselves. Whatever those in Paris might say, the English geologists were convinced of two things—that the tools were manufactured by humans and that they were truly ancient—despite Boucher de Perthes's sloppy methods and more elaborate, flamboyant claims.

Bit by bit, in this isolated locale and that, the swell of evidence for human antiquity was growing. But it was widely disregarded, often disbelieved, and generally buried in obscure, local publications.

This was more or less the case in 1848, when a skull that was later recognized as a Neandertal was unearthed on Gibraltar as military fortifications were being constructed. The specific details of the discovery are now obscure, the only clue being the minutes of the Gibraltar Scientific Society for March 3, 1848, which state that the secretary "presented a human skull from Forbes' Quarry, North Front."

No further comments are made and to all appearances, no further notice was paid. The skull was stowed in the small museum on the island with other and various relics and curiosities. There it sat, awaiting its rediscovery for more than a decade. The bones had been there for thousands of years before they saw the light of day again; a few more couldn't hurt. No one looked, no one saw, no one cared. Yet.

2

Not *My* Ancestor

1856–1865

Against this dark tapestry of ignorance, relieved only by glimmers of evidence for human antiquity, the Neandertal fossils now in Fuhlrott's hands stood out like a beacon. Poor Fuhlrott may well have hoped these extraordinary fossils would ensure his entry into the scientific elite, but it was not to be. The Neandertal fossils shed new light, but instead of bringing understanding, they brought only controversy, confusion, and criticism.

Part of the difficulty lay in the dating of the remains. Until the time of the fossils' discovery, three general approaches to establishing the antiquity of human ancestry had been tried. The first was Biblical: calculating the generation lengths and numbers of "begats" in the Bible from Adam and Eve to Jesus. This famous calculation, made in the 1600s by James Ussher, Archbishop of Armagh, led to the widely known date of 4004 B.C. for the creation of the world. An extension of this literary approach led antiquarians to consult Roman as well as religious writings, on which they based the notion of uncivilized, pre-Celtic peoples as the original inhabitants of Europe. The story of human history then could be seen as a series of tribal wanderings and migrations across the largely uncivilized world. These tribes became races, their habits became distinct cultures and languages, and the family of man could be traced more or less directly, at least in theory, back to the Garden of Eden itself.

Lacking hard evidence of the ancestors, imaginative scholars turned to the study of languages their descendants spoke. They charted what amounted to an evolutionary tree of the development of languages—a whole group of the more "superior" ones, called Aryan, being derived from ancient Sanskrit. Comparative, though sometimes laughably naïve, linguistic studies became an increasingly popular means of tracing the relationships and contacts among these ancient tribal groups or races. In vain, Thomas Henry Huxley pointed out the fatal flaw in logic: "Physical, mental and moral peculiarities go with blood and not with language. In the United States the negroes have spoken English for generations; but no one on that ground would call them Englishmen, or expect them to differ physically, mentally or morally from other negroes."

The second approach was archeological, based on the association of ancient stone tools—when everyone could agree which ones were tools—with human skeletal remains. By looking at the sequence of remains, a sort of hierarchy or seriation of artifact types was derived, so that metalworking peoples were more recent than those who made clay pots and produced ground or polished stone axes, who were in turn preceded by those more primitive still, with only flaked tools. The general framework of such an approach may have been correct, but the details were fuzzy. Besides, seriation of the tool types revealed next to nothing about the people themselves.

The third was paleontological and relied on the association of either stone tools or, preferably, the skeletal remains of ancient humans themselves with extinct mammals. Because the focus of this work was in Europe, it involved finding traces of humans or their presence in the same levels with extinct mammoths or woolly rhinoceroses, giant elk, cave hyenas, and the like: all species now recognized as coming from the late Pleistocene, between about 130,000 and 10,000 years ago, when Europe was periodically glaciated. (The Pleistocene epoch in its entirety lasted from about 1.8 million years to 10,000 years ago.) A variant on this approach was strictly geological, in which the depth and type of the deposit overlying the bones or tools could be taken as indicative of the antiquity of the finds. This approach was particularly useful, and generally accurate, in regions where the geological sequences of strata were well known and readily recognizable without confusion. Because no independent means of dating deposits, such as the radiometric methods now in use, had yet been developed, what was actually achieved was a seriation of strata or ages whose duration was open to speculation rather than an actual calibration of the antiquity of the fossils in any particular geological formation.

Supplementing these approaches, but by no means resolving the controversies, were studies of the embryological development and anatomy of various living mammals. Comparative anatomy, as this field was generally known, provided direct evidence of the structural similarities between any two creatures that were in hand. It was a vibrant and important field, led in the nineteenth century by such intellectual giants as Georges Cuvier and Paul Broca in France, Richard Owen and Thomas Henry Huxley in England, and Ernst Haeckel in Germany.

What was not immediately apparent either was the weighting that ought to be given to different features: Was it more important if two species resembled each other in the teeth or in the shape of the skull? Were feet more telling than, say, shoulders, or shoulders more indicative than skulls? What was *not* asked was how long these differences took to evolve, for the notion of descent with modification—Darwin's classic definition of evolution—had not yet been introduced.

Comparative anatomy successfully established the broad framework of the resemblances among different species without excessive difficulty. From the time that the first specimens of them reached Europe, it was apparent that the great apes—the chimpanzee, gorilla, and orangutan—were anatomically very similar to humans. Somewhat less similar, but still strikingly reminiscent of humans, were the lesser apes—gibbons and siamangs—followed by monkeys and lower primates. Nineteenth-century illustrations of chimps in top hats riding bicycles, or of such events as "A Day at the Zoo" or "A Visit to the Monkey House," demonstrate graphically that the public was well aware of the comical resemblance between certain humans and other primates.

Still, scientists, though equally cognizant of the echoes of humanity among the apes (or vice versa), engaged in technical debates about the precise relationships. By the 1860s, Huxley in England and Broca in France were in firm agreement that humans were indeed strikingly similar to the chimpanzee, while in Germany, Haeckel championed the smaller Asian ape, the gibbon, as our closest relative.

But what the Neandertal skeletal remains supplied was an entirely novel type of evidence, for while they were obviously human in the broad sense—that is, as opposed to being apes or monkeys —they were not like the modern humans that anyone knew. They were different, and nothing so different had ever been considered closely before. That these fossils had actually been found in geological deposits that suggested some considerable antiquity—thus providing a second line of evidence—was a bonus.

Whether Fuhlrott immediately appreciated what a blockbuster the fossils were, we shall never know. At the very least, he knew they would have an important bearing on what we would now call human evolution. What we do know is that he sought professional help, from Hermann Schaaffhausen, the professor of anatomy at the nearby University of Bonn. Together, the schoolteacher and the professor studied the remains and prepared to announce their findings to the scientific community.

The venue they chose was the periodic meeting of the Lower Rhine Medical and Natural History Society at Bonn. Based on inspection of a plaster cast provided by Fuhlrott, Schaaffhausen made his preliminary announcement at the meeting on February 4, 1857, roughly six months after the initial discovery of the fossils. After this meeting—and, one suspects, following upon some sweet persuasion—Fuhlrott "to whom," in Schaaffhausen's words, "science is indebted for the preservation of these bones . . . brought the cranium from Elberfeld and entrusted it to me for more accurate anatomical examination."

By the June 2 General Meeting of the Natural History Society of Prussian Rhineland and Westphalia, also held in Bonn, Schaaffhausen had prepared a more detailed account. He had also wisely extended the courtesy to Fuhlrott of asking him to attend and to present his own paper, describing the circumstances of the find. It was a significant honor for a schoolteacher and amateur natural historian to speak at such an occasion, when many of the great professors of Germany might be present, and Fuhlrott undoubtedly was flattered at the thought. But the event itself must have fallen far short of the accolades and praise Fuhlrott had every right to expect.

Fuhlrott delivered his paper first, stressing the geological evidence for the antiquity of the bones that were "covered to a thickness of 4 or 5 feet with a deposit of mud, sparingly intermixed with rounded fragments of chert [a type of rock commonly used for tool manufacture]" and the clear association of the various bones into a single skeleton: "Of this I was assured in the most positive terms by the two labourers who were employed to clear out the grotto, and who were questioned by me on the spot."

Flimsy as this hearsay evidence seems by modern scientific criteria, Fuhlrott's procedure of seeking information from workmen, rather than conducting the dig himself, was standard at the time. He also pointed out the dendritic deposits (mineral deposits arranged in a linear, branching pattern) on the surface of the fossils. Dendritic deposits were then believed to be a good sign of antiquity and fossilization because they had recently been noted on bones of cave bears and other extinct forms by Professor H. von Meyer, a colleague of Schaaffhausen's at Bonn. Unbeknownst to Fuhlrott, that same Professor von Meyer was about to repudiate his own criterion for antiquity and was to join with a similarly named colleague at Bonn, Professor August Franz Mayer, to become one of the most vocal critics of the Neandertal remains.

9. Hermann Schaaffhausen, the German biologist who announced the original Neandertal skeleton to the scientific world, with Johann Karl Fuhlrott, the schoolteacher who recognized the fossil as an ancient human. Schaaffhausen fought for the acceptance of evolutionary biology in Germany throughout the late nineteenth century.

Following Fuhlrott's paper, Schaaffhausen stood to deliver his anatomical analysis. It was a strongly worded, directly stated pronouncement, suggesting that Schaaffhausen, like many another German Herr Doktor Professor, was used to respect for his firmly held opinions.

> The conclusions at which I arrived were: —1st. That the extraordinary form of the skull was due to a natural conformation hitherto not known to exist, even in the most barbarous races. 2nd. That these remarkable human remains belonged to a period antecedent to the time of the Celts and Germans, and were in all probability derived from one of the wild races of North-western Europe, spoken of by Latin writers; and which were encountered as autochthones [indigenous peoples] by the German immigrants. And 3rdly. That it was beyond doubt that these human relics were traceable to a period at which the latest animals of the diluvium still existed; but that no proof in support of this assumption, nor consequences of their so termed *fossil* condition, was afforded by the circumstances under which the bones were discovered.

He then proceeded to describe and to illustrate the most extraordinary bones any of the attendees had ever seen.

He started with the long, narrow skull, a large-brained, heavy specimen. Perhaps its most remarkable feature—the one that startled observers and led them to attribute savagery to its owner—was the strong, bony ridge that protruded ominously over each eye. The lowering brow was completed by a low, brutish forehead. The braincase was capacious, but elongated front to back rather than being gracefully domed. At the nape of the neck was a pronounced bony bulge that came to be known as the occipital "bun" or "chignon."

In an odd twist of events, the cranium itself was to become the focus of attention—the bone of contention, as it were—in part because of the tremendous popularity of phrenology in the latter part of the nineteenth century. Started in Vienna by a physician, Franz Joseph Gall, the science of phrenology held that the shape of the skull revealed the mental and especially moral characteristics of the owner of that skull. The science was greatly popularized in America and England by the Fowler family, entrepreneurs who produced and sold diagrams and porcelain busts of the head, carefully marked to show the areas in which different qualities were housed. These aids enabled students of phrenology to judge such qualities as the amativeness, honesty, domestic propensities, or knowing faculties of their friends by the sizes of the bumps on their heads. Couples contemplating marriage regularly went to have their heads "read," to see if they were compatible. This widespread belief was cleverly played upon by Oscar Wilde in his famous *Picture of Dorian Gray*, in which the deteriorating moral character of the central figure is recorded on his portrait rather than on his face.

Although rarely explicit in the discussions of the Neandertal fossils, this implicit belief in the link between the skull and character was clearly evident in the controversy that ensued. Time and again, the cranial features were paramount even though the actual evidence that pertained to many of the arguments could be derived only from examination of the limb bones.

Of these, there were several. Both humeri, or upper arm bones, were recovered, but they differed from one another. The right was stout, with a large head for articulation with the scapula, or shoulder blade (part of which was also recovered), and a strongly built shaft with big ridges for the attachment of powerful muscles. The accompanying bones of the lower part of the right arm, the radius and ulna, were also present. But the left humerus, though incomplete, was markedly more slender than the right, and the left ulna was shortened and distorted.

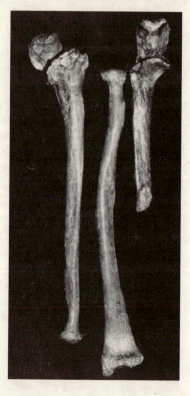

10. The forearm bones of the original Neandertal skeleton from the Feldhofer grotto,
seen from the front. On the right are the
two normal bones (the complete radius and
upper half of the ulna) from the right arm.
On the left is the fractured left ulna, with
the upper end turned outward just below
the elbow. The break healed in this awkward
position long before death; the resultant
disuse of the left arm led to a reduction in
the size of the bones of that arm. The genuinely pathological condition of the left ulna
supported accusations that this was not a
new type of extinct human but was simply
a diseased individual—charges used to reject
evolutionary ideas in general.

An injury in life had broken that ulna near the elbow joint. Long
disuse of the injured arm made the left humerus and ulna smaller than
the stout ones on the right. This was because the break had healed
improperly, leaving a lump of pathological bony tissue that prevented the
left elbow from being bent to an angle of less than about ninety degrees.
This circumstance, undoubtedly a source of pain to the original owner
of the ulna, was to prove the bane of the existence of the nineteenth-
century "owners" as well. Alert to the possibility of the claims that were,
indeed, shortly to be made, Schaaffhausen carefully observed that this
ulna "presents no sign of rachitic degeneration" but only of a poorly
healed fracture. His remarks fell on deaf ears.

The femora, or thigh bones, were also remarkable for their stoutness,
large joints, and exaggerated muscle markings. In an attempt to emphasize their normality, Schaaffhausen compared them to some recent bones
of an exceptionally large person that were kept in the Anatomical
Museum at Bonn, labeled " 'Giant's-bones' . . . with which in thickness

the foregoing [Neandertal remains] pretty nearly correspond, although they are shorter." In addition, though Schaaffhausen omitted mention of the fact, the femora curved along their length; the curvature in itself is normal in humans, but was carried to an unusual extreme in the fossil.

The left ilium, or upper part of the hipbone, was also preserved, as were some robust ribs so strongly built that there was debate as to whether they belonged to some carnivore of which no other trace was preserved.

Schaaffhausen's published paper shows that he chose an interesting strategy for organizing his argument. The first paragraph recounts the bare facts of the discovery and first scientific presentations of the Neandertal remains, as might be expected. But it closes with a strongly worded summary of the main conclusions of his study of the remains. Only after the conclusions were made clear did he present, for the next sixteen and a half pages, the evidence, measurements, and comparisons upon which he based his opinions.

Thus, instead of leading his colleagues through a careful chain of reasoning and supporting evidence that would bring them inevitably to his conclusions, Schaaffhausen baldly and boldly set out his convictions first, leaving them either to follow his backtracking through the evidence or simply to accept his word for the truth of his statements. Very self-assured scholars, who know no one will doubt their authority, might use such a strategy. So, too, might a man who fears he may be shouted down before he has time to present his arguments and so wishes to drive home his major points at the beginning.

What Schaaffhausen asserted most strongly was that the bones were not pathological (except the once-fractured left ulna) but represented a normal individual of a new type of human. He also emphasized that they were very ancient, being both pre-Celtic and antediluvian: in fact, fossil.

In this, Schaaffhausen had correctly identified the key issues that were shortly to become the subject of bitter dispute. He knew his audience well and perceived where the newness and importance of the Neandertal material lay. He also thought he had found direct evidence supporting his theory of the mutability of species and the descent of humans from apes, which he had published in 1853 in a volume entitled *The Stability and Transformation of Species*.

Unfortunately for Schaaffhausen and Fuhlrott, the former's dogmatic assertions and political position were not sufficient to insure acceptance of these ideas. Schaaffhausen's conclusions were soon challenged by a scientific audience consisting initially of Germany's major figures in natural history. Only later did dissenters from the majority view speak up and only later still did the debate spread to the rest of Europe.

The rejection of Schaaffhausen's ideas within his own country was perhaps inevitable. As it was in France in the mid-nineteenth century, German science was rigidly hierarchical and strongly centralized. As Paris was in France, Berlin was the center of everything in German academic life. A few highly influential academic posts were occupied by individuals whose power was greatly extended by additional appointments or by special commissions to the government. A professor at Bonn, like Schaaffhausen, was almost bound to come off badly in a challenge to the establishment views.

It was an interesting admixture of individuals who responded to Schaaffhausen's bombshell, delivered at that extraordinary June 2 meeting and later published in full. Unfortunately for Fuhlrott and Schaaffhausen, not one took their side.

The most important respondent was the man who personified, indeed dictated, the establishment's views: Rudolf Virchow. To Schaaffhausen, Virchow's opinion meant more than that of any other scientist at the time. And Virchow was having none of Schaaffhausen's fossil man, for reasons that become clear when Virchow's personal and intellectual histories are considered.

Virchow was born in 1821, the son of a farmer in Pomerania, a Polish region of the German empire where one was either a Junker—a Prussian aristocrat—or a peasant. The young Virchow could boast of neither family name, nor inherited money, nor good looks. He was small, wiry and brown-haired, with a sallow complexion, a thin, beaky nose, and piercing, unforgiving eyes that always accused the subject of their focus of doing less than he or she should have.

In fact, a reminiscence by one of his students after Virchow's death speaks of passing a portrait of his former master, years after his death, and once again feeling Virchow's urging to do more, to do it better—of feeling, in fact, the guilt of not measuring up to the inflated expectations that his students, employees, and colleagues always suffered from.

Lacking family, grace, and beauty, Virchow was nevertheless gifted with astonishing brilliance and his deep determination to succeed. From an early age, Virchow's open ambition was to show the world that he was not simply as good as anyone else but better: to win his rightful place as a leader of Germany. His drive doubtless sprang from his sense of inferiority, of being the poor, ugly boy with the unfashionable accent and

11. Rudolf Virchow, the founder of modern pathology and ardent opponent of evolution in any form. By proclaiming several normal Neandertal fossils to be pathological, he delayed their acceptance in Germany as archaic humans until the late nineteenth century.

the family of no distinction. In a peculiar way, his handicaps fed his self-confidence and produced an invincible conviction of the rightness of his instincts and beliefs. His arrogance, even as a young man, was astounding in its proportions. He tore through his youth, winning prizes and excelling in all the sciences, and entered into medical training in Berlin.

Virchow's outstanding intelligence and hard work won him a scholarship to one of the best schools in Germany, the Pepinière, a division of the Friedrich Wilhelm Institute of the University of Berlin that trained young men for a medical career in the Prussian army. As a scholarship boy—a "Pepin"—Virchow was acutely aware that he was considered to be socially inferior, a feeling only accentuated by his continual struggle to find the money to pay for clothes, books, and other needs. Along the way, he acquired the patronage of several powerful men of the very aristocratic class that he so mercilessly criticized once his education was complete.

Though he was obviously headed for success, no one spoke of his charm, his wit, his physical prowess, or his warmth: only of his intelligence, hard work, and outspoken criticism of anything he thought was morally or, worse yet, intellectually dishonest. In later years, when he had attained positions of power and influence, Virchow cultivated a cadre of dedicated young men who surrounded him in his professional life. If they could live up to his standards of behavior, his coterie were the recipients of great kindness and favors. If they failed him—for example, by such outrages as taking jobs he had not procured for them or marrying without his permission—they found themselves scorned and rejected.

It was Virchow's destiny to become the founder of modern pathology, a science peculiarly suited to his skeptic's personality. Virchow's pathology emphasized factual detail, the meticulous weighing of evidence, and the deep distrust of intuition. This flavor was, no doubt, produced in part by Virchow's own predispositions. Such was his influence, as an intellectual giant in nineteenth-century Germany, in structuring the science of pathology that the whiff of Virchowian skepticism and the image of the hard-nosed, unrelenting pathologist has lingered until today.

To Virchow, his pathology studies were the careful stalking and identification of the enemy, that which endangers life and order and goodness, an enemy that must be fought and utterly destroyed if possible. This cool, merciless battle against enemies (usually in human form) was an endeavor in which Virchow engaged again and again during his varied career as scientist, politician, and anthropologist. He became a vigorous opponent of any idea he felt was metaphysical, romantic, or speculative, and there were many such ideas in nineteenth-century Germany because of the rise of the romantic and reactionary movement known as *Naturphilosophie*.

Naturphilosophie, led and inspired by the works of philosopher Friedrich Wilhelm Joseph von Schelling, combined a sort of romantic mysticism—a nostalgia for a medieval era of chivalry and feudalism—with a philosophical style of natural history built upon the notion of the oneness of God and Nature. All beings were perfectible if they were allowed to evolve toward their destiny; all organisms represented variations on the theme of the archetypal organism, whose characteristics could be identified by careful study; and all the natural world was sacred, though the best and most perfect expression was in the German countryside.

While the strength of this approach to natural history was that it got scientists out to capture and observe specimens in their natural habitats, it also gave rise to unadulterated speculation and nonsense about organisms. Several main proponents of natural philosophy in the 1830s and 1840s fumbled with evolutionary ideas and also toyed with the ancient idea of the spontaneous generation of life, giving both an equally bad name in Virchow's mind.

Virchow's two best-known theories stand out in sharp contrast to the abstract, romantic philosophizing about nature that characterized most biologists in Germany in the first half of the nineteenth century. His ideas were deeply revealing of his personality and thought processes.

Looking carefully, the "most minute and most careful microscopy," and recording objectively were his methods.

The first of his major ideas concerned the origin of cells themselves and was a large part of Virchow's thesis as a senior medical student in the 1840s. "*Omnis cellula a cellula,*" Virchow declared. "All cells come from other cells." He then set out to prove, in irrefutable, scientific detail, that such a thing as spontaneous generation was not and could not be true. It was an open attack on the views of well-respected scholars much his senior.

The very structure of Virchow's epigram reveals a firmly held belief that living things are as they have always been, that they can have come only from other living things just like themselves. Virchow's later work on characterizing races and tracing racial migrations reflects the same type of belief: Celts came from Celts, Germans came from Germans, and so on. Things were always largely as they are now. What's more, Virchow was a firm polygenist, believing that the different races had different origins. The man who espoused such views could not possibly accept a human ancestor like a Neandertal.

As was to happen repeatedly with Neandertal fossils, it was not just science but also politics that led to their misinterpretation. Another of Virchow's theories proclaimed that disease and illness were simply a matter of a rogue cell or cells, a vicious revolt by a part of the organism against the good of the whole. Virchow drew explicit parallels between the organism, comprised of individual cells organized (perhaps at some sacrifice to the individual's good) for the benefit of the whole, and the state, which Virchow believed must be similarly organized. Thus, in Virchow's view, the organism, like the state, was made up of individual units that carried out their own life-functions and also cooperated— through a division of labor, each carrying out the task for which it was best fitted—in the formation of a higher, collective being.

If there were no such well-ordered system—if organisms and whole species, like cells, could step outside their natural positions and boundaries—the result would be disease, chaos, and ruin. In fact, in later years Virchow was to express the idea that it was only through what we would now call mutants or evolutionary experiments that anything new might arise. In short, he suggested that the founders of new species or new types of organisms were literally and by definition pathological, since they were deviations from the normal.

For Virchow, the idea of human antiquity, of our descent from a more apelike form, and of evolutionary theory itself was associated with political ideals that were utterly unacceptable. He was a liberal fighting the establishment and yet fiercely patriotic. What he hoped for was the Marxist revolution, in which each would be allotted or assigned to his or her rightful place in the society, *not* on the basis of heredity and family, but on the basis of abilities. He was a socialist of sorts, a champion of the people, and yet still a believer in elitism, but only under a system that would permit gifted individuals of nondescript background (like himself) to rise to the top.

The net result of this complex pattern of beliefs and principles was that Virchow tried to suppress the acceptance of evolutionary ideas or of any hominid fossils by every means possible until he died in 1902.

The main ground on which the Neandertal fossils were attacked in Germany was singularly Virchow's own: the specimens were declared to be clearly pathological. The instigator of the initial attack was Professor Mayer, Schaaffhausen's colleague from Bonn. His arguments now seem ludicrous and were certainly delivered with a heavy-handed, Germanic humor. Fuhlrott's poor skeleton was considered point by point. For example, Mayer observed: "This flexure [of the thigh bones] is not normal, and is observable, like the inward flexure of the tuberosities of the ischial bones [of the pelvis], in those who have been riders from their youth up." Added to this inferred lifetime in the saddle, Mayer deduced that the Neandertal individual probably had had rickets as a child, thus accentuating the curvature of the legs. In the end, he proposed that the skeleton was not ancient at all, but belonged to a Mongolian Cossack soldier of Tchernitcheff's army, one of the Russian hordes that went through Germany to attack France in 1814. After being wounded, Mayer supposed, the Cossack conveniently crawled into the cave to die.

Finally, he explained the unusual features of the skull: "The prominence of the superciliary arches is in part, . . . occasioned by the corrugator supercilliorum muscle, but this need be but weak if it has only to lift the already raised outer lamella of the frontal bone." In other words, Mayer proposed that usual or habitual exercise of the muscles of the forehead might cause the bulging of the superficial layer of the bone over the orbits until they form the hefty browridges observed on the Neandertal cranium.

As Huxley archly summarized Mayer's argument:

> Given a rickety child with a bad habit of frowning (say from the internal flatulent disturbances to which such children are especially

liable), and the result will be a Neandertal man! [In Mayer's view]
. . . the Neandertal man was nothing but a rickety, bow-legged,
frowning Cossack, who, having carefully divested himself of his
arms, accoutrements, and clothes (no traces of which were found),
crept into a cave to die, and has been covered up with loam two feet
thick by the "rebound" of the muddy cataracts which (hypotheti-
cally,) have rushed over the mouth of his cave.

Huxley's presentation of the case makes it sound so absurd that it is
difficult to imagine anyone believing Mayer's claim, even for a moment.

And yet, Mayer's assertion that the skeleton was pathological and
rachitic was endorsed by Virchow, the great pathologist himself. Rickets
was a well-known and common disease of the nineteenth century; Virchow was not only familiar with it, he had written a definitive description and diagnosis of the disease in two works published in 1853 and 1854.

What is so astonishing about Virchow's pronouncement is that he, of
all people, should have seen clearly that the bones of the Neandertal
arms and legs were extraordinarily stout, bespeaking a muscular individual of supremely athletic habits, rather than the weakened and slender
bones of an undernourished, calcium-poor, rachitic sufferer. He had
himself described the way in which the hardening or calcification of new
bone was retarded in rickets, and the long bones developed unusual
curvatures caused by incomplete fractures. As Schaaffhausen pointed out,
and Virchow's eyes cannot have failed to see, "[There is] an uncommon
thickness of the other bones of the skeleton, which exceeds by about
one-half the usual proportions."

How is it Virchow can have denied his eyes, in an ultimate betrayal
of his long-held credo of honesty and adhering to the evidence at all
costs? A combination of factors seems to have come into play. Most
important was Virchow's blanket belief in the immutability of species
and organisms even down to the cellular level. If a species was mutable,
it was therefore diseased, pathological: the enemy.

Virchow's later assertions that the origin of any new type of organism
lay, by definition, in a pathological founder reveals the internal consistency in his interpretation of the Neandertal remains. Although they
were not pathological in the clinical sense of being diseased—except,
most unfortunately, for the once-broken ulna—the Neandertal remains
were pathological in Virchow's terms in that they were unlike modern
humans: they represented a deviation from humanness.

Underlying all this was his deep dislike of evolutionary ideas in general and their political implications in particular. In this regard, he fought acceptance of the Neandertals because they implied that evolution occurred, and he fought evolution because it too closely resembled the romantic deification of Nature practiced by the natural philosophers. Their woolly-headed, poetic appreciations of the glories of Nature probably made Virchow shudder to the depths of his intensely pragmatic, focused, laboratory-inhabiting self. It was a revolutionary view of biology that Virchow found deeply repellent.

Ironically, Virchow had been a revolutionary of sorts only a few years before. Asked by the government to conduct a medical survey of Upper Silesia, where a typhus epidemic was raging, Virchow delivered a blistering indictment of the government's inept handling of the catastrophe and recommended (among other things) "full and unlimited democracy, or education, freedom and prosperity" as the cure. Just after this blunt and public criticism, he went to fight at the barricades in Berlin in the abortive revolution of 1848 against the repressive, conservative monarchy headed by a king turned natural philosopher, Frederich Wilhelm IV. The king, to Virchow's disgust, devoted his energies to trying to re-create the medieval utopia he envisioned.

Following the fighting in 1848, Virchow was so well known as a liberal protester against the Prussian aristocracy that he was fired from his post at the Charité Hospital in Berlin. For some time, the German government seemed to be trying to starve him out or buy him off, or perhaps he was simply being rescued by some Prussian patron. After five long months of unemployment, he was offered a junior professorship at a provincial university, Würzburg, effectively exiling him to a remote position in the country and forcing him to leave his friends, job, fiancée, and once-promising future. However, the minister of culture refused to forward the request for his appointment to the King of Bavaria unless Virchow changed his political views and guaranteed that he would not make Würzburg "a playground for . . . [his] hitherto demonstrated radical tendencies." The Würzburg Senate rejected the minister's former demand but, as Virchow wrote to his parents, "the second, however, it has put to me. I have replied that I have no intention of acquiring a playground for radical tendencies." It was a proud, even arrogant reply, but he discontinued publication of his radical journal and adopted a less public role that he referred to as "observer."

This circumspection was apparently sufficient, for the job was offered and accepted; Virchow rapidly became one of Würzburg's renowned academic stars. Despite his paltry pay at Würzburg, some years later Virchow turned down a position at Zürich, which would have conveniently removed him from Germany. He was offered a special government grant to travel abroad and study for two years: he refused. Finally, he was asked to take a fact-finding tour through the Spessart region of Bavaria, where famine and disease rampaged, to investigate health conditions. The intent may have been to busy him with medical work, so that his troublemaking would cease, or to see if he was still so implacable. He was, almost.

This offer he accepted, and turned in another indictment of government mismanagement and neglect of the populace; however, he praised the government for its intervention, which meant that only typhoid and not typhus, too, was ravaging the poor. He proposed radical reforms, widespread education, a more even distribution of resources, and an end to the bleeding of the country's resources to line the pockets of the aristocracy. It was an accurate, but extremely critical, assessment of a complex disaster.

Astonishingly, this bold move seemed to produce the result desired by Virchow. True, serious changes in government were underway, but these had the effect more of consolidating the German empire under the Prussian leadership of Bismarck and his cronies—the very factions that Virchow criticized most bitterly—than of empowering the peasants.

Why, then, was the ultimate effect of Virchow's blistering criticism of the status quo that he was offered a professorship in Berlin at the tender age of thirty-five, after seven years of exile? The government even acceded to his demand to build a new pathological institute for him and to add a new department to the Charité. The most logical explanation is that, because Virchow was now internationally recognized for his medical research, he was difficult to ignore; it was, in a sense, an embarrassment not to have him in Berlin. He may also have been valued for his blunt honesty, however uncomfortable his outspokenness was, and for his suggestions about improving the lot of the people, which might lessen their tendency to revolt. Finally, it may have been a decision based along the lines of a remark made famous by Lyndon Johnson, who pointed out that it is better to have a troublemaker inside the tent, pissing out, than outside the tent, pissing in. It was certainly preferable to have Virchow preoccupied with building departments, institutes, museums, and scientific societies in Berlin, where they could keep an eye on him, than in the provinces taking public potshots at the ruling powers.

Whatever the cause, once Virchow took over the professorship in Berlin in 1856, he was an unstoppable and irresistible power in German biological science and considerably less inclined to rock the boat. The Neandertal remains were pathological and did not establish human antiquity or evolution, and that was that. What's more, Virchow argued a few years later, the healed fracture of the arm and apparent old age of the Neandertal individual showed that he could not possibly have belonged to a primitive hunter-gatherer society, in which Virchow believed an injured hunter could not have survived. Therefore, the individual was from a sedentary, agrarian society and obviously recent.

His disdain of Darwinian evolutionary theory, which hit Germany with an almost audible zing in 1860, became the party line. In that year, Heinrich Georg Bronn, a paleontologist from Heidelberg, translated into German Darwin's great work, *The Origin of Species*. But Bronn chose to omit the telltale and daring line, "Light will be shed upon the origin of man and his history." He had the further audacity to append to the volume some critical remarks of his own, so that the only form in which the work was available to German speakers carried the seeds of disbelief.

Bronn knew the feelings of the times and predicted accurately how the leaders of German science would react. Darwin's work was quickly and harshly reviewed in several major scientific journals. Virchow himself attacked Darwin's ideas as poorly supported and unproven—strange opinions, indeed, of the work that overwhelmed all of the British reviewers with its meticulous documentation and detail.

In Germany, the crucial circumstance leading to the rejection of evolutionary theory was that Darwin's masterful presentation of the idea *followed* the discovery and description of the Neandertal remains. With no preestablished context of evolutionary theory, and with a strongly centralized scientific community led by Virchow, the Neandertal fossils were soundly rejected at first. But in Britain, the same fossils enjoyed a very different reception.

The entire sequence of events, and the depth of the controversy over the Neandertal fossils, was reversed in England. Little was known in English scientific circles of Schaaffhausen's and Fuhlrott's work until 1861. In the meantime, the British were busily fighting another battle. Three Englishmen were to play pivotal roles that would forever change our understanding of human evolution: Alfred Russel Wallace, Charles Darwin, and Thomas Henry Huxley.

The battle's origins can be traced back to September 1855, when

12. Portrait of Alfred Russel Wallace working in the tropics. This image, probably made after the fact, depicts Wallace writing his important articles on evolution and the origin of species.

Wallace, an unknown, impoverished, self-educated man, had published an eye-opening paper in the *Annals and Magazine of Natural History* in London. This paper, entitled "On the Law which has Regulated the Introduction of New Species," contained the essence of the ideas of evolution that were to become known as Darwin's and, only coincidentally, as Wallace's.

Born in January 1823, Wallace was the eighth of nine children of an inept businessman and sometime publisher of magazines doomed to failure, Thomas Vere Wallace, and his wife, Mary Anne née Greenell. The family had left fashionable and expensive London for Usk, a small market town on the Welsh border, some years before. The family's fortunes fell from middle class until they hovered perilously close to being working class. Most of the children were sent out as apprentices, due to the lack of family funds, and Wallace enjoyed only seven years of formal schooling before he followed his siblings out into the world at fourteen. An unusually tall boy, reaching six feet two inches, Wallace was a painfully shy but diligent young scholar with a strong interest in natural history.

In 1834, Wallace was apprenticed to a land surveyor, while the young gentleman Darwin was seeing the world on the *Beagle*. Two years later, Wallace was packed off to his brother John, a carpenter in London, where he took to wearing spectacles for his weak eyes, worked ten-hour days, and read and attended lectures at the Hall of Science, a working-man's club, in the evenings. There he listened to fiery speeches by Robert Owen, who fought for higher wages for workers and the abolition of child labor, and who discussed Malthus's theories of population increase and competition for resources.

It was a new sort of education for Wallace, but it did not continue long. Once again, family pressures caused Wallace to leave London in 1837 and join another brother, William, who was working in the country-side as a surveyor. As they traveled the road, mapping and surveying, they collected fossils and other geological curiosities. It was the year Darwin, just back from the voyage of the *Beagle*, began writing down thoughts in his first notebook on the transmutation of species.

Darwin was not simply the older and richer of the two, he had the immense advantages of a privileged education and an influential family. Nonetheless, Wallace's eyes were opened to the order and beauty of science when a small book on botany that he purchased with a precious shilling suddenly enabled him to identify and classify the plants he encountered. Seeking still more information, he sought help from a bookseller, who suggested Loudon's *Encyclopedia of Plants*—a wonderful volume costing several pounds, far more money than Wallace had at his disposal. Hayward, the bookseller, allowed the eager young man to borrow a copy, from which he copied out immense amounts of informa-tion. He began creating his own collection of plants, each pressed and identified. Attending a flower show at Swansea, Wallace was stunned by his first orchid and conceived a passionate desire to see the tropics, where such wonders bloomed.

Unnoticed by Wallace, his brother was having difficulty keeping enough business to employ them both. His father's death in 1843 scat-tered the impoverished family still further. In 1844, while Darwin was living happily at Down House and working slowly on an essay present-ing his species theory, Wallace landed a post as a schoolteacher in Leicester. For once he had a job with enough free time to build up his herbarium and frequent the public library.

A chance meeting in Leicester with a self-taught insect enthusiast from a modest background, Henry Walter Bates, radically changed Wallace's life. Not only were they in instant sympathy—Bates was perhaps the first man Wallace had ever met who truly shared his love of natural history—but Bates's astonishing collection of hundreds of beetles broadened Wallace's interests to include entomology. Here he shared a lifelong enthusiasm with Darwin, whose acquaintance Wallace had yet to make, for Darwin was ever among the most avid of beetle collectors. Their lives were disparate and yet oddly parallel.

This idyllic period of happy rambles and shared collecting trips was rudely interrupted by the realities of life: Wallace's brother William died, leaving considerable debts, and Wallace resigned his teaching post, returning to work as a surveyor, because these were in demand and commanded much higher salaries than before, to pay off his brother's debts. By 1848, through extraordinary work and frugality, Wallace had amassed what seemed to him a huge amount of money: one hundred pounds. By odd coincidence, in the same year, Darwin's father died, leaving him forty thousand pounds.

Wallace and Bates continued to correspond, reporting excitedly to each other when they read Darwin's *Voyage of the Beagle* and Lyell's *Principles of Geology*. There was, of course, no thought in the nineteenth-century, class-bound society of Britain that men such as themselves could hobnob with the scientific gentry whose books they were devouring. Wallace became fascinated by the species question, and he and Bates both longed to depart for the tropics to solve it. A chance reading of a Victorian travelogue, W. H. Edwards's *Voyage Up the River Amazon*, hardened their daydreams into action: they would go.

With little money, no educational credentials, and no connections, neither Wallace nor Bates could hope to be invited to be a ship's naturalist, as Darwin had been for the *Beagle*, or be taken on a navy ship as surgeon-naturalist, as Thomas Henry Huxley had been aboard the *Rattlesnake*. They hit upon the idea of collecting natural-history specimens for museums and wealthy amateurs. They found an agent, Samuel Stevens, who was to handle their financial affairs for years, and set out on the HMS *Mischief* for the Amazon in 1848.

For four years, the two friends tramped the tropics, bewildered and amazed by the abundance of new plants and animals that surrounded them, beset by hardships, disease, hunger, and biting insects, set upon by leeches, ticks, and vampire bats. It was their second education, a telling addition to their book learning. From it, both Bates and Wallace published accounts of their adventures and findings.

Among Bates's most enduring contributions was his work on the role of mimicry (now known as Batesian mimicry), published in 1860–61 but conceived during his and Wallace's South American adventures. As he collected butterflies, Bates noticed that some species so closely resembled others that two could hardly be distinguished until they were actually in his hands. The more numerous type, in such circumstances, was bad-tasting or had some other chemical defense against predators; the mimic took advantage of this by posing as its unpalatable partner. Batesian mimicry was obviously dependent upon natural selection, the mechanism that would work to keep the mimic sufficiently similar to the prototype to be protected. No halfway mimicry or general resemblance would suffice.

For Wallace, one benefit of his Amazonian travels was that it developed his interest in human races, particularly those generally viewed as brutal savages. Unlike most explorers of the day, Wallace, in his writings, shows clearly that he *liked* the Indians he encountered and admired their ability to survive "absolutely independent of civilization" through the use of their knowledge, skills, and ingenious tools.

Here Wallace differed sharply from Darwin, who had been horrified and utterly taken aback by his first encounter with peoples who were neither agrarian peasants nor urban factory workers. Indeed, in a subtle, but common, kind of racism, Darwin identified the living Tierra del Fuegians he encountered on the *Beagle* voyage with relict populations of human ancestors, a survival of more ancient types as a sort of living fossil. In *The Descent of Man*, Darwin looked back on his *Beagle* voyage and concluded:

> There can hardly be a doubt that we are descended from barbarians. The astonishment which I felt on first seeing a party of Fuegians on a wild and broken shore will never be forgotten by me, for the reflection at once rushed into my mind—such were our ancestors. These men were absolutely naked and bedaubed with paint, their long hair was tangled, their mouths, frothed with excitement, and their expression was wild, startled, and distrustful. They possessed hardly any arts, and like wild animals lived on what they could catch.

In short, Darwin the gentleman, used to refined manners and genteel ways, could hardly credit these creatures with being members of his own species—a common enough view at the time. The nature of humanity, and whether it was inherent (genetic) or learned, would be debated for years to come.

A more tangible product of Wallace's Amazonian trip was his publications. In addition to a travelogue, Wallace published a monograph on *Papilio*, a genus of rare and beautiful butterfly. His innovation was not the presentation of thirty-eight different species of butterflies, but his classification, which was based on both the appearance and the ecology of the species. He understood, and proposed, that this group of closely allied species—implying their common descent—were simultaneously limited in their distribution and encouraged in their divergence by geography.

Wallace's return to England was bedraggled—the ship went down, destroying the last shipment of precious specimens—but not disastrous, because his agent Stevens had providentially insured the specimens for at least a part of their value. His aim was to publish, though he had rescued little from the sinking ship. There was, however, a tin containing drawings and notes on palm trees. When no publisher would risk it, Wallace published *Palm Trees of the Amazon* at his own expense. The 137 pages and 48 plates, with careful detail and technical descriptions, attracted some notice in scientific circles in London.

It was the beginning of Wallace's reputation. *Palm Trees* certainly came to the attention of the botanist at Kew Gardens, Joseph Hooker, one of Darwin's closest, lifelong friends. Wallace attended some lectures by Huxley—whose brilliance and knowledge cowed him—and frequented the Insect Room at the British Museum, where he saw Darwin, who later could not remember this meeting. Inevitably, Wallace's shyness and social background made him reticent and uncomfortable in the presence of such men.

While Darwin labored on at a snail's pace, working on his notebooks and ideas about the origin of species, Wallace decided to undertake another voyage. In January 1854, he set out for eight years of travel in southeast Asia, especially the Malay peninsula. Late in 1854, while a guest of the White Rajah of Sarawak, James Brooke, Wallace wrote his paper for the *Annals and Magazine of Natural History*, proposing the Sarawak Law. The most essential point therein, as Wallace emphasized with italics, was that *"Every species has come into existence coincident both in time and space with a pre-existing closely allied species."* He clearly suggested that the preexisting, closely allied species serves as the ancestral stock from which the new species arises under the influence of geography and environment.

The response in England, unknown to Wallace, was extraordinary.

Lyell, the geologist, read Wallace's essay on November 26, 1855. Two days later, he started keeping his own scientific notebook on the species question. Six months later, in April, Lyell went to Down House to see Darwin, writing in his diary, "With Darwin: On the formation of Species by Natural Selection (Origin Query?)" and noting in his journal that he and Darwin had discussed Mr. Wallace.

For Darwin's part, he read and annotated "Wallace's Paper," copying out Wallace's ten points of evidence and his interpretation of the origin of species. It was compelling stuff. Wallace proposed that the analogy of the branching tree was the "best mode of representing the natural arrangement of species and their successive creation," arguing that the resemblances among species and the geographic distribution of closely related species could be explained if they arose as new branches springing from the same trunk, some of which might be pruned or destroyed by changed circumstances but others of which would survive. Darwin scribbled in his annotations: "Can this be true?" Although he had been working on his own theory of evolution and the origin of species for eighteen years at that point, Darwin had obviously missed a trick or two that Wallace had discovered.

In distinct contrast to Wallace, whose continual scrambling for knowledge and money pushed him into more rapid thinking and prompter publication, Darwin's life history and background permitted, perhaps even encouraged, his infinitely slow pace.

On February 12, 1809, Charles Darwin was born into a well-known and well-to-do family, one of six children of Robert Waring Darwin and Susannah Wedgwood Darwin, from the wealthy and illustrious china-making family. Darwin had a comfortable, love-filled childhood, despite the death of his mother when he was eight years old. His beloved father was a much-respected physician and a large man, six feet two inches, from whom Darwin inherited his height and substantial wealth. Darwin's paternal grandfather was Erasmus Darwin, of *Zoonomia* fame, and his maternal grandfather was Josiah Wedgwood.

As a child, Darwin was distracted from all else by natural history. He collected insects, birds, birds' eggs, minerals, beetles, and practically everything else he could get his hands on. In his *Autobiography*, he recalled with "deep mortification" that his father once said to him in a rare fit of exasperation: "You care for nothing but shooting, dogs and rat-catching, and you will be a disgrace to yourself and all your family."

In 1825, "as [he] was doing no good at school," Darwin was sent off

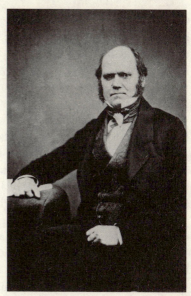

13. Charles Darwin in 1857, the year in which he was agonizing over the publication of Wallace's papers on the origin of species and writing his own book on the subject.

to Edinburgh University to study medicine. Over the next two years, he found his work by turns fearfully dull and repellently disgusting. In short, he did not take to the medical profession well, a fact he explained as being in no small measure due to his family's wealth.

Despite the family fortune that Darwin would eventually inherit, his father was determined that he be trained in something useful. Rather than letting his son turn into an idle, sporting man, Robert Darwin suggested that Charles study to become a clergyman. In 1828, the young Darwin entered Christ's Church College of Cambridge University, where he stayed for a full three years. His total of five years of university studies provides a striking contrast with Wallace's meager seven years of elementary school.

Darwin's response to Cambridge was, at first, as lackadaisical as his endeavors at medicine:

> . . . my time was sadly wasted there, and worse than wasted. From my passion for shooting and for hunting and when this failed for riding across the country I got into a sporting set, including some dissipated, low-minded young men. We used often to dine together in the evening, though these dinners often included men of a higher stamp, and we sometimes drank too much, with jolly singing and playing at cards afterwards.

Given Darwin's exceedingly quiet, reclusive life for most of the intervening years between his youth and the writing of these words, it is difficult to judge whether he was actually a young rake and ne'er-do-well or whether he was simply an ordinary young gentleman sometimes given to high spirits but whose greater fault may have been simply a lack of focus and motivation.

Fortunately for science, Darwin also fell in with John Stevens Henslow, the renowned professor of botany, and his tutor, Adam Sedgwick, the geologist. These two men must have managed to strike some spark in Darwin's intellect and, after graduation, Henslow secured for Darwin the post as ship's naturalist on the HMS *Beagle*. Such an occurrence was Darwin's heart's desire and, though his father strongly objected, the young man was left with an out: "If you can find any man of common sense, who advises you to go," his father said, "I will give my consent."

His uncle obliged, and Darwin consoled his father that he would be forced to become less extravagant, saying, "I should be deuced clever to spend more than my allowance whilst on board the *Beagle*."

His father replied, "But they all tell me you are very clever."

Fortunately, the young Darwin was clever enough to have his eyes opened and his brain excited by the things he saw on the voyage of the *Beagle*. During the five years of travel, from 1831 to 1836, Darwin grew up emotionally and intellectually, seeing for himself the influences of climate, geography, and habitat on the wondrous new wealth of birds, insects, plants, and animals to which he was exposed. He learned to see and think for himself.

Upon returning to England, he lived on his income—no sunken ship and half-insured cargo for Darwin—and, like Wallace, began to write up his ideas and observations. He also became an active figure in various scientific societies and married his cousin, Emma Wedgwood, as their respective families had wished for years.

As mentioned, in 1837 Darwin opened his notebook on the transmutation of species. Judging by the rate of publication of his other studies, this one should have been finished in a year or two. Instead, somewhere along the way, he slowed down and began to drag his feet. The bright young man underwent a metamorphosis in reverse. Unlike insects, he went not from a crawling larva to a winged form, but backwards.

He developed a constellation of physical ailments involving head, stomach, and nerves that came and went with convenient regularity. A number of diagnoses have been suggested, ranging from Chagas' disease, transmitted by parasites that he may have picked up in South America, to profound hypochondriasis. Whatever the cause, he struggled against his ailments to work, stopped going out, and eventually found visits from even his closest friends too disturbing. He worked intermittently on his "big book" on the origin of species, but seemed never to be drawing any nearer to completion. Whether physically ill or not, it seems clear that Darwin could not bring himself to express his heretical ideas openly—such expression being a dangerous tactic, as he was later to advise others.

It is not quite clear when Darwin first read Wallace's Sarawak paper but, whenever it was, it spurred Darwin into ending his dithering and endless deliberations. Sometime early in 1856, perhaps during the April visit, Lyell urged Darwin to write his views out pretty fully. Darwin's response was typically hesitant:

> With respect to your suggestion of a sketch of my views, I hardly know what to think, but will reflect on it, but it goes against my prejudices. To give a fair sketch would be absolutely impossible, for every proposition requires such an array of facts. If I were to do anything, it could only refer to the main agency of change—selection—and perhaps point out a very few of the leading features. . . . I do not know what to think; I rather hate the idea of writing for priority, yet I certainly should be vexed if any one were to publish my doctrines before me.

Lyell realized Wallace was rapidly closing in on a theory that Darwin had been struggling with for years and Lyell urged him to get on with it; Darwin was worried.

In 1856–57, in letters to his close friends Lyell the geologist, Hooker the botanist, and others, Darwin begs over and over for their opinions—"I very much want advice and *truthful* consolation if you can give it. . . . I am in a peck of troubles and do pray forgive me for troubling you." The same questions spin round and round in these letters: Should he publish an abstract? Is it justifiable if it is at the urging of friends? May he name them as these friends? Don't they think an abstract in book form is better than publication in a journal, where he might have to *beg* an editor and council to publish? He also emphasizes, repeatedly, how long he had been working on his theory, stating in some letters it is eighteen years—though his son, editor of his *Life and Letters*, states it can have been only seventeen—and in others that it is nineteen years. These letters have the ring of an anxious and insecure man seeking approval and support from his powerful friends for something he intends to do that he feels may not be quite right or may not be received well.

Wallace wrote to Darwin on October 10, 1856, in a letter now lost, apparently asking if Darwin or any of his learned friends had read the Sarawak paper, to which Darwin replied on May 1, 1857. Darwin's letter was calm; it had been a year, more or less, since he had read Wallace's paper and begun preparing his own works for publication at Lyell's urging. His letter praises Wallace for the excellence of his Sarawak paper—with which he agrees in almost every word—and emphasizes with an exclamation point that he, Darwin, has been working on the subject for twenty years. He also alludes to a theory, now being readied for publication, too extensive to be explained in a letter.

Wallace was thrilled by Darwin's letter and boasted to his old friend, Bates, "I have been much gratified by a letter from Darwin in which he says that he agrees with 'almost every word' of my paper." His response to finding out that Darwin is working on a similar theory shows no hint of Darwin-like anxiety over being scooped:

> He may save me the trouble of writing more on my hypothesis, by proving that there is no difference in nature between the origin of species and of varieties, or he may give me trouble by arriving at another conclusion; but, in all events, his facts will be given for me to work upon.

If Wallace's Sarawak paper apparently provoked a flurry of anxiety over publication in Darwin's circle, it was nothing compared with the stomach-churning shock Darwin experienced when he received what is now known as Wallace's Ternate paper. In the early summer of 1858, Darwin received the manuscript sent to him by Wallace, who asked with his usual charming modesty and naiveté if Darwin would pass it on to Lyell if he thought it had merit. Wallace's work was entitled "On the Tendency of Varieties to Depart Indefinitely from the Original Type." It contained a perfectly straightforward, elegantly simple exposition of evolution, powered by the mechanisms of the struggle for existence and natural selection.

It must have been a dreadful moment, as Darwin read Wallace's words and slowly realized that these lucid phrases and perceptive sentences explained the very theory Darwin had been struggling to articulate for twenty-one years. He wrote to Lyell in despair on June 18, 1858:

> [Wallace] has to-day sent me the enclosed, and asked me to forward it to you. . . . Your words have come true with a vengeance—that I should be forestalled. . . . Please return me the MS., which he does

not say he wishes me to publish, but I shall, of course, at once write and offer to send to any journal. So all my originality, whatever it may amount to, will be smashed.

A week later, Darwin wrote his friend again. He was patently wrestling with both his conscience and his pride, wondering, in a tormented spasm of guilt, whether it would be dishonorable of him to publish materials on the origin of species that he had written years before. Could Lyell and his dear friend Hooker advise him? His letters (there are several—in itself an indication of his terrible anxiousness) show that he hoped for support and yet squirmed at confronting and revealing to others his own naked ambition and pride. In one letter, he moaned piteously, "I am quite prostrated and can do nothing. . . . It is miserable in me to care at all about priority."

Added to the professional disaster that Wallace's work presented, Darwin was suffering a more personal crisis. His household was decimated by disease. First his young son, Charles, born mentally deficient, died of scarlet fever. Then the child's nurse contracted the disease. In short order, his fifteen-year-old daughter Henrietta came down with diphtheria, which then spread to her nurse. Darwin the devoted father was beside himself with grief and fear for his family, at the same time that Darwin the dedicated and dogged scientist was contemplating the shattered fragments of his life's work. It was, without question, the worst few weeks of his comfortable and usually sheltered life.

Some have argued that Darwin and his friends Lyell and Hooker engaged in an outright conspiracy to preserve Darwin's priority, intentionally usurping the honors and fame that were rightly due Wallace. This is probably a harsher judgment than is fair. Quite probably, Lyell and Hooker never believed that Darwin would actually finish his big book, whereas the up-and-coming Wallace was bound to, so that giving their friend the priority in terms of a small paper on the subject would not be so telling. In any case, the negotiations to publish Wallace's paper in the Linnaean Society journal jointly with Darwin's were a "delicate arrangement."

The arrangement, constructed by Lyell and Hooker, was for Wallace's paper to be read before the July 1, 1858, meeting of the Linnaean Society in London, *following* a very similarly titled paper by Darwin: "On the Tendency of Species to form Varieties; and on the Perpetuation of Varieties and Species by Natural means of Selection."

Thomas Huxley was not party to Darwin's anguish or Lyell and Hooker's maneuverings in 1858. Why was Huxley excluded, not asked for

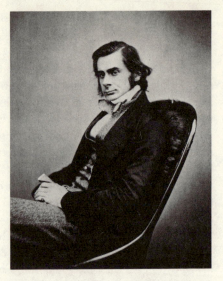

14. Thomas Henry Huxley as a dapper young man. He was a prominent natural historian, educator, and later public defender of the ideas of a reticent Charles Darwin.

help or advice? Was he less close to Darwin, more difficult to reveal weakness to? Did Darwin fear Huxley's sharp tongue and his lightning-flash judgment? It is impossible to know. It is clear, however, from Darwin's letters following the publication of *The Origin of Species* in the subsequent year that he awaited with real anxiety Huxley's response to the work ("If I can convert Huxley I shall be content. . . . I long to learn what Huxley thinks. . . .") and is delighted beyond measure when the pronouncement is favorable.

Huxley was not, quite, from the same background as Darwin, Lyell, and Hooker. While of respectable, educated background, Huxley's family lacked one crucial attribute the others shared: wealth. Huxley was born May 4, 1825, in what was then a quiet little country village, Ealing, a few miles from Hyde Park Corner, the seventh of eight children born to George and Rachel Withers Huxley.

Most of what little is known of his early life comes from his *Autobiography*—and Huxley openly proclaimed that "Autobiographies are essentially works of fiction, whatever biographies may be." He wrote of his resemblance to his adored mother, in her piercing black eyes and extreme rapidity of thought. Quickness of wit was the very essence of Huxley throughout his life. Whether from his mother or father, he also inherited a square jaw and a thick mane of dark hair that, set off by the flashing dark eyes, made the young Huxley a pretty child and a handsome young man.

Although his father was a schoolteacher, there never seemed to be enough money for the large Huxley household, which was situated over a butcher's shop, though their deprivations could not compare with those of the Wallaces. Because his father taught there for a time, Huxley attended Great Ealing School, then thought by many to be one of the finest public (private, in American terms) schools in England. Whatever its overall quality, the young Huxley was unhappy and later recalled that

> the society I fell into at school was the worst I have ever known. We were average lads, with much the same inherent capacity for good and evil as any others; but the people who were set over us cared about as much for our intellectual and moral welfare as if they were baby farmers. We were left to the operation of the struggle for existence among ourselves, and bullying was the least of all the ill practices current among us.

As with Darwin's assessment of his misspent youth, it is difficult to know how to interpret these words of Huxley's. Perhaps he, like many another sensitive and intelligent boy, found his school full of ruthless, juvenile bullies more concerned with social power and sports prowess than things of the mind. Those were the only two years of formal schooling Huxley was to endure until he entered medical school.

While Wallace was saving money for his trip, and Darwin was starting to withdraw into his myriad illnesses, Huxley was starting to shine. In 1839, at age fourteen, Huxley began an apprenticeship with his brother-in-law, Dr. Cooke, working in the squalid slums of the East End of London. It left him time to read voluminously, carry out experiments in science, and teach himself languages. There were neither ten-hour days followed by evenings at a workingman's club and scrimping and saving to buy a single book, like Wallace, nor happy idling away an excellent education, like Darwin.

Brilliance will out, however. In 1842, the year Darwin retired to Down House, Huxley dared to take an open examination in botany—a subject in which he had received little or no formal instruction—and came in second, winning a silver medal. Soon thereafter, his performance on yet another exam won him a merit scholarship for medical studies at the Charing Cross Hospital. Back in school and eager to learn, he regularly carried off prizes in anatomy, chemistry, and physiology. He also read everything he could and conducted such meticulous studies of anatomical structures that his first scientific paper, describing and naming Huxley's layer at the root of the hair cell, was published when he was but nineteen.

After three years at Charing Cross, Huxley won the gold medal for anatomy and physiology, his special love—what he called the mechanical engineering of living machines. To earn a salary, Huxley joined the navy as a physician. Though this could have been routine medical drudgery, the naval explorer Sir John Richardson noticed Huxley's talents and recommended him to be assistant surgeon aboard the HMS *Rattlesnake*, which was then leaving on a four-year journey. Part of the ship's mission was to compile a thorough collection of specimens from the South Seas.

The parallels to Darwin's pivotal voyage on the *Beagle* are striking and yet not entirely accurate. On his voyage, Huxley, like Darwin, grew up, learned to think, captured, dissected, and drew everything. The crucial reference on Huxley's voyage was not Lyell's but the French biologist Buffon's volumes. Their prominence on his shelf led the sailors to nickname his endless specimens "buffons." But unlike Darwin, Huxley was no broad-minded natural historian, interested vaguely in anything and everything. His powers of concentration were greater, his focus much narrower; he wanted to know how animals were put together, how they *worked*.

Among the treasures Huxley acquired on this voyage was one of the heart: the acquaintance of a Miss Henrietta Heathorn, a charming young lady from Sydney. An attraction developed almost immediately, and the engagement was sealed before the *Rattlesnake* sailed on. The patient Henrietta was to wait seven years for her Hal, as she called Huxley, to be in secure enough circumstances to marry.

Huxley began publishing by mailing manuscripts back to England during the voyage, stepping up the rate after his return. Instead of taking comfortable rooms and devoting himself to his work, Huxley needed a job. He persuaded the navy to give him paid leave, and then to extend it not once but twice. He begged the navy for grant support for his publications, but was denied. It was a constant scramble for funds and freedom to work. Very soon, his efforts were handsomely rewarded, first with election to the Royal Society within months of his return and, in the next year, with the Royal Medal. Some years later, to help out one of his suddenly widowed and impoverished sisters, Huxley sold his Royal Medal for fifty pounds.

Huxley finally left the navy in January 1854, with no other prospect in sight. Within months he had some part-time teaching jobs and, in November, became professor of natural history and paleontology at the Government School of Mines and naturalist to the Geological Society in London. With amusing lack of foresight, he ungraciously declared at the time that he had no interest in paleontology or fossils whatsoever.

In 1855, a few months before Wallace's Sarawak paper was published, Huxley was finally able to send for his beloved Nettie, but she arrived in England unwell. A physician who examined her declared she had only six months to live. Huxley replied, "Well, six months or not, she is going to be my wife." She was, in the end, to outlive him. It was an unusually close and loving marriage; their friends often referred to the Huxleys, romping with their seven children, as "the happy family." Upon his death, Henrietta found her husband had kept a flower she had worn at one of their first meetings.

By the time *The Origin of Species* was published, Huxley had discovered his matchless gift for words—for speaking and writing with a clarity, precision, and sparkling turn of phrase that captured his listeners and readers—partly through the series of public lectures that his new post required him to give. Huxley became a polished and confident speaker and by 1858 was already widely acknowledged as the finest lecturer and essayist on scientific subjects. Though his remarks gave the impression of being off-the-cuff, Huxley once said, "I always think out carefully every word I am going to say. There is no greater danger than the so-called *inspiration of the moment*, which leads you to say something which is not exactly true or which you would regret afterwards."

Darwin could see that Huxley would be (and was) an influential ally. And evolutionary theory was to need Huxley's skills. Neither Darwin nor Wallace was ever comfortable with public speaking; indeed, Darwin was unable to attend a meeting of the Geological Society, much less to deliver a stirring lecture to a crowded hall. What sad fate would have overtaken Darwin's evolutionary synthesis but for Huxley's ability as a speaker?

Perhaps Huxley was spared Darwin's misery over the problem posed by Wallace's work because Huxley had criticized, severely, an earlier, vaguely evolutionary work called *Vestiges of the Creation*. As would become apparent, however, Huxley's opinion was ripe to be changed by Darwin's words.

While Wallace's paper was a new and original work, sweated out of his brain in the isolation of the jungle, Darwin's Linnaean Society paper was simply an extract of his letter to the American botanist Asa Gray, in 1857, discussing the principle of divergence coupled with an extract from his 1844 essay. Placing it first and pairing it with Wallace's fully formed paper was a fairly naked attempt to demonstrate publicly that Darwin's ideas had paralleled and preceded those of Wallace. Wallace, of course, knew nothing of the arrangement until months later. On July 5, 1858, after the Linnaean Society meeting, Darwin encouraged Hooker to write and break the news to Wallace and "exonerate" him. A few days later, Darwin wrote Hooker gratefully:

> Your letter to Wallace seems to be perfect, quite clear and most courteous. I do not think it could possibly be improved, and I have to-day forwarded it with a letter of my own. I always thought it very possible that I might be forestalled, but I fancied that I had a grand enough soul not to care; but I found myself mistaken and punished; I had, however, quite resigned myself, and had written half a letter to Wallace to give up all priority to him, and should certainly not have changed had it not been for Lyell's and your quite extraordinary kindness. I assure you I feel it, and shall not forget it. I am *more* than satisfied at what took place at the Linnaean Society.

And so, too, was Wallace, who had never expected his humble ideas to be presented to the most eminent men of science in Britain. He wrote Darwin to thank him for his kindness—a letter received with a sigh of relief by Darwin, who still felt guilty and who disclaimed any responsibility for leading Lyell and Hooker to "what they thought was a fair course of action."

To everyone's surprise, Darwin now worked flat out on his book, which was published just more than a year later: November 24, 1859. Typically, he sent prepublication copies and almost groveling letters expressing his humble hopes of receiving their favorable responses to most of the great men of science: Lyell, Hooker, Huxley, his old professor J. S. Henslow, Asa Gray and the zoologist Louis Agassiz in America, botanist A. De Candolle in France, John Lubbock (who achieved dual fame as an archeologist and as the institutor of Bank Holidays in England), the geologist Hugh Falconer, Alfred Russel Wallace himself, and dozens of others.

By the actual date of publication, the book was already the topic of everyone's conversation. The first printing of 1,250 copies sold out on the first day, on which Darwin had an offer to translate it and print it in French, which later fell through because the French publishers hesitated to support it. By February 1860, he was corresponding with Heinrich Bronn, who made the fateful German translation omitting Darwin's single, timid sentence about man. An American printing also followed rapidly.

Though Darwin feared the response of each man whose opinion he respected, he was on the whole elated by the reception from the scientific community. Huxley applauded Darwin's work and reported he is "sharpening up his claws and beak in readiness" to defend Darwin against the "considerable abuse and misrepresentation which, unless I greatly mistake, is in store for you." His entire life Huxley enjoyed a good fight, especially if it involved tweaking the nose of a pompous public figure. The battle over *The Origin of Species*, one of Huxley's finest, provided ample opportunity for such sport.

As an opening salvo, Huxley ghostwrote a thoughtful but favorable review of Darwin's book in the London *Times* in December 1859, forcing it into the public eye for a fair trial. In April 1860, he published a brilliant review under his own name in the *Westminster Review*. During these first few years, Darwin kept a personal tally of the converts and almost-converts to his theory. Huxley was well up on the "convert" list, but other reviewers were not so kind. Sedgwick, the Cambridge geologist and former professor of Darwin's, wrote a scathing review in the *Spectator*, expressing his "detestation" of the theory and its "intensely mischievous" effect, calling Darwin's facts and documentation "a string of air bubbles." Others were as critical or even savage.

As anticipated, Darwin's friends—most prominently Huxley—sprang to his defense and replied to many of the reviews. The showdown came at the famous June 30, 1860, meeting of the British Association at Oxford, in which Huxley faced off with Bishop Wilberforce in front of an excited audience of between seven hundred and a thousand people. Ironically, Huxley was present only because Robert Chambers—the anonymous author of *Vestiges of Creation* whom Huxley had so soundly trounced for inaccuracies and errors—had urged him to fight Wilberforce face-to-face.

The chair of the meeting was Henslow, Darwin's former professor from Cambridge. Wilberforce spoke first, and in "dulcet tones . . . ridiculed Darwin badly, and Huxley savagely." He then made the fatal mistake of asking Huxley whether it was on his grandmother's or his grandfather's side that he was descended from an ape. This was a cunning insult. Not only did it misrepresent what Darwin had said but also cast an implied and uncalled-for aspersion on the honor of Huxley's family.

Huxley, given such a ripe opportunity, in one reply vanquished his opponent.

I asserted, and I repeat, that a man has no reason to be ashamed of
having an ape for his grandfather. If there were an ancestor whom
I should feel shame in recalling, it would be a *man* [i.e., Wilberforce
himself], a man of restless and versatile intellect, who, not content
with an equivocal success in his own sphere of activity, plunges into
scientific questions with which he has no real acquaintance, only to
obscure them by an aimless rhetoric, and distract the attention of
his hearers from the real point at issue by eloquent digressions, and
skilled appeals to religious prejudice.

The fight was out in the open now; Huxley's verbal sword flashed, drew
blood; the tension rose; a lady fainted and was carried out; and shortly
thereafter the meeting broke up. Darwin, of course, had not even been
present when the ultimate battle was fought for his ideas; he was at
home, nursing a bad headache.

From this point, the tide turned. Even Lyell, one of the most powerful
scientific men in England, who long hesitated to endorce Darwinism
fully, changed his view to such an extent that he published a book
entitled *The Geological Evidence of the Antiquity of Man* in 1863. As
Huxley later reviewed the period:

The publication of the Darwin and Wallace papers in 1858, and still
more than that of the "Origin" in 1859, had the effect upon them
of a flash of light, which to a man who has lost himself in a dark
night, suddenly reveals a road which, whether it takes him straight
home or not, certainly goes his way. That which we were looking
for, and could not find, was a hypothesis respecting the origin of
known organic forms, which assumed the operation of no causes
but such as could be proved to be actually at work. We wanted, not
to pin our faith to that or any other speculation, but to get hold of
clear and definite conceptions which could be brought face to face
with facts and have their validity tested. The "Origin" provided us
with the working hypothesis we sought. . . .

Even a cursory glance at the history of the biological sciences
during the last quarter of a century is sufficient to justify the
assertion, that the most potent instrument for the extension of the
realm of natural knowledge which has come into men's hands, since
the publication of Newton's "Principia," is Darwin's "Origin of
Species."

It was badly received by the generation to which it was first
addressed, and the outpouring of angry nonsense to which it gave
rise is sad to think upon. But the present generation will probably
behave just as badly if another Darwin should arise, and inflict upon
them that which the generality of mankind most hate—the neces-

sity of revising their convictions. Let them, then, be charitable to us ancients. . . . Let them as speedily perform a strategic right-about-face, and follow the truth wherever it leads.

When, in April 1861, the zoologist George Busk translated Schaaff-hausen's description of the Neandertal remains into English, most of the British scientific community had already been partly or wholly converted to Darwin's ideas. The odd trio —Wallace, Darwin, and Huxley—were unquestionably responsible. Wallace had prepared the way and spurred Darwin into actually completing his book, a well-nigh miraculous event unlikely to have transpired under any other circumstances. Darwin wrote *The Origin of Species*, a masterful work precisely because of its diffuse nature and reticence. Without seeming argumentative, its endless flood of small detail and innocent example accrue, page after page, impercepti-bly nudging the reader toward the conclusion that evolution occurs and must occur, through the agency of natural selection. But once the idea was presented, a Huxley was needed, one who could state the evidence and implications more clearly and cleanly than Darwin, one who relished a good, witty argument.

The role of class and influence, as well as temperament, in effecting this acceptance was substantial. No theory put forth by only a self-educated, almost working-class man like Wallace could ever have swept British science as did one suggested by the Cambridge-educated gentle-man with the right connections, Darwin. No defender of the theory could have been more effective than one with the right manners (a good school) and a sound profession, combined with a certain middle-class scrappiness and ambition, like Huxley.

At this point, the only public mention of the Neandertal fossils in English had been a cryptic, unsigned remark in the *Westminster Review*, describing the fossils as "the ruin of a solitary arch in an enormous bridge, which time has destroyed and which may have connected the highest of animals with the lowest of men." This remark, attributed by some to Huxley—who was a frequent contributor to the magazine and who had taught himself German as a teenager—gives only the mildest hint of what was to come. What remained to be debated was what the Neandertal fossils were.

As Busk's remarks show, human antiquity per se was not the problem:

> The fact of the geological antiquity of Man, or, to use other words, of his long having been contemporary with extinct animals whose

remains are universally regarded by geologists as "fossil," has apparently been fully established, though rather, perhaps, from the discovery of his works than of his actual remains, under certain geological conditions. It has become a matter, therefore, among others, of extreme interest to determine how far it may be possible, from the scanty remains of his bones as yet discovered, to ascertain whether, and in what respects, the priscan [pristine] race or races may have differed from those which at present inhabit the earth.

Busk, like everyone to follow, focused on the unusual aspects of the skull, especially remarking on the large, projecting, and apelike browridges that show "a very savage type." No other "ancient" skull known to him showed the development of the supraorbital ridges to comparable extent. He opened the question, of little real importance but the subject of endless pedantic debate, of whether the prominent browridges were caused by an expansion of the underlying frontal sinus or by a thickening of the frontal bone itself.

Though Busk accepted Fuhlrott's secondhand assurances of the geologic placement and hence antiquity of the Neandertal remains, others did not. C. Carter Blake, a rather pugnacious gentleman and amateur geologist/geographer/anthropologist clearly biased against foreign scientists, thought otherwise. Writing in the *Geologist* in September 1861, Blake made the skull the real point of his discussion. He noted the large size of the braincase "not cerebrally inferior to the Papuan or Negro races" and observed it showed "none of the other characters which so prominently differentiate the human from the simian sub-kingdoms." He concluded there was no reason to suppose the Neandertal skull represented a distinct species—an interesting denial since no one had yet suggested in print that the Neandertal remains represented a new species. It was obviously being thought and perhaps even said, if not published.

But a year later, Blake's position had shifted. He had by then inspected a cast of the cranium, lent him by Huxley. Though he reiterated that the skull was still not a distinct species, he remarked:

> The apparent ape-like, but really maldeveloped idiotic character of its conformation is so hideous, and its alleged proximity to the anthropoid *Simiae* of such importance, that every effort should be made to determine its probable date in time. . . .
>
> There are several suspicious circumstances connected with the Neanderthal cranium, *e.g.* the pathological enlargement of the coronoid process of the left *ulna* [the end of the forearm bone at the elbow], apparently from an injury during life; the peculiar rounded

shape and abrupt curvature of the ribs, analogous in their appearance to those of a carnivorous animal. . . . All these characters are
compatible with the Neanderthal skeleton having belonged to some
poor idiot or hermit, who died in the cave where his remains have
been found. They are incompatible with the evidences which must
be left in a Westphalian bone-cave of a normal healthy uninjured
human being of the *Homo sapiens* of Linnaeus.

Blake's argument was a tour de force in muddled reasoning. Yet an
anonymous remark (was it Blake himself writing?) in the *Medical Times
and Gazette* of 1862 supported him, concluding that "A theory of rickets
and idiocy would, we suspect, go some way towards unravelling the
mystery."

Blake also liked the theory put forward by his friend Joseph Barnard
Davis, a medical man. Barnard Davis suggested that the peculiarities of
the skull might be due to premature closure of some of the sutures of
the skull, so that growth was exaggerated in other planes. Such abnormalities were known.

Finally, as the foreign associate of the Société d'Anthropologie de
Paris and the self-appointed spokesman for the French view in England,
Blake reported that his French colleague, Dr. I. F. Pruner-Bey, also
favored the "idiot" hypothesis. Pruner-Bey's work suggested the skull
was little more than that of a Celt, perhaps an idiot Irishman, even
though he noted its large braincase.

To this suggestion, his fellow countryman, brain expert, and founder
of the Société d'Anthropologie de Paris, Dr. Paul Broca, retorted:

The whole of M. Pruner Bey's [*sic*] arguments repose on one basis,
the knowledge whether the peculiar form of the Neanderthal skull
is pathological. As we have never seen such a skull, and do not wish
to admit that it belonged to a race of which no other vestige remains
to us, we are forced to seek a morbid origin for the peculiarities
which it presents. . . . Idiocy, competent to produce a cranium of
this kind, is necessarily microcephalic [tiny-brained]; now this skull
is not microcephalous, therefore it is not that of an idiot.

The responses to the Neandertal remains in France were complex.
Broca and his fellow members of his newly founded Société d'Anthropologie de Paris represented a significant challenge to the scientific
establishment of France. At the Muséum National d'Histoire Naturelle,
the legacy of Cuvier and his antievolutionary ideas held sway.

In contrast, Broca and his colleagues believed in evolution, but only

15. Paul Broca, the founder of French physical anthropology in the nineteenth century. Although he embraced human evolution, Broca never accepted the Neandertals as ancient and archaic humans.

up to a point. In their eyes, species were obviously not fixed and invariable; species transformed themselves (or were transformed) over time. This was clearly evolution of a sort, harking back to Lamarck's ideas on transformism. But all of the theories, including natural selection, were inadequate as a complete explanation of the mechanism behind evolution, Broca's group felt. Thus, they accepted that both natural selection and descent with modification (evolution) occurred, without ever wholeheartedly endorsing "Darwinism."

At the very least, this perspective on evolution led to a freer discussion of the subject. In 1859, Broca—a well-respected surgeon and professor at the Faculté de Médicine in Paris—wanted to found a new organization to consider the broader study of man. As Broca expressed it:

> Ethnologists regard man as the primitive element of tribes, races, and peoples. The anthropologist looks at him as a member of the fauna of the globe, belonging to a zoological classification, and subject to the same laws as the rest of the animal kingdom. To study him from the last point of view only would be to lose sight of some of his most interesting and practical relations; but to be confined to the ethnologist's views is to set aside the scientific rule which requires us to proceed from the simple to the compound, from the known to the unknown, from the material and organic fact to the functional phenomena.

Broca's struggle, although ultimately successful in founding what Huxley later described as "one of the most powerful instruments for the advance of anthropological knowledge," is a classic illustration of the extent to which Darwin's ideas were perceived as dangerously radical. It would seem an innocent thing for a prominent anatomist and physiologist to propose to found a scientific society for the study of mankind, but it was not so.

The trouble started in 1858, when Broca wanted to communicate his findings on the fecundity of "human hybrids"—that is, the offspring of interracial marriages. The Société ethnologique de Paris (Ethnological Society of Paris) had dwindled out of existence ten years before—it had been interested only in documenting the habits, customs, and language of the different races of humans in any case—so Broca delivered his remarks to the Société de Biologie (Society of Biology). He either failed to realize or did not appreciate fully how deeply opposed the president of the Société de Biologie, Rayer, was to his findings that such hybrids were fully fertile, and to the implication that human races represented only minor variations within a single species rather than quite different biological entities. As a result, Broca was asked to "desist" from further communications and, in frustration, decided to start up a Société d'Anthropologie de Paris—focusing on what would now be called biological anthropology—with at least twenty members.

This proved a surprisingly difficult task. Six members of the Société de Biologie joined but few others would. In 1859, though he had only nineteen potential members, Broca approached the government authorities for permission. They responded with classic bureaucratic obstructionism, by sending him from office to office until he eventually ended up with the prefect of police, who was convinced that anthropology was a cover for an antigovernment conspiracy. Broca's request for the society was eventually granted, under two conditions: first, that he, Broca, would be held personally responsible for any revolutionary sentiments expressed that might attack the government, church, or general social order; and second, that a plainclothes policeman was to attend every meeting and report back fully on what transpired. The beleaguered Société d'Anthropologie de Paris had only started meeting a few months before *The Origin of Species*—a revolutionary document if ever there was one—was published. Little wonder that a group of scientific rebels who already espoused the principle of zoological continuity between humans and animals welcomed his words.

In England, the furor over the *The Origin of Species* was no less disturbing to the status quo, but the ruling powers were considerably less centralized and oppressive. In 1860, Huxley began a series of public

lectures for "the workingman"—members of the working class who
were trying to better themselves—taking as his subject the relation of
man to the lower animals. The lectures were published in 1863 as a series
of essays entitled *Evidence as to Man's Place in Nature*. These essays show
the myriad anatomical and even behavioral connections that link humans
with other primates, an especially sharp-edged observation since one of
Huxley's major critics, Richard Owen, had striven in vain to find at least
one distinct anatomical feature in humans not shared by apes. Anticipating—correctly—the outcry from the public at large, Huxley answered:

> It is not I who seek to base Man's dignity upon his great toe, or
> insinuate that we are lost if an Ape has a hippocampus minor. On
> the contrary, I have done my best to sweep away this vanity. I have
> endeavored to show that no absolute structural line of demarcation,
> wider than that between the animals which immediately succeed us
> in the scale, can be drawn between the animal world and ourselves;
> and I may add the expression of my belief that the attempt to draw
> a psychical distinction is equally futile, and that even the highest
> faculties of feeling and of intellect begin to germinate in lower
> forms of life. At the same time, no one is more convinced than I of
> the vastness of the gulf between civilised man and the brute; or is
> more certain that whether *from* them or not, he is assuredly not
> *of* them.

Huxley's was a subtle point, but one that won over his audience: the
continuity between humans and other animals does not detract from the
inherent specialness of humans.

In the next essay, he took up the issue of human fossils. Huxley
presented the initial detailed comparison of the known fossil human
skulls—the adult Engis skull, discovered years before by Schmerling in
Belgium but ignored for so long, and the Neandertal remains—in the
context of a discussion of primate anatomy in general. This emphasized
his contention that humans, and their ancestors, were simply another
type of primate. He worked not only from drawings and photographs
but also from detailed plaster casts of the original specimens—a procedure that allowed him to compare two skulls when the originals were in
different places. This, too, proved a technical revolution that has endured
to modern times. And he created and used, for the first time, a series of
measurements that soon became standard for comparing crania metri-
cally. No longer would vague, waffling comparisons of the subjectively
judged resemblances among any oddly assorted group of skulls suffice.
Huxley oriented all of the skulls in the same way, using anatomical

landmarks, and *measured* them systematically. Thus, in a single essay Huxley transformed such anthropological studies into science. He also argued strongly that it was a pressing task to document the variability in normal human crania with these techniques so that the degree of difference among fossil crania could be assessed.

He deduced from his cranial studies that the Neandertal cranium was unlike the Engis remains—a point on which modern anthropologists would agree. The Engis cranium is, in Huxley's words:

> . . . a fair average human skull, which might have belonged to a philosopher, or might have contained the thoughtless brains of a savage.
> The case of the Neanderthal skull is very different. Under whatever aspect we view this cranium, whether we regard its vertical depression, the enormous thickness of its superciliary [brow] ridges, its sloping occiput [back of the skull], or its long and straight squamosal suture [joining of two bones on the side of the skull], we meet with ape-like characters, stamping it as the most pithecoid of human crania yet discovered.

But, he added, the brain is so large and the long bones so indicative of a European of middle stature that the whole skeleton is clearly human, if somewhat savage. He concluded:

> And indeed, though truly the most pithecoid of known human skulls, the Neanderthal cranium is by no means as isolated as it appears to be at first, but forms, in reality, the extreme term of a series leading gradually from it to the highest and most developed of human crania.
> . . . the fossil remains of Man hitherto discovered do not seem to me to take us appreciably nearer to that lower pithecoid form, by the modification of which he has, probably, become what he is.

With true Huxleyan delight, he reiterated these observations in 1864 while gleefully demolishing the opposing opinions of Pruner-Bey, Mayer, Schaaffhausen, William Turner, and William King.

It was King's challenge that is most interesting in retrospect. In 1863, William King, a professor at Queen's College, Galway, in Ireland, and a former student of Lyell's, argued at a meeting of the British Association that the Neandertal fossils represented a new species of human, *Homo neanderthalensis.* This fact alone will strike modern biologists as bizarre, because a new species can now be named only if a technical, anatomical

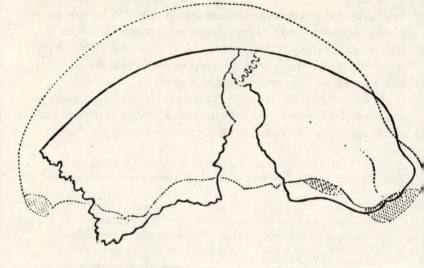

~~~ EGUISHEIM   ······· NEANDERTHAL

16. Comparison of the contours of the braincases of Feldhofer grotto Neandertal cranium and a recent human cranium, published in 1868 by Paul Broca. This drawing reflects the then common view that the Neandertal skullcap, although low and large-browed, was not very different from many recent human skulls.

description of the fossil explaining in what way it is distinct from other, similar species appears in a periodically published journal. No mere scientific paper read at a meeting, albeit ever so learned, would suffice to name a new species today.

In the written version of his British Association paper, published in January 1864, King reviewed the find and its features, closing his paper with these remarkable passages:

> The distinctive faculties of Man are visibly expressed in his elevated cranial dome—a feature which, though much debased in certain savage races, essentially characterizes the human species. But, considering that the Neanderthal skull is eminently simial, both in its general and particular characters, I feel myself constrained to believe that the thoughts and desires which once dwelt within it never soared beyond those of a brute. The Andamaner [inhabitant of the Andaman Islands, off the coast of India], it is indisputable, possesses but the dimmest conceptions of the existence of the Creator of the Universe: his ideas on this subject, and on his own moral obligations, place him very little above animals of marked sagacity;* [see

below] nevertheless, viewed in connection with the strictly human conformation of his cranium, they are such as to specifically identify him with *Homo sapiens*. Psychical endowments of a lower grade than those characterizing the Andamaner cannot be conceived to exist: they stand next to brute benightedness.

Applying the above argument to the Neanderthal skull, and considering . . . that it more closely conforms to the brain-case of the Chimpanzee, . . . there seems no reason to believe otherwise than that similar darkness [such as that experienced by the chimpanzee] characterized the being to which the fossil belonged.

King's case was simply that the Neandertal remains represented a new species because its anatomy suggested that it experienced moral "darkness"—another point startling today when phrenology is no longer regarded as a valid science. Equally astonishing is the offhand remark King made in the footnote denoted by the asterisk in the above quoted passage:

A paper advocating the views contained in this article was read at the last meeting of the British Association, held in Newcastle-upon-Tyne. In that paper I called the fossil by the name *Homo Neanderthalensis* [*sic*]; but I now feel strongly inclined to believe that it is not only specifically but generically distinct from Man.

In short, King asserted that the fossil should not even be included in the genus *Homo*, much less in the species *Homo sapiens*, without offering any line of reasoning or evidence and without suggesting what the appropriate new generic name ought to be. Incredibly, after casually dropping such a bombshell in print, King made no further comment on the issue.

In 1864, as the discussions over the Neandertal remains flourished, Busk remembered the Gibraltar skull, which he had been sent some years before by a Captain Broome. He looked at it again and saw its close resemblances to the Neandertal cranium. With Hugh Falconer, the paleontologist, Busk presented it at a British Association meeting at Bath. Their opinion, as expressed by Falconer, echoed Huxley's:

If you hear any remarks made, you may say from me, that I do not regard this priscan pithecoid man as the "missing link," so to speak. It is a case of a very low type of humanity—very low and savage, and of extreme antiquity—but still man, and not a half way step between man and monkey.

This shows the early popularity of the phrase *missing link* that has since become so widely recognized as referring to human ancestors. More important at the time was the opinion that the skull, though human, was unlike modern human skulls. Falconer suggested to Busk that they call it *Homo calpicus*, from the ancient name Calfe for Gibraltar.

Their efforts were rewarded with a grant for £165, so that Busk and Falconer could sail to Gibraltar and encourage further excavation. There Captain Broome, the garrison commander who had first sent Busk the cranium, offered indefatigable help to the pair. Ironically, this generosity and helpfulness brought Broome's scientific endeavors to the attention of his superiors, who promptly cashiered him for using military prisoners in private excavations.

Although many prominent English and French scientists favored the Neandertal as a genuine, archaic human, the matter of finding true fossil human remains did not die down. In Abbeville, Boucher de Perthes was once again stirring up controversy with a new find, a jaw from the site of a gravel pit at Moulin Quignon. In retrospect, after the partial skeleton from Neandertal and the complete skull from Gibraltar, it is hard to believe that anyone could have taken this poor bone so seriously. But the Moulin Quignon jaw became a cause célèbre almost overnight.

On April 9, 1863, Boucher de Perthes announced in the local newspaper, *L'Abbevillois*, that he had found a human jaw associated with Acheulian hand axes at Moulin Quignon. From the geology, he concluded that the human bone came from the oldest part of the deposits, thus establishing great antiquity for fossil humans. It was thoroughly modern in its anatomy and in no way resembled the jaw one might imagine would fit the Neandertal cranium. At last, here was the maker of the ancient stone tools found with extinct Pleistocene mammals, Boucher de Perthes proudly claimed.

But was it? *L'affaire Moulin Quignon*, as it might be called, was to prove a tortuous and painful episode. At its conclusion, Boucher de Perthes was to write to Hugh Falconer, "Vous m'avez tué!" ("You have killed me!")

3
L'Affaire Moulin Quignon
1865–1885

Boucher de Perthes, now in his middle seventies, must have been smug with satisfaction over his latest find. It had been some years since the English geologists and paleontologists—Lyell, Prestwich, Flower, Evans, and Falconer—had given their stamp of approval to Boucher de Perthes's flints and hand axes. It had started with a visit from Falconer, who wrote to Prestwich in 1858, describing his first inspection of Boucher de Perthes's material:

> He showed me "flint" hatchets which *he had dug up with his own hands* mixed *indiscriminately* with the molars of *E[lephas] primigenius*. . . . Abbeville is an out-of-the-way place, very little visited, and the French *savants* who meet him in Paris laugh at Monsieur de Perthes and his researches. But after devoting the greater part of the day to his vast collection, I am perfectly satisfied that there is a great deal of fair presumptive evidence in favour of many of his speculations regarding the remote antiquity of these industrial objects, and their association with animals now extinct.

Among the French, only Rigollot supported him, but because Rigollot was a former skeptic, his belief in the authenticity of the flaked Acheulian hand axes did much to redeem Boucher de Perthes's tattered reputation. Still, he had a lingering infamy as a man with an idée fixe, one who believed so strongly in human antiquity that his judgment was sometimes blinded. But now, surely, he had the find of finds that would silence his skeptics.

As early as 1859, rumors and scurrilous stories were circulating that Boucher de Perthes was being fooled by modern, counterfeited stone tools. Because of the near-universal practice of paying workmen to excavate and rewarding them for good finds, the door was wide open to fakery. Indeed, the Abbeville area was notorious for it, perhaps because of Boucher de Perthes's unbridled enthusiasm. One of the probably apocryphal stories involved Madame Ducatel, a cousin of the archeologist Vayson de Pradenne. While walking through the streets of Abbeville, she passed a peasant who was sitting on his doorstep, diligently chipping stone. When asked what he was doing, he replied, wide-eyed, "I am making Celtic axes for Monsieur Boucher de Perthes."

17. Cartoon in the journal *L'Illustration du Midi* of 1863, caricaturing the study of the Moulin Quignon jaw at the Académie des Sciences in Paris. This modern human lower jaw, believed by Boucher de Perthes to belong to the maker of his ancient tools from Abbeville, was certainly planted by a local worker paid for making important "discoveries."

Nonetheless, the English scientists were convinced that many of Boucher de Perthes's finds were genuine. Although cruder than the hand axes from other sites, such as St. Acheul, the Moulin Quignon specimens had a distinctive bright yellow color. After reading of Boucher de Perthes's latest remarkable discovery, Prestwich and Evans hurried to Abbeville, followed a few days later by Falconer. The three arrived in Abbeville within a few days of the announcement, meeting up with Jean-Louis-

Armand de Quatrefages, a famous naturalist from the Académie des Sciences in Paris.

The first question to be settled was whether one of the workmen had "found" the jaw and the associated tools. Boucher de Perthes insisted that he had extracted it with his own hands on March 28, 1863. De Quatrefages, impressed, took the jaw to Paris with him for further examination; Falconer carried an isolated molar tooth from the jaw to London for George Busk and an anatomist, Sir John Tomes, to inspect. But, before the English scientists left Abbeville, an incident occurred that seriously undermined Prestwich's and Evans's faith in Boucher de Perthes's claims.

Prestwich recounted the damning story in a letter to Edouard Lartet on May 5, 1863:

> We were, however, both at once struck with the form of all the flint implements, with the [unusual] sharpness of their angles, and with their peculiar soiling. We, however, reserved our opinion and went to take a look at the pit. Unfortunately a fall of gravel had taken place, and the section was covered up so that we could only see one end of it. That there was a black band [from which the fossil and tools were said to have come] was evident, and one fact struck me in favour of the probable authenticity of the specimens, which was, that heretofore all the specimens of the flint implements had been obtained from the ochreous gravel, and it seemed to me that if ignorant workmen wished to imitate the real specimens, they would rather have adopted the usual matrix than have sought one which was exceptional. As we were walking to St. Giles from Moulin Quignon, one of the men took two specimens from his pocket and gave them to me. These were both from an ochreous or ferruginous matrix, and it seemed at once evident to us that they were both false. I therefore took the opportunity to wash one at the first cottage we came to. All the soil came off immediately, and left the flint quite fresh and clean and sharp. This further evidence satisfied us both then that some imposition was practised, and immediately we got back to Abbeville I at once told M. Boucher de Perthes of our doubts and suspicions about the workmen. He did not see it in the same light that we did, even after he had himself washed one of the specimens. . . . I only much regret that M. de Perthes did not mention in a sufficiently pointed manner our doubts to Dr. Falconer and M. Quatrefages, as it might have led to a stricter examination of the flints on the spot and more reserve on the part of my friend. It was only in fact after washing and close inspection that the nature either of the jaw or of the flints could be determined. They were all so much soiled and that seemingly with intent.

Without ever dropping his polite tone—for he and Falconer had found Boucher de Perthes gracious and charming—Prestwich then enumerated several suspicious features of the flints, including their sudden abundance when six or eight previous visits had yielded none. He was troubled by the material.

Edouard Lartet, the recipient of Prestwich's account, was on his way to becoming a major figure in the study of human prehistory in France. Born in April 1801, he lived his whole life in Gers, where he practiced law. He became fascinated by a mastodon tooth found by a peasant in his village and took up paleontology in his thirties. Among his greatest early discoveries were the first two species of fossil apes, one known as *Dryopithecus*, long thought to be a chimpanzee ancestor, and the other, *Pliopithecus*, a gibbonlike creature. But Lartet sought, and found, evidence of human antiquity, too. Though he was not rewarded with Neandertal remains, Lartet and his English collaborator and financial supporter, Henry Christy, were responsible for the discovery of cave sites from the Upper Paleolithic that yielded tools and objects made by the earliest humans with modern anatomy.

Lartet's early papers on the evidence for an ancient human occupation of western Europe, like Boucher de Perthes's, were soundly rejected by the Académie des Sciences. But by 1861, Lartet had excavated the famous site of Aurignac, which had a distinctive and specialized set of flaked stone tools that clearly attested to the presence of ancient people. Setting up sequential cultural stages that would provide a relative dating of finds was a major concern at this time. On the basis of his work, Lartet proposed an innovative scheme for classifying the evidences of ancient humans by the species of extinct animals with which they were associated:

> Thus, in the period of Primitive Man we shall have the Age of the Great Cave bear, the Age of the Elephant and the Rhinoceros, the Age of the Reindeer, and the Age of the Aurochs [an extinct type of oxen]; much after the manner recently adopted by the archeologists in their divisions of Stone Age, Bronze Age, and Iron Age.

Then, in 1861, Lartet began finding and recognizing the first signs of prehistoric art made by early humans. Working in the Vézère Valley with Christy, Lartet recovered some marvels of prehistoric art—wonderful objects, like the engraved mammoth on a piece of fossil ivory recovered from La Madeleine in 1864—that captured the public imagination when they were exhibited at the International Exposition in Paris in 1867. Few stone tools or oddly shaped bones had the immense public appeal of these Upper Paleolithic art objects, even though the Neandertal fossils were more ancient. But the mixed reception to his work up to the mid-1860s made Lartet, too, supportive of Boucher de Perthes's struggles against the stony beliefs of the academicians in Paris.

Unfortunately, Busk and Tomes, upon inspecting the Moulin Quignon tooth and sawing it open, discovered still more convincing evidence that it was not fossilized. In Falconer's words: ". . . it proved to be quite recent; the section was white, glistening, full of gelatine, and fresh-looking." The tooth was not stained, infiltrated, and filled with sediments from the distinctive black bed, as might have been expected.

The English felt the point was settled (the finds were fakes or planted); so did the French (the finds were real). The differing and equally strong opinions of the French and English over this matter led to a novel suggestion. They would set up an international commission, to be convened in Paris during May 1863, which would examine the evidence and pronounce on the authenticity of the finds.

The English contingent was comprised of Prestwich, Falconer, Busk, and Dr. William Carpenter, vice president of the Royal Society of London. From the Institut, the French sent de Quatrefages; Lartet; two geologists, Jules Desnoyers and Achilles Delesse; and the Belgian zoologist Henri Milne-Edwards. They were joined by several other well-recognized authorities in paleontology, prehistory, and related fields. The French were determined to defend their national honor; the English were, regretfully, determined to keep some clumsy fakes from muddying further the already murky waters of human antiquity.

After four days of argument and evidence, the English were still convinced that all of the "black bed" material from Moulin Quignon was false, probably made recently by an individual using a metal hammer, as were some (but only some) of the specimens from other sites near Abbeville. The French did not agree, nor could the commission reach a consensus on the jaw. The evidence of its freshness, lack of staining, and close anatomical resemblance to a pre-Roman jaw from Britain was presented; the French were dubious and unwilling to concede.

The unhappy commission then embarked for Abbeville itself to examine the site and to confront Boucher de Perthes. One account of the proceeding suggests that a visit to Moulin Quignon revealed that the vital "black bed" had been quarried out of existence in the meantime, though the more nearly contemporary account in Prestwich's *Life and Letters* does not mention this point. In any case, the commission found itself deadlocked. There was only one point of agreement: "The jaw in question was not fraudulently introduced into the gravel-pit of Moulin Quignon [by Boucher de Perthes]: it had existed previously in the spot where M. Boucher de Perthes found it on the 28th March 1863."

This lukewarm assertion of his innocence, rather than his correctness, was hardly the type of scientific acclaim and vindication that Boucher de Perthes yearned for. Though he was elected a foreign correspondent to the Geological Society of London the next month, following on the heels of the debacle of the inquiry, he was not assuaged by this honor. Bitterly he wrote to his English friends, from whom he had expected support that was not forthcoming, accusing Falconer of "killing" him.

Desperately, Boucher de Perthes continued to excavate at Moulin Quignon. He took to calling in impromptu commissions (the mayor, stray geology professors, local doctors, lawyers, librarians, priests, and the like) to witness the event whenever he found something, or thought he was about to find something, of significance. He must have become a nuisance in this regard, as in his frequent, fervent publications of his new finds in *L'Abbevillois*. Soon, the English and French scientists stopped coming to look at his material or paying any real attention to his claims. Boucher de Perthes died in 1868, believing to the end that he had been misjudged and wronged over *l'affaire Moulin Quignon*.

The counterfeit stone tools and planted bones—for such they surely were—foreshadowed a later and much more deliberate forgery that was to confuse and confound paleoanthropologists for many years. At Moulin Quignon, there was probably little intention to foil the progress of science. Almost certainly, the motivation was a transparently simple one: if M. Boucher de Perthes would pay good money for hand axes, and promised even better bonuses for bones, why shouldn't the workmen indulge him and enrich themselves? Who would be harmed?

What became clear in the debate over the Moulin Quignon material was the power of national pride to blind the eyes of learned men to the suspicious character of the finds. The French not only failed to see the evidence when it was shown them, but they also never formally admitted that the Moulin Quignon jaw was intrusive—that is, a much more recent bone deliberately placed in older sediments. In time, they simply stopped speaking of it. The lessons that should have been learned from Moulin Quignon were not. Somehow, the episode did not sensitize anyone to the extreme vulnerability of the field to fraud or deceit by the unscrupulous.

As to the source of the vulnerability, much depends upon geological context, and once a fossil or tool has been removed from the ground, only the excavator can know where it came from. The meticulous documentation of excavations through photographs, measurements, and drawings had not yet developed. Indeed, very few of those involved in the search for human ancestors during this period actually excavated the sites themselves. Once paleontologists and anthropologists began to wield shovels themselves and started keeping rigorous plans, maps, and notes, it became much more difficult to plant remains—unless, of course, the excavator was also the hoaxer.

What was being sought in the latter half of the nineteenth century was fossil material of a type that no one had ever seen before: the bones of Neandertals or other human ancestors. Searching for the novel and unknown is always treacherous ground. These scientists, like all others, formed expectations—sometimes formalized as hypotheses—of what they thought they would find. When they were surprised, they either questioned the reality of the find or were forced to go back and rethink their logic to see where they went wrong. In either case, the object itself was considered with great care and attention. But when those expectations were met, there was a natural tendency *not* to inspect the object so critically. And in paleoanthropology, the great power of fraud has lain in the hoaxer's ability to meet expectations and thus escape detection.

After Moulin Quignon, the English thought they were immune to the problem, no doubt: it was a question of French shortsightedness. The shoe was to be on the other foot in fifty years' time, when the greatest scientific fraud in all of paleontology was to be perpetrated on the blind-eyed British.

L'affaire Moulin Quignon also exemplifies the rather confused ideas in the mid-1860s about what fossil humans should look like. That any knowledgeable scientist would take the Moulin Quignon jaw seriously as a human fossil appears difficult to fathom in retrospect. Yet, despite the support for the Neander Tal fossils as an archaic, prehistoric human, few knew what to expect. Clearly, many—especially those who were uncomfortable with the idea of human evolution at all—still expected human fossils to look just like modern humans; it was only a matter of finding the specimens in the appropriately prehistoric context.

For now, all was progressing quietly. In 1865, the English archeologist and neighbor of the Darwins, John Lubbock, published his immensely influential book, *Pre-historic Times*. In it, Lubbock tackled the immense job of summarizing all that was known to date of "the principles of pre-historic archaeology; laying special stress upon the indications which it affords of the condition of man in primeval times." Despite the fledgling state of the field—this book made *prehistory* a household word in England for the first time—Lubbock had a lot of material to cover. He began by elaborating upon the then popular scheme of classifying archeological remains into the Iron, Bronze, and Stone Ages, in order of increasing antiquity. Lubbock suggested that the most ancient period ought to be subdivided into the Paleolithic (meaning "old stone") Age, for that time in which the implements were simply flaked, and the Neolithic (meaning "new stone") Age, for the period in which stone was polished and ground and gold began to be used as ornamentation. This chronological framework was immediately and universally adopted; only many years later was it modified, so that the Paleolithic was further subdivided into Lower (earliest), Middle (intermediate), and Upper (most recent) Paleolithic.

Several elements of Lubbock's framework are important. For one thing, it implied a universal, linear progression of successive stages in human evolution, as demonstrated by the techniques used by various types of humans to work materials. It was supposed implicitly that the Neolithic, for example, occurred everywhere in Europe simultaneously or that all Paleolithic sites were approximately contemporaneous. But, as Lubbock observed:

> In order to prevent any misapprehension, it may also be well to state, at once, that for the present, I only apply this classification to Europe, though, in all probability, it might be extended also to the neighbouring regions of Asia and Africa. As regards other civilized countries, China and Japan, for instance, we, as yet, know nothing of their pre-historic archaeology. It is evident, also, that some nations, such as the Fuegians [from Tierra del Fuego], Anda-maners [from the Andaman Islands], etc., are even now, or were very lately, in an Age of Stone.

Part of the difficulty was that technological sophistication or progress was being muddled with biological evolution. Thus, in the mid-1800s it remained a lingering doubt in Europeans' minds whether the primitive peoples they encountered on their voyages and explorations were truly human. Could a Tierra del Fuegian like Jemmy Button be lifted up out of his barbaric culture—by Captain Robert FitzRoy of the *Beagle* in 1830—whisked off to England on a sailing ship, dressed and given rudimentary lessons in the English language, manners, and mores, and so by education be transformed into a "human" like the Londoners he astonished?

Apparently, he could; and few thought it high-handed, immoral, or wrong to conduct such experiments or to return Button summarily to Tierra del Fuego on the *Beagle* voyage that included Darwin three years afterwards. In fact, many admired Captain FitzRoy for his noble attempt to uplift such a savage. If the nonindustrial peoples, particularly hunter-gatherers, were fully human, they were simply holdovers, lingering representatives of earlier stages of development that could and should be improved through education. Button's story is simply an unromanticized version of Eliza Doolittle's, so exquisitely satirized years later in George Bernard Shaw's *Pygmalion*.

The firmly held conviction that benighted savages, prone to the most immoral and revolting practices, could be civilized proved extremely important in world affairs. The "white man's burden," as Kipling was to call it in 1899, was to go throughout the world bringing the ignorant and uneducated into the modern world. Telling the natives of the Word of God, showing them the dignity, cleanliness, and proper moral standards of a civilized person ("Always dress for dinner") was the responsibility that came with the good fortune of being born British (or French or German). What's more, study of the ways, anatomy, language, and technology of "savages" or "barbarians" could be used to fill in the gaps in the archeological record. As Lubbock explained this approach:

> Although our knowledge of ancient times has of late years greatly increased, it is still very imperfect, and we cannot afford to neglect any possible source of information. It is evident that history cannot throw much light on the early condition of man, because the discovery—or, to speak more correctly, the use—of metal has in all cases preceded that of writing. . . . Deprived, therefore, as regards this [early] period, of any assistance from history, but relieved at the same time from the embarrassing interference of tradition, the archaeologist is free to follow the methods which have so successfully been pursued in geology—the rude bone and stone implements of bygone ages being to the one what the remains of extinct animals are to the other. . . . Much light is thrown on our fossil pachyderms, for instance, by the species which still inhabit some parts of Asia and Africa . . . and, in the same manner, if we wish clearly to understand the antiquities of Europe, we must compare them with the rude implements and weapons still, or until lately, used by the savage races in other parts of the world.

The second great wave of imperial expansion was about to sweep the world, and Lubbock's book reveals the attitudes that fostered it.

The second point about Lubbock's book is that its organization is very revealing of the implicit objectives of prehistoric research at the time. The book is organized, not starting with the oldest finds and ending with modern material, but in reverse chronological order. In short, the origins of the present—be it anatomy, technology, language, or custom—were being traced *backwards* into the past. The point was not to discover what was there in the past but to find out how the modern world came to be.

The influence of this point of view is subtle but real. Virtually all recent books on human evolution or archeology start with the oldest evidence, showing dead ends, extinctions, lost knowledge or habits, and a few survivals—the picture becomes that of a pruning away of myriad possibilities until the present day is reached. Viewed this way, the past seems to be a record of marvelous evolutionary experimentation, of richness selected upon, of multiplicity and pluralism regrettably shrunk down to greater paucity. But the standard nineteenth-century approach to the past, as exemplified by Lubbock's book, lends itself to interpreting the fossil and archeological record as a teleological or even moral tale. Because the end (modern civilization) is known, all else becomes stages along the way to that end; evolution is progressing *toward* something. The archeologist or paleontologist is thus following a chain of links back into the past, in a linear array, rather than charting the proliferation of different creatures or tools, only some of which survive. In the nineteenth century, there was little thought or appreciation given to diversity. They were connecting the dots in straight lines, not drawing the branching patterns of bushes or trees.

Finally, Lubbock, as had Lyell two years before, openly endorsed the genuineness and antiquity of human fossils in this book. Those propositions were becoming more acceptable, at least in England, but were far from settled in France and Germany.

In France, evolutionary ideas and anthropological interests were still closely tied to left-wing politics, which is why Broca faced such difficulty in founding the Société d'Anthropologie de Paris in 1859. By 1864, another rebellious young anthropologist was on the scene in Paris. Gabriel de Mortillet had just returned from fifteen years in exile, spent mostly in Italy and Switzerland, and had promptly joined Broca's *société.*

Born in 1821 to a middle-class family, de Mortillet had been schooled as a child by Jesuits, though he soon rejected this influence thoroughly.

As a youth, he studied engineering at the Conservatoire des Arts et Métiers, in Paris, and natural history at the Muséum National d'Histoire Naturelle, but—like many a young man caught up in exciting times—he paid more attention to politics than to his studies. He followed events avidly as the Second Republic of France fought for political control. During the summer of 1848—the so-called June Days of the twenty-third to the twenty-sixth—a bloody civil war broke out in Paris, with barricades in the streets separating the dissatisfied or unemployed workers, the hotheaded students, and the out-and-out radicals from the Republican armies.

De Mortillet was in the thick of it. His inflammatory publications in the late 1840s railed against the church, the autocratic rule of the state, and the power of the bourgeoisie. In 1848, he published a work calling for the nationalization of banks, railroads, and all large businesses and even, in an excess of revolutionary zeal, arguing that "the right to live is superior to property rights. A man whose very existence is threatened can seize the property of another, and can steal with a clear conscience." These were not popular words, especially among those who held considerable property. The Republican army, under General Louis-Eugène Cavaignac, moved in and eventually killed at least fifteen hundred rebels and arrested twelve thousand more, which decapitated the insurrection. Small wonder that one who endorsed such trouble-making views was among those sentenced to prison; de Mortillet sought exile instead.

His work abroad focused on natural-science museums, fossils, and geology and led him to reject the antievolutionary views that still dominated the scientific establishment in Paris. When he returned in 1864, he immediately launched an open attack on the old fogies at the Académie des Sciences who persisted in such Cuvierian nonsense. One of his main vehicles was a journal he founded and edited himself: *Matériaux pour l'histoire positive et philosophique de l'homme"* (*Material for the Positivist and Philosophical History of Man*). De Mortillet was ready and willing to support, even fight for, evidence of human ancestry as soon as it presented itself.

He had not long to wait. In 1865, he was invited to give a survey of prehistoric research at the Italian Scientific Congress held at La Spezia. His talk was so successful that it resulted in the formation of the Congrès Internationale d'Anthropologie et Préhistoire Archéologique (International Congress of Anthropology and Prehistoric Archeology), with himself as secretary.

Soon after this gratifying recognition came the discovery of another fossil. The recent publicity and attention given to fossil finds had left the Belgian government anxious to know if it had any more prehistoric treasures. Schmerling had found the Engis skull in Namur province thirty years before; were there others? Happily, Edouard Dupont, a Belgian geologist surveying the Namur province for the Ministry of the Interior, found the large cave of Le Trou de la Naulette and in it, a human lower jaw, an ulna (forearm bone), and a metacarpal (hand bone). The fossils were separated from the surface by four stalagmitic strata, indicating great antiquity.

Unlike the Neandertal fossils from Feldhofer, the La Naulette jaw was sealed in its geological bed with extinct Ice Age mammals: mammoths, woolly rhinos, reindeer, boar, mouflon (a wild sheep), and others. Its antiquity was thus difficult to question. And, unlike the Moulin Quignon jaw, the La Naulette mandible was not modern in its anatomy.

Most observers remarked that the jaw lacked the protruding chin seen in modern humans. The front of the mandible sloped backwards from the teeth to where the chin should have been; the chin was receding or

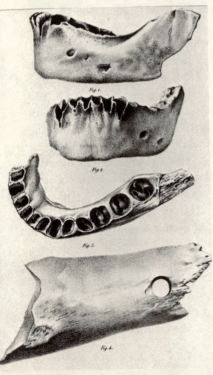

18. Drawings of the lower jaw of a Neandertal found by Edouard Dupont in the Trou de La Naulette, Belgium, in 1866, and an artificially pierced bone from the same cave. Though the jaw showed archaic features and had been found in clearly ancient deposits, few were ready to be convinced of the existence of pre-modern human ancestors such as the Neandertals.

even apelike in profile. Equally significant, the sockets, or alveoli, for the teeth (which had all, unfortunately, fallen out of the jaw after death) suggested to some that the canine or eye tooth was unusually large, as in apes or monkeys.

The prominent French anatomist Broca gave one of the first detailed analyses of the new fossil, saying:

> This mandible, contemporary with the mammoth, was it human? M. Dupont was in doubt at first. Several naturalists took it for the jaw of an ape; M. Dupont then went to Paris to consult M. Pruner-Bey, who hesitated in his turn. Here is the mandible; I demonstrate without doubt today that it came from a human. But it must be well understood that its conformation closely resembles that which we have considered until now to be characteristic of apes' jaws.

Broca then compared the jaw systematically with those of a chimp, a modern Melanesian, two Neolithic jaws, and one from a modern Parisian, showing that the various primitive features of the La Naulette jaw could be fitted into a continuum with the other specimens. Although the La Naulette jaw was the most apelike among the others, it was nonetheless human in Broca's opinion. Although he stopped short of wholeheartedly accepting Darwin's theory of evolution—on the grounds that it remained to be proven—Broca clearly recognized that the La Naulette mandible was "the first fact that furnishes anatomical evidence to the darwinists. It is the first link on a chain that extends from man to the apes." Thus, he saw human fossils in terms of what they implied about evolutionary theory.

Like the Neandertal remains from Germany, Broca concluded, the La Naulette jaw was human but showed more simian tendencies than any other specimen yet known. Anticipating some opposition to his views, Broca declared boldly in words that echoed Huxley's speech at Oxford:

> As for me . . . I would much rather be a perfected ape than a degraded Adam. Yes, if it is shown to me that my humble ancestors were quadrupedal animals, arboreal herbivores, brothers or cousins of those who were also the ancestors of monkeys and apes, far from blushing in shame for my species because of its genealogy and parentage, I will be proud of all that evolution has accomplished, of the continuous improvement which takes us up to the highest order, of the successive triumphs that have made us superior to all of the other species . . . the splendid work of progress. . . .
>
> I will conclude in saying: the fixity of species is almost impossi-

ble, it contradicts the mode of succession and of the distribution of species in the sequence of extant and extinct creatures. It is therefore extremely likely that species are variable and are subject to evolution.

But the causes, the mechanisms of this evolution are still unknown.

Not everyone was so sanguine about having apish ancestors or about evolution, for at this point a curious and haunting inversion occurred. In his writings about La Naulette, Dupont explicitly denied an extraordinary claim about the Neandertal fossils that had never yet been made (in print): that they were the remains of a cannibalistic feast. He argued that the fossils were naturally broken and located within a cave but were not associated with worked stones or hearths—items for which he deliberately searched. For all his care, he uncovered only broken animal bones and the three human bones. Perhaps he was indirectly responding to the charge of cannibalism that had been raised before, by a Monsieur Spring, who was writing of the more modern finds at Chauvaux, Belgium. Spring

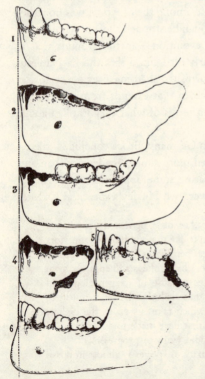

19. Comparison of the La Naulette mandible (no. 2) to those of a chimpanzee (no. 1) and four modern humans (nos. 3, 4, 5, and 6) from a paper by Paul Broca. On the basis of several features, Broca argued that the La Naulette mandible was the most primitive of this series of human jaws, rather than being close to the chimpanzee mandible.

had found shattered human and animal bones mixed together in hearths and took this as logical evidence that both animals and humans had been treated as food. But Dupont's finds did not include such evidence.

Bizarrely, the claim that Neandertals were cannibals started here—with a case that particularly *did not* suggest cannibalism—and has persisted, lingering about Neandertal remains like a poisonous miasma, until the present day. A purported summary of Dupont's findings, written in English by C. Carter Blake, stated that Dupont believed the La Naulette remains showed evidence of cannibalism. Was it mistranslation, misunderstanding, or carelessness? Then, in 1930, Aleš Hrdlička, a physical anthropologist at the Smithsonian, again attributed to Dupont the claim that the La Naulette remains showed signs of cannibalism. Hrdlička was an obsessively careful man and was fully fluent in French. Perhaps the problem was that he read, remembered, and unconsciously inverted Dupont's original denial, or that he placed more weight on later, unsupported accusations.

Dupont's motivation may well have been a subtle one. As the twentieth-century anthropologist William Arens has observed, there is no more universally common way of distancing oneself from other people than to call them cannibals. It is one of the ultimate insults, one of the definitive signs of nonhumanity. Like incest—a charge with which it is often coupled—cannibalism is one of the most universal taboos, one of the most repellent and uncivilized behaviors. Though Dupont's implicit, original motivation may have been to avert this accusation, the charge was to stick. Neandertals—for the La Naulette jaw was soon explicitly linked with the Neandertal remains from Feldhofer—were not only apelike, they ate their own kind. There was no clearer way to show how different they were from human beings.

This low opinion of the savagery and simian qualities of the individual from whom the La Naulette jaw came prevailed over Broca's more rational view. Pruner-Bey, and his English friend Blake, spoke of enormous, projecting canines, a point picked up by Darwin and cited in his 1871 book, *The Descent of Man*. Darwin apparently did not notice the distinction between estimating the size of teeth from their sockets, as did Broca, and speaking with conviction about the size and projection of the teeth themselves, as did Blake and Pruner-Bey. Yet Blake, in a rare moment of restraint, said:

> Its [the La Naulette jaw's] undoubted resemblance to the jaw of a
> young ape I shall not venture to deny; nevertheless, I shall not

attempt to offer any theory respecting the mental or social status of the individual, or of his or her complexion, stature, or probable appearance.

Others were not always so cautious.

Some years later, prompted to respond by the evolutionary enthusiasm of his compatriot Hermann Schaaffhausen for the La Naulette mandible, Rudolf Virchow replied in his increasingly predictable manner. He was convinced that the only feature distinguishing the La Naulette jaw from those of recent humans was its apparent lack of a chin. Recognizing the specimen for what it is, the mandible of a young adult, he argued that all of the supposedly apelike characteristics were reflections of the backward sloping of the front of the jaw. After actually studying the original specimen in Brussels through the courtesy of Dupont, Virchow then claimed that there was a pathological hyperostosis, or bony growth, just below the front teeth and above where the chin ought to be. This had caused the abnormal receding slope of the region and the apparent absence of a chin. The argument would be defensible, if curious, except that all modern assessments of the specimen agree that no such growth exists. Once again, Virchow had invoked his own particular specialty and denied the fundamental principle of honest observation to "bury" a fossil human. His conclusion was the same as always; the La Naulette mandible was no more indicative of human evolution or ancestry than the original Neandertal remains.

The ulna and the metacarpal received little attention. Dupont described the ulna as incomplete, small, and "normal." Recent restudy of these two bones shows that, unlike the jaw that is markedly Neandertal in form, the hand and arm bone more closely resemble bones of recent humans than those of Neandertals.

De Mortillet seized upon the La Naulette mandible as providing the opportunity for which he had been waiting. He proposed a grand new synthesis of human prehistory, in which cultural (as shown by the stone tools) and physical (as shown by the bones) evolution proceeded hand in hand through a series of glacial and interglacial periods recently recognized by a Scottish geologist, Archibald Geikie. Between 1867 and 1873, in a series of papers and books, de Mortillet elaborated his linear framework for considering human evolution, drawing on the work already accomplished by Lartet and Lubbock.

According to de Mortillet, the Paleolithic could be subdivided still further. The most recent, postglacial cultures were the Magdalenian (named after La Madeleine, where Lartet had found the engraved picture of a mammoth) and before that, the Aurignacian, named for the material excavated by Lartet at the Aurignac Cave. Still earlier came the Solutrean, named for an extraordinary French site first discovered in 1866. Le Solutré yielded modern-looking human remains mixed into a vast deposit consisting mostly of the fossilized bones of wild horses intermingled with beautifully worked, flaked stone tools. The preceding culture, the Mousterian, coincided with a glacial period and was named after the collections from a site called Le Moustier, in an area referred to as the upper shelter, which had been excavated by Lartet shortly before. (Another part of Le Moustier, known as the lower shelter, would in the future yield human remains under circumstances deeply insulting to the French national pride.) All of these periods, de Mortillet hypothesized, contained people similar to modern humans. Finally, before the glacial Mousterian culture was the Chellean period, named after the site of Chelles, and which de Mortillet believed was associated with Neandertals.

Brave as de Mortillet's attempt was to synthesize geological, archeological and paleontological evidence into one grand pattern, he fell prey to the fatal temptation to speculate. Thus, at the most remote end of his linear progression of cultural and physical stages, he erected another that was to cause endless trouble. He proposed that, before the Chellean culture of the Neandertal race, as he called it, there had existed another species, which he at first called *Anthropopithecus* and later *Homosimius*, who had used a special type of stone tool called the eolith. This was a term coined by a Belgian geologist, Rutot, from the prefix *eo-*, meaning "dawn," and the suffix *-lith*, meaning "stone." In its original meaning, eoliths were stones that had not been flaked into standard shapes or tool types but were simply utilized pieces in naturally broken forms. This, of course, meant that practically every fragment of flint broken by natural causes that was found qualified as an eolith. As these were supposed, according to de Mortillet, to be evidence of the activities of the earliest sort of human ancestors, the record of human evolution suddenly stretched back a very long way indeed. But few heeded de Mortillet's claims for eoliths until later; only his synthesis of stages was important.

For the French, this synthesis implied, significantly, a linear, continual evolutionary *progress* through time, rather than the jerky, catastrophe-interrupted record of stasis that the remnants of Cuvierian thought would suggest. It was what de Mortillet called "*la loi de progrès de l'humanité*" ("the law of the progress of humanity"). It was gradual, smooth, continuous, and moving always toward betterment and perfection. What remained now to be achieved was social perfection, for which de Mortillet and other left-wingers were fighting vigorously according to their notions of utopia.

The idea of progress was supported by the emerging field of ethnography, which focused on the study of the lives, customs, and beliefs of living, non-Western peoples generally at the time regarded as "primitive." Ethnographers tended to agree that humanity had progressed through different stages of cultural development or "evolution," with Europeans obviously having come farther than the rest. Two books expressed this view most clearly. In 1871, Edward Tylor, an Englishman, published *Primitive Cultures: Researches into the Development of Mythology, Philosophy, Religion, Language, Art and Customs*, one of the first systematic cross-cultural studies. His conclusions were closely paralleled by a book by the remarkable American, Lewis Henry Morgan. Unlike Tylor, who simply traveled and observed, Morgan lived with and studied various American Indian tribes at a time when "going native" was viewed with general horror; though he did not live continuously with the Iroquois, he spent enough time with them to develop a deep respect for the tribes he came to know. He wrote up his results in several books, the most influential being *Ancient Society; or Researches in the Lines of Human Progress from Savagery through Barbarism to Civilization*, a title that says it all. Like Lubbock, Morgan and Tylor believed that living tribal peoples represented in some way the lifeways and habits of our ancestors. Morgan codified this notion as a three-stage developmental model, in which humans progressed from Savagery through Barbarism to Civilization. Various aspects of a culture—its food sources, technology, and social rules—enabled the researcher to determine how far it had progressed toward civilization.

For those who held this view, the Neandertals and other prehistoric humans were simply fitted into preexisting stages, pigeonholed for reference, and used to reinforce the "evolutionary" view of human history and progress. This is most wonderfully illustrated by what is probably the first artistic depiction of a Neandertal, a drawing that appeared on the front page of the July 19, 1873, *Harper's Weekly*—a publication subtitled tellingly *A Journal of Civilization*—showing a Neandertal couple in their shelter. The dramatic scene is described by the anonymous author:

> Yet, however divided the views of *savants* may be, the artist whose drawing we present to the reader, has followed his own judgment

in giving an ideal representation of the Neanderthal man. A more ferocious-looking, gorilla-like human being can hardly be imagined. The savage stands almost in the attitude of an ape, before his den, where his female companion is seen slumbering, enveloped by shaggy furs. Always ready for attack or defence, he holds in his hand a hachet of primitive character, consisting of a chipped flint set in a wooden handle; his spear, likewise armed with a flint blade, leans against the rock. A bull's skull and other bones, one of them a split marrow-bone, attest the wild man's success as a hunter. Thus is supposed to have lived the contemporary of the mammoth!

While de Mortillet and the popular press spoke of a unilineal progress in human evolution, the French establishment was creating its own synthesis, although they did not incorporate the geology and the archeological finds as de Mortillet had. In 1873, de Quatrefages and his assistant at the Muséum National d'Histoire Naturelle, the young Ernest Jules Hamy, attempted to solidify the links among various fossil human remains and understand their relationship to modern races. Throughout Europe, there were major debates between the monogenists—those who, like de Quatrefages and Hamy in France, Darwin and Huxley in England, or Haeckel in Germany, believed that all races arose from a single, common stock—and the polygenists—such as Broca and Pruner-Bey in France, Blake and Barnard Davis in England, and Virchow in Germany—who thought the races had separate origins.

De Quatrefages and Hamy proposed that Europe had originally been inhabited by a dolichocephalic (long-headed) race of people, with a cranium like that from the Neander Tal or Gibraltar and a jaw like that from La Naulette. They called this the Cannstadt race after a robust, large-browed skull that had been discovered in 1700 near Cannstadt, Germany. Found during work around a Roman oppidum, the skull itself was almost certainly Roman and of no great antiquity. It was only the first of many skulls, from places such as Staegnaes, Switzerland; Puy en Velay in southern France; Olmo, near Florence, Italy; Enguisheim near Colmar, France; and Clichy, near Paris, France, all almost certainly remains of Neolithic or later humans, fully modern individuals who happened to have somewhat thick skulls, low foreheads, and relatively large brows. The continued discovery of such skulls during the nineteenth century only gave further credence to the existence of a Cannstadt race and prolonged confusion between its dubious members (robust modern humans) and legitimate Neandertal finds. De Quatrefages and Hamy participated vigorously in the confusion, seeing the original Neandertal and the Gibraltar crania as extreme examples of this Cannstadt "type." There had been no real evolution, they argued—both were, after all, the intellectual descendants of Cuvier—there had only been a migration of racial groups.

The idea was that this aboriginal, long-headed race had been displaced by the broad-headed or brachycephalic Aryans moving up from Asia. The longheads had evolved into the Lapps, Finns, and Basques, whereas the broad-headed Aryans had developed into the Germans, English, and other "superior" European races. The Aryan "question," as it was known, was invented not by de Quatrefages and Hamy but by linguists; the contribution of de Quatrefages and Hamy was to try to tie the Aryan race to specific fossil specimens. Though de Quatrefages and Hamy had their doubts about Darwinian evolution, not to mention the descent of man from the apes, they could support a certain limited type of transformism in which all of these major racial groups arose from one major stock.

In 1868, half a dozen skeletons of essentially modern anatomy had been uncovered in the cave of Cro-Magnon in southwestern France. The specimens were found by railroad workers, who badly mixed up the parts of the different individuals. These skeletons seemed to reinforce the idea that links could be drawn between fossil and modern races. Louis Lartet, the son of the now-deceased Edouard and himself a geologist, had continued his father's work in the Vézère Valley. Cro-Magnon proved to be a magnificent site, yielding stone tools, carved reindeer antlers, ivory pendants, quantities of shells apparently pierced for stringing, and the bones of five or more individuals. The conditions (to the extent that they could be reconstructed by Lartet after the fact) were suggestive of a deliberate burial; the associated animal bones and geologic setting indicated substantial antiquity. These were, argued de Quatrefages and Hamy, representatives of a lost but anatomically modern race that they called Cro-Magnon Man, whose descendants could be clearly found among the inhabitants of the Dordogne region today. In a real sense, de Quatrefages and Hamy were entirely correct, for the Cro-Magnon remains are tall and muscular but little different in basic anatomy from modern humans.

As usual, Virchow was scathing. Because he was a confirmed polygenist, explicitly believing that the modern races were descended from separate stocks much like themselves, Virchow was unlikely to view the de Quatrefages-Hamy synthesis with favor. He was busily building his power base in Berlin, founding the Berliner Gesellschaft für Anthropologie, Ethnologie und Urgeschichte (known in English as the Society of Anthropology)—of which Virchow, naturally, became the president—and taking charge of its illustrious publication, the *Zeitschrift für Ethnologie* (*Journal of Ethnology*).

Like Huxley in England—though for different reasons—Virchow was trying to stamp out the Aryan myth. One source of Virchow's dislike for the natural philosophers was the political and social implication of their ideas, which grew stronger and stronger as the nineteenth century progressed. The very first whisperings of a Nazi-type racism, of the identification of the perfect human type with the healthy, outdoorsy, blond, blue-eyed Aryan youth of Germany, were integral parts of the *Naturphilosophie* as the middle of the nineteenth century approached.

Virchow's distrust and dislike of *Naturphilosophie* and evolutionary ideas were coming to a head. In the 1870s, Virchow actually attempted to eradicate the stereotype of the blond, blue-eyed German youth by conducting a massive scientific study of the skin, hair, and eye color of thousands of German children. Though he was able to show that most Germans did not conform to this Aryan prototype, he could not shake the widespread conviction that this was what true Germans *ought* to be like. For his part, he was more convinced than ever that the different races had always been separate and had always been much as they were now: evolution was an unproven, dangerous, and romantic idea.

Besides, Virchow had asserted strongly before and reasserted in 1874 that the fossil specimens in question were both pathological and recent. Ancient humans were like the skeletons from Cro-Magnon—like modern people—not like those diseased and distorted Neandertal and La Naulette remains. Virchow was correct, of course, in recognizing that de Quatrefages and Hamy had seized upon a ragbag of different fossils (most poorly dated even by the loose standards of the day), from all over the map, to try to put together a coherent story. Nonetheless, their flawed synthesis was one of the first times anyone had tried to place all of the fossils in context and connect them with modern races.

Virchow's cynicism and criticism were taken seriously. Because the Prussian empire was burgeoning during the 1860s and 1870s, the great Prussian scientist, Virchow, now enjoyed an unparalleled influence that spread far beyond the German borders of today. The expansion of the Prussian empire had begun in 1861, when Wilhelm I had succeeded his brother—who had blossomed into flamboyant insanity—to the throne.

The liberals, like Virchow, hoped for reforms in Prussia; instead, in 1862, Wilhelm I appointed the archetypal Prussian Junker, Otto von Bismarck, to the position of prime minister.

To Virchow, Bismarck symbolized all of the aristocratic, militaristic traits that he most despised; Bismarck's "Blood and Iron" program of German unification was nothing less than the brutal conquest of Germany by Prussia. Virchow took direct action, running for and being elected to the Prussian Diet in an opposition seat. But there was no stopping Bismarck. In 1865, Virchow's criticism of Bismarck was so extreme and their personal enmity had reached such heights that Bismarck challenged the professor to a duel. Virchow declined.

In 1866, the Prussian empire defeated Austria in the Seven Weeks War, annexing a large territory to create a powerful new state, the North German Confederation, now the dominant power of central Europe. This reinforced the intellectual domination of the German elite in Berlin, led by Virchow, over those in less important centers of learning, such as Vienna. In 1870, the defeat of the French in the Franco-Prussian War had much the same effect. Though Virchow hated the Prussian military machine, and worked against it, the political domination of most of Europe by the Prussian empire only enhanced his position.

But all was not in accord within German science. When translated into German, Darwin's words fell on at least one set of receptive ears: those of Ernst Haeckel, who in 1861 was newly appointed *privat docent* (lecturer) of zoology at the University of Jena. Jena had long been the nursery of both *Naturphilosophie* and evolutionary ideas, however ill formed, in Germany. Haeckel read Bronn's translation and immediately grasped the power of Darwin's theory to explain the natural world. Trained by both the great men of natural philosophy, such as Johannes Müller, and (for a time) by more rigorous, modern German scientists including Virchow himself, Haeckel had no trouble accepting evolutionary theory as correct. Indeed, not knowing that Bronn had excised the only reference to man's place in nature—the question of questions, in Huxley's terms—Haeckel set out not only to defend and to promulgate Darwin's ideas but also to rectify Darwin's omission and apply these ideas to humans.

By this time, Haeckel was rapidly becoming Virchow's antithesis, his bête noire in scientific Germany, whereas he had once been Virchow's protégé. Born in February 1834, Haeckel came from a conservative, Protestant, well-to-do family in Potsdam. His father, a lawyer, was interested in *Naturphilosophie*, especially Goethe's works. The young

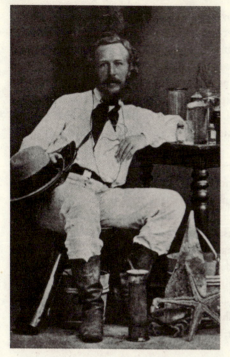

20. Ernst Haeckel as a young naturalist in Heligoland, on the North Sea. As a professor at Würzburg, Germany, and a flamboyant proponent of *Naturphilosophie* and evolution, Haeckel became the archenemy of Rudolf Virchow, who used his position as one of the foremost scientists in Germany to suppress evolutionary ideas.

Ernst was a born naturalist with a fascination for botany and a taste for the out-of-doors, inclinations fostered by his mother. He did well in school and found his teachers sympathetic and stimulating. An assessment of his character and qualities, written by his teachers upon his graduation from secondary school in 1852, was extraordinary:

> Full of warm reverence for his teachers, amiable and agreeable toward his schoolfellows, thoroughly obedient to the regulations . . . in all respects exemplary and pure. . . . Endowed with excellent talents, he has exhibited during the whole of his school time the most praiseworthy diligence in order to develop them conscientiously.

It is an assessment of a young man about to set off for medical school that would make any parent's heart glow with pride. The young Haeckel had charisma and the ability to win friends; exemplary conduct; intelligence and diligence; a love of natural history; and strong Christian belief (which was later to falter). Added to this, he was large, strong, and handsome.

In autumn of 1852, Haeckel departed for Würzburg to study natural history and medicine. By November, he had started attending evening lectures of the Physical Society, the president of which was one of his future professors, Virchow: his first sight of this intellectual giant of German science. Ironically, he found that Virchow was physically small, wiry, unappealingly sallow, and sharp-nosed—a quick-stinging wasp of a man. Still, the young Haeckel was so impressed that he described the evening to his parents in detail. With typical emphasis on facts, not ideas, Virchow had delivered a lecture on the subject of cretinism in lower Franconia.

Aside from providing glimpses of his exposure to Virchow and others, Haeckel's letters to his parents detail his personality clearly. His concerns and escapades were the normal student ones: he wanted to give up medicine; he had taken part in madcap student pranks and charades; he was fascinated with his studies; he had been for a soul-restoring walk in the mountains; he was meeting his friends for coffee and discussions; he had run out of money; he needed such-and-such a book to be sent to him; he had learned to drink champagne. But above all, the flamboyant, romantic style of his thought and writing, and his emotional devotion to his family and friends, are shown most vividly. He might have been pursuing scientific knowledge, but his thoughts and soul were those of a die-hard romantic.

Haeckel's letters describe his reverence and respect for Virchow's learnedness and intelligence. He daily acquired writer's cramp by attempting to transcribe every word Virchow uttered. That accomplished, he then spent three or four hours ruminating and digesting Virchow's words for every one hour of lecture, so far did the professor's breadth and depth of knowledge exceed the student's. Haeckel tried to explain to his parents Virchow's rationalist and reductionist view of life, in which living organisms are the

> sum of the functions of the individual organs. . . . The entire living body is divided into a number of individual seats of life, the specific activities of which are dependent upon the nature of their elementary parts, therefore, in the last instance, upon the cells of which the entire body is composed.

Indeed, to Haeckel's mind, there was a flaw: Virchow did not explain "the chief point of all, namely the relation of the soul to this organized complex whole of independent seats of life which are bound to matter." To Virchow, of course, the soul was a philosophical, nonexistent abstraction; there could be no possible discussion of it whatsoever.

Haeckel continued in words that show how dissimilar the professor and the student were:

> . . . this rationalistic, materialistic conception of all the apparitions of life has emanated altogether from the whole character of Virchow. Everywhere, in his works and words, you confront with clear and biting sharpness the absolutely matter-of-fact man: strong contempt and highly refined derision for all those who think differently from him, religious rationalism . . . , and, in addition, extraordinary firmness of character.

Haeckel also noted Virchow's "clear, logical sharpness . . . his fine but caustic wit . . . his high self-consciousness." How foreign Virchow's view of life was to this exuberant young man who wrote of "magnificent trees, somber mountain slopes, lovely meadow lands and romantic masses of rock on the banks of its mountain rivulet, which dashes wildly over bowlders [*sic*] and forms graceful cascades."

In the summer of 1854, Haeckel traveled to Heligoland, on the North Sea, to study sea invertebrates, a topic that was to become his greatest scientific specialty. Here, too, his romantic, aesthetic appreciation of his subject could not be more diametrically opposed to that of the cold and analytical Virchow. Haeckel was overjoyed and enchanted with his specimens: "the most delightful little jellyfish"; the "most magnificent starfish . . . of a magnificent purple color and one-half to three-quarters of a foot in diameter . . . the most marvelous polyps, crabs that live in shells, etc., etc." He recorded, too, the "deep, calm, pleasurable contemplation of the individual wonders of nature." He loved being in the open air, hiking, collecting specimens, breathing deeply of clean air, and exercising his muscles more than his brain cells.

Despite their philosophical and psychological differences, Haeckel was drawn by Virchow's brilliance and worked hard to become his "Royal Bavarian assistant at the Pathologico-anatomical Institute at Würtzburg," in the summer of 1856, just before Virchow's departure for Berlin. With a brutal disregard for human emotions, the first job Virchow assigned his new assistant was a postmortem on a fellow medical student, a merry friend who had died suddenly of acute tuberculosis. It was the first unpleasant task of a long summer of rotting corpses, stench, and filth. Try as he might, Haeckel could not repress his natural enthusiasm and subjectivity or emulate Virchow's cold, objective style.

The formal employer-employee relationship between the two men terminated at the end of the summer of 1856, apparently cordially. In the next few years, Haeckel produced a masterful monograph on the radiolaria, the unicellular marine organisms he had studied in Messina, Italy. It was such a monumental work, and so widely praised, that he was offered a position at the University of Jena, which he happily accepted. It was a mere four years after Haeckel's summer of service to Virchow that the bitter conflict between the two began to brew.

Haeckel, the grand, romantic theorist, the lover of life, immediately took to Darwin's ideas. The sweep and scope of Darwin's examples, the sheer grandeur of the hypothesis, appealed to him; for the very same reasons, Virchow despised it. Haeckel became, in effect, Darwin's Huxley in Germany: the chief explainer, defender, and proponent of Darwinian evolution. Like Huxley, he drew the fire and seemed to relish the blast. And like Huxley, he drew upon his own expertise to elaborate Darwin's ideas.

Haeckel was soon writing and lecturing to large audiences on the unity of life and its origin from the Monera, primitive unicellular sea creatures that he believed had formed from chemical compounds in the sea. Not only did he invoke a pet hatred of Virchow's, the spontaneous generation of life, but he also argued that the developmental history of an embryo repeated its evolutionary history as it progressed from the simpler to the more complex. This idea came to be encapsulated as the slogan "Ontogeny recapitulates phylogeny."

The heresy implicit in human evolution as espoused by Haeckel caused him no inner qualms. Haeckel completely abandoned Christian religion in 1864, following the sudden death of his beloved wife, and turned instead to beliefs based on natural philosophy that unified God and Nature, body and soul, matter and spirit. He proselytized for the notion of Darwinian and specifically human evolution with the zeal of the newly converted. He became an expert in ape anatomy, favoring especially the gibbon as our closest relative (in which he was mistaken).

In fact, Haeckel's enthusiasm for his new beliefs was so boundless that one of his biographers felt that Haeckel had "concentrated on himself . . . all the hatred and bitterness which Evolution excited in certain quarters" and that "in a surprisingly short time it became the fashion in Germany that Haeckel alone should be abused, while Darwin was held up as the ideal of forethought and moderation." Haeckel's vigorous defense of evolutionary ideas provoked a gentle reproof from his new hero, Charles Darwin, who wrote:

> Your letter of the 18th [May, 1867] had given me great pleasure, for
> you have received what I said in the most kind and cordial manner.

You have in part taken what I said much stronger than I had intended. It never occurred to me for a moment to doubt that your work, with the whole subject so admirably and clearly arranged, as well as fortified by so many new facts and arguments, would not advance our common object in the highest degree. All that I think is that you will excite anger, and that anger so completely blinds every one that your arguments would have no chance of influencing those who are already opposed to our views. Moreover, I do not at all like that you, towards whom I feel so much friendship, should unnecessarily make enemies, and there is pain and vexation enough in the world without more being caused. But I repeat that I can feel no doubt that your work will greatly advance our subject, and I heartily wish it could be translated into English, for my own sake and that of others.

Haeckel's enthusiasm remained undiminished. In 1868, with no hard evidence but only logic, Haeckel published a human "pedigree" or phylogeny, showing a single human lineage from the apes through an extinct, hypothetical ancestor. Because Haeckel believed that speech was the hallmark of humanity, he named his missing link *Pithecanthropus alalus*—the ape (*pithec-*) man (*-anthropus*) without speech (*alalus*). This was, not incidentally, the first time the metaphor of a tree had been used to express evolutionary relationships. Virchow, naturally, responded negatively to the coining of names for objects that didn't even exist. Soon, the dark, sallow, slightly built Virchow was locked in a tooth-and-nail struggle with his onetime student, who could have modeled for the perfect Aryan type.

The battle between Virchow and Haeckel for power and control of German science raged for years, reaching its height in 1877 when they exchanged vehement insults and naked accusations of reciprocal idiocy at a scientific congress at Munich. Ostensibly, the argument was over Haeckel's push to have evolution taught in the schools, an idea to which Virchow was deeply opposed because he regarded evolution as unproven and highly speculative. Virchow also feared that such a move would bring more Haeckelian mysticism and nonsense into the classrooms, like Haeckel's extraordinary new theory of heredity in which each cell had its own soul and its own subunits (plastidules), which in turn possessed inherited memory.

The bitterness arose in part from their utterly different views of the world and their divergent styles. It was compounded by Haeckel's enthusiasm and flair, which led him to publish sloppily conducted work and to generalize too freely on flimsy evidence to make a point—attributes that Virchow must have regarded as mortal sins in a student he had personally nurtured. The vast popular audience to whom Haeckel now spoke didn't care about or understand Virchow's bitter points. They understood Haeckel's compelling words and accepted them as wondrous truths. The more Haeckel's popular regard grew, the more contemptuous and scathing Virchow became.

And Haeckel's fame and popular influence grew far beyond what anyone could have anticipated. Though Virchow was ever the greater genius, Haeckel had the charisma and ability to communicate. His popular lectures on human origins were packed; the written versions of his public lectures, *Natürliche Schöpfungsgeschichte* (*Nature's Story of Creation*, first published in 1868) and his later work, *Die Welträtsel* (*The Riddle of the Universe*), sold hundreds of thousands of copies in every European language.

While it is tempting to see this struggle for the power over people's minds in Germany as a battle between a sunny, charming hero, Haeckel, and a dour, coldhearted villain, Virchow, there is an important twist to these historical events. For Haeckel's confused thinking and tremendous powers of persuasion led him ever deeper into the development of eugenic theories, into an explicitly racist interpretation of survival of the fittest that became the foundation of Nazi doctrine. Evolution, Haeckel asserted, was an elitist theory. Evolutionary theory showed the essential rightness of determining who were the most fit individuals (those of Aryan descent) and placing them on top of society, to rule and reproduce, while the unfit (largely personified by Jews, for whom Haeckel had an open aversion and distrust, and the mentally deficient) must be prevented from breeding, for the good of all.

It was in large part this overtone of racial favoritism, of vicious elitism, that fired Virchow's condemnation of human evolution and Haeckel himself. Because, in Germany, evolution, eugenics, romanticism, and muddled science were irrevocably tied to human fossils, the human fossils must be rejected—and Virchow, founder of the Berliner Gesellschaft für Anthropologie, Ethnologie und Urgeschichte and the Ethnological Museum, editor and publisher of the major scientific and anthropological journals, did everything in his considerable power to accomplish this aim. Only Haeckel dared to defect. While his defection was not entirely successful within Germany, Haeckel found a more sympathetic audience in England, where a young protégé of Huxley's, E. Ray Lankester, became Haeckel's chief translator.

In France, a similar struggle for scientific power developed. The establishment scientists ensconced in the Muséum National d'Histoire Naturelle, led by de Quatrefages and Hamy, were still skeptical about evolution and preoccupied with race. They were attempting to describe in tremendous detail the "typical" skulls of the different ethnic and racial groups, a feat celebrated by the publication in 1882 of *Crania Ethnica*. The antiestablishment group centered around the genial surgeon Broca and included de Mortillet on its more pugnacious fringes. This group participated in the Société d'Anthropologie de Paris and in 1872 founded the journal *Revue d'Anthropologie*, of which Broca was the editor.

Broca's continuing surgical responsibilities gave him ample opportunity to study the human brain, a field in which he rapidly became one of the acknowledged experts. In particular, one patient—left speechless by a brain lesion—provided the occasion for a significant discovery after his death. In the postmortem, Broca found that the lesion had damaged only one special region on the left side of the brain, now called Broca's area. He deduced that here was the center for the control of the muscles that produce articulate speech—one of the first times that such a specific function had been localized to a particular region of the brain. It made Broca the scientific heir to phrenology. But more important, it was a dramatic demonstration that the human brain was an integrated whole comprised of discrete, functional units, much like a finely tuned but very complex machine. This provided invaluable support for the positivist and materialist views of Broca, de Mortillet, and their colleagues, and was powerful evidence against the vague, semimystical views of the human mind then held by the establishment.

The basis of Broca's anatomical work was his firm belief that he had to understand the patterns of variation, not simply the ideal types, of human form in order to understand the significance of anatomical differences. This conviction led him to invent an assortment of scientific instruments, many still in use today: gadgets for measuring various angles and dimensions of skulls and brains with new precision and accuracy. Broca thus became one of the first to use statistical concepts, albeit simple ones, to investigate the variation in human skeletons.

Along with his other responsibilities, Broca hoped to found a school of anthropology in Paris. Despite the immense difficulties of such an undertaking, he was so well respected and liked as a scientist and gentleman that, in 1875, the dean of the faculty of the Ecole des Hautes Etudes granted him space to start up, but no money. Broca turned to the members of the Société d'Anthropologie, who pledged thirty-five thousand francs to set up the school. Unfortunately, their firm commitment to the school, combined with their reputation as left-wing protesters, alarmed the minister of public instruction, who attempted to block its opening.

At last, on December 15, 1876, the Ecole d'Anthropologie (School of Anthropology) opened despite the government's lack of help and cooperation. The school was granted a permit to operate on only a year-by-year basis; the permit specified by name the individual professors who were authorized to teach. This close control continued until 1878, when the institution was officially recognized and approved. The Société d'Anthropologie, the Ecole d'Anthropologie, and Broca's personal research laboratory were united under the grand title of l'Institut d'Anthropologie (the Anthropological Institute).

The open admission and free tuition that were basic principles of the school echoed the radical opinions that had originally earned de Mortillet his exile. Indeed, the founding of the school represented an alliance between Broca's group, who were interested in being able to study the physical aspects of anthropology without hindrance, and de Mortillet's followers, who needed a power base from which to push their political program. De Mortillet could never have aspired to become founder and director of such a school because the government was so justifiably wary of his activities. But Broca was another matter, and he was widely enough respected to start the school and be named director. Broca's student and heir apparent, Paul Topinard, became assistant director, but fully three of the original six academic chairs at the school were claimed by de Mortillet and his cronies.

Once entrenched, de Mortillet's group developed an increasingly strident and outspoken view of anthropology as a revolutionary instrument, deviating more and more from the interests of Broca's group. De Mortillet's scheme of linear progression in evolution was now given a further twist: the story of human evolution became an instructive, moral tale. The apparent lack of burial rituals at the older sites said to de Mortillet that religion was a recent, and undesirable, invention. Rather than being benighted and barbaric, early humans had been noble savages personified, living in peace and honor until religion and priests brought trouble and confusion to the world through their attempts to suppress freedom and natural instincts.

André LeFevre, Charles Letourneau, and others who were soon to join de Mortillet at the Ecole wrote what were explicitly called "combat articles," defending materialism and evolution and attempting to evict superstition and harmful, religious beliefs from the people's minds. They linked physical, cultural, and moral changes into a single evolutionary pattern, though they did little to reform the establishment's conservative views. For example, it was not until 1878 that the Académie des Sciences elected Darwin a correspondent—and then it was in the botanical section, for his studies of plants, rather than for his evolutionary theory.

By 1879, Broca's sincere efforts to establish anthropology as a scientific discipline based on medicine and natural history, and his tremendous contributions to medical science, were acknowledged. The left wing of the Senate nominated Broca for election as a permanent senator representing science; the right, or monarchical side, opposed this idea vigorously but lost. In February 1880, Broca was feted at a banquet to commemorate this signal honor. His speech of acknowledgment and thanks was a clear indication of his beliefs:

> They would not have thought of me if they had not known with what certainty they could count upon my devotion to republican principles; and, if among many others not less trustworthy and more skilled in political knowledge, they have chosen a man of science, it is because they hold science in high consideration, and believe that to serve science is to serve one's country. . . . Were I superstitious, I should believe, from the great happiness I experience to-day, that some great danger was threatening me.

It was. Five months later, at the age of fifty-six, Broca was dead. With the premature demise of this respected figure, the struggles for power at the school intensified. De Mortillet's group assumed more and more control; they eventually succeeded in taking over and removing Broca's successor, Topinard, from his tenured position as director.

Political squabbles and struggles generally took precedence over science for some years, but the fossils continued to accumulate. In 1874 and 1876, pieces of Neandertal fossils had been found in deposits in northern Wales, at Pontnewydd, and in southern France at Rivaux. In August 1880, part of a Neandertal child's mandible was found at Šipka, in Moravia; a few years later, early remains of modern humans were found elsewhere in Moravia, at Mladeč and Brno. However, the importance of the finds in Wales and France was overlooked and unappreciated until they were reexamined more than one hundred years after their discovery; similarly, the human remains from Mladeč were viewed simply as establishing the easternmost extent of the territory occupied by the modern-

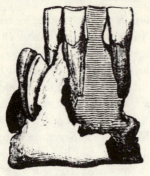

Anterior view

Right-side view

Posterior view

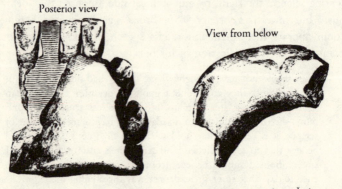

View from below

21. Four views of the fragment of a Neandertal lower jaw from Šipka, Moravia, Czechoslovakia, found in 1880 by Karel Maška. It is the front of a normal mandible of a Neandertal child with unerupted teeth. This is one of the specimens Rudolf Virchow tried to explain away as abnormal rather than as archaic.

looking but ancient Cro-Magnons. But the jaw from Šipka created much more of a stir.

The Šipka mandible was discovered by Karel Maška, a schoolteacher turned prehistorian who is now generally regarded as one of the founders of central European Paleolithic archeology. The excavation—one of the most carefully conducted in the era—showed neatly that the specimen was found among cultural debris and hearths. There could be no questioning its association with Mousterian (Middle Paleolithic) tools and extinct animals. There was only the question of its significance for human evolution, to be debated by the same scientists playing the same roles.

Schaaffhausen published a short note in the same year the fossil was discovered, declaring it to be a member of the species *Homo primigenius*—the name then gaining popularity in Germany for Neandertals. His old adversary Virchow was quick to reply, stating—not surprisingly—that the Šipka jaw was another pathological but otherwise completely modern specimen.

This time, however, Virchow gave the facts a bizarre twist. The Šipka fossil was only the broken front of a jaw, with three of the four incisor teeth in place. The adjacent three teeth—the canine (eye tooth) and the premolars (bicuspids)—were preserved, but had incompletely formed roots and had not yet erupted through the gum by the time the individual died. Virchow, like any other competent anatomist, would have known that a child's incisors erupt between six and seven years of age and the canines and premolars erupt between eleven and thirteen years. Thus, logically, the jaw represents a child older than six or seven and younger than eleven to thirteen: probably an eight- or nine-year-old. Because it was a Neandertal, the jaw was unusually robust and large for such a young child. Therefore, Virchow asserted that it was an adult with an abnormal or pathological eruption pattern that made it appear to be an immature individual, rather than accept that it was a child with a large jaw. Yet another fossil thus entered an intellectual limbo, hovering between being accepted as a legitimate Neandertal and being ignored as pathological and modern.

While Virchow was denigrating the Šipka fossil, Broca's successor, Topinard, had taken another, careful look at the La Naulette mandible and published his conclusions in 1886. His paper expresses clearly some significant changes in thinking.

Topinard repeated Broca's argument that the Darwinian theory of evolution, though still controversial, was supported by finding transitional forms in the fossil record. Since most evolutionary biologists had relied on the study of living species as the source of evidence about evolutionary processes, this was an important, new realization. In fact, Haeckel in Germany at the time thought that the fossils were largely irrelevant. Further, Topinard openly suggested that such material was beginning to be found, as in the mixture of apelike and humanlike features in the La Naulette mandible. It was what you would expect to see if Darwin's ideas were correct, he maintained. While the La Naulette mandible was too fragmentary a fossil to constitute definite proof, he conceded, it was certainly a step in the right direction.

Next, he stressed the close relationship between anatomical form and function. This was a long-held paradigm, almost a truism of anatomy. But

22. Paul Topinard, one of Paul Broca's successors, in the anthropological section of the Muséum National d'Histoire Naturelle in Paris. In 1886, Topinard produced a masterful study of the La Naulette jaw, ending with a prophetic call for new fossils.

Topinard, again following Broca's lead, took it one step further by emphasizing that anatomical comparisons among specimens could only be interpreted in light of the function of the different features. He stressed, as had Broca, the need for studies of form and function to be quantitative, to incorporate careful, reproducible measurements taken in a standard way; only then could anthropology be scientific.

Topinard's quantitative comparisons led him to some interesting conclusions. The mandible had an ape-human mix of features; it was extremely similar to the new Šipka mandible; and there was no support whatever for Virchow's contention that La Naulette and Šipka were both pathological.

Topinard's closing words of this paper were to be prophetic: "The wisest course, gentlemen, is to abstain from all conjectures and to await the discovery of new specimens. It is the archeologists who must discover them and turn them over to us, since it is our role to decipher their significance. We are counting on them."

In early July 1886, at a Belgian site called Betche-aux-Rotches, Topinard's wish was to be granted, sooner and more magnificently than he could ever have expected.

4

Shuffling into the Light

1886–1905

Paul Topinard called for more fossils in 1886, thinking they would clarify the myriad remaining questions in his mind about fossils like those from Gibraltar, the Neander Tal, and La Naulette. And in a real sense, the new fossils that were about to turn up crystallized the amorphous and conflicting opinions about Neandertals into a solid basis from which to proceed.

In July 1886, as if made to order, two Belgians—a lawyer and amateur archeologist, Marcel de Puydt, and a geologist from the University of Liège, Marie Joseph Maximin (known as Max) Lohest—made a fateful find. Once again, they were working in the richly fossiliferous province of Namur that had already yielded the Engis skull to Schmerling and the La Naulette mandible to Dupont. Their find in the cave at Spy d'Orneau was so remarkable that the establishment in France began to entertain new ideas and, even in Germany, people began to doubt Virchow's authoritative dismissal of fossil humans.

The cave was under a limestone promontory known locally as the Betche-aux-Rotches, on a hillside overlooking a small valley. It had been known since early in the 1880s as one that yielded many fossils and stone tools; it was well worked and thoroughly disturbed by amateurs when Lohest and de Puydt started their systematic work in 1885. However, they found that the flattened terrace at the mouth of the cave had not yet been dug over. In it, at one of the lowest levels, they found two almost perfect skeletons of Neandertals. The bones were found with Mousterian artifacts—an association that was to become so common that Mousterian tools were taken as prima facie evidence of Neandertal presence.

Lohest, though a geologist and paleontologist, was a specialist in Paleozoic fishes, and de Puydt was an archeologist with even less knowledge of osteological remains. Lohest invited Julien Fraipont, an anatomist also at Liège, to work with him in describing the two Spy skeletons.

23. Maximin Lohest (left), Marcel de Puydt (center), and Julien Fraipont (right). In 1886, Lohest and de Puydt discovered two Neandertal skeletons in place at the site of Betche-aux-Rotches, at Spy d'Orneau, Belgium; and Lohest and Fraipont subsequently described the fossils, establishing for the first time that the Neandertals were not pathological modern humans but true, archaic fossil humans.

Fraipont was born in 1857, only a few weeks before Lohest. They were from similar backgrounds, Lohest's father being a doctor of law and a merchant and Fraipont's being a banker. But Lohest's family never seemed to expect him to join the family business, and he went from secondary school to the faculty of philosophy and letters at the University of Liège. After some years, he transferred to the School of Mines, receiving an honorary diploma in engineering in 1883. He was a young geologist still establishing his reputation at the time of the Spy discoveries, and did not become professor of geology until 1897.

Fraipont, after secondary school, went straight into the family bank and was soon operating as a sort of junior partner. Bored, he began attending zoology courses at the University of Liège in odd hours, working under Edouard Van Beneden. He became so fascinated that, at age thirty-one, Fraipont disappointed his family by abandoning his promising banking career to become Van Beneden's *préparateur*. It proved a good move in the long run, though. In a few years, he was promoted to assistant and in the mid-1880s began teaching his own courses in paleontology, animal geography, and systematic zoology at the university. He rose rapidly and in 1886 was appointed professor.

Between Lohest, the fish expert, and Fraipont, the authority on protozoa and hydrozoa, they somehow produced a remarkably creditable piece of work on Neandertals. The monograph that the pair wrote in record time (it was published in 1887, only about a year after the discovery) was a work of the highest quality for the nineteenth century. It showed without doubt that the remains were "eminently Neanderthaloid" and unquestionably old. The excellent documentation of the context in which the remains had been found silenced all arguments about antiquity. The precision and detail of the measurements and descriptions set an equally high standard. Because Fraipont and Lohest were able to show skeletal remains from almost the entire body—in unimpeachable geological context—their assessments were extremely persuasive.

They even suggested—though it was never explicitly stated—that the two Neandertal individuals from Spy were intentionally buried. They

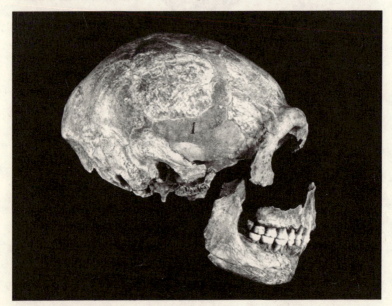

24. The skull of the Spy 1 Neandertal. The close resemblance of the Spy braincase, brows, and limb bones to those from the Neandertal and La Naulette convinced almost all observers that the Neandertals were normal, extinct, and ancient fossil humans.

based this on the position of the skeletons in the ground, for many of the bones were still articulated, as in life, and even those not actually touching the adjacent bones to which they would have been attached were close to their original anatomical position. Yet, not having strong proof of burial, they did not pursue the issue. After all, no one expected to find human burials or other rituals at so remote a period in time, and de Puydt and Lohest were clearly not seeking evidence to support such a claim as they dug through the levels and uncovered the skeletons.

Here, at last, was a look at a whole (or almost whole) Neandertal. Neither skull was complete, but the form was clear: the cranium was long and low—in fact, extremely dolichocephalic, which allied it with the more primitive races—with strong, protruding browridges like those in the Gibraltar and original Neander Tal crania. The face, though not complete, was heavy. The jaw exhibited "brutal depth and solidity," combined with the receding chin that had already been seen on the La Naulette mandible. The canine teeth were not enormous and protruding, contrary to Pruner-Bey's and Blake's surmise; still, overall the skull had a very pithecoid look to it. As Huxley had, Fraipont and Lohest felt that these Neandertals were human, but very apelike humans, rather than intermediates between apes and humans.

The postcranial bones—those of the body rather than of the head—were both immense and immensely revealing. The limbs were strongly built, with short and dense bones and large joints, like those from the original Feldhofer specimen. The anatomy of the leg bones attracted new attention but not, this time, as a result of supposed equestrian habits or disease. Fraipont and Lohest came to a telling conclusion:

> The men of Spy, when standing upright, must have had the thigh (femur) angled obliquely from the back at the top to the front where it met the lower leg (tibia), which was also inclined at an angle sloping backwards to the ankle.

In other words, they believed that Neandertals stood and walked with bent knees, as an ape does when it walks bipedally. Now this interpretation of Neandertal anatomy was grafted onto the previous one of glowering, apish facial features—a striking image, wrong in many regards, that was to endure long and be taken as fact.

Shortly after this conclusion was published, Topinard, still at this point the director of the Ecole d'Anthropologie and editor of the *Revue d'Anthropologie*, brought to Fraipont's attention a work by a Dr. René

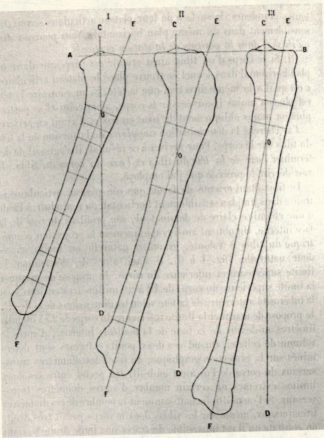

25. Julien Fraipont drew these sketches in 1888, illustrating the angle of the tibial plateau, or the upper surface of the shin bone. He believed erroneously that the tibial plateau must be horizontal for normal human gait and stance. The backward slope, or retroversion, of the tibial plateau in the Spy 2 specimen (middle) led him to suggest that Neandertals had habitually bent knees, like a chimpanzee (left), and unlike a modern human (right).

Collignon that had been published in the *Revue* in 1880. In this paper, Collignon pointed out the importance of the angle of the anatomical region known as the tibial head or plateau: the relatively flat pair of facets on the tibia (the large bone of the lower leg) that meet and support the femur at the knee. Collignon argued, and Fraipont accepted, that this plateau had to be almost perfectly horizontal, and perpendicular to the long axis of the tibia, in order for the knee to be extended and the leg straightened. If the tibial plateau was tipped backwards—a condition called tibial retroversion—then the knee must be kept bent habitually.

Here was a way to test Fraipont's and Lohest's ideas about Neandertal walking. When Fraipont measured the angle of the tibial plateau on the single intact tibia from Spy, he found that it was, indeed, retroverted, at an angle of about eighteen degrees. When he measured a series of chimpanzee, gorilla, and orangutan leg bones, Fraipont found that they had even higher angles of retroversion; a series of modern human and Neolithic skeletons showed lower, more nearly horizontal angles of retroversion. Thus, Fraipont concluded, the anatomy of the Spy Neandertals proved that he was right about their bent-kneed, shuffling, and imperfectly upright gait—another example of their simian character.

It sounded a perfectly reasonable, well-founded conclusion, and it contributed materially to the overall assessment of Neandertals as brutish, savage, and primitive. Upright, proud, striding posture was what honest, decent *humans* engaged in; hunched, bent-kneed, shuffling postures were for the dark, the troglodytic, the bestial ancestors. Unfortunately, Fraipont's conclusion was wrong. It was to take seventy years before Neandertals were restored to upright posture and almost a hundred years before the true meaning of tibial retroversion would be understood.

Fraipont, as the anatomist, assumed greater prominence as the fossils were studied and described. Lohest, as the geologist, went back to mineralogy and tectonics, although it was he who played a crucial role with the Spy remains in the early twentieth century.

When the local landowner, the Compte A. de Beaufort, gave permission to de Puydt and Lohest to excavate at Spy, he demanded that their finds be turned over to the Belgian state upon completion of their studies, a practice which is today almost universal but which was then unusual. Independent of the roles each played in the actual study of the material from Spy, Fraipont ended up with control of the animal bones and stone tools, while Lohest kept the human fossils and worked-bone tools and ornaments from the more recent layers that overlay the Neandertals. Fraipont honored his part of the agreement, donating his portion to the University of Liège; Lohest did not, claiming that the human remains were his personal possession. The fossils remain today the property of the Lohest family, although they are stored in the Royal Belgian Institute of Natural Sciences (l'Institut royal des Sciences naturelles de Belgique) in Brussels. Repeated attempts to have them turned over to the Belgian state have been to no avail.

Indeed, Lohest treated the fossils as the greatest treasure of his life, with the result that the Spy fossils have been surprisingly well traveled since their discovery. In 1914, when the Germans invaded Belgium, the fifty-seven-year-old Lohest became convinced that the German armies were seeking these national treasures in order to "liberate" them. He removed them clandestinely from the laboratory at the University of Liège, where they had been studied, and concealed them in a chest in his home—it is said under a pile of blankets and linens, where they nestled, invisible, for years. His surmise, which might have seemed fanciful obsession, proved correct: the Germans searched for the fossils in vain. The material reemerged after World War I; however, in the process of "going into hiding," the bones of the two Neandertal individuals became thoroughly intermixed. In the 1920s, when the American physical anthropologist Aleš Hrdlička visited Lohest to examine the fossils, it was no longer possible to tell what had been found with what; he had to resort them completely, based on anatomical characteristics and logic. Hrdlička also found that several small pieces listed in the original report by Fraipont and Lohest were missing—perhaps squirreled away in another hiding place, now forgotten?—and they have never reappeared.

It is also reputed that the fossils traveled to France, bundled in a suitcase tied to the back of the Lohest family car on the eve of World War II, for similar reasons. While these dramatic escapes saved the fossils from exportation to Berlin and certain destruction during the bombing of that city, these events took their toll on the fossils, producing some minor damage and loss. Recent Belgian physical anthropologists find it all a source of some embarrassment, though these incidents have served as a delicious source for folklore and embellishment.

The Spy fossils were so well documented, so complete, and so similar to those from Neander Tal, La Naulette, and Gibraltar that they were difficult to ignore. They forced a revision of the predominant opinion. Arguments that they were pathological or idiots began to look a little silly. As a retrospective and slightly whimsical review of the initial debates over the Neandertal remains, written in 1896, put it:

> The man of the Neander valley remained without honor, even in his own country, for more than a quarter of a century, and was still doubted and reviled when his kinsmen, the men of Spy, came to his defense, and a new chapter was added to the early history of the human race.

These skeletons proved to be the funerary decorations of the pathological interpretation of the Neandertals everywhere except Germany, and even there, doubts crept in despite Virchow's valiant efforts to refute them. Many began to think that maybe there had been not one or two individuals but even a whole species of fossil humans with these unusual anatomical features. Edward Drinker Cope, an American paleontologist known far better for his spectacular fossil dinosaur finds in the American West than for his contributions to human evolution, resurrected William King's name, *Homo neanderthalensis*, as the appropriate scientific term for this group. The press were already calling it the Neanderthal Man. Unknown to the prominent scientists busily pronouncing on these fossils and their significance, a determined young Dutchman was embarking on a course of action that was to prove more important than all of their pontificating.

Marie Eugène François Thomas (known as Eugène) Dubois was born the son of a country apothecary in the French-speaking border town of Eijsden, the Netherlands, in 1858. His father was pleased when the boy showed scientific inclinations and encouraged him in botany and chemistry. On his own, Dubois developed an interest in fossils, collecting from deposits so close by that he could see them from his bedroom window. His parents chose to send him to a state high school, despite the fact that many Catholics like themselves found its emphasis on the sciences disturbing. Perhaps they shared the independence of mind that manifested itself so clearly in Dubois when he grew up.

In 1877, though his father wanted him to study pharmacy, Dubois characteristically insisted on going his own way and registered at the University of Amsterdam to study medicine. This course led him to abandon the Catholic faith, because he felt it hindered clear thinking. There was no contest in his mind when religion and science came into conflict. He discovered he had little interest in the practice of medicine per se. He quickly specialized as an anatomist, being appointed assistant to his professor, Max Fürbringer, in 1881. He soaked up evolutionary works by Darwin, Wallace, and Haeckel. Fürbringer had himself been a student of Haeckel's at the University of Jena. It was undoubtedly Fürbringer's influence that brought to life the importance of the missing link mentioned in Haeckel's books. Fürbringer treated the clear-eyed, square-jawed, and rather handsome young man as a protégé, recommending him for various teaching jobs and leading him to expect that, when Fürbringer returned to Germany, Dubois would inherit his position.

Dubois was not entirely happy, however, for he loathed teaching and was becoming disenchanted with anatomy. Dubois was an intelligent man, but one who preferred the all-important first step or initial insight to the slow slog of careful data collection. Research was simply not as interesting as he had expected. He was restless and perhaps anxious to make his name and be recognized. Waiting for Fürbringer to decide to leave so that he could move into his position was hardly the sort of bold move Dubois liked. He began to flirt with paleontology again, going to look for fossils at the Neolithic flint mines near Rijckholt during his vacations.

What finally propelled him to quit his job suddenly and take off for the East Indies is not entirely clear. He fell out with Fürbringer over a study of the larynx, in which Dubois thought Fürbringer wanted too much credit and denigrated the independence and value of Dubois's work. Although Dubois agreed at the time to alter his manuscript to show that it was built on prior work by Fürbringer, he harbored a grudge and in later years claimed that Fürbringer had "swindled" him out of his rightful recognition.

Finally, rather than publish the larynx study with the changes he so disliked, Dubois simply took off for the East Indies. He seems to have broken his ties with Fürbringer abruptly, refusing to answer his adviser's letters. Apparently Dubois would not discuss their differences further; the situation was abundantly clear to him. In the end, Dubois's formal farewell to the man who had done so much for him was a letter received after Dubois departed.

Along with considerable intellectual independence—what some might call pigheadedness—Dubois was also terribly concerned about the recognition of his ideas, or what he called his "intellectual property rights." Throughout his life, he showed a paranoia that others would steal his ideas and receive credit for them. Photographs taken before his departure for the Indies show his likable, open, wide-eyed demeanor—in some he is clean-shaven, in others, bearded—but his pride and perhaps touchiness are evident in his forthright gaze and erect posture. Here was a young man who was going his own way.

Although the need to get away from his adviser and stand on his own feet was strong, Dubois had another motivation that he himself described as more important. He went, explicitly, to find the missing link: an outstanding contribution to biology that would make his name instantly. He was convinced he knew how and where to find such a fossil, although

26. A young Eugène Dubois and his wife, Anna, just prior to their departure for Java, where he was to find the *Pithecanthropus* fossils, now known as *Homo erectus*

his attempts to obtain sponsorship from the Dutch government were unsuccessful. Instead of giving up his plan, he joined the Royal Dutch East Indies Army as a medical officer, which would guarantee him a salary and a house in the East Indies. He packed up his young wife, Anna, who must have been a patient woman, and left everything he had ever known behind to follow his destiny. It was an astonishing exercise in hubris, all the more amazing because it worked.

He arrived in Padang, Sumatra, on December 11, 1887, assigned to an army hospital—a job that left him frustratingly little time for exploration and research. Now that he had gotten to Sumatra, Dubois once again attacked the problem of official support and recognition. An article he published in 1888 was a thinly disguised attempt to persuade the government to support his project; it was entitled "On the Advisability of Research on the Diluvial Fauna of the Dutch Indies, Especially of Sumatra." The article showed clearly the imaginative train of reasoning Dubois had followed, enumerated as five points.

First, following Darwin, Dubois believed that human evolution must have started in the tropics because humans had lost the apelike fur they surely once had. The cold, even glacial, Pleistocene era in Europe was no climate in which to give up such a useful means of keeping warm. This was supported by the fossil evidence now known from Europe, which consisted of anatomically modern humans or pathological types, such as the Neandertal remains, about equivalent to the lowest races of humans alive at the time.

Second, the apes that were our closest relatives were all tropical in distribution, and because the tropics were the only regions in which the climate had not radically changed, it was there that one ought to seek the common ancestor of apes and humans.

Third, new fossil materials suggested that Asia, not Africa, was the home continent for human origins. Dubois cited in particular the "Siwalik chimpanzee" or *Anthropopithecus*, a fossil ape whose jaw had been found by Richard Lydekker in 1878 in an area now on the border between India and Pakistan. Lydekker had hypothesized, on the basis of this find and an orangutanlike canine tooth from the same deposits, that ancestral apes had inhabited the Punjab region. The difficulty was that the Punjab region was part of British India. However, on both modern evidence (Wallace's work) and fossil remains (the work of the Dutch geologist Karl Martin), there were many reasons to think that the Indian subcontinent had shared its fauna with the islands of the East Indies for many, many years. Thus, there was every reason to hope that fossil primates and even human ancestors might be found in the Indies.

Dubois's fourth point was that, like Haeckel, he favored the gibbon as particularly closely related to humans. Gibbons walk upright on two legs; gibbons have skulls that are globular, not burdened with massive crests or bony ridges; gibbons have faces that are less protruding than those of other apes: all of these are resemblances to humans. And because gibbons were found in the Indo-Malayan archipelago and not on the Asian mainland, Sumatra was an excellent place to look for their ancestors.

Finally, Dubois observed that all the fossil human remains of importance to date had been found in caves, which were to be found in abundance on Sumatra.

These were Dubois's logical points. But he was enough of a statesman to know that logic does not always win the day. The final thrust of the paper was that these points were so obvious and so clear that foreign scholars would soon be flocking to the Dutch East Indies because of their great potential for improving the understanding of human and general mammalian evolution. Dubois closed his argument with a cunningly phrased query:

> And will the Netherlands, which has done so much for the natural sciences of the East Indies colonies, remain indifferent where such important questions are concerned, while the road to their solution has been shown?

How could the government ignore such a challenge? While waiting for a response, Dubois was nothing if not persistent. He requested a transfer from the busy coastal hospital at Padang to the convalescent hospital inland at Pajakombo, where his duties would be less demanding. In his spare time, he began exploring nearby caves, turning up bones of apes (orangutans and gibbons), rhinos, tapirs, elephants, deer, cattle, and pigs. He promptly sent a report on his independent work to the Dutch East Indies government.

His strategy worked remarkably well, garnering support from his superiors in the army medical corps, the Indisch Comite van Weten-schappelijk Onderzoek (East Indies Committee for Scientific Research), and a number of influential colonial officials. At home, support was rising, too: Martin, the geologist at Leiden; Max Weber, the zoologist; and the Committee for the Promotion of Research in the Natural Sciences in the Dutch Colonies all came over to his side.

His stubborn perseverance paid off; on March 6, 1888, he was seconded to the director of Education, Religion, and Industry with the express charge of carrying out paleontological research on Sumatra and possibly nearby Java as well. He received, in addition, two engineers and fifty convicts to carry out the excavation.

Having conquered so many obstacles, Dubois must have expected immediate success, but it was not forthcoming. On October 27, 1889, he wrote a letter to F. A. Jentink, director of the Rijksmuseum van Natuurlijke Historie (the National Museum of Natural History) that was so full of niggling complaints and excuses that it is almost amusing. Although he seems to whine about working conditions, he also jokes that the fossils are "diluviania," or relicts of the Biblical Flood—a precept he clearly did not uphold. It was all a fiasco.

Later that year, he gave up on Sumatra and headed for Java, in which he had had little interest previously, but which suddenly looked more promising. A mining engineer had just discovered a fossil human skull near the village of Wadjak (modern spelling Wajak). It was sent to Dubois by C. P. Sluiter, the curator of the Royal East Indies Society of Natural Science, who didn't quite know what to make of it. Dubois did: though it was fossilized, he viewed the skull as fully human, but nonetheless the "first representative of the primordial people of Java," an assessment not too different from today's. It was not what he was looking for, so Dubois put off cleaning the rock adhering to the skull and formally describing it for twenty years. But, characteristically, he refused to let any other professionals examine it in the meantime. He might have no burning interest in the specimen himself, but it was *his*.

The move to Java marked Dubois's collaboration with two new corporals from the engineering corps, G. Kriele and A. De Winter. Dubois also embarked on a new strategy, carrying out excavations in open sites as well as in caves. Dubois settled at Toeloeng Agoeng, some distance from any of the sites being excavated, visiting them at intervals and otherwise awaiting Kriele's and De Winter's written reports or better yet, the wooden crates containing fossils wrapped in teak leaves that they sent along when anything was found. The banks of the Solo River— sometimes referred to by the local name, Bengawan—proved rich in mammalian fossils. In September 1891, a locality known as Trinil, after a nearby village, began to yield remains that were to fulfill Dubois's proud ambitions.

Along with boxes and boxes of animal bones, Trinil gave up first a molar tooth and then a staggering skullcap, or calotte, of the missing link Dubois had come to the Indies to find. Initially, Dubois adopted the generic name Lydekker had most recently given to the Siwalik chimpanzee, *Anthropopithecus*, using the trivial name *javanensis* to indicate the place of origin. More than this was difficult to do, for Dubois had no comparative collections of either modern or fossil bones. He wrote frantically to Holland, asking Max Weber to send him a chimpanzee skull immediately; it did not arrive until late in 1892. In the meantime, he tried to estimate the cranial capacity (brain size) of the calotte, even though it was filled with rocky matrix that Dubois hesitated to remove.

With the onset of monsoon season, excavations at Trinil were halted until the following spring. In August 1892, the workers at Trinil uncovered a virtually complete left femur at what they believed was the same level that had yielded the tooth and the calotte the year before. Now Dubois had both ends of the creature, and what a curious beast it was.

Here was the surprise: the femur was nothing like that of a chimpanzee, orangutan, or gorilla. Although there was a bony growth of pathological bone out of the middle of the shaft—a growth Dubois, as a physician, recognized as having resulted from a wound or injury of some sort—there was little doubt about the functional anatomy of the femur. He wrote in his report:

> This being was . . . in no way equipped to climb trees in the manner of the chimpanzee, gorilla, or orangutan. . . . On the contrary, it is obvious from the entire construction of the femur that this bone fulfilled the same mechanical role as in the human body. . . . Taking this view of the thigh bone, one can say with absolute certainty that *Anthropopithecus* of Java stood upright and moved like a human.

This unanticipated evidence moved Dubois to change the name by which he referred to his new treasure from *Anthropopithecus javanensis* to *Anthropopithecus erectus*, indicating his belief its posture was upright.

But in late December 1893, having calculated and then recalculated the cranial capacity of the incomplete skull as best he could, Dubois changed the name again. The creature was upright, and Dubois had estimated to his own satisfaction that the cranial capacity must have been around 1,000 cc (versus 410 in a chimpanzee and 1,300–1,400 in living humans). It seemed no longer correct to ally it with the Siwalik chimpanzee; it was quite a different sort of thing. Instead, Dubois selected a name that he felt indicated greater resemblance to humans, and a name he surely knew from his student days: *Pithecanthropus*—Haeckel's generic name for the man-ape or missing link—*erectus*, for its upright stance. Dubois did not use *alalus*, the trivial name that Haeckel had coined, meaning "speechless." He may have felt *alalus* was inappropriate, because the portion of the skull that remained gave no clue as to the verbal capabilities of the creature. However, with Dubois's predilection for setting himself apart from others and going his own way, he may also have felt it far preferable to create his own, distinctive name than to adopt someone else's.

In 1894, Dubois published his first detailed account of the new discovery, with drawings of the fossils and comparisons to the skulls of three gibbons and one chimpanzee (all he had). While the description of the remains in the brief monograph was competent, especially considering the handicaps of working in the colonies far from museums and up-to-date publications, the documentation of the geological setting of the finds was abysmal. Frankly, Dubois had been at the diggings only infrequently, and De Winter and Kriele seem to have kept neither meticulous notes nor maps of any kind. Dubois failed to include even a sketch of the geological section of the riverbank and was distressingly vague about the exact positions of the finds, of which he was certainly ignorant. It was not, as far as he was concerned, the important issue. It would be foolish (*thöricht*) to doubt that the fossils came from a single individual, he asserted confidently.

What he did cover thoroughly were the implications of the find, as he saw them. Dubois traced the descent of man from a gibbonlike form, which he dubbed *Prohylobates* ("toward the gibbon"), through Lydekker's *Anthropopithecus*, on to the new *Pithecanthropus erectus*, and then to modern humans. The fossil skull showed distinct resemblances to gibbons, in Dubois's opinion, but the conclusions were clear and simple:

> From a study of the femur and skull it follows with certainty that this fossil cannot be classified as simian. . . . And, as with the skull, so also with the femur, the differences that separate *Pithecanthropus* from man are less than those distinguishing it from the highest anthropoid. . . . Although far advanced in the course of differentiation, this Pleistocene form had not yet attained to the human type. *Pithecanthropus erectus* is the transition form between man and the anthropoids which the laws of evolution teach us must have existed. He is the ancestor of man.

He did not compare his material to the Neandertal fossils, because he considered those fossils both pathological and modern. All in all, compared with Fraipont and Lohest's solid monograph on the Spy fossils, which was full of geological and anatomical measurements and detailed notes, Dubois's publication looked dubious indeed.

The rumbles of criticism were heard even before the monograph officially appeared. Dubois's quarterly report to his superiors, which contained the meat of his findings, had been transcribed and published in the *Tijdschrift van het Koninklijke Nederlandsch Aardrijksundig Genootschap* (*Journal of the Royal Dutch Geographic Society*). J. A. C. A. Timmerman, the editor, took the extraordinary liberty of sniping in print at Dubois's conclusion that the East Indies were the cradle of the human race, adding the comment: "This last conclusion really does seem to have been made rather hastily."

Hastily made was to be one of the kinder assessments. When the monograph became available in late 1894, the remarks from the European scientists were even more negative. For example, the Swiss anthropologist Rudolf Martin referred to "airy speculative constructions" that "collapse spontaneously" when examined carefully. Even a fellow countryman and anthropologist, Herman F. C. ten Kate, declared himself more willing to be *thöricht* than to assume that pieces found widely scattered belonged to a single individual. At this time, not one of the paleontologists or anthropologists criticizing Dubois's work had seen the fossils themselves, or casts of them, nor had any of them heard Dubois speak on the topic.

One of the earliest lengthy responses came from Léonce-Pierre Manouvrier on January 3, 1895, at a meeting of the Société d'Anthropologie de Paris. By then, Manouvrier was rapidly becoming one of the preeminent anthropologists in the Western world. His opinion of Dubois's finds was crucial.

Born on June 20, 1850, Manouvrier was one of twelve children in a family in the village of Guéret, in the Creuse region of central France. He left home and moved to Paris to pursue medical studies, later serving as a practicing physician during the Franco-Prussian War of 1871. Though he never returned to live in the Creuse area, he also never severed ties completely. He remained active in local scientific societies, becoming an ardent crusader for the protection of the countryside and rivers against the depredations of the quarries and factories.

In 1878, Manouvrier took a step that was to change the course of his career. Following up on his longtime interest, he volunteered to become Broca's assistant and preparator at the Ecole d'Anthropologie. He quickly specialized in studying the relationship of the brain and the skull, completing his thesis two years after Broca's premature death in 1880. He subsequently became professor of physical anthropology at the Ecole d'Anthropologie in 1885, director of the Laboratory of Anthropology at the Ecole Pratique des Hautes Etudes (Practical School of Higher Studies) in 1900, and assistant director of the physiological research station of the Collège de France in 1902.

From his formal introduction to physical anthropology in 1878 until his death in 1927, Manouvrier led a life that was a textbook example of devotion and promotion through the anthropological and physiological

27. Léonce-Pierre Manouvrier, successor of Paul Broca at the Ecole d'Anthropologie in Paris. He championed both Eugène Dubois's interpretation of the *Pithecanthropus* fossils as early humans and a gradualist view of progress through human evolution.

laboratories of Paris. He was clearly the academic and intellectual successor to Broca, responsible for training and influencing most of the next generation of physical anthropologists. His laboratories attracted aspiring young physical anthropologists from all over the world. One of his students in the 1890s, the Bohemian-born American Aleš Hrdlička, was to model his career on Manouvrier's, and try—in vain—to re-create an American version of the Ecole d'Anthropologie on the shore of the Potomac.

Manouvrier was a man completely absorbed in his work, overflowing with so many ideas that only a small proportion of them ever made it into print even though he had a plethora of publications on myriad subjects. His laboratories were places for stimulating discussions as well as practical experiments. And he was known to spend long nights, sometimes until the first light of dawn, walking through the streets of Paris with colleagues, students, and friends, deep in discussion on whatever philosophical or scientific topics presented themselves.

Manouvrier is most often remembered as the man who, in the late nineteenth and early twentieth centuries, brought French physical anthropology to its first maturity. One of his most important contributions was the idea that three factors apart from inheritance—environment, habitual patterns of behavior, and body size and proportions—can have a profound effect on the skeleton. Thus, he explained the tibial retroversion seen in the Spy fossils to their activity patterns in life, arguing correctly that this feature said little about their ability to stand upright.

Manouvrier also used similar arguments to buttress the concept of evolution as it was understood in France—or transformism as it was often called in the late nineteenth century. If the body was so malleable, Manouvrier reasoned, then some type of evolution powered by a Lamarckian mechanism must be a reality. Though he did not believe that Darwinian natural selection was more than a trivial filter acting on abnormal individuals—a common enough position during this era— Manouvrier lent his unreserved support to the concept of evolution. Indeed, he threw the power of his impressive academic positions behind evolutionary theory and influenced many others to accept it.

Middle-aged and a bit stout in the closing years of the nineteenth century, Manouvrier sported a graying Van Dyke beard and a calm, well-disciplined manner. But his conservative appearance and impeccable credentials as a prominent member of the academic establishment belied his political views. His underlying conviction that an individual could change himself substantially applied to social as well as scientific concerns. He believed wholeheartedly in the nineteenth-century notions of progress and the ability of individuals to pull themselves up by their bootstraps: genetics were not destiny, an issue that was to become increasingly tendentious.

Manouvrier was also one of the foremost authorities in anthropometry, or the science of measuring human shape and form. Like Topinard, Broca's other prominent student, Manouvrier believed in measurement as a way to make observations objective and accurate. He was among the first to devise a way to predict stature (how tall an individual had been) from the lengths of individual long bones, an approach now refined with statistical techniques unavailable to Manouvrier at the time. Manouvrier's approach fitted well with the popular attempts at the turn of the century to read psychological and philosophical attributes from skeletons. It was a sort of phrenology of the entire body, an unscientific—but at the time entirely credible—way of dealing with the physical variability of humans.

Indeed, the Institut d'Anthropologie was a leader in such studies of human anatomy, and the course Manouvrier took was strongly influenced by the physiologist Etienne-Jules Marey. Though Manouvrier taught at the Institut, he also maintained a research position in Marey's laboratory (of which he became the assistant director), where innovative studies of human and animal locomotion were being conducted. As a result, Manouvrier's interests shifted from purely descriptive anatomy—

measurement for measurement's sake—toward an understanding of what the differences in anatomy meant in terms of function that Huxley would have found familiar.

Manouvrier's investigations into brain size were to yield fascinating implications that went far beyond what might have been expected. One of his most important findings—which contradicted the earlier work of Broca—was that there is no meaningful difference in brain size between males and females. The apparent difference detected by Broca and others was simply a function of the larger body size of males; large bodies had large brains, and small bodies small brains, but the proportion was constant. This discovery had an immediate and dramatic effect on French educational policy, so that more intellectual and professional opportunities were opened up for women.

This, then, was the man who would interpret Dubois's fossils, who would evaluate Dubois's evaluation, in France. Manouvrier's presentation began by summarizing Dubois's main points about the Trinil fossils: that the bones came from an animal intermediate between the great apes and humans; that it had an upright posture (hence the name *Pithecanthropus erectus*); and that it represented a true human ancestor derived from gibbons. But, Manouvrier went on:

> Unhappily, the tooth having been found one meter from the femur and fifteen meters from the cranium, it was not absolutely certain that these three pieces derived from a single individual. M. Dubois affirms most energetically his conviction in this regard, but doubt imposes itself.

This was the first and most common line of attack: the skull, tooth, and femur did not belong to the same body. Dubois might assert that it was foolish to question the relatedness of the three finds, but his word for it was simply insufficient. The lack of geological detail and documentation left Dubois open to such accusations.

Manouvrier voiced the opinion of many when he argued that none of the traits seen in the femur were sufficient to differentiate it from a thoroughly modern and completely human femur. The pathological excrescence of bone on the femur was of a type known in humans and was remarkable only in that it was such an extreme case, he added. (Indeed, most scientists today still believe the femur is that of a modern human. Certainly, now that many femora of *Pithecanthropus*, known today as *Homo erectus*, are known, the Trinil femur stands alone in resembling a modern human and is quite different from the others.)

As for the tooth, it was somewhat apish and could easily belong to the skullcap. Manouvrier agreed with Dubois's estimate of the cranial capacity of *Pithecanthropus*—about 1,000 cc—which would have made the individual a microcephalic idiot if it were as large in body size as the femur suggested. But Manouvrier was inclined to doubt that the skull was pathological. Instead, he felt that there were meaningful similarities between the calotte and the Neandertal skulls, especially in terms of the large browridges. He closed his discussion by saying that perhaps, just possibly, Dubois had found one of those intermediates between humans and apes that evolution predicted. As the debate developed, Manouvrier was to come more and more to support Dubois's ideas: one of the few, along with de Mortillet, who did. It may be that Dubois's facility with the French language made acceptance of his ideas by Francophones easier.

In Germany, the reception to Dubois's find was a clear case of déjà vu. Wilhelm Krause, speaking at a meeting of Virchow's society, by then known as the Berliner Anthropologische Gesellschaft (Berlin Anthropological Society), was especially snide, declaring that *as an anatomist* he could make short work of Dubois's nonsensical ideas. Since Dubois was an anatomist himself, or had been at Amsterdam, this slur on his professional competency was a low blow. To Krause, the skullcap belonged to a giant gibbon; the tooth was also simian; the femur was human, and that was that. The association of the remains in the ground, if such there were, was of no significance because "in river banks the most disparate things lie next to and on top of each other. . . ." The only crumb he tossed in Dubois's direction was a remark that Dubois had thus brought to light a new, large species of gibbon and showed that modern humans had apparently existed in the late Pliocene (the age to which the remains were generally attributed).

Of course, Virchow, the founder of the society, its most eminent member, and its president for life, attended the meeting and had his own contribution to make to the discussion of Krause's lecture. He pointed out that the description of the geology and circumstances under which the finds were made was totally inadequate. Playing cruelly on Dubois's own words, he declared it would be *thöricht not* to consider that the fossils came from different creatures. The skull probably came from a large gibbon, as the femur might have, although it differed very little from a human. The tooth was too damaged to say anything much about it. Dubois's claim to have discovered the missing link was based on flimsy speculation that did not stand up to scientific scrutiny. He had found a very interesting gibbon.

Virchow also flatly denied all resemblances to humans; some were suggesting that the skullcap was human. The browridges were large, as all agreed, but there was a narrowing or waisting of the cranial vault just behind these browridges—a feature known as post-orbital constriction—which Virchow asserted never occurred in humans. What's more, Dubois was in error about the cause of the pathological bone on the femur. Virchow, as the foremost pathologist of Europe, believed that the best diagnosis was that it had been caused by an infection, probably in the spinal column. The healing process would have rendered the individual immobile; he must have been cared for by others, which implied that the individual was human and not the same species as the individual from which the calotte came. Nonetheless, contradictorily, Virchow would not rule out the possibility that the femur was that of an ape.

Predictably, there was one man in Germany who disagreed with Virchow: Ernst Haeckel. The two were bound to take opposite sides of any argument at this point, so far had their enmity developed. Besides, Haeckel was greatly flattered by Dubois's use of the name *Pithecanthropus* and by the tactful letter Dubois had sent saying that he regarded the finding of the missing link a way to express his gratitude for Haeckel's influence. Both Dubois's interpretation of the finds as the missing link and his phylogeny or family tree received Haeckel's firm approval. In fact, he tried to get the University of Jena to give Dubois an honorary doctorate (they considered Dubois too controversial to go through with it). But even Haeckel, so inclined to believe Dubois, had some doubts about the femur and noticed the resemblances between the Trinil skullcap and the crania from the Neander Tal and Gibraltar. Though Haeckel had had little time for fossils before, now he thought that both *Pithecanthropus* and the Neandertals were transitional forms on the chain linking man and ape.

The reception of the monograph in England was equally contentious. It was a new era; the old giants were mostly gone. Lyell had died in 1875, Darwin in 1882, and Huxley in 1895 after an illness of some months' duration, just as the *Pithecanthropus* debate was raging. The current generation of leaders, though competent, was simply not of their stature. There was no one of sufficient brilliance, conviction, and position to lead paleoanthropology in Britain at the time, so opinions were tinted every conceivable hue.

There were assessments that unwittingly reiterated the reception of the original Neandertal fossils. Lydekker, the paleontologist who had found and named *Anthropopithecus* in the Siwaliks, thought that the remains came from a microcephalic human. Daniel J. Cunningham, an anatomist speaking at the Royal Dublin Society, criticized Dubois for failing to compare the skullcap with the Neandertal remains or with crania from other savage races. While the Trinil calotte reminded him of a microcephalic, it was strikingly similar to the Neandertal crania. Could microcephalics represent atavisms, throwbacks to an ancestral condition? Cunningham's conclusion was that a direct line of descent could be traced from *Pithecanthropus* through Neandertal to modern humans. He repeated this line of argument in other talks and publications throughout the year, including a lecture on February 13, 1896, to the Anatomical Society of Great Britain and Ireland.

At this particular talk was an ambitious young Scottish anatomist, Arthur Keith, then newly appointed as senior demonstrator in anatomy at the London Hospital. Keith was to become one of the foremost authorities on human fossils in Britain. He had been born in 1866; he had just turned thirty years old a few days before Cunningham's talk. The fourth son of the former Jessie Macpherson and John Keith, a small farmer, Keith was trying hard to make his name in London scientific circles. Dubois's *Pithecanthropus* seemed a perfect vehicle.

It was a pivotal juncture in a long struggle. Although funds were tight in the Keith household, young Arthur had managed to attend the University of Aberdeen in medicine. He was an unsophisticated country boy who had some difficulty pronouncing his *r*'s, and it made him the brunt of student jokes that wounded his considerable pride. Still, his performance was laudable. He won an award for distinguished performance in anatomy: a copy of Darwin's *The Origin of Species* inscribed by his famous professor, John Struthers. Keith also won a handsome scholarship that paid for his last three years of medical school, by finishing first on a competitive exam. After graduating in 1888, he desperately sought employment; eventually, he took up an assistantship with a Mansfield physician, Dr. Trevor Jones, who as a young doctor had prospered by working in West Africa, gaining experience and saving money. Though he liked his English mentor, when a former professor recommended Keith for a job in Siam (now Thailand) as a physician on a gold-mining project, Keith leapt at the chance. It offered a good salary, a house, servants, paid passage out and back, and opportunities for adventure and research. Keith appealed to Jones to release him from his contract, on the grounds that it was a golden opportunity such as Jones had also enjoyed as a young man. Sentiment won out, and Keith left for Bangkok.

As Dubois had done in Sumatra, Keith fulfilled his medical duties ably—though malaria and drink took a fearful toll on the rest of the European population—and used his spare time overseas to further his scientific career. He collected plants for Joseph Hooker at Kew Gardens, dissected monkeys and apes, and developed a lifelong interest in races. In 1892, Keith returned to Britain to study at University College, London, and at Aberdeen again. In 1893, the work he had started in Siam comparing the ligaments of apes and humans won him the first-ever Struthers Prize, named for the very man who had taught him anatomy.

In 1894, at just about the time that Dubois's monograph was first published, Keith accomplished his academic goals: he was elected a Fellow of the Royal College of Surgeons and received his M.D. from Aberdeen—a degree that in Britain requires completion of an original research project—for a study of primate musculature. So Keith had every credential with which to speak authoritatively about ape and human anatomy, though he had little experience of fossils at this point. And he was not one to let an opportunity to exercise his knowledge pass.

In the discussion that followed Cunningham's talk, Keith rose to speak, observing that both the age and the association of the fossils with one another were open to question, because they were on the banks of a river that flooded annually. He thought the molar was too apish for either the skull or the femur.

Keith's slow and somewhat painful manner of speaking was in marked contrast to his often stinging literary style, which was to develop in later years to almost Virchowian sharpness. Just a hint of this is shown in one of Keith's papers about *Pithecanthropus*, in which he reversed his original stance about the femur, seeing it as evidence for a much larger thesis:

> It seems to me . . . [now] highly probable that the frame of man reached its perfection for pedal progression long before his brain attained its present complex structure. If one conceives this probable or even possible, there is no hindrance to awarding the femur to the Bengawan woman [*Pithecanthropus erectus*]. . . . We can [now] say with some assurance that man has not changed much since the Tertiary period of the earth's history closed . . . for the purpose of giving us a clue to the human line of descent, the fossil remains at present known assist us not a single jot.

In other words, Keith now maintained that the femur, though very modern, belonged with the other fossils and showed that the body of man's ancestors became modern long ago, well before the brain did. Thus, a modern-legged *Pithecanthropus* with a Neandertal-like, apish head was entirely reasonable but not very helpful. It is an important point, but not as much for the reception of the *Pithecanthropus* remains as for its glimpse into Keith's thinking. In the mid-1890s, Keith was still young and not yet a leader in scientific opinion. But, in twenty years' time, this belief of Keith's that the brain evolved later than the rest of the body was to have a crucial influence on the reception of other fossils yet to be examined.

Sir William Turner was another who pronounced on Dubois's fossils. Turner was a perfect example of a man who had risen from an ordinary background through hard work and force of character rather than outstanding intelligence. Throughout his career, Turner published frequently, even voluminously, on primate and human anatomy—a total of 276 publications on the subject. He tried his hand at many topics, including Neolithic skulls from Scotland and studies of the human brain. His energy, amiability, and conscientiousness in societies and committee work made him a prime candidate for various offices; he was generally not selected for the quality of his research—which seems, in retrospect, competent but pedestrian. He became a prominent and highly visible anatomist of his day. By 1894, Turner was a Fellow of the Royal Society (of both London and Edinburgh) and had been knighted; he was chairman of anatomy at the University of Edinburgh, editor and founder of the *Journal of Anatomy and Physiology*, and president of the Anatomical Society of Great Britain and Ireland: a formidable figure with great influence.

As is true of many who savor committee work and report-writing, Turner thoroughly enjoyed a chance to pontificate on scientific matters. Thus, he delivered extensive remarks about the Javan material on February 4, 1895, in a lecture at the Royal Society of Edinburgh. A pompous man, he was much given to reminding audiences of his opinions on the subject of human evolution that he held over the previous thirty-odd years. There is an air of "of course, I told you so" about his talk, though the papers in question are sometimes sufficiently ambiguous that they could later be used as support for either of two contradictory opinions. He started by reviewing his stand on the Neandertal question:

In a paper . . . thirty-one years ago . . . I showed that the Neanderthal characters are closely paralleled both in skulls of existing savage races, and even in occasional specimens of modern European crania. . . . The conclusion above arrived at is now so generally accepted, that anthropologists not unfrequently refer to specimens of the crania of both savage and civilized races, which they are examining, as possessing Neanderthaloid characters.

. . . [Fraipont and Lohest] had not sufficiently taken into consideration the influence which position of attitude would exercise in modifying the bones of the [Neandertal] limbs, and the effects which would be produced by occupation, habit, and muscular action on the bones, when in the plastic stage of growth. In the memoir which I published in 1886 . . . I called attention to the squatting attitude assumed by so many savage races. . . . Characters which . . . [Messrs.] Collignon and Fraipont thought to be indicative of an inability to attain, in the full sense, the erect attitude, were due to the customary position of squatting, which both ancient and modern savages assumed when at rest. We have no evidence, therefore, that Quaternary man was not as capable of raising his body to the erect attitude as men of the present day. . . .

Having eliminated Neandertals as a possible transitional type, Turner then turned to *Pithecanthropus*. The first flaw in Dubois's work, in Turner's eyes, was that he had such a limited collection of apes for comparison—stuck, as he was, in some obscure Dutch colony. So Turner produced his own measurements on a grand total of two chimpanzees, two orangutans, and seven gorillas—little better than Dubois's effort. Dubois had also erred in comparing the skullcap only with skulls of European, civilized races; he should have looked at the savage races, in which case the 1,000 cc capacity would correspond to that in perhaps twenty crania (out of a "large collection" Turner had at hand) from India, Australia, the Andaman Islands, and such places. The tooth was probably unrelated to the cranium, and the femur, if only Dubois had examined a sufficient number to know it, was entirely within the normal range of variability for humans. All in all, Turner was not convinced of Dubois's claim that he had found a transitional form, and besides, he really hadn't done the work properly.

Aside from Haeckel, Manouvrier, and later de Mortillet, Dubois's sole enthusiastic supporter came from America: Othniel Charles Marsh, a paleontologist at Yale. Though most of his career was spent on dinosaurs and fossil horses, Marsh had no qualms about dabbling in human evolution. He wrote an influential paper, speaking flatteringly of Dubois's "admirable" publication that showed him "to be an anatomist of more than usual attainments, and fully qualified to record the important discovery he had made." Though Marsh did not entirely agree with Dubois, he concluded:

> . . . he has proved to science the existence of a new prehistoric anthropoid form, not human indeed, but in size, brain power, and erect posture, much nearer man than any animal hitherto discovered, living or extinct. . . . There can be no doubt that the discovery itself is an event equal in interest to that of the Neanderthal skull.

To Dubois, who regarded Neandertals as pathological humans only misguidedly seen as bearing on human evolution, this was a backhanded compliment indeed. Marsh also described what had happened on September 21, 1895, at the Third International Congress of Zoologists at Leiden, where—at long last, after months of long-distance criticism—Dubois and his fossils came face-to-face with his detractors.

Dubois's reception couldn't have been worse if it had been prearranged. Virchow, one of his most outspoken and powerful critics, was the chairman of the meeting. Virchow's position was clear; he brought along his own specimens to illustrate his points and show how Dubois had been mistaken. Various specimens of human races and apes were also extracted from the Leiden Museum collections, for comparison. Naïvely, Dubois invited Marsh, Virchow, and William Flower to come an hour before the meeting to have some time examining the fossils before it all began. Dubois certainly knew he was not preaching to the converted at Leiden; he had heard and read the criticism. Perhaps he thought seeing the fossils would alter his opponents' views, though the experience had no apparent effect on Virchow's feelings.

Still, Dubois's strategy was useful, for Marsh was deeply impressed by the apparent antiquity of the heavily fossilized remains. Their condition was simply not convincingly apparent in the drawings and photographs in the monograph. Manouvrier was similarly impressed when he saw the material on Dubois's visit to Paris the next month, and so would others be. But not Virchow.

Dubois had also seen that the lack of geological data was working against him, so in his talk he presented a description of the locality, some information about the associated faunal material that indicated a Pliocene age, and a geological section with the position of the fossils marked on it. This wealth of new information fairly effectively covered up the fact that he really didn't know precisely where the fossils came from. The audience was somewhat reassured.

Dubois also emphasized his contention that the femur was not human, citing comparisons to four hundred femora that he had made with Manouvrier's help since returning from Java. He stressed that the skull showed both human and apelike traits, hence the divergence in opinions; these simply proved its transitional nature. The incomplete cranium was not like the pathological Neandertal or Spy skulls, which had larger braincases.

The most dramatic new evidence was saved for last. Dubois produced a new molar that he said had been found only three meters from the skullcap, thus supporting his argument that only one individual was represented. This second molar is something of a mystery: the most authoritative, modern treatment of Dubois's material suggests it was a battered monkey molar found years before and conveniently reclassified as human to silence the arguments over the association of the finds. The idea was that another fragment somehow made it seem more likely that all the pieces were derived from a single individual. Logically, this argument makes no sense, because if there were two individuals present, there would be an even greater chance of finding still another piece of one of them. Emotionally, it was very effective.

This strategy for "proving" that fossil bones found separately came from one individual foreshadowed in an eerie way what was to occur twenty years later in the case of the fraudulent Piltdown skull. That find occasioned the next great debate over the association of fossil remains and, as at Leiden, another tooth was conveniently found to "prove" that the first few fossils came from one individual. Was someone at that meeting in Leiden who would later be involved in the Piltdown hoax?

Dubois undoubtedly shifted a few opinions in his direction. But at the close of the discussion, few agreed with him wholeheartedly, and the only unanimity was that the finds were most important. The statements to this effect smack slightly of a sop to the discoverer, recalling the outcome of the inquiry at Moulin Quignon thirty years before. And, like Boucher de Perthes, Dubois was far from satisfied. He felt he was being misunderstood and vilified.

His only recourse, and his inclination in any case, was pigheaded persistence. Dubois took to the lecture circuit, speaking emphatically at each stop: Liège, Brussels, twice in Paris, London, Edinburgh, Dublin, Berlin, and Jena. Showing the fossils to his colleagues and "clarifying" his points helped Dubois's cause to some extent, as several authorities came to accept at least some of his conclusions. But almost no one entirely agreed with Dubois, and the debate and controversy continued for years, leading to the publication of at least eighty articles, papers, and books on the subject by the year 1900.

Many were struck with the fossils' resemblance to Neandertals, once a contentious issue in itself. Now Neandertals were securely within the fold as either very primitive or explicitly ancestral humans with some apelike characteristics. In fact, at Liège, Dubois examined the Spy Neandertal fossils for the first time and declared he had been mistaken: they were not pathological, and they did look a good deal like *Pithecanthropus*. It is one of the few times Dubois changed his mind about anything and significantly, it was not about his own material.

In Berlin, he argued furiously against the almost uniform rejection of his ideas led by Virchow, who maintained steadfastly that the remains were those of a gibbon. Not only was *Pithecanthropus* not proven to be a transitional form between humans and apes, Virchow and his cronies argued, but such proof was not going to be found because evolution in itself was a wildly speculative myth. As the diversity of opinion over human evolution grew in Germany, Virchow's rigidity in rejecting it and in slashing at anyone who did not follow his lead grew. He denied that evolution had occurred; he denied that the fossils had any bearing on human evolution; and yet he sent a young man, Vaughan Stevens, out to Malacca to search for "the missing link," by which he appears to have meant the most primitive race of modern humans rather than a transitional ape-human fossil. Virchow was aging, and contradicted himself from time to time, but he was still the most influential biologist in Germany. When he spoke of Dubois's work as "mistaking individual, preconceived teleological notions for scientific evidence" and rallied his colleagues to "beware of weakening the public's faith in the certainty of scientific research," most in Germany followed his clear lead.

Dubois tried a new line of attack, though it failed to sway Virchow. To support his position, Dubois presented his work on the relationship between brain size and body size—the first of a long series of studies that were to occupy much of the rest of his life. The general approach had been pioneered by his primary supporter, Manouvrier, though Dubois refined it greatly. He was able to demonstrate that mammals have a regular ratio of brain size to body size, implying that one could be predicted from the other. While predictable, the ratio was not constant;

as Dubois compared species of different sizes, it became apparent that bodies increase in size faster than brains. That is, he observed correctly that large animals generally have less brain per pound of body than do small animals.

What did this have to do with *Pithecanthropus*? Now that the matrix had been cleaned out of the skullcap, Dubois could make a more accurate (and only slightly smaller) estimate of cranial capacity. To maintain an apelike proportion of brain size to body size, with a brain of 900 cc the body would have to become absurdly enormous: approximately 230 kg. Therefore, the fossil skullcap could not belong to a giant gibbon. If, on the other hand, the brain size to body size ratio typical of humans were used, then *Pithecanthropus* must have had a body size of about 19 kg, an equally ridiculous answer given the size of the femur. The only way a reasonable estimate of body size could be obtained was if an intermediate proportion of brain to body size were used, showing the intermediate status of *Pithecanthropus*.

In 1896, Dubois produced a reconstruction of the entire skull—cranium plus mandible—and all of the teeth of *Pithecanthropus*. In light of the utter lack of evidence for much of this reconstruction, its resemblance to the anatomical facts as later finds showed them is remarkable. His defender, Manouvrier—now almost completely converted to Dubois's cause—produced his own reconstruction, featuring a less apelike jaw and more human teeth. De Mortillet also announced his agreement with Dubois, seeing in *Pithecanthropus* the fulfillment of the prediction he had made about a transitional ape-man, which he had called *Anthropopithèque*.

For years, the debate rose and fell like a tide in France, Germany, England, and the United States. Dubois stolidly elaborated and explained his thoughts over and over again; others changed their minds by slow degrees; still others remained fixedly and bitterly opposed to all that was being said.

From all this wrangling, a substantial number of scholars came to accept *Pithecanthropus* (at least the cranium) as a transitional form, seeing it in a context that was clearly evolutionary. Those who already believed in evolution such as Haeckel, Manouvrier, and de Mortillet, found the fossil easiest to accept. The main holdouts were those in Germany who were heavily influenced by Virchow's resistance to evolutionary ideas.

Most of the evolutionists suddenly appreciated that the features of

Pithecanthropus placed it not between humans and apes, but between Neandertals and apes. Instead of three dots in a row—humans, Neandertals, apes—now there were four. Because the Spy remains had confirmed that their anatomy was normal, and because the focus of the argument had shifted to *Pithecanthropus*, Neandertals were instated firmly as good human ancestors. Many in Britain, including Keith, Cunningham, and the geologist William Sollas, placed both Neandertals and *Pithecanthropus* in the direct line of human evolution.

Despite the growing acceptance of parts of his ideas, the blunt criticism and cruel gibes aimed at Dubois embittered him. He rarely shifted his own ideas by a single millimeter, but he was both angry and deeply hurt that so few others altered their beliefs to his. Middle age had transformed Dubois from an open-faced young man to a portly, solid loner with a double-breasted coat and luxuriant mustache. He began to tire of combat, to weary of everyone else's stubbornness in persistently disagreeing with him. In 1898, he accepted a professorship in crystallography, mineralogy, geology, and paleontology at the University of Amsterdam, not a particularly illustrious post. His salary was less than he had earned ten years before as a mere lecturer in anatomy—and he was the man who had found the missing link.

Dubois plunged into his work on the relationship between brain size and body size that had started with the intent of showing *Pithecanthropus*'s intermediate position. One of his last public statements about *Pithecanthropus* for the next twenty years was the life-size, full-body statue of the species that Dubois produced for the World Exhibition in Paris in 1900. The male figure is erect, but has a divergent big toe, like an ape's, apparently for climbing trees. The arms are elongated and apish, as are the palms of the hands; the thumb, as in an ape, is markedly shorter than the other fingers. The loins are discreetly concealed by a brief saronglike garment meant to be of animal hide.

What is most astonishing is the facial expression. The figure has a small cranial vault, a slightly protruding jaw, and a hairless face. He stares in quizzical puzzlement at the deer antler he holds in his hand, tines pointed toward his abdomen—a feature doubtless meant to convey Dubois's conviction (later proved correct) that *Pithecanthropus* made and used tools. But somehow, the statue's stance suggests that *Pithecanthropus* might be about to plunge the antler into his own stomach in a suicidal move. This suggestion would seem ridiculous if the statue had not been made at a time when Dubois was himself deeply disillusioned and embittered. He was about to withdraw from the very scientific endeavors that he had counted on to bring him fame and respect.

For many years after 1900, Dubois neither published on his own fossils nor allowed anyone else to see them. In his house, the glass fronts of the cabinets that held them were covered in newspaper. His obstinacy was so extreme that rumors circulated that he had converted back to Catholicism and destroyed the fossils, or that he had buried them under his dining-room floor, but these were baseless allegations. As he aged, and endured more criticism, his fears of being usurped grew stronger. In time, he grew into a suspicious-eyed, unhappy old man.

Feeding Dubois's suspicion and mistrust was the recent behavior of Gustav Schwalbe, an anatomist from the University of Strasbourg. Born in 1844, fifteen years earlier than Dubois, Schwalbe had trained as a physician, specializing in comparative anatomy of apes and humans. Like Haeckel, he was a vehement supporter of Darwinism; unlike Haeckel, he thought the fossil record had much to tell about evolution. "A zoology of mammals," he wrote, "without paleontology is an extremely deficient [science] that can provide only highly incomplete information on the evolutionary history of the entire mammalian group with its individual members." And Schwalbe was entirely prepared to take on Virchow, being a well-established anatomist of senior rank himself.

In spring of 1897, the energetic Schwalbe visited Dubois to examine the fossils in person. Dubois was delighted, but his generosity to a fellow scientist on this occasion turned out badly. Starting in 1899, Schwalbe published an exhaustive comparative study of the Trinil *Pithecanthropus* cranium that grew to several hundred pages, seriously dwarfing Dubois's own monograph. Much of the study was published in a new journal Schwalbe had founded, *Die Zeitschrift für Morphologie und Anthropologie* (*Journal of Morphology and Anthropology*), ostensibly to foster the development of physical anthropology as a science but undoubtedly to escape Virchow's editorial stranglehold on the other anthropology journals in Germany.

Schwalbe's study of Dubois's fossil was endlessly thorough and presented new methods for measuring and comparing skulls in a standardized way. He showed in great detail how the cranium differed from that of a gibbon; he expounded for pages on the many features in which *Pithecanthropus* occupied an intermediate position between Neandertals and apes. Between 1901 and 1906, spurred on by his work on *Pithecanthropus*, Schwalbe began publishing the results of another lengthy study,

28. Gustav Schwalbe, the German paleontologist who strove, through his studies of
the Neandertal and *Pithecanthropus* fossils,
to make human paleontology into a legitimate science at the turn of the century

this time of the Neandertal remains. Here, his major point, repeated
throughout his writings, was that Neandertals were distinctly different
from modern humans (even savage races) and that the name *Homo
primigenius* should be applied to such remains. That Neandertals were
a distinct and extinct species became Schwalbe's cause célèbre. Its acceptance was eased, no doubt, by a dearth of violent opposition, for Virchow
had died on September 5, 1902, at the age of eighty-four.

In addition, Schwalbe offered two different possible phylogenies based
on all of the information then available about fossil humans. The first
was that *Pithecanthropus* was directly ancestral to modern humans, on
the one hand, and Neandertals—an extinct side-branch—on the other.
The second phylogeny postulated that evolution had proceeded from
Pithecanthropus directly through Neandertals (*Homo primigenius*) to
modern humans (*Homo sapiens*), without branching. At the time,
Schwalbe seemed to prefer this unilineal scheme, though he later expressed somewhat greater assurance in the first. But, as he said:

> I lay little value on a decision whether the fossil skulls under
> consideration belong to the direct ancestral lineage of humans or
> represent side-branches of the ancestral lineage. For in the latter
> case also, the ancestors must have looked similar to the preserved
> remains of *Pithecanthropus* and *Homo primigenius*. In a pure zoo-
> logical sense *Homo primigenius* is an intermediate between *Homo
> sapiens* and *Pithecanthropus erectus*.

To Schwalbe, the details of phylogenies were insignificant compared with
the importance of establishing that *Homo primigenius* and *Pithecan-*

thropus erectus were outside the range of normal human variability and must each, on anatomical grounds, be a separate species.

For the field, it was a much-needed breakthrough in scientific method and clear thinking. For Dubois, it was an embarrassment and the fulfillment of his worst fears about his fellow scientists. He had allowed another access to his precious fossils and his right to have the most or even the only authoritative opinion had been usurped. Many years and much maneuvering would be needed before Dubois would let another scientist glimpse his prizes.

By the end of the century, much had been accomplished in the study of human evolution. It had taken almost fifty years, but evolutionary theory was now widely accepted, two forms of fossil humans were known and had been studied thoroughly, and Neandertals had moved into, out of, and back into the direct lineage of human ancestry. The poor Neandertal who had died in the Feldhofer grotto so many years before had reemerged into the hotspot of controversy. He had been labeled variously as modern, idiotic, and pathological, yet few still upheld these views. The more recent charges of cannibalism and bent-kneed gait still stuck to Neandertals, as did that of general moral depravity.

A major factor in Neandertal's new acceptability as a fossil ancestor of humans was the fact that the recent barrage of attacks on Dubois's *Pithecanthropus* had drawn most of the fire for some years. It is fascinating that the accusations of incompetency and misinterpretation leveled at Dubois on the subject of *Pithecanthropus* were nearly identical to those applied to the Neandertal remains. In fact, were an X substituted for the name of the fossil, it would be impossible to tell from the content of most scientific papers which of the two was being referred to. Had nothing been learned?

Not enough. The response was still more emotional than scientific. The animal within still frightened people. Neandertals looked more familiar, less apish, and less threatening now only because *Pithecanthropus* glowered out of our past with a still more savage gleam in its eye. As the scientists congratulated one another on their learning, on their new objective measurements and techniques, some fossils were being uncovered in Croatia that resurrected the nightmare once again.

5

The Proper Study of Mankind

1906–1918

If Dubois's discovery of a still more primitive form of human fossil, *Pithecanthropus*, made Neandertals seem more acceptably human, it was but a temporary reprieve. In an out-of-the-way place, an out-of-the-ordinary young man had been excavating since 1899, with extraordinary results that now began to reach the outside world in hints and whispers. His work was to speak darkly of the beast in human ancestry.

Dragutin Gorjanović-Kramberger, christened Karl Kramberger and known to most as Gorjanović, was born in 1856. He was thus metaphorically a child of human evolution. Born in the year when the first Neandertal fossils were found, he never knew a time when evidence of human antiquity and evolution were not talked of, even if they remained controversial in the small city of Zagreb, the capital of Croatia. In fact, in 1871 the idea of human evolution was hotly debated in Zagreb following a public lecture by Spiridion Burina, a Vienna-trained zoologist, at the National Museum, who had the audacity to entitle his talk "On the Antiquity of Human Kind." At fifteen, Gorjanović was at a perfect age to understand the issues and relish a theory that so upset his staid and stodgy elders. Unlike the first generation of scientists dealing with human fossil remains, he did not suffer from the shock of confronting a theory that contradicted deep-seated training and prejudices.

In the mid-nineteenth century, Zagreb was working hard to overcome its reputation as a backward, provincial, and peripheral city. In a sense, Croatia as a whole was trying to struggle out of a status comparable to that of third world nations today; it was underdeveloped, poor, rural, and

29. Karl (Dragutin) Gorjanović-Kramberger, the Croatian paleontologist who excavated, described, and interpreted the large sample of Neandertals from Krapina

lacked opportunities for education or advancement of its citizens. With improvement in mind, the National Museum was founded in 1846; it took almost twenty years for the Croatian Academy of Arts and Sciences to be founded, and the University of Zagreb followed still later. Into this world, Gorjanović was born the son of a shoemaker and innkeeper, Matija Kramberger, and a widow, Terezija Dušek, née Vrbanović; he was the only child of the couple's marriage, joining the three others from his mother's first marriage.

Like so many who became prominent students of human evolution, Gorjanović was fascinated by natural history as a young boy. He spent many hours perusing the "museum" put together by the family's neighbor, Slavoljub Wormastiny, a pharmacist and taxidermist for the National Museum, or poring through the collection of fossil fish that was the pride of the postal clerk, Mr. Gönner. Gorjanović himself ventured often to the nearby village of Dolje, to see whether the quarrymen had turned up any fossils they could let him have for his own "museum."

Despite his father's modest profession, the boy attended a "prestigious" elementary school, where he was assessed by his teachers for his "exemplary diligence," "discipline," and "average mental capacity [combined with] . . . constant earnest endeavor"—hardly an unreservedly enthusiastic endorsement. Still, the boy went on to secondary school and then went to the Teachers Academy: a good deal of education for a Croatian boy at that time. Instead of settling for becoming a schoolmaster, Gorjanović had still higher ambitions. He left Croatia and enrolled at Zürich University—an expensive proposition and a real advancement for an innkeeper's son of "average mental capacity." He soon transferred to Munich University to study paleontology under Karl Zittel, where he began to come into his own, distinguishing himself in examinations. Gorjanović's international education shows both the domination of German science—Munich was considered a much better place than Zürich—and the intellectual poverty of Croatia, which could not boast a university or, indeed, many secondary schools suitable for training what was now clearly a bright young man.

Zittel was an exacting morphologist who demanded that his students dissect and draw the details of anatomical structures, comparing first-hand the features of one vertebrate with another. It was a good education and one that instilled in Gorjanović the useful habit of drawing everything he studied, as well as taking notes. His notebooks are filled with sketches of specimens, geological sections, and the like. In 1879, at twenty-three, Gorjanović received his doctorate in natural sciences from the University of Tübingen, for a study of the fossil fish of the Carpathians.

He returned home, where intellectual conditions had been improving. While he had been away, the University of Zagreb had been revamped and revitalized, and the Croatian Academy of Arts and Sciences and the National Museum were striving for international respectability. Government funds were available for training, enabling Gorjanović to go to Vienna for a year to learn more about geology and to broaden his background in paleontology. In 1880, Gorjanović returned home again, this time to take up a post as curator for the mineralogy and geology department at the National Museum in Zagreb.

It was an ideal position for an enthusiastic young man; so little work had been done in Croatia that the opportunities for fieldwork were nearly endless. To complete his happiness, he fell in love with Emilija Burijan, a young woman of Czech descent who was assimilated as a Croat. She in turn liked the handsome young scientist, with his luxuriant hair, carefully upturned mustache, and tidy beard, and they married in 1881. National pride in Croatia was blooming, so in 1882, he hyphenated his father's Germanic surname Kramberger with the Croatian Gorjanović. Why he selected that name, other than its national origin, is unclear; it was neither his mother's nor his wife's maiden name. When asked why he had lumbered himself with a cumbersome, hyphenated name, he replied, jokingly, "There are a lot of Krambergers, but good-for-nothings are among their ranks, so it is much to my advantage to be called Gorjanović." Indeed, to his Croatian colleagues and followers, he became known merely as "Gorjanović."

He was a whirlwind. In addition to marrying, conducting fieldwork, and changing his name, Gorjanović was publishing several scientific papers a year, mostly on fossil fish. But because the scientific community was tiny, he was often called upon to work on other aspects of paleontology or geology and even to pronounce upon such important points as how to pipe water into the city of Zagreb. It may have been a small pond, but Gorjanović was a big fish. He set up the Croatian Natural History Society, founded the Mountain Climbing Society, and was appointed professor at the University of Zagreb. In 1892, he became an associate member of the Academy of Arts and Sciences and the following year, he was made director of his department at the museum. He was instrumental in forming the Geological Survey of Croatia as well.

By the late 1890s, Gorjanović had an impeccable reputation in Croatia as a scientific expert and was at least known to paleontologists and anatomists in the rest of Europe. There are hints in the letters from better-known European paleontologists that Gorjanović was viewed as a good man, hardworking but hopelessly on the periphery of the important intellectual currents, as scientists in poor, provincial areas often are. But, as is also so often the case, it took only one fortuitous find to move Gorjanović from periphery to the thick of things.

In August 1899, Gorjanović was tramping though the countryside collecting fossils and rock samples, his favorite summer occupation. He stopped at Krapina to take a look at a site from which some extinct rhinoceros and buffalo bones had been sent to the museum. Either in the company of the discoverers—the schoolteacher, Mr. Rehorić, and his colleague, Mr. Kasimir Semenić—or acting upon their instructions (the record is not clear), Gorjanović went to the foot of a hillside a few hundred meters from the center of town. Some twenty-five meters above the stream was an open cave from which sand for building had been taken for years. He later described his first impressions:

> At quite some distance from the open cave it was possible to discern several dark bands running more or less parallel in the light yellow exposed sandstone cliff. Upon reaching the cliff I was struck, noting the composition of those bands as containing ash, charred sand and charcoal, that I was looking at a whole sequence of hearths, repeated time and time again in that 8- to 9-meter tall sandstone cliff. At once it was utterly clear that beings had resided therein who had lit fires, but nearby such a hearth site I came across a fragment of flint-like stone that had been shaped for use. And moreover I observed bits of animal bones, and extracted—this was then the first time—a single human molar. The honorable reader can readily

imagine how this discovery thrilled me beyond belief! Why, I was standing on the threshold of a primeval human settlement unlike anything previously discovered in our land.

Fortunately, Gorjanović seemed to understand from his first glimpse of the site how important it was—and was able to convince the mayor and people of Krapina that sand-quarrying must stop immediately. Quite clearly, Gorjanović saw that this site represented his chance to emerge from obscurity into the international arena.

30. Excavations at Krapina at the turn of the century. The man in the black suit and hat is probably Karl (Dragutin) Gorjanović-Kramberger, and the suited man in boots next to him is most likely his assistant, Stjepan Osterman.

He returned with his assistant, Stjepan Osterman, a University of Zagreb student, in September. Excavation was carried out by a deliberate, systematic plan, with the entire vertical expanse divided into nine levels, themselves each subdivided into cultural layers. Each object—fragment of bone, chip of tooth, or stone tool or flake—was marked with a number reflecting its stratigraphic position. Gorjanović or Osterman supervised the digging themselves. Geologic sections and sketches were carefully recorded in Gorjanović's notebooks. It was an admirable approach, as good or better than Lohest's and de Puydt's at Spy—well above the general standards of excavation at the time. The first field season lasted thirty-three days and yielded human fossils—attributed by Gorjanović at first to *Homo sapiens* but clearly Neandertals—as well as extinct mammals, stone tools, and remains of hearths.

Curiously, the numbers of human versus animal bones recovered by Gorjanović, and then taken to the museum in Zagreb, are similar. Normally, archeological sites contain hundreds of times more animal bones—food refuse—than human remains, because over time each human eats more than one animal. This fact shows clearly that Gorjanović was selective in what he retained. He took immense care to identify even the smallest pieces of human fossils from Krapina. In addition to large and obviously human bones, the Neandertal fossils include small pieces of vertebrae, ribs, and hand and foot bones. In contrast, the animal fossils are usually the "better" pieces—the more identifiable jaws with teeth, skulls, or major limb bones, rather than scraps and fragments. Despite Gorjanović's evident pains to collect them, some of the smaller Neandertal specimens remained uncataloged by him, lying in separate boxes in his desk or sometimes even mixed in with the animal bones, where they lay unrecognized until the 1980s. But such selectivity in collection was common, almost standard, at the turn of the century. Most important, he had lots of Neandertal fossils, and he recognized them from the outset.

Word spread quickly through Croatia that early humans had been found. Gorjanović spoke at local and regional scientific meetings, presenting his preliminary results and his conviction that he had found representatives of de Mortillet's Mousterian people, and met with some of the usual criticisms. Gorjanović was at a considerable disadvantage. He was utterly inexperienced in analyzing human fossils—indeed, he had spent little time on mammals at all—and he had not seen any of the exciting discoveries of the last forty-three years that filled the pages of the scientific journals. He had probably read mostly German accounts—Gorjanović's remarks often pay homage to Virchow's opinion—so that he was at least familiar with the issues.

On December 16, 1899, Gorjanović addressed the Croatian Academy of Arts and Sciences. He referred to the La Naulette and Šipka remains, accepting their pathological status as proclaimed by Virchow, and announced:

And so, of the jawbones we know with certainty to be Diluvial, of those that are known, these specimens from the Krapina Diluvial are not only the most complete, but come from fully normal individuals, and display certain features not found on recent man.

As is common with scientists from small, isolated establishments, Gorjanović also indulged in some bragging about the uniqueness and importance of his find. It was an occasion for an excusable display of national pride:

The limited perimeter within which such traces were found, along with the way they were covered by layers of earth, and, particularly the animals contemporary with this man, namely the bones of extinct animals, and then the remains of the man himself, are those circumstances that make Krapina not only the foremost, but—I can freely claim—the most classic site known today. Aside from the site itself, the remains of human skeletons, particularly the jawbones with teeth, are as such unparalleled in the world.

He was, of course, absolutely right, but few paid any attention, even when he lectured in Vienna. Who was this fellow with the unpronounceable name, the Eastern European accent, the convoluted syntax, and the George V beard and mustache? What did he know about fossil humans anyway?

Not much, of course, so when his other duties permitted, Gorjanović embarked on a thorough study of the skeletons of modern human races stored in Vienna and Budapest. Even in these early years, Gorjanović did his best to use the newest approaches to his fossils. He used fluorine dating to try to establish the great antiquity of the remains (though he was able to get only two samples analyzed) and later used X rays—soon after their discovery in 1895—to study the internal structure of the fossil bones.

Excavations resumed in the summer of 1900, with Gorjanović supervising the work in person and making daily notes on the numerous finds. He directed workmen in using dynamite to blast off part of the overlying sediments, or overburden—a procedure that some recent scientists have suggested might have contributed to the fragmentation of the fossils. In 1901, Gorjanović contracted tuberculosis, probably exacerbated by overwork. He took time off to rest and recuperate. Excavations began again in 1902, under Osterman's control, and Gorjanović was back at the site in the summer of 1903.

Word was beginning to come from Croatia that Gorjanović had found something of real importance, however improbable a major discovery in that remote area might seem and however inaccessible Gorjanović's publications in Croatian were. The find was mentioned by Gorjanović to Johannes Ranke, a German anthropologist, in a letter that appeared in Virchow's journal, *Korrespondenzblatt der Deutschen Gesellschaft für Anthropologie, Ethnologie und Urgeschichte* (*Correspondence to the German Society for Anthropology, Ethnology and Prehistory*), in 1900, despite the fact that Ranke was deeply opposed to the idea of human evolution. There was also a note in a Viennese journal. Many anthropologists and anatomists wrote inquiring about the finds, which had not yet been described in any detail in print, and some even had the audacity to ask Gorjanović to send them the original fossils. Clearly, the world at large was dubious about his ability or competence to describe and analyze the material or perhaps simply thought he was too ignorant to understand its importance.

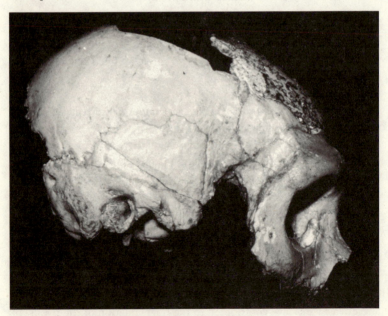

31. A Neandertal cranium from Krapina, known as the "C" skull, found by Karl (Dragutin) Gorjanović-Kramberger. It is the most complete cranium among the hundreds of bones of Neandertals excavated by Gorjanović between 1899 and 1906. The darker piece on the forehead was fitted onto the skull in 1978 by Milford Wolpoff, who recognized it among the skull fragments saved by Gorjanović.

Not only the sheer number of fossils but also their fragmentation proved a difficulty. Hundreds of specimens were collected, eventually amounting to almost a thousand fragments of human fossils, three thousand animal bones, and a thousand stone tools or flakes. Cleaning, labeling, gluing, and reconstructing the fossils were demanding tasks. Hermann Klaatsch, a pushy man and a well-known anthropologist at the University of Heidelberg, was among the first to visit in person and helped in the repair of one of the more complete skulls.

Klaatsch, the son of a well-to-do Berlin physician, had himself studied medicine under Karl Gegenbaur, a friend and colleague of Haeckel's. As a young professor of anatomy at Heidelberg, he had been among those who, following Virchow's lead, challenged Darwinian evolution. He was an ambitious and abrasive young man—one of his contemporaries referred to him as an "arrogant wind-bag" and another remembered him as having "the vigorous body and mind we so often meet with among Prussians." He was ever alert to opportunities to build his career or secure his position, such as finding excuses to demonstrate his support for Virchow. In 1899, Klaatsch argued forcefully that examining fossil human remains, such as the original Neandertal cranium, for apelike features was a waste of time; even the earliest fossils known to him were fully human and completely modern in their anatomy.

To gather evidence in support of his convictions, Klaatsch traveled extensively over the next several years, visiting sites and examining as many fossil human remains as he could. His journeys took him as far as Java and Australia, where he collected information on aboriginal customs (he regarded many of these to be atavistic) and arts as well as on early humans. He published frequently on a wide range of topics and rapidly acquired a noteworthy reputation. Presumably, his trip to Zagreb was conducted for the same purpose: to see for himself that there were no signs of "pithecoid" anatomy among the Krapina fossils.

Klaatsch perhaps also hoped to stake a claim to the material for himself by establishing an early friendship with the Croatian scientist. In any case, he kept writing Gorjanović, impatiently urging him to publish his material. Excavation continued until 1905, a year that was particularly successful; most of the Neandertal fossils were recovered in this year, and Gorjanović was getting near to publication.

Just when Gorjanović had become convinced that the Krapina remains showed evidence of cannibalism is unclear. It was obviously on his mind in 1902, for in that year Klaatsch wrote in one of his nagging letters:

Due to the great theoretical importance that your findings possess, it would be marvelous indeed if one could come to the Museum in Zagreb and take a look [at the new material]. How do you stand with further excavation[?] Now that you have squeezed the lemon with your great strength you mustn't leave it at that. Are there not other places in the Krapina vicinity that might provide opportunities for new discoveries? Wouldn't it be wonderful if we could convince our fellow colleagues that Paleolithic cannibals did truly exist?

Friendly as the tone of this letter appears to be, it hums with barely concealed desires. Klaatsch was clearly hoping that Gorjanović would hand over the precious human fossils to him and then go off somewhere else to dig for more. After all, Klaatsch seemed to think, Gorjanović was a fish expert and fieldworker while he, Klaatsch, was the human anatomist and an expert on prehistoric man. The fossils were someone's ticket into the brightly lit heart of anthropology, and Klaatsch lusted after them. Though he had done nothing to find the fossils, he prodded Gorjanović from afar and waited greedily for the naïve Croatian to hand over the glorious material he had excavated with such care.

But Gorjanović was not such a fool as to relinquish the important fossils he had worked so hard to find. He resisted, firmly, Klaatsch's attempts to insinuate himself and usurp the fossils. When the descriptions and analysis of the Krapina fossils were published at length, it was in a monograph with only one author: Gorjanović. *Der Diluviale Mensch von Krapina in Kroatien* (*Diluvial Man from Krapina in Croatia*) was published in 1906 in German; it was a substantial work of 277 pages with fourteen plates of photographs of the Neandertal fossils. It was detailed, thorough, and more than competent, and its quality seems to have surprised many anthropologists in western Europe.

Perhaps pointedly, Gorjanović dedicated the work not to Klaatsch but to another German anatomist, Gustav Schwalbe, whom Gorjanović considered the leading expert on prehistoric humans because of Schwalbe's recent and extensive studies on Neandertals and *Pithecanthropus*. Schwalbe's letter acknowledging receipt of the work is telling:

I was delighted that you sent me your work and showed me this honor that I hold very dear. . . . Your illustrations are instructive in many respects and I will do my best to read this with close attention. At present this is not possible because I am busy with my lectures, but I will do so at the first opportunity.

It is a kind and tactful letter but one distinctly lacking any real enthusiasm for the work or its intellectual significance. It implies that Schwalbe expected the monograph to be second-rate and not very interesting; it was more important to prepare his lectures than to read it, since in all probability (he may have thought) it would maunder on and on for endless pages about tediously insignificant or even misidentified scraps of bone and stone.

Once Schwalbe had read the work, the tone changed from polite disinterest to one of open excitement. Schwalbe wrote a second time:

> Your book shows for the first time all parts of the skeleton of *Homo primigenius* and in this way it presents an astounding picture of one human species. It will serve me in my further research. I commend you on a work that delineates the important point that the *Homo primigenius* represents for all time [i.e., that Neandertals are a distinct fossil species]. It is most kind of you to dedicate the work to me.

There was more. Along with descriptions of the Neandertal remains, Gorjanović's monograph presented geological and stratigraphic information and a preliminary discussion of the archeological remains and animal bones. It also put forth the idea that all of the tools were of the Mousterian type, a point still largely accepted, and suggested (on the basis of the tools and the animals) that the Neandertal remains came from a single time period, probably the warm, Riss-Würm interglacial period between the last two ice ages (the interval between 127,000 and 73,000 years ago). His erroneous conviction that the human fossils were all contemporaneous, not challenged until the latter part of the twentieth century, caused Gorjanović to abbreviate the discussion of the stratigraphy and geology, omitting much information he had recorded in his notebooks.

One of the most enduring ideas put forth in Gorjanović's monograph concerns cannibalism: that dreaded, bestial practice with which Neandertals had been associated before. Gorjanović saw that the Krapina fossils, though they represented many different skeletons, were consistently broken up, disarticulated, and scattered through the deposits. There was no way to tell from the distribution of bones which head belonged to which set of ribs, or which femur had once been attached to which tibia. What's more, every one of the large bones that would have contained edible marrow was splintered. Some of the Neandertal bones even showed signs of having been burned or exposed to fire. Finally, many of the individuals whose remains were found at Krapina were not yet adult, which Gorjanović thought was another sign of cannibalism. He wrote most fully about this idea in a series of essays eventually published under the title *Pračovjek iz Krapine* (*Prehistoric Man from Krapina*), in which he painted a vivid picture of his "Krapinci" in surprisingly cheerful and nonjudgmental words:

> He appears to be a human of wild appearance due to his low forehead and the thick ridges over the eyes. His nose was blunt and broad, and jaw more or less like a snout, protruding forward. This wild appearance was certainly enhanced by longish hair, and a bearded countenance.... These people walked on two legs—though they may have been somewhat bent at the knees—and they used two hands to work with, necessary for defense and food gathering and to work with tools etc.... Prehistoric man was about 160 cm tall.... The principal task facing prehistoric man was the collecting of food, which consisted mostly of the meat of forest animals, wild cattle, fish, and most probably, various plant roots and fruits. The crude tools that man took with him to the hunt were . . . quite limited. He needed cunning and courage to grapple with the wild inhabitants of the forests and meadows who surrounded him. . . . No doubt he was attacked on his territory from time to time by neighboring hordes who may not have had such abundant hunting grounds[.] This human was a hunter and a traveller[;] under such conditions there were life and death struggles. People fell on each side, and the victors proceeded with the dead as they did with the catch from a good hunt. These men ate their fellow tribesmen, and what's more, they cracked open the hollow bones and sucked out the marrow.... Aside from this, other human bones were found even skulls—that had been smashed and charred by fire. We will soon hear that this prehistoric man proceeded precisely as he did with animal bones, i.e. without the slightest sense of order he tossed them around the cave.

While certainly damning, Gorjanović's words lack the open horror and loathing previous accounts of Neandertal life had featured. He sounds somehow more scientific, detached, even matter of fact, thus reinforcing the image of Neandertals as even more effectively than if he had given way to scandalized disapproval.

The notion that the Krapina Neandertals were cannibals met with mixed reviews. In the next twenty-five years, as authoritative textbooks on human evolution proliferated, different authors varied in their degree of acceptance of Gorjanović's interpretation. In France, the influential

Marcellin Boule would note that the bones were charred, but refrained from leveling any accusations. In England and the United States, the response ranged from statements that the bones were both burned and broken, linked to challenges that this proved cannibalism, to acceptance of the idea softened by the speculation that it occurred only in response to the threat of starvation. Only Aleš Hrdlička, the Bohemian-born American anthropologist and frequent correspondent of Gorjanović, accepted cannibalism at Krapina without reservation. He also repeated the claim that the La Naulette jaw had been fragmented by cannibals—a charge that was specifically refuted by Dupont in his original description of the La Naulette remains in French. The ugly specter of man-eating-man had been raised again, and somehow indelibly colored the image of Neandertals, even though it took time to mature and become more widely accepted.

After publication of his 1906 monograph, Gorjanović finally received the respect he deserved. In early 1907, just months later, Gorjanović was declared Court Counselor and received the Golden Chain award from Emperor Franz Josef of the Austro-Hungarian Empire (of which Croatia was then a part). Later, at the end of World War I—in a gesture reminiscent of Huxley's selling his Royal Medal—Gorjanović donated the Golden Chain to be sold so that the proceeds might be used to treat military invalids. Gorjanović was a local, regional, and national hero. Both now and for the rest of his life, Gorjanović was almost the only scholar to publish on the Krapina material. He never refused to let others examine his fossils, but he never encouraged them to publish on them, either.

As had Dubois after his monograph on the Trinil fossils appeared, Gorjanović immediately embarked on the lecture circuit, visiting Nuremberg, Vienna, Frankfurt, Cologne, Brussels, Strasbourg, Budapest, and Munich. Oddly, he did not go to Paris, London, or any American cities; perhaps less attention was paid to his finds there. Certainly, the linguistic difficulties were greater, and in the 1920s, Gorjanović was insulted to find out that the French were only then bothering to try to read any of his publications (most of which by then were in German).

In any case, the Croatian had a far more pleasant time during his travels than had the Dutchman; where the latter had met with argument, opposition, and disbelief, the former was lauded for his fascinating and important discoveries. Fortunately for Gorjanović, Virchow had died in 1902, so he did not have to fight the predictable pathology battle.

Aside from establishing Gorjanović's reputation in human evolution studies and giving him a lifetime's supply of fossils to work on, the Krapina finds opened a whole new challenge to the scientific community. If the Spy skeletons had shown that Neandertals were not simply pathological humans, the Krapina fossils confirmed it. Krapina yielded remains of not two but as many as two to three dozen individual Neandertals, well represented by many bones, and scattered jaws and teeth that brought the total number of individuals up to about seventy. Astonishingly, these individuals ranged in age from young children to adults. It was the first time anything approaching a biological population of fossil humans—rather than an individual or two—had been available for study. It called for a new appreciation and thorough study of anatomical variation among the remains, which Gorjanović embarked on with enthusiasm in between his other projects, such as making a geological survey of Croatia. In years to come, he published detailed studies of the teeth, the jaws, and the scapula (shoulder blade), as well as works on the stone tools, mollusks, and various species in the mammalian fauna from Krapina.

In Gorjanović's mind, the Krapina remains demonstrated that Neandertals were directly ancestral to modern humans, as Schwalbe had proposed. Many agreed with him, but not Klaatsch. In a series of publications between 1901 and 1910, Klaatsch insisted that modern humans such as Cro-Magnons were contemporaneous with Neandertals and thus not their descendants. He tried to demonstrate that the Krapina remains included an anatomically modern species that he called *Homo aurignacensis* in addition to Neandertals or *Homo primigenius*: a contention that Gorjanović hotly denied.

About the same time that Gorjanović's monograph on Krapina was published, this great find was upstaged a bit by the flood of new fossils that were found or resurrected. First there was the Gibraltar skull: somehow the fate of this fossil was to be overlooked, perhaps because the bone was obscured by an extremely hard, stony matrix that was difficult to remove. Discovered in 1848, the Gibraltar skull was recognized as Neandertal in 1864 by Hugh Falconer, in 1865 by George Busk, and again in 1869 by Paul Broca. Nonetheless, it languished for many more years in the Hunterian Museum at the Royal College of Surgeons, in London—despite the fact that it was the only known Neandertal in which the face and the base of the skull were preserved. The first detailed description of the skull was written in 1907 by, remarkably enough,

William Sollas, a prominent English geologist at Oxford with only a passing competency in anatomy. (His penchant for pronouncing on anatomical subjects was a habit that did not endear him to his anatomist colleagues.) Just two years later, the skull was studied again by the Italian Giuseppe Sera, who observed that the base of the skull told an important tale, being flatter and less sharply angled than in modern humans and in this respect, much more akin to apes.

The new flurry of activity about the Gibraltar skull was nothing compared with the immense impact of an enigmatic mandible from Mauer, near Heidelberg, found in 1907. Though Klaatsch—now famous for his work on fossil humans—would once have laid claim to this fossil, he had moved on to the University of Breslau, so it came to his former colleague at Heidelberg, Otto Schoetensack, who was also an anatomist and paleontologist. Schoetensack was familiar with the gravel pits owned by Herr Joseph Rosch near the village of Mauer, because fossils of extinct Pleistocene mammals had turned up there periodically over the previous twenty years. Rosch had kindly donated the entire menagerie to the University of Heidelberg and agreed to keep his eyes open for more.

On October 21, 1907, Rosch sent word to Schoetensack that the human fossil they had been waiting and hoping for had made its appearance some eighty feet below the surface. A delighted Schoetensack took the next train to Mauer and, on arrival, found a virtually complete lower jaw—broken in two by the workmen's shovels, but easily and obviously refitted into a whole.

The jaw is massive and boasts a complete set of teeth. Although the robustness of the jaw is pithecoid, there are no projecting canines as seen in apes. To the contrary, Schoetensack found the teeth entirely human and unusual only in the large size of the pulp cavity. The ramus (the vertical part of the jaw behind the tooth row that rises to meet the cranium in the jaw joint) is exceptionally broad and low. The chin, as in Neandertals, is simply not there; the front of the jaw recedes noticeably.

With this primitive morphology, and the great antiquity indicated by its deep placement in the sediments, Schoetensack felt he had a tremendously important find. He promptly published a monograph in 1908, declaring the jaw to be a new type of human, *Homo heidelbergensis*. No one doubted that it was probably the oldest fossil human known from Europe, much older than the Neandertal remains. In 1909, the American anthropologist George Grant MacCurdy reviewed the find in a *Smithsonian Report*, saying:

That the lower jaws of La Naulette, Spy and Krapina represent one and the same stage in the evolution of *Homo sapiens* there is no longer any doubt. That this stage is intermediate between recent man and *Homo Heidelbergensis* [sic] a careful comparison of the specimens in question furnishes ample proof. The lower jaw from Mauer is therefore pre-Neanderthaloid. That it also exhibits pre-anthropoid characters gives it a fundamental position in the line of human evolution. Dr. Schoetensack is to be congratulated on his rich rewards for twenty years' vigil.

Some even thought the mandible went with creatures like Dubois's *Pithecanthropus*—which in turn raised the unwelcome (but fortunately transient) thought that the Heidelberg jaw was a fossil gibbon, not a human at all.

No sooner had the Mauer mandible attracted everyone's attention than another fossil stole the scene—more for the circumstances of its discovery and study than for its intrinsic qualities. On March 7, 1908, a German-Swiss researcher who was to become among the most despised scoundrels of all time (in the view of French anthropologists) made a spectacular discovery.

Otto Hauser was by many accounts a difficult and unpleasant person; it is said he had been a sickly child with a lame leg and that his boyhood illnesses accounted for his boorish, quarrelsome ways. Whatever the cause, he irritated and offended almost everyone—especially everyone French—with the exception of the ambitious Hermann Klaatsch, who became his collaborator. One of the reasons for his unpopularity was that he was both an amateur, having no academic affiliation or training, and a commercial archeologist. That is, he dug and then sold the antiquities he found to museums or private collectors. His first ventures, in Switzerland, caused such resentment and scorn among his compatriots that he swore he would never work there again. Embittered, he moved his operations to France, using his parents' wealth to lease or buy large tracts of land in the Vézère Valley where Lartet had worked. He hired large numbers of workmen to scour the caves on the hillsides for hand axes and other treasures, which he then sold to cover his expenses, or so he said.

Of course, he was not the only treasure hunter in the Vézère Valley, which has been described as being overrun at the time by burrowing amateurs like hordes of moles. But Hauser had the unhappy distinctions of a German accent and education—in a time when the French dislike

Fouilles O. Hauser 1911

Laugerie intermédiaire voir le Guide O. Hauser
„Le Perigord Préhistorique 1911"

32. Otto Hauser (in the foreground), a Swiss antiquarian much despised by the French for his boorish personality and habit of finding prize fossils on French territory, excavating near Les Eyzies-de-Tayac in the Dordogne in 1911 (from a postcard distributed by Hauser)

of the Germans was growing from heartfelt to rabid—and of commandeering for profit some of the choicest localities in the "Dordogne district, . . . the most ancient and the most valuable archives in France." Among his other flaws was having lots of money. A photograph of him in the early 1900s shows a portly, well-dressed man in a dark suit with a light-colored waistcoat and stiff collar. He sports a bowler hat and generous, sweeping, dark mustaches, and sits in a smart, two-wheeled carriage pulled by a dark-colored horse.

Although his image seems inoffensive, the response to Hauser in person was quite different. Contemporary French accounts are doubtless biased against Hauser, but they nonetheless reveal numerous sources of resentment; they are, in fact, a sort of primer for slander. Hauser is depicted thus:

> . . . an unsympathetic appearance, limping, a gross eater and a formidable drinker. . . . He presented himself at first as a very modest individual and a "regular fellow" to various archaeologists and workers. But once he had procured his documents and papers for working in the Dordogne and the general region of Les Eyzies, his attitude changed. He became proud, arrogant, fatter still, and showed himself immediately to be a jealous rival in the manner typical of the country in which he was educated [Germany]. He would do anything for anyone when he was seeking his authorizations and permits. Money, promises, threats, orgies offered and shared in, all were treated as fair game by this character. Miserable from the start, one saw him progressing bit by bit, throwing money out the windows and seeking to crush all the inhabitants of the country with his haughtiness and insolence. . . . But his frequent orgies scandalized the honest and peaceful population of Eyzies and of Bugue, at the same time that his brutal, victorious attitude toward conquered countries revolted them.

Most unforgivably, Hauser eventually found something really good. The French flatly hated him for it, as the remarks quoted above show. Hauser, in turn, called the French prehistorians "dilettanti, sensation-mongers, and picnickers."

What Hauser found was a complete skeleton of an adolescent in a rock shelter in the village of Le Moustier, immediately below the shelter that Edouard Lartet had excavated and for which he named the Mousterian culture. Its location and significance made it a nearly sacred site to the French. Knowing that his find would have to be authenticated or he would surely be accused of lying about its stratigraphic position or antiquity, he had the workmen rebury the skeleton, and quickly summoned witnesses. The first visitors, on April 10, included the mayor and a municipal counselor, who presumably had little idea what they were seeing but signed a document that the skull appeared to be *in situ*—that is, in its original, undisturbed position in the ground. Hauser recorded the event with a photograph. In June, he showed the remains to various visiting Germans and in July, to some Americans.

But the real tribunal was yet to come. He invited an impressive list of

33. Postcard advertisement for the excavations of Otto Hauser in Les Eyzies-de-Tayac, Dordogne, about 1911. An Aurignacian (early Upper Paleolithic) engraved stone is in the upper left, the skull of the Le Moustier Neandertal adolescent is in the upper right, and the museum and headquarters of Hauser's excavations, with the Swiss and French flags flying, are shown in the middle. Tourist information is provided at the bottom in German, French, and English.

scientists to witness the "rediscovery" of the same skeleton on August 10, 1908, including Klaatsch and Virchow's son, Hans, now an anthropologist—all Germans. Not one French anthropologist, paleontologist, or geologist was invited—hardly surprising, because the establishment had done everything in its power to get rid of Hauser, but another cause for wounded pride.

Hauser published a reasonably full account of the fossil early in 1909, in *L'Homme Préhistorique*, noting that it was a Neandertal skeleton

> that had been buried as we have found him, with his body in an attitude as if he were sleeping. . . . The figure reposed on its right side: its arm supporting its head; its cheek resting on its elbow; the right hand placed on the back of the head; the back turned upwards, the left shoulder lifted up towards the lower jaw. The left arm was extended straight ahead; in the immediate region we found, at a time when we didn't yet know that the terrain we were exploring

contained a skeleton, the most beautiful hand-axe that the site has
ever yielded. . . . The entire right side of the figure rested on a sort
of pavement or bed of flints, . . . a sort of "stone pillow."

A complete Neandertal skeleton—the first well-documented burial—
with beautiful stone tools, too? Found by that scoundrel Hauser? The
French were spitting in fury.

Then, on August 26, 1909—little more than a year since the tribunal
at Le Moustier attested to the finding of the first skeleton—Hauser
found another. This time, he was working at a cave site known as Combe
Capelle, also in the Dordogne region. At the bottom of a level containing
Aurignacian tools (now thought to be between about thirty thousand
and thirty-five thousand years old), Hauser found this second skeleton,
buried with shell ornaments. He telegraphed to his collaborator
Klaatsch, who hurried from Breslau to the Dordogne. The excavation—
carried out with plenty of witnesses—showed that a crude grave had
been scooped out of the earth in the cave. The body was again in a
position known as a "crouch burial"—meaning the arms and legs were
tightly flexed, perhaps even bound up—and Aurignacian stone tools had
been left near the body. But this skeleton was fully modern in its
anatomy: a Cro-Magnon type, not at all Neandertal, even though it came
from the level only inches above the Mousterian (Neandertal) level.

Working with Hauser over the next few years, Klaatsch began promulgating several theories that now seem especially nasty and unpleasant. He
made the Combe Capelle specimen the type of a new fossil human
species, *Homo aurignacensis*. Retreating from his stand that apes had
nothing to do with human ancestry, Klaatsch used the Combe Capelle
specimen as the basis of a new, polygenist theory. Although the human
races had been modern in anatomy for a long time, according to
Klaatsch, they had not all arisen from a single ancestor (which implied
they were not all the same species). In fact, the different racial groups
could be traced to different apish ancestors. The Negroid racial stock, for
example, was derived from Neandertals, which in turn arose from a
gorillalike ancestor. The Caucasians were clearly a different story. The
Caucasians derived from *Homo aurignacensis*, and earlier still from an
"invader" from Asia that had its evolutionary roots among those of the
large Asian ape, the orangutan.

The implication was that Neandertals had many brutish aspects and
few signs of civilization or culture, although they clearly made stone
tools and buried their dead. Neandertals were dated to the Middle

Paleolithic period and used Mousterian tools. The type found in the immediately adjacent geological layer, just above the Mousterian-Neandertal layers, has been called by various names: Aurignacian man, Cro-Magnon man, Upper Paleolithic man, or early modern human. It was a different matter altogether. People of this type had different, more sophisticated tools and displayed tremendous artistic talents in the form of the breathtakingly beautiful painted murals of bison, mammoth, horses, reindeer, and other beasts, which adorned caves in France and Spain. These incredible artworks simply reinforced the remarkable differences between Neandertals on the one hand and Cro-Magnons on the other. This psychological gulf between two types of humans so close together in time was puzzling and troublesome. How could bestial, beetle-browed, even cannibalistic Neandertals have evolved so rapidly into tall, slender hunters capable of producing such art?

In 1923, Klaatsch proposed an answer, based on a lurid interpretation of the Krapina remains, that epitomized the thinking in many minds. He suggested that the Neandertals had been killed and cannibalized during a bloody struggle against modern humans (*Homo aurignacensis*) for survival, the battle of Krapina. Thus, there was no evolution of one to the other; there was only the extermination of a lower type of humans by a higher one. It was an image that lingered long in people's minds, even if it sounded suspiciously like a justification for interracial warfare and extermination. No one liked Klaatsch much, or Hauser either, so this theory and the differentiation of the Combe Capelle fossils into a separate species were not widely accepted.

From the French point of view, the supreme insult came in the ultimate disposition of the fossils. After excavation, Hauser sold the pair of priceless skeletons, one from Le Moustier and the other from Combe Capelle, to the Museum für Volkerkunde (Ethnological Museum) in Berlin. The price was 125,000 francs. It was a vast sum of money at the time and could not be matched by the French, who were gnashing their teeth over the whole affair and never forgave Hauser. Many Germans were little happier, because it seemed a fortune to pay for old bones. Even Hauser was miserable over the whole arrangement, because the Swiss bank into which the money was paid failed shortly afterwards and he lost nearly all of it. In the end, it seems, he had sold what the French regarded as their national treasures for next to nothing.

Ironically, these fossils that the French regarded as looted were to be looted from Germany, too. During World War II, the Le Moustier and

Combe Capelle fossils disappeared from their Berlin home, along with much of the archeological wealth in the Museum für Volkerkunde. The Le Moustier skull turned up in St. Petersburg (then Leningrad) in the 1950s, in crates taken from Berlin at the close of the war, but its limb bones and all of the Combe Capelle fossils seem to have vanished forever.

When war broke out in Europe in 1914, Hauser found himself in awkward circumstances. His bitterly resented association with the German government led to accusations that he was a spy, "a servant of German science." His workrooms were broken into and vandalized; he received two hundred francs in compensation, which he regarded as paltry and the French regarded as overly generous. His mail was seized and opened, on the grounds that he was transmitting information to the Germans. Finally, he was warned by local people he employed that worse was in store for him, so he fled home to Switzerland. The French government seized Hauser's land in the Vézère Valley. In Switzerland, Hauser published a series of popular books about prehistoric life, vivid in their imaginative re-creation of the habits of our ancestors and scathing in their thinly disguised caricatures of the French prehistorians and anthropologists he had known.

Hauser was never to return to work in France, nor did he excavate elsewhere with notable result. It is said that in later years Hauser used to visit the Museum für Volkerkunde in Berlin with his wife, solemnly laying a large bouquet of flowers on top of the glass cases that held the skeletons from Le Moustier and Combe Capelle. Perhaps Hauser had some feeling for those whose bones he had disturbed, after all, or perhaps he was just revisiting and honoring the fruits of his greatest triumph.

Among those who gnashed their teeth most furiously at the sale of the skeletons was Marcellin Boule, then a professor at the Muséum National d'Histoire Naturelle. Boule took Hauser's triumphs as personal insults. His acidic commentary on the Le Moustier skeleton, written in the 1920s, attacks Hauser's scientific work:

> The scientific value of this relic is markedly diminished by the poverty of significant stratigraphic or palaeontological data, and especially by the deplorable manner in which it was extricated and stored. The reconstruction of the skull by Klaatsch, a professor of anatomy, is a positive caricature.

Klaatsch was dissatisfied with a second reconstruction, for he was attempting a third when he died, apparently of the malaria he had caught

34. Marcellin Boule, the French paleontologist who described the La Chapelle-aux-Saints Neandertal in his 1911–1913 monograph. Boule's seminal analysis of the Neandertals led to his becoming the doyen of human paleontology in France between the world wars. This picture was taken in his later, well-established years; pictures of him as a younger man show him sporting a luxuriant mustache, a goatee, and the same self-confident look.

in Java. One of the museum technicians completed the job, unfortunately filling in the missing pieces with plaster so cleverly painted that no one could any longer tell what was the original and what was added. It was only in the 1920s that the skull pieces were reassembled in an anatomically reasonable fashion by the German anthropologist Hans Weinert. This long-bungled reconstruction shows that Gorjanović was foresighted indeed not to let Klaatsch get too close to the Krapina fossils.

Of the Combe Capelle specimen, Boule was equally critical, remarking:

> An attempt has been made to establish it as the type specimen of a particular species under the name *Homo aurignacensis*, and the German anthropologist Klaatsch propounded the most extravagant hypothesis with regard to it. As a matter of fact, as we shall see later, it . . . is nothing more than a variety of the Cro-Magnon Race.

Boule was to remain Hauser's archenemy for life. Part of the problem may have been that Hauser had the audacity to sell a fossil Boule would dearly have loved to study—and to the Germans, of all people. Part of the problem was also the differences in nationality, family background, and training.

Born in 1861 in Montsalvy, Boule had studied first at the University of Toulouse. He was not of a wealthy family like Hauser's and achieved his education and professional opportunities through merit rather than money. At Toulouse, Boule was befriended by one of his teachers, the eminent archeologist Emile Cartailhac, and received degrees in natural and physical sciences, specializing in geology. In 1887, he earned a coveted teaching certificate and went to the Muséum National d'Histoire Naturelle on scholarship. There he met Edouard Lartet and the man who was to become his closest friend and mentor, the paleontologist Albert Gaudry. Gaudry easily enticed Boule to shift his primary interests from geology to paleontology. With his old friend Cartailhac, Boule began publishing studies of various Mousterian rock shelters. Boule taught for a few years and then returned to Paris for further study. In 1888, he published a long and important article that reviewed the geological contexts of every known fossil human—including a few only purportedly fossil humans. This established him as one thoroughly in command of the relevant literature, even if it did little to further his firsthand experience with the fossils.

During the 1890s, Boule gradually took control over what was to become one of the major anthropological journals, *L'Anthropologie*. It had been formed in 1890 by Cartailhac, Hamy, and Topinard, who merged the previously existing *Revue d'Ethnologie*, edited by Hamy, with the *Revue d'Anthropologie*, edited by Topinard. The new journal provided a single outlet for physical anthropological and related research in France; it was also the main organ in this field expressing the views of scientists opposed to the *Bulletin de la Société d'Anthropologie de Paris*, once Broca's journal and now edited by his successors at the Ecole d'Anthropologie. By 1894, the editorial board of *L'Anthropologie* had been expanded to include Boule and René Verneau, among others. By the time the year was out, Boule and Verneau had become coeditors, positions that they were to retain until they relinquished control to their students in the 1930s. Without question, Boule dominated both Verneau and, increasingly, much of French physical anthropology through this journal. It became a convenient vehicle through which Boule could express his opinions, passing judgment on all new finds and, whenever the slightest opportunity presented itself, publishing fervent diatribes castigating Hauser.

Boule completed his doctorate in natural sciences in 1892 and took up a job as Gaudry's *préparateur*. His rise in his profession was steady but not meteoric. Two years after this appointment, Boule became an assistant professor. Six years later, he stood in for Gaudry, who was on leave, as interim professor in 1900–1901. Finally, when Gaudry retired in 1902, his protégé Boule became full professor and head of the laboratory of paleontology.

The special relationship between Gaudry and Boule lasted many years and was of unusual closeness—one modern historian of science describes Boule as Gaudry's disciple, and it is perhaps not too strong a word. Gaudry was Boule's teacher, father-figure, mentor, role model, closest friend, collaborator: his inspiration and guide. Naturally, Boule shaped his career on Gaudry's.

For his part, Gaudry had always carefully avoided the thorny thickets of human evolution—not because the subject was of no interest, but because it was professionally dangerous. It was his strategy for keeping evolutionary paleontology alive at the Muséum National d'Histoire Naturelle when the museum was still dominated by Cuvierian antievolutionists. Probably there was no spoken agreement, only a tacit understanding that, as long as only animals were studied, Gaudry would be allowed to continue his work and writings about evolution. If he stepped over the bounds and began writing on unacceptable topics, there would be trouble. So Gaudry practiced scientific diplomacy, though occasionally he tiptoed close to the edge, as when he published an account of the fauna associated with the Chancelade skeleton, a Cro-Magnon find made in 1888, without commenting on the human fossil itself.

Once he took over from Gaudry, Boule felt his task was "widening the path" blazed by Gaudry and venturing upon the "agonizing problem of human origins" now that human evolution was regarded as more acceptable and even exciting. It was his duty, his calling, even his sacred trust to follow up on Gaudry's lead and carry his tradition of work into new realms that were denied Gaudry himself.

But how to do this without any human fossils to work on? Boule had written briefly about some Cro-Magnon skeletons discovered at Grimaldi, Italy, in 1901, in excavations in which Prince Albert I of Monaco—fanatically interested in human prehistory—participated. The Grimaldi finds seemed to suggest that anatomically modern humans also lived in Mousterian times, as did Neandertals, further complicating the problems of the one being the ancestor of the other. All the Grimaldi skeletons were deliberately buried, as is reasonably common with Upper Paleolithic human remains; their bones were colored with red ocher that was presumably applied to the flesh, and shell ornaments and other decorations surrounded the skeletons.

But the analysis of the Grimaldi remains was not given to Boule but to Verneau, who was still deeply concerned with the questions of race and racial migrations that had captivated the scientists in the late nineteenth century. He came to a bizarre conclusion, proclaiming that the oldest two (of four) skeletons found in the Grotte des Enfants at Grimaldi were a distinct, Negroid race. Because L. Testut, an anthropologist at the University of Lyons, had recently declared the Chancelade skeleton found near Périgueux in 1888 to be that of an Eskimo, the notion of racial migrations suddenly assumed almost ludicrous proportions, with extremes of modern racial groups wandering helter-skelter across the French countryside and then dying out. With the acuity of hindsight, it is easy to see that both Testut and Verneau were confusing anatomical variations—some of which are a function of habits and behaviors during life—with clusters of anatomical features that are genetically associated with racial groups. In fact, determining the racial origin of a single skull is not always a simple matter, even with modern knowledge and statistical techniques, and it seems unlikely that Verneau or Testut had examined many Eskimo or African skulls. However improbable their pronouncements may have sounded at the time, they posed a difficult political, social, and anatomical problem. The Prince of Monaco was involved in the Grimaldi excavation, and he had given Verneau the fossils to analyze. The Prince himself subsequently became a prominent patron of paleoanthropology, founding the Anthropological Museum of Monaco and in 1906 taking "under his protection" the thirteenth meeting of the International Congress of Anthropology and Prehistoric Archeology, the future of which seemed dubious at the time. It was best not to make trouble about the interpretation of the Grimaldi finds.

Boule needed a good fossil human of his own to work on. The bitter irony was that the Neandertal skeleton that was to be the highlight of Boule's career as a paleoanthropologist was discovered on August 3, 1908, just one week before Hauser's great German tribunal at Le Moustier. Two young French brothers, Amédée and Jean Bouyssonie—both recently ordained as priests—were excavating in a small cave near the village of La Chapelle-aux-Saints, south of Brive-la-Gaillarde in the Corrèze region of central France. They found what was then the most complete, and what was to become the best known, Neandertal.

The Bouyssonie brothers formed part of a newly active "modernist" movement within the French Catholic Church. Amédée, the elder by ten years, was actively debating the relationship between science and nature (including evolution), on the one hand, and the Catholic faith, on the other. It was all part of a struggle to find a compromise that would enable him and others like him to retain their religious faith and yet reconcile it with the increasingly incontrovertible evidence of evolution and other laws of nature. In time, he came to believe in what is now called orthogenesis—a sort of "directed" evolution that proceeds in its own way, through its own mechanisms, yet with the occasional and "providential" intervention of a Supreme Being.

One of the major centers for this modernist movement was the seminary of Saint-Sulpice at Issy-les-Moulineaux, near Paris. Jean Bouyssonie had spent 1897 and 1898 there, sharing a room with the young Henri Breuil, who was to become a renowned expert on Paleolithic art. This was the beginning of a long friendship in which the young seminarians—soon to become abbés—shared both their religious studies and their passion for prehistory. Despite Breuil's later prominence, it was perhaps more passion than science on his part. After his death, French colleagues from the generation following his spoke of him as *un antiquaire de génie,* "an antiquarian of genius." While this sounds like an

35. The small cave known as the Bouffia Bonneval at La Chapelle-aux-Saints, after the discovery of the Neandertal skeleton. From left to right: Josef Bonneval, the servant of the Bonneval family (he was unrelated to them), who owned the cave and lent his services to the Bouyssonie brothers to help with the excavation; Mr. Bouygés, a local bourgeois who wanted to be in the picture; Mr. Bru, a neighbor; and Félix Bonneval, the son of the landowner, at age sixteen. Josef Bonneval discovered the Neandertal skeleton by sinking his pick into the side of the braincase.

unqualified compliment, it is a remark that all but calls Breuil a clever antiquities dealer, little better than Otto Hauser. Together with the Bouyssonies, in 1897 Breuil visited many of the prehistoric sites in the region of Brive-la-Gaillarde.

During the summer of 1908, as they had for many previous summers, the Bouyssonies cycled the thirty kilometers from Brive through the countryside to the village of Gines, near La Chapelle-aux-Saints. Their objective was to combine a visit with their cousins with their perpetual search for prehistoric tools. Outside La Chapelle-aux-Saints, they excavated a small cave known locally as the Bouffia Bonneval—*bouffia* being local dialect for "foxhole" and Bonneval being the name of the landowner. As Monsieur Bonneval felt the young abbés were getting excessively tired and dirty carrying out this work for themselves, he lent them the services of a servant, Josef Bonneval, who only coincidentally shared the same surname as his employer. Thus, it was Josef Bonneval who was wielding the pickaxe on August 3, 1908, when it struck something with a hollow thud: the side of the skull of a remarkably complete Neandertal skeleton.

The topography and stratigraphy of the small cave were straightforward. The cave was small, only 6 meters long and varying in width from 2.5 to 4 meters; the ceiling rose only 1 to 2 meters above the floor. The entire floor of the cave was covered by an archeological layer, formed of a "magma" of broken animal bones and flint tools, embedded in a hard, yellowish earth. The animal bones included extinct reindeer, ibex, horse, rhinoceros, wolf, and other Pleistocene species; the tools were clearly Mousterian. As for the skeleton, the abbés, joined by a Louis Bardon, published an account of its placements and discovery in *L'Anthropologie*—Boule's journal:

> The man that we have found was *intentionally buried*. He was deposited at the bottom of a trench dug into the marly soil of the cave; this soil, white-colored and hard to dig, is distinctly different from that of the archaeological layer. This grave or trench . . . was almost rectangular, with a width of 1 meter, a length of 1 meter 45 centimeters, and a depth of about 30 centimeters.
>
> The body was oriented in it approximately east-west, lying on its back, the head to the west, touching the edge of the hole in one corner and wedged in place by several stones. The right arm was bent, going back towards the head; the left arm was straight. The legs were also bent back towards the right.
>
> Over the head were placed three or four large fragments of long

bone; over them, still articulated, was the end of a large bovid metatarsal, the two first phalanges and one second phalanx [bones of the lower leg and hoof]. Evident proof that the leg was placed there with its meat on—perhaps as nourishment for the dead person—(proof also that the grave had never been disturbed). Around the rest of the body were a great number of quartz flakes, of dressed flints, several fragments of ochre, broken bones, etc., as in the rest of the archaeological layer.

Breuil recommended to the Bouyssonies that they send the skeleton to Marcellin Boule. Why Boule? For one thing, his 1888 essay on human paleontology had shown him to be a knowledgeable young man, up-to-date on all the most recent finds. More important, Breuil and Boule had been students of Cartailhac together at the University of Toulouse. The network of connections and influence smoothly linked Boule to the Bouyssonies, via Breuil, and the brothers sent Boule the skeleton for analysis. Here at last was the fossil Boule had longed for.

This was a fateful decision, for Boule as well as for Neandertals. Boule was ready and waiting for such an opportunity to prove that human fossils could be studied in the same rigorous manner as any other aspect of paleontology. He also had some ideas, though possibly not explicitly acknowledged ones, about how evolution worked. Boule's previous studies of different mammalian groups had yielded some interestingly consistent conclusions. He had found, repeatedly, that mammalian groups had originated earlier than had been thought and that putative ancestors were often collateral dead ends merely paralleling what had been thought to be their descendants. In other words, Boule, and Gaudry before him, found branching patterns peppered with extinctions and dead ends. Coupled with his writings on Grimaldi suggesting a brief period of time separating Neandertals and Cro-Magnons, Boule's conclusions on the La Chapelle-aux-Saints Neandertal were almost predictable.

With this intellectual background, Boule set to work on the Old Man ("Vieillard") from La Chapelle-aux-Saints, as the skeleton came to be known. He took great care to publish interim reports and preliminary portions of his study as rapidly as possible, because his nemesis Hauser was busily finding more fossils.

Boule, and many other French paleontologists and anthropologists, treated the La Chapelle-aux-Saints remains as if they were the first good evidence of a Neandertal burial, despite Hauser's slightly earlier discovery of the Le Moustier burial and suggestions that the Spy skeletons had

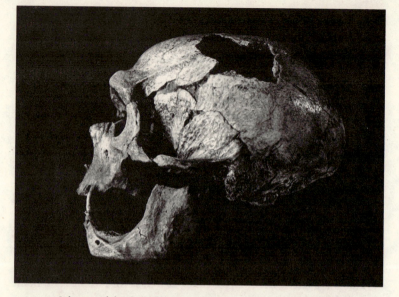

36. Side view of the skull of the La Chapelle-aux-Saints Neandertal found in 1908. As a result of the study by Marcellin Boule, this specimen served as the basis of the image of the Neandertals as brutish and semihuman, a dead-end side-branch in human evolution. Although this individual was only about thirty years old when he died, he had already lost most of his cheek teeth, resulting in the open-mouthed appearance.

been buried. But somehow the reassuringly human habit of burying the dead with some ceremony and with grave goods apparently intended to make the afterlife of the deceased easier did not change the basic image of Neandertals. Large browridges weighed more heavily than burials.

Boule's preliminary assessments of the La Chapelle-aux-Saints skeleton appeared in *L'Anthropologie* starting in December 1908. In them, he emphasized that the remains were found in a deliberate burial, that they were unquestionably Neandertal, and that (Virchow's blustering in the previous century notwithstanding) the morphology of the skeleton was normal and nonpathological, though simian in many respects.

The year 1909 saw yet another discovery in the Dordogne region, at La Ferrassie. Since 1899, two prehistorians, Denis Peyrony and Dr. Louis Capitan, had been exploring this rock shelter, which yielded many fine artifacts. On September 17, 1909, Peyrony, Capitan, and a Monsieur Raveau discovered some human bones in one of the layers. As was by then the fashion, they summoned a tribunal, including Boule, his collaborators at La Chapelle-aux-Saints Bouyssonie and Bardon, Cartailhac, Breuil, and a Monsieur Feaux, who had excavated at Chancelade. In a stratigraphic layer identified as being the same as that at La Chapelle-aux-Saints, the team uncovered an adult male Neandertal skeleton, again in a flexed position in an excavated grave. Mousterian stone tools were found in the layer as well. In 1910, Peyrony found a second skeleton, this time an adult female. Dubbed La Ferrassie 1 and 2, the two skeletons were shipped off to Boule's laboratory, where they were used as stand-ins for parts missing in the La Chapelle-aux-Saints skeleton during the writing of Boule's monograph. Additional discoveries of the skeletons of five children buried at La Ferrassie were made in subsequent years, too late to be used in Boule's monograph. In fact, Boule never bothered to describe the La Ferrassie sample properly. After all, he probably reasoned, what was there to say about Neandertals after La Chapelle-aux-Saints?

Then, in 1910, Henri Martin—a medical practitioner and a good friend of Boule's—discovered bones of two more Neandertals, at the site of La Quina. Martin had been exploring the region since 1905, when he had given up his lucrative Parisian practice and had moved to the Charente region. It was some years before Martin's move that the La Quina rock shelter had been discovered at the foot of a cliff as a result of a road cut, thanks to the sharp eyes of a local amateur archeologist named Gustave Chauvet. It was Chauvet who first found and collected the exquisite Mousterian tools, including a type that was to come to be known as a Quina scraper. But the monied Parisian moved in, bought the site in its entirety, and closed it to (other) amateurs in a peremptory fashion that nurtured considerable local resentment.

Martin, too, was soon finding Mousterian tools and bones of extinct animals in the old rock shelter that ran for a considerable distance along the foot of a cliff. Although his manners were less than gracious, Martin's scientific acumen was sharp. In 1910, his years of digging were rewarded with human material: two tali (ankle bones), which he recognized as being Neandertal. More important, Martin realized that the peculiar angle of the head of the talus in Neandertals did *not* indicate that their big toes were divergent from the other toes in an apelike fashion—an analysis that was published and of which his good friend Boule could not have been unaware, though he was later to disregard it. Then, in September 1911—just before the first installment of Boule's monograph was published—Martin found a skeleton of an adult Neandertal in a burial. He had little time to make sense of the find before Boule's work began to appear.

Boule's monograph was published in the *Annales de Paléontologie* in four installments between October 1911 and March 1913. Publishing a work such as this in installments was an unusual approach that can probably be attributed to Boule's anxiety that Hauser would preempt him. In any case, the monograph was immediately a classic, a study of such thoroughness and merit that it established the paleontology of humans—paleoanthropology, as it would later be called—as a scientific discipline.

His conclusions were to have a more lasting impact on the image of Neandertals than any previous work. Boule's work was scientific, detailed, rigorous; it was methodologically unimpeachable and followed closely the procedures he had used in earlier studies of other mammalian fossils. He described each part of the skeleton systematically and compared it to other Neandertal material, apes, and humans. When the work was finished, he could stand back and say with satisfaction that now "the science of paleontology is *one*, whether concerned with man or animals." It was exactly the outcome he had been hoping for.

What is remarkable is that, despite Boule's evident scholarship and care, the monograph is also astonishingly wrong in many of its conclusions. He took the Old Man of La Chapelle-aux-Saints as the "type" of Neandertals—not in a formal taxonomic sense, but psychologically—and painted a detailed picture of Neandertal anatomy that became the received truth. And this truth showed Neandertals as terribly primitive and apish, in no way a possible ancestor of the glorious Cro-Magnons who followed them so quickly in time. Neandertals could only be an extinct and remote relative of modern humans.

Because Boule had been troubled by the rapid turnover between Neandertals and modern humans before he laid eyes on the Old Man, his results are hardly surprising. At every turn, Boule emphasized the physical similarities between Neandertals and apes and distanced the fossil humans from living people. He reconstructed the vertebral column of Neandertals as much straighter than that of modern humans, giving rise to a stooping posture and slouching gait. Boule's Neandertal had a forwardly thrust head—which somehow highlighted its elongated shape, protruding face, and large browridges—perpetually bent knees, and a widely divergent big toe. The drawing in his monograph imprinted itself on the minds of anthropologists everywhere. It was the perfectly imperfect troglodyte: the brute, the savage. And, of course, it was not Boule's or anyone else's ancestor.

Boule concluded that the Old Man was probably over fifty years old at the time of death, an opinion based on the extent to which the bones of the braincase had fused together. This idea of age was reinforced by the extensive signs of degeneration on the skeleton. The Old Man had lost most of his molar teeth before death, suffered from severe arthritis of the lower neck, back, and shoulders, had lived long enough to heal a broken rib, and had a badly deteriorated left hip. Without question, the Old Man had had a hard time of it. His physical condition is all the more remarkable in the light of more recent assessments of his age, which place him at about thirty at the time of death.

While Boule was not blind to most of these abnormalities, his aim was to present a real, true, "normal" Neandertal. Thus he noted these lesions and injuries only briefly, trying to discern how the skeleton would have looked without them. The missing or diseased portions of the La Chapelle-aux-Saints skeleton were "filled in" by reference to the remains from La Ferrassie—though, ironically, he mistakenly took the fractured hip region of La Ferrassie 1 for normal (if peculiar).

Though he clearly saw the diseased state of his precious Neandertal, he was blind to the real significance of these pathologies. Depite the accuracy of his observations, Boule's reconstruction of this not-so-old man of La Chapelle-aux-Saints was seriously inaccurate. Perhaps the fact that Boule himself was fifty in 1911 lent passion to his denial that the Old Man walked and moved less spryly (or less normally) than a younger Neandertal might have.

From the perspective of more modern analysis, many of the features he enumerated as apish and contributing to a shuffling, bent-kneed gait are neither pathological nor unheard-of in modern humans. One problem was that the methods of functional anatomy—of analyzing an extinct species to determine its posture, gait, and habitual behavior—were in their infancy at the time. This meant that he was simply taking the wrong measurement at times and was misunderstanding its significance at others. Another problem was the recurrent plague of variability; it was not known how much normal, modern humans (or apes or fossil humans) varied in their anatomy or how to determine the level of difference that was meaningful. Simply put, the morphology typical of Neandertals—so muscular and strong or hypertrophied, in technical terms—represents in many ways the extreme among modern humans, but no one knew enough about human morphology to understand this.

For example, Boule was impressed by the muscularity and massiveness of the hip region, attested to by the strongly ridged markings where muscles had attached and by the thickness and substance of the bones. He believed, wrongly, that the thigh could not have been positioned so as to straighten the hip completely. He also noticed the retroverted tibial plateaux—as had Fraipont and Lohest in the Spy material—and accepted that this meant that the knees could not be straightened either, even though two studies (one of them by Manouvrier) in the 1890s had shown that some modern humans with normal gait and posture also showed tibial retroversion. Boule noted Manouvrier's conclusions and then, amazingly, simply ignored their implications for the Neandertals. Boule also placed the big toe well apart from the other toes, as it is in apes who use the foot for grasping—a mistake based in part on a faulty reconstruction of missing portions of bones and in part on measurements that do not capture the functioning of the foot very well. In this, Boule must have deliberately ignored Martin's work on the La Quina material.

Boule made similar errors in his interpretation of the vertebral column, of the La Chapelle-aux-Saints skeleton, one of the most important regions for reconstructed posture. His conclusions were based on a comparison of human and ape anatomy. Normal modern humans have a double S-curve to their spines. Viewed from the side, a human spine curves toward the front of the individual at the neck and again at the lower back; the intervening thoracic region, where the ribs are, bulges backwards, making a curve that is concave to the front. In contrast, apes have spines that bulge backwards from top to bottom in a single arc that

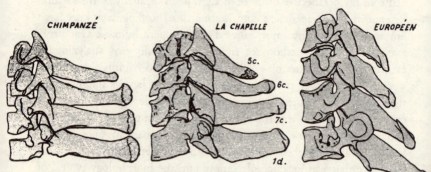

37. The last three cervical (neck) vertebrae and first thoracic (chest) vertebra of La Chapelle-aux-Saints 1 compared with those of a chimpanzee (left) and a modern European (right), as depicted by Marcellin Boule in 1912. The horizontal spines of the La Chapelle-aux-Saints vertebrae were considered by Boule to indicate a chimpanzeelike head posture for the Neandertals.

is concave to the front. Of course, Boule's reconstruction of the La Chapelle-aux-Saints remains showed a distinctly apelike curvature. Part of the anatomical support for this interpretation came from the vertebral spines, the fingerlike, bony projections of the vertebrae that can be felt as hard bumps along the back of the neck. In the La Chapelle-aux-Saints skeleton, the vertebral spines of the lower neck are long and thus superficially resemble those of a chimpanzee. Yet, as early as 1886, the anatomist Daniel J. Cunningham had noted similar, if slightly less massive, vertebral spines in modern humans—a publication of which Boule was probably aware, but which he apparently discounted.

His unwillingness to attribute a human curvature to the Neandertal spine showed in another telling detail. Each vertebra has a roughly cylindrical portion known as its body, which is separated from the bodies of the vertebra above and below by disks, which are unfortunately prone to "slipping" in life. The vertebral bodies of the skeleton were damaged in the region of the lower back, so Boule modeled the missing parts with clay. His repairs made the vertebral bodies wedge-shaped, so that they were taller in front than in the back. While the only way to arrange such wedge-shaped vertebrae in anatomical position is in a lumbar curvature like that seen in modern humans, Boule managed to ignore what his own hands had created when he stacked the vertebrae to make an entire spinal column.

It would seem that the failings of Boule's reconstruction must be attributed to something other than the arthritis and other physical abnormalities suffered by the Old Man of La Chapelle-aux-Saints. Although technically Boule was studying that single individual, he borrowed freely from the largely nonpathological remains from Neandertal, Spy, and La Ferrassie in his analysis. As mentioned, human paleontology was in its infancy, and the knowledge of how to conduct a functional analysis or what was the normal range of variability was equally immature. These shortcomings of the state of the science—or art—did not necessarily give him free rein in making inferences. He repeatedly ignored relevant work conducted by colleagues and consistently selected the interpretation among the alternatives that made Neandertals less human. How could he do this and yet produce one of the most influential monographs ever written in human paleontology?

Boule's aims, when he began the study, were complex. He openly desired to expand the purview of his laboratory to include human evolution, and he did. He hoped to establish human paleontology as a rigorous science; this he achieved, too. He was also inclined to believe that Neandertals had nothing to do with human ancestry, and his anatomical analysis succeeded in expelling these brutish forms from the human family tree. Neandertals were doubly fossil—both ancient and extinct—Boule could assert, without having to explain the tricky issues of why or how they had become extinct or who the ancestors of modern humans were if they were not Neandertals.

His conclusion, in turn, provided evidence for a branching pattern in evolution, a bush rather than a straight line, such as he had found in other studies. Not incidentally, this finding contradicted the unilineal scheme of human evolution suggested by Gabriel de Mortillet, of the Ecole d'Anthropologie, and supported by his colleague Léonce Manouvrier. In the early twentieth century, as in the late nineteenth, the Ecole d'Anthropologie was the clear rival to the Muséum National d'Histoire Naturelle, where Boule worked, and embarrassing de Mortillet was always a welcome outcome to a study. Boule had previously attacked de Mortillet viciously on various grounds, calling his scheme a "mirage of doctrines" and a "mummy which he encircles every day with new bandages" to protect it from criticism. That de Mortillet's scheme was echoed by the German anatomist Schwalbe may have made it all the more pleasing that Boule's study indicated something to the contrary. Boule did not deliberately and knowingly slant his results; it was only that he saw, readily, that which was agreeable and was oblivious to elements suggesting uncomfortable implications.

In producing a monograph of such high quality, Boule consolidated his role in human evolutionary studies, both at home and abroad. Prince Albert I of Monaco himself came to Boule's lab to inspect the Old Man of La Chapelle-aux-Saints and stayed on into the evening to ask Boule to "prepare for him a plan of organization for an institute of human paleontology." The Prince was prepared to donate the building and an endowment of 1,600,000 francs. The building, a magnificent one, included bas-relief sculptures of Neandertals as well as Upper Paleolithic and more recent peoples engaged in hunting, carving art, or fishing, as was appropriate. The skull of La Chapelle-aux-Saints was even carved below the Prince's family shield, over the lintel of the main doorway. It was a fitting tribute to Boule, to human paleontology, and, ironically, to the poor, diseased, and prematurely aged Old Man from La Chapelle-aux-Saints.

Boule didn't need to be asked twice. He promptly drew up the plan that, on December 15, 1910, made him professor and head of the Institut de Paléontologie Humaine (Institute of Human Paleontology), with his old friends the Abbés Henri Breuil and Hugo Obermaier, both experts in prehistoric art, as his first two appointments. Breuil, in archeological studies, had been demonstrating congruent results to Boule's, overturning the nineteenth-century paradigm of culture progressing in a universal and predictable sequence through set stages of development. Breuil's work suggested a more complex, less predictable, and "bushier" pattern of cultural development and differentiation. Breuil argued that the Aurignacian—the early Upper Paleolithic culture associated with anatomically modern Cro-Magnons in western Europe—must have come from outside the region. To his eyes, the Aurignacian tools had nothing to do with the preceding Mousterian culture, which after all had been fashioned by those brutish Neandertals.

In terms of ideas, Boule's work also secured him an even clearer ascendancy. Intellectually, his work provided a major alternative—what was to become known as the pre-Sapiens theory—to Schwalbe's and de Mortillet's unilineal scheme. He became *the* man in France to evaluate and pronounce upon anything to do with human evolution; his intellectual dominance of French anthropology became comparable to that of Cuvier years before. In fact, even before the monograph appeared, the gist of Boule's conclusions seemed to have reached England, perhaps through accounts of various lectures he delivered.

The concept that Neandertals could be securely removed from human ancestry was received with open arms by at least one Briton, Arthur Keith. Keith was by then no longer a fledgling scientist; in 1908, he had been appointed Conservator of the Hunterian Museum (of anatomical specimens) at the Royal College of Surgeons in London, following in George Busk's shoes. He was determined to use this new position as a springboard to consolidate his position as a major figure in anthropology in England. He developed a sharp, rather sarcastic style of writing that he used to defend his ideas and criticize dissenters. At forty-two, Keith was still tall and slim, with fair hair and handsome features that had worn well as he entered middle age. Even so, photos of him never show a relaxed, confident, and happy man—only a tense one, with anxious eyes that seem to worry what others are thinking or doing.

Soon after his appointment to the Hunterian, he set out to build an impressive collection and mount an exhibit on early humans in England. Thus, he tried to secure or at least restudy all of the significant fossil

38. Arthur Keith in 1912. Keith was the young British anatomist who, with Marcellin Boule of France, rejected the Neandertals from human evolution, believing in the great antiquity of sapient humans. He promoted various dubiously ancient skeletons, including Piltdown, and engaged in furious debates with Arthur Smith Woodward, a paleontologist at the British Museum of Natural History, over the proper reconstruction of the Piltdown cranium.

human material in the country, placing it in context with the European discoveries. Such an exhibit would, of course, emphasize the importance of the British finds—despite the greater magnificence of the material being discovered in France—and would establish him as Britain's foremost expert in fossil humans: a doubly satisfying outcome.

Keith had espoused Neandertals as human ancestors before, but sometime early in 1911 he underwent an abrupt aboutface. The reasons for Keith's reversal of opinion have never been clear; various interpretations, including sinister ones, can be put on it. But the fact is that, before Boule's monograph began to appear—but after Boule had telegraphed his punches by presenting his major points in brief published summaries—Keith began suggesting that the modern human type had a great antiquity and was not descended from Neandertals.

Keith's arguments are based on an interesting selection of unpromising specimens. First, astonishingly, he reviewed the evidence about the infamous Moulin Quignon jaw and "came to the conclusion that it was an authentic document." For some years, no one else in Britain and few in France had accepted the very dubious Moulin Quignon mandible as genuinely ancient. Why did Keith? Perhaps because the Moulin Quignon mandible fit with ideas he was forming on the basis of other, English specimens that he examined for his exhibit. These were two other fossils whose antiquity he (but not everyone) accepted and whose anatomy was entirely modern (and not at all Neandertal): Galley Hill and Ipswich.

Galley Hill Man had been found in 1888 in Kent, in the gravel of the hundred-foot terrace of the Thames River by workmen quarrying for the chalk that underlay the gravel. As was by now a usual story, a local amateur—a "black" or dark-haired Scot named Robert Elliott—had asked the workmen to keep an eye out for flint implements or fossils. When the fossils were first being described in 1894, six years after the discovery, he wrote:

> It was on one of my fortnightly visits that I was informed by a man, named Jack Allsop (who had for a long time looked out and saved for me any implements or stone of similar shape . . .), that he had found a skull under the gravel. This I could hardly credit at first; but on asking him to show it to me, he produced it in several pieces from the base of a pillar of laminated clay and sand, where he had hidden it. I asked where the rest of the bones were. He pointed to the section opposite this pillar, and a few feet from it, and told me that he had left the other bones undisturbed for me to see; and there, sure enough, about 2 feet above the top of the chalk and 8 feet from the top of the gravel, portions of bone were projecting from a matrix of clayey loam and sand. . . .
>
> We carefully looked for any signs of the section being disturbed [which would indicate that the skeleton was a burial and thus came from a more recent time period], but failed.

In retrospect, asking where the "rest" of the bones were is an unusual question, if it accurately describes what occurred. Asking *if* there were any other bones would seem a more obvious query because finds comprising largely complete skeletons are quite rare unless a burial is encountered. Was there something about the circumstance that subconsciously suggested to Elliott that it was a burial, despite his denials? It is impossible to know without photographic or proper written documentation, of which there was none.

Indeed, unknown to Elliott, another amateur more sensitive to the importance of documentation was on the scene and tried to make a photographic record of the bones' position. The master of the school that overlooked the site, Matthew H. Heys, was also interested in prehistory and had been on the spot when the skull was uncovered. When Keith began studying the remains in 1910, he asked Mr. Heys to recount the discovery. Heys remembered seeing the skull partially exposed and telling the workmen to leave the skull *in situ* until he could return with a photographer.

> To my utter astonishment and indignation, a day or two after, and before I could get a photographer, I found they had been removed

by Mr. R. Elliott, then a stranger to me, and without their having been photographed. My anticipated possession of them was thus thwarted.

Heys, too, believed the overlying geological beds to be undisturbed, quoting Jack Allsop as saying, "The man or animal was not buried by anybody." Allsop, Heys, Elliott, and later, Keith, all believed the skeleton to be contemporaneous with the flint artifacts found in the gravel, which were dated by their style to the Chellean culture, the one prior to the Mousterian culture generally associated with Neandertals.

Testimony well after the fact notwithstanding, there were many well-founded doubts about Galley Hill Man's antiquity. When the find was described to the Geological Society in 1895, John Evans—one of the deeply skeptical English geologists who had been involved in the Moulin Quignon debacle—pointed out how unlikely it was that a complete skeleton would be preserved unless it were in a burial. Boule, who was shown the skeleton in Paris in 1909, scoffed at it as mere "bric-a-brac." But Keith believed in it. In 1915, he argued cleverly but convolutedly that the Galley Hill remains probably did represent a burial, but a pre-Mousterian, pre-Neandertal one in which the grave was dug only into the deepest part of the gravel, thus leaving the overlying gravel undisturbed, as Allsop, Heys, and Elliott had asserted.

He also believed, with comparably fervent faith, in the Ipswich skeleton, which in anatomy matched the Galley Hill fossil—and modern humans—very well indeed. The find consisted of a partial skull with large pieces of the major limb bones, arranged in a crouch burial. At first, Keith was stunned by the modernity of the Ipswich skeleton, whose stratigraphic position led him to expect it would be Neandertal or transitional between Neandertals and modern humans. But it was not so; it was, Keith admitted, like finding a "modern aeroplane in a church crypt which had been bricked up since the days of Queen Elizabeth." While this metaphor would suggest that Keith felt there was something wrong with the dating—as, indeed, there was, because both Galley Hill and Ipswich are intrusive burials of modern humans—he chose the other course: believing that humans with modern anatomy were much older than had been realized and that they coexisted with the more primitive Neandertals. As had Boule in France, Keith advocated abandoning the linear theory of human evolution for a bushier one, with more than one branch evolving at once.

Just why Keith changed his mind and adopted this belief has puzzled many scholars, both at the time and later. If it had followed upon Boule's monograph, which made a strong and apparently thoroughly scientific case that Neandertals were not direct human ancestors, Keith's metamorphosis would be more comprehensible. Perhaps he simply anticipated the way the wind was about to blow, for a widespread conversion to Boule's notion that Neandertals were doubly fossil followed shortly, or perhaps he was simply scrambling for a good fossil in hopes of consolidating his position in Britain as Boule had in France. Certainly everyone, French and English alike, was hoping that the now-expected ancient human fossil with advanced anatomy would be found in his bailiwick.

The time was thus ripe for the curious events that occurred starting sometime in 1908, according to the official story, which almost certainly incorporates a generous dollop of lies. In the last analysis, the fossils recovered in Sussex starting in that year were outright forgeries that misled nearly everyone interested in human evolution for years. It is one of the most bizarre, convoluted, and professionally embarrassing episodes in the entire history of the study of human evolution.

If the Moulin Quignon mandible was a deception—and the specimen was surely planted—then the fossils of Piltdown were a deluxe, special-edition hoax. *Eoanthropus dawsoni,* as the new species came to be known in scientific circles, was a master forgery, an exercise in deceit so cunningly contrived that the twisting maze of actions and words cannot even yet be completely unraveled.

The main accounts of the discovery come from Charles Dawson, for whom the fossil was named. He was a solicitor with a boundless enthusiasm for ancient tools and fossils, who longed for the great discovery that would earn him an FRS (Fellow of the Royal Society), who may have given in to the temptation to create that discovery when searching for it failed to yield results. The kindest assessment is that it is difficult to exonerate Dawson, the harshest that he must have been involved. And he almost certainly had a learned accomplice.

Dawson, son of a barrister, was born in 1864 in Fulkeith Hall, Lancashire, but grew up mostly in Sussex, where he resided as an adult. As a boy, Dawson was encouraged by his headmaster at school to become a keen geologist and archeologist. At twenty-one, he was elected to the Geological Society, where he had already met Arthur Smith Woodward, then a young man proud to be an assistant in the geology department at the British Museum of Natural History in South Kensington. Dawson maintained a lifelong enthusiasm for geology, but there is no evidence that he ever grasped the principles of the scientific method. He was one of those whose eagerness and willingness to believe engulfed whatever common sense and caution he possessed.

The famous John Cooke portrait of the Piltdown men—the scientists (and Dawson) who were involved in the debates over the fossil—shows him to be a soft-faced man, bald, with gold-rimmed glasses, full cheeks, and a bushy mustache. He was large, genial, cheerful, garrulous, and impossible to dislike, from all accounts, but also, perhaps, thoroughly gullible. By far the most telling description of him comes from the pen of Père Pierre Teilhard de Chardin, who met Dawson in 1909 when Teilhard was a Jesuit priest-in-training:

> Visiting a local quarry near here [Hastings, England], we were astonished to see the manager prick up his ears when we talked to him of fossils. He had just discovered a huge bone of the pelvis of an iguanodon [a dinosaur] and had [received] a telegram from Mr. Dawson announcing his intention to visit the quarry. I have learnt since that the iguanodon was found pretty well intact, bit by bit, and that the fragments were being packed in a case to be sent to the British Museum. Mr. Dawson turned up while we were still on the spot, and immediately came up to us with a happy air, saying "Geologists?"

The lean, lanky French intellectual, with the wry sense of humor and clever turn of phrase, and the stocky, rotund English solicitor, positively bouncing with indiscriminate enthusiasm, must have made an interesting pair.

Teilhard de Chardin was rapidly earning his own formidable reputation, both as a scholar in the study of human evolution and later in life, as author of almost bafflingly mystical writings on the Catholic Church and evolution.

Born in 1881 to an aristocratic family in Sarcenat, Teilhard seemed destined since childhood both for paleontology and the church. His schoolteachers often found him distracted, gazing out the window and thinking of fossils or geology rather than of his lessons. In 1898, he entered the Jesuit order, long known for its scholarship, and was sent first to Aix-en-Provence and then to the isle of Jersey. At twenty-four, he took up a position in Cairo, teaching physics and chemistry. He used the opportunity to study the Eocene strata and fossils of Egypt while he was there. Between 1908 and 1912, Teilhard was stationed at the Jesuit House at Hastings, England, where he combined studies of theology with his passion, vertebrate paleontology. In this way, he met up with Dawson and became embroiled in the Piltdown affair.

In 1912, he left England to study with Marcellin Boule, in Paris. Ten years later, he completed a doctoral thesis at the Sorbonne on the Eocene fossils of France. In years to come, Teilhard played pivotal roles in the discovery and description of many famous human fossils, of which Piltdown was the first. It marked his entry into a field in which he was to develop widely acknowledged expertise and luck: he was often at the right place at the right time to participate in significant discoveries.

Although paleontology was his absorbing passion, Teilhard was also known for his wicked sense of fun and somewhat puckish sense of humor. Indeed, his fondness for practical jokes, and his decidedly peculiar reluctance to talk about the Piltdown affair in later years, have led some to suggest that Teilhard was either the forger or the confessor of the forger, a position that would have bound him to secrecy. From all accounts, Teilhard seems to have known something—or perhaps to have felt that, as the only foreigner involved, the finger of accusation was bound to point at him. It was one of many tightropes he walked during his life. In his later years, Teilhard's religious (or evolutionary) theories were to get him into trouble with church authorities. At various points in his career, he was forbidden by the church to teach or to publish his evolutionary ideas and was exiled to remote outposts. Nonetheless, he developed an elaborate theory that human evolution was now proceeding toward the development of a higher, collective consciousness, a sort of superorganism of social morality. The church found his notions verging on blasphemy and exceedingly unwelcome, even though most of his great philosophical works were published only posthumously.

Teilhard was a tall, elegant man with an aquiline nose, kindly eyes, and prominent wrinkles, from smiling, at the sides of his mouth. He was only thirty years old when the Piltdown affair began, and still engaged in the lengthy training required of Jesuits; he was to be ordained in 1912, after meeting Dawson and before finding a crucial tooth of Piltdown Man. As Teilhard later recounted the discovery, however, it would seem that Dawson pointed him to the spot where an observant man could hardly fail to find the tooth.

As the story goes, Dawson began taking an interest in the unusual gravel quarried from a shallow pit located along the drive of Barkham Manor, where Dawson served as steward and thus went periodically for

39. Workers at Piltdown in 1912 or 1913. From left to right: Robert Kenward, Jr., the son of the family who lived on the estate where the fossils were found; Charles Dawson, the solicitor and amateur antiquarian who discovered the fossils; Venus Hargreaves, a laborer; Chipper the goose, who appears in several photographs at Piltdown; and Arthur Smith Woodward, the paleontologist from the British Museum of Natural History

meetings. In classic manner, Dawson asked the workmen (including a laborer with the delightful name of Venus Hargreaves) to keep an eye out for stone tools or fossils. In 1908, it is said, some fragments taken by the workmen to be of a "coconut" because of their dark-brown color and thin, curved shape were recovered and recognized by Dawson as pieces of a human cranium. Repeated visits by Dawson up until 1911 eventually yielded more pieces of the same skull as well as a fossil hippo tooth. Dawson wrote about the finds to his longtime friend and contact at the British Museum of Natural History, Arthur Smith Woodward, an expert in fish and reptiles.

Smith Woodward, a small, intense man with pince-nez, little hair, and a graying goatee and mustache, was then keeper (head curator) of geology at the British Museum. Like Dawson, he was born in the north of England—Macclesfield—but to a less exalted family; Smith Woodward's father was a silk-dyer, and his son attended the local grammar school rather than a fancy boarding school. Both men were born in 1864, making them forty-eight in 1911. Hard work and determination brought Smith

Woodward to Owens College, in Manchester, where he studied paleontology with W. Boyd Dawkins, who proclaimed Woodward "the best student in Geology and Palaeontology of his year." Perhaps it was also this hard work, or the struggle to rise above his background, that left Smith Woodward apparently humorless, unimpassioned, and "externally rather cold."

Whatever his personal shortcomings, Smith Woodward had climbed far and fast since joining the British Museum at the age of eighteen in 1882. In 1885, he was elected to the Geological Society and was a regular and active pontificator at many meetings. In 1892, he rose to assistant keeper of geology at the museum and, in 1896, he received the Royal Society's Lyell Medal for his many contributions on fossil fish. In 1901, he had been promoted to keeper of geology, the position he would maintain until retirement. At the time of the Piltdown affair, he was a well-respected and well-established scholar, known for his serious and energetic approach to fossils if not for his charm or wit. Smith Woodward was a man who took himself seriously—so seriously, some have suggested, that it was to let the hot air out of his balloon that the Piltdown hoax was conceived. In any case, he maintained a relationship through the years with Dawson, who—in exchange for the proud title of honorary collector for the British Museum—happily handed over his best fossil discoveries. So it was naturally to his old colleague Smith Woodward that Dawson took the chocolate brown bits and pieces of fossil from Piltdown in May 1912.

On June 2, 1912, Dawson was delighted to lead Smith Woodward and his new friend, Teilhard de Chardin, on a visit to the site near Barkham Manor. They found some eoliths and scraps of extinct fossil animals easily. Impressed, Smith Woodward decided that he and Dawson would continue to work the site over the summer—one presumes Teilhard was otherwise occupied. They did so, assisted ably by Venus Hargreaves and, inexplicably, by a large white goose named Chipper, both of whom appear regularly in photographs of the excavation. It was a successful summer, at least by the forger's standards.

By autumn of 1912, rumors were flying about the new fossil human that had been uncovered in Sussex. In November, someone—it has not been determined who—leaked information to the Manchester *Guardian*, which printed the story on November 21.

There seems to be no doubt whatever of its genuineness, and more than a possibility of its being the oldest remnant of a human frame yet discovered on this planet. . . . It will be extremely interesting to learn how far it bridges the gap between the skulls of the most man-like apes and the most ape-like man so far known to science, but the fact that it has been unhesitatingly recognised as human and not simian would appear to indicate that more than half the difference must still remain.

It was an artfully constructed leak that smoothed the way for an utterly unquestioning acceptance of the material. "No doubt whatsoever of its genuineness . . ." What an interesting tack to take: to raise and dismiss the specter of the fossils not being genuine (in this context, of course, "genuine" would be taken to mean genuinely ancient) with a single phrase that slips so easily past the eyes and into the consciousness of the reader.

The newspaper story heightened the excitement that the vague rumors had started and ensured a record turnout for the December 18, 1912, meeting of the Geological Society of London, at which Smith Woodward and Dawson presented the material. They gave it a formal scientific name, *Eoanthropus dawsoni* (Dawson's dawn-man), and declared it to be the true and most ancient ancestor of modern humans. What they showed were a number of fragments of the cranium—remarkable for its large braincase, vertical forehead, and generally refined appearance— with a distinctly apelike jaw. They confidently presented a reconstruction that featured a complete cranium and mandible full of teeth, showing that the evolution of the large brain and modern face preceded the evolutionary loss of the simian jaw. Thus, by the end of the Pliocene (the estimated age of the finds), they maintained that there were two distinct human lineages: that of Piltdown, evolving toward humans, and the other including Neandertals, deteriorating toward extinction. No degenerate, brutish, beetle-browed Neandertals lurked in their family tree.

From this point onward, the story becomes complicated. Enormous discussion ensued over the Piltdown material. The antiquity of the material was questioned, but not with especial seriousness. Many geologists inspected the site and declared it to be of Pleistocene or even older Pliocene age. The associated animal fossils (which were also planted and probably had come from North Africa) played an important role in convincing everyone of the bed's antiquity.

The Smith Woodward-Dawson reconstruction was challenged as inaccurate, most passionately by Arthur Keith. Keith favored a reconstruction with a significantly larger braincase—a major point of contention

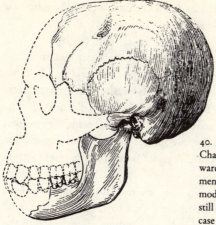

40. The Piltdown skull, as reconstructed by Charles Dawson and Arthur Smith Woodward in 1913. Subsequent anatomical arguments with Arthur Keith led them to modify the reconstruction slightly, but it still gave the impression of a human brain case with an ape's jaw.

in the blizzard of papers and counter-papers by Keith, Smith Woodward, and their respective supporters over the next few years. Though he ardently contested the Smith Woodward reconstruction, Keith was in any case justifiably delighted to find confirmation of his pet theory that the modern human form was very ancient. It simply added piquancy to the debate that Smith Woodward himself had declared Keith's ideas "an amusing heresy" not long before. Keith lost no opportunity to skewer his intellectual opponents on this score or on the matter of their anatomical blunders in reconstructing the skull. Keith's rise to extreme prominence over this affair, and the way the fossils so neatly dovetailed with his otherwise peculiar views of Moulin Quignon, Galley Hill and Ipswich, have contributed to the case that Keith was in on the forgery.

Some scientists—particularly those in the United States, well away from the tremendous blossoming of British pride at having found the earliest human ancestor—questioned whether the jaw and cranium belonged together. (As was to be proven much later, their doubts were well founded. The jaw has proved to be that of a modern orangutan, broken, altered, and stained to match the cranium, which is genuinely fossil, without being of great antiquity, and also genuinely modern in anatomy.) Prominent American scholars, such as the mammalogist Gerrit Miller, Jr., and physical anthropologist Aleš Hrdlička, both of the Smithsonian, and paleontologist William King Gregory of the American Museum of Natural History, voiced their ambivalence about the association of the jaw and the cranium. Of all the "dualists," as they came to be called, Hrdlička was alone in accepting the mandible as an ancient chimpanzee's and believing that the cranium came from an intrusive, modern human skeleton. It was shades of *Pithecanthropus* all over again.

Across the channel, Marcellin Boule echoed their doubts. He was enthusiastic about the presence of an essentially modern human braincase in the Pliocene or Lower Pleistocene; such a find fulfilled his predictions and justified his rejection of Neandertals from human ancestry. But somehow, like Miller, Hrdlička, and Gregory, Boule had difficulty accepting the mandible as part of the same creature. He even argued that the fossils represented two distinct species, using *Homo dawsoni* for the braincase and *Troglodytes* (an old genus name for the chimpanzee) *dawsoni* for the jaw.

And as with *Pithecanthropus*, in time another tooth was found—a canine tooth, picked up by Teilhard on a visit to the site in 1913, that showed a distinctly apelike character. As had Dubois's flourishing of the second *Pithecanthropus* tooth at a meeting attended by the young Keith, the new Piltdown tooth persuaded at least some skeptics of the validity of the association of the different remains.

The fact is that the original fossils were selected and broken with tremendous insight, betraying a keen understanding of exactly which anatomical features needed to be present and which absent to convince. Whoever the forger was, he was a clever fellow who knew exactly what he was doing and how eagerly the "fish" would rise to the bait. It was not a forgery intended to be discovered easily. Indeed, the forger covered his tracks so well that virtually everyone significantly involved with the fossil has been accused at one time or another.

The second Piltdown find, the canine tooth, speaks of the same intelligence and keenness of apprehension, for it exactly fulfilled Smith Woodward's prediction in his reconstruction and neatly repeated Dubois's ploy when his word was doubted. A third and more mysterious discovery followed, conveniently timed to dampen the rising swell of doubt from the United States that the jaw and cranium were associated. In 1915, at a site whose precise location he somehow neglected to disclose to anyone before his early death, Dawson found additional fragments of a skull of another *Eoanthropus*, a molar tooth, and bits of rhinoceros bones, somewhere a mile or two from the original site. They were, literally, finds "made to order." If dark-eyed doubt did not quite die in American or French academic circles, its cries were stifled, and the baying of deep suspicion was postponed for years.

In the meantime, nearly the entire scientific coterie of Britain believed in the fossils without hesitation. At the British Museum, Smith Woodward accepted them because they were his and because they placed him in the enviable position of overturning previous theories about human evolution. Fossil fish, Smith Woodward's area of expertise, would never reap so much glory or attention. At the Royal College of Surgeons, Keith accepted the finds because they showed the modern human form to be ancient, as he had said. At the University of Manchester, the irreverent Australian Grafton Elliot Smith, a brain specialist and anatomist, accepted the fossils because they supported his pet notion that the evolution of the brain was the first and most crucial development in the evolution of humans. At Oxford, William Sollas—the foremost geologist pronouncing on human evolution—believed that erect posture was the first step toward modernity, with enlargement of the brain following shortly thereafter. This exemplified his belief that evolution occurred piecemeal, with some regions of the body evolving faster than others. In fact, the Piltdown remains so neatly met his expectations that he wrote in 1915 that the Dawn Man "had, indeed, been long previously anticipated as an almost necessary stage in the course of human development."

In France, though he had reservations about the jaw, Boule accepted the Piltdown cranium because it showed he was right in expelling Neandertals from human ancestry. The Abbé Henri Breuil, Boule's colleague at the Institut de Paléontologie Humaine, was, like Boule, comfortable with a branching pattern of evolutionary development and disliked the older, linear theories espoused by de Mortillet and others. Thus Breuil, as a leading archeologist, was also entirely prepared to accept Piltdown as real. In fact, as historian of science Michael Hammond has observed:

> Providentially, this discovery proved the fruitfulness of the great wave of theoretical speculation that had swept the [anthropological and paleontological] community just before Piltdown's dramatic emergence. . . . It seems to have occurred to no one to check systematically all parts of so plausible a fossil discovery.

Though by 1918 the debates and discussions over their interpretation had given rise to a bibliography of over 120 titles by more than fifty scientists, the Piltdown fossils were nonetheless accepted as legitimate fossils. Smith Woodward and Dawson suffered none of the humiliation that blighted Boucher de Perthes's life after the Moulin Quignon jaw came to light. Though doubts persisted about the association of the jaw and cranium, Piltdown was seen as an early, brainy human ancestor or near-ancestor for many years to come.

The effect of Piltdown on the scientific study of Neandertals was stifling. If Boule's monograph had unceremoniously booted Neandertals out of the family tree, Piltdown had dug their graves anew and buried them. Neandertals were simply uninteresting, an irrelevant degenerate side-branch.

Besides, as Keith eloquently wrote in July 1915 in the preface to the first edition of his authoritative work on human evolution, *The Antiquity of Man*:

> The events of the year have revolutionised the outlook of all of us; we have burst suddenly into a critical phase in the evolutionary progress of mankind; we have had to lay aside the problems of our distant past and concentrate our thoughts and energies on the immediate present. Liège and Namur, which figure in this book as the sites of peaceful antiquarian discovery, have become the scenes of bloody war. And yet, amidst all the distractions of the present time, the author hopes there may be some who will wish to survey the issues of the present fateful period from the distant standpoint of a student of man's early evolution.

It was no time to think of fossils. World War I—the Great War, the War to End All Wars—had broken out following the assassination of Archduke Ferdinand and his wife on June 28, 1914. Bitter fighting, hardship, unthinkable horrors, and the need for undreamed-of courage were to batter the world for four long years, until Armistice Day, November 11, 1918. Europe, England, the United States: all were changed forever. It would be impossible to think of mankind—or even to look in the mirror and think of oneself—in the same way again.

6

An Okapi of Humanity

1918–1939

Arthur Keith in England and Marcellin Boule in France had things nicely arranged to their liking now. They were set up as the recognized authorities on matters of human evolution in their respective countries. In the aftermath of the war, these two men kept Neandertals as firmly at bay, psychologically, as their countries had their enemy in war, excluding both from the charmed circle of true humans. The wave of postwar optimism and elation only thinly veiled the uncomfortable revelations of human nature that war had brought; scientists and the public alike were all too eager to pick up the pieces of their shattered lives and return to a feeling of safety, security, and rationalism.

Keith was knighted in 1921—no higher official acclaim was possible in Britain. Sometimes endorsing and sometimes contesting his lead in England was a host of prominent "Piltdown men": the anatomist Grafton Elliot Smith and the paleontologist Arthur Smith Woodward (both later knighted), and the geologist William Sollas. Keith thought of himself as the preeminent paleoanthropologist of England, and so perhaps did Smith Woodward assess his own stature, but both were surpassed in enduring influence by Elliot Smith. Time and again, students trained by Elliot Smith were strategically placed to become the leaders of the next generation. He sent them in all directions, like doves from the Ark, until some returned bearing fossils that opened up new intellectual territories. Being in museum positions, neither Keith nor Smith Woodward had the opportunity to inoculate so many of the next generation with their ideas.

Boule, for his part, now had almost complete control of French paleoanthropology, save for a few awkward dissidents at the Ecole d'Anthropologie. Through his dual associations with the Muséum National d'Histoire Naturelle and the Institut de Paléontologie Humaine, Boule controlled the most important institutions and enjoyed the prerogative of filling other positions with his protégés. He left his mark on Pierre Teilhard de Chardin, who was at this point at the Collège de France, Jean Piveteau at the Sorbonne, and Henri Vallois at the Institut de Paléontologie Humaine. Only after Boule's death did any of these former students really grapple afresh with the problems of human evolution; before then, they were simply his acolytes.

Boule and Keith each consolidated his position by forging an international alliance with the other. What distinguished humans from apes, these pundits agreed, was the evolution of a large brain that ruled with intelligence and moral force over people's more bestial instincts. The consensus seemed to be that, if our brains had made us what we are, then perhaps our brains could save us from another miserable episode of devastating war. It was time to turn back to the comfort of authoritative science.

Similar feelings manifested themselves as a tremendous flowering of the public interest in human evolution, which had been but a spindly seedling before the war. In 1911, both Keith and Sollas published books synthesizing all that was known of human ancestry in reassuringly tidy terms and a deep, baritone voice. Keith followed this up with another book in 1915, the popularity of which can be shown by a brief glimpse of its publishing history. There were two printings in 1915, one in 1916, and another in 1920; a revised, second edition came out in January 1925 and was reprinted in autumn of 1925 and again in 1926; an American second edition appeared in 1928, and so on. Similar works—commanding summaries—were written in 1915 (revised in 1916 and 1918) by Henry Fairfield Osborn and in the 1920s by George Grant MacCurdy in the United States, Elliot Smith in England, and Boule in France (the revisions of which were continued after Boule's death until 1957 by his former student, Vallois). In the fragile years between the two world wars, new discoveries invariably made the popular press and lectures propounding new or old theories were given to packed houses who wanted it all explained to them.

The work of German anthropologists, representing as they did the product of the defeated nation, was largely discounted and ignored in

France and England. But within Germany, anthropology remained a lively field. Ernst Haeckel had outlived Virchow, his bitter opponent, and was now a beloved national and international figure, though he never commanded the ironfisted power over the academic community that Virchow had enjoyed. Haeckel continued to be fascinated with the differences between the various races, integrating his views of the moral and intellectual characteristics of those races into his grand, flamboyant schemes of the evolution of life. The blond, blue-eyed, Aryan German of athletic build and vigorous temperament was to Haeckel obviously morally, mentally, physically, and, indeed, evolutionarily superior to other types.

During and after the war, Haeckel's thoughts on racial differences and social causes turned more and more to the wisdom (as he saw it) of eugenics: the practice of deliberately encouraging superior "types" to reproduce while severely discouraging reproduction by inferior groups. Coupled with his strongly nationalistic romanticism and powered by his undeniable gift for stirring the emotions with his words, Haeckel's doctrines had tremendous appeal to many Germans. They were a warming antidote to the cold miseries of military defeat and the ensuing economic depression.

In 1919, those in the newly founded German Workers' Party took special note of Haeckel's ideas, even though—or perhaps because—he died in that year. The party continued to use and develop his ideas as the basis of their principles when the party's name was changed the next year to the Nazionalsozialistische Deutsche Arbeiterpartei, the Nazi Party. By the time Adolf Hitler, an intense, dark-haired young man, took over leadership of the party in 1921, Haeckel's ideas were already beginning to take on the mystical aura of the prophetic. Haeckel became the symbol, the patron saint, of the darker side of German imperialism. His vision of a genetically superior elite, born to rule, was twisted and distorted by Hitler, who made Jews and the "inferior" Slavic peoples responsible for the hard times and humiliating defeat suffered by the Germans. Only by eliminating such contaminating elements could the true Germans be restored to their proper ascendancy in the world, Hitler argued with increasing fervor in the 1920s and 1930s. Sadly, his reassertion of German pride was so welcome that many averted their eyes from its uglier implications.

Although the origin and nature of humanity were central issues, the actual facts that were recorded in the fossil record itself played little role in these political developments; indeed, the fossils themselves had never been a matter of great concern to Haeckel. Outside Germany, German disgrace was strong enough that any tattered remnants of support for Schwalbe's original theory of a Neandertal stage of human evolution disintegrated into broken threads. Even Schwalbe himself recanted after reading Boule's monograph on La Chapelle-aux-Saints, declaring that he now favored the notion that Neandertals did not stand on the direct lineage to modern *Homo sapiens*. He was the major advocate in Germany of Dubois's *Pithecanthropus* as a human ancestor, perhaps leading to both Neandertals and modern humans, until his death in 1916. Even though Schwalbe never accepted that anatomically modern humans, such as Galley Hill or even Piltdown, were contemporaneous with Neandertals, his opinion was widely discounted. To non-Germans, there was every reason both to embrace Piltdown, the intelligent ancestor, and to expel Neandertals, the bestial caveman, from our lineage.

The view was not quite the same from the other side of the Atlantic. As a nation, Americans had proved themselves during the war to be brave but oddly naïve: rich in goods and opportunities, strong and optimistic, but young and inexperienced. They had been on the winning side of the war. But as paleoanthropologists and paleontologists, Americans were struggling against this not-entirely-flattering stereotype for international recognition as serious scientists. It was a difficult fight, for several reasons.

First, there was the somewhat paternalistic attitude taken by the British, and to some extent other Europeans, toward Americans. Whereas England, France, and Germany had traditions of many years' duration in anthropology—had founded great schools, scientific societies, and museums in the mid-nineteenth century—the United States had been preoccupied with its Civil War at the time. While the Europeans were wrestling with intellectual issues, the Americans were squabbling over their fragile nationhood. Only now, in the early twentieth century, was the United States beginning to boast of experts who could offer university programs in anthropology per se. The British, in particular, tended to regard Americans at this time as amusingly uncivilized and had for many years exported their writers, musicians, artists, and actors on American tours, with a distinct air of bringing culture and learning to the ignorant colonials.

Although the evolution of humans was one of the hottest topics of the day, no significant fossils had been found in the Americas. True, there had been some claims, but these proved both peculiar and embarrassing. In a series of papers in the early 1900s, Florentino Ameghino, an Argentinian paleontologist of Italian extraction, had described a handful of fossils that he regarded as the true and original ancestors of humans. With an imaginative disregard for much of the evidence amassed so far, Ameghino believed that humans had not evolved from a common ancestor with anthropoid apes—chimps, gorillas, and orangutans—but had rather arisen directly from a South American monkeylike ancestor.

Based on a few fossil fragments found by his brother, Ameghino named the earliest ancestor *Homunculus patagonicus*, proclaiming it the "Ancestor of the Monkeys of the Old and New Continents." By 1909, Ameghino had knitted several other misidentified primate fossils from poorly documented or misunderstood geological contexts into an elaborate and fanciful scheme of human evolution that conformed to the facts as well as a hand-me-down sweater fits its recipient. Ameghino claimed that humans evolved from the small early primates such as *Homunculus* through at least four intermediate forms directly to modern *Homo sapiens*. Conveniently, all of this had occurred, Ameghino asserted, within his home province of Buenos Aires, from where sapient humans had then spread to cover the entire globe.

It was a virtuoso performance of misunderstanding, sloppy science, and chauvinism that reflected like a fun-house mirror the intense local pride and the sometimes slender claims of the French and English to the earliest human ancestors. The difference was that Ameghino's fossils in no way supported his claims—many were not fossilized at all and at least one, the skullcap known as *Diprothomo*, so loosely resembled its description as to defy belief. When the first physical anthropologist in America, Aleš Hrdlička—anxious to evaluate this important claim—examined the fossil in 1910, he was dumbfounded.

"It proved at every point antagonistic to the notion that had been formed of it on the basis of the published data," Hrdlička wrote, describing further his "incredulity as to its being the relic in question." Hrdlička soon realized that Ameghino's interpretation was warped by equal parts of pride and anatomical ignorance, which led him to hold the fossil in an orientation that made its morphology appear bizarre.

Hrdlička felt it was his duty, his calling, to puncture the ridiculous balloon Ameghino was floating aloft and to show the world that not all scientists in the Americas were fools. He had no credible fossils of his own, so his options were reduced to those of professional skeptic. He spoke and published frankly on the matter of early humans in the New World. After extended study, Hrdlička's assessment of the South American evidence for early man paralleled his suspicions of the North American evidence:

> Under these circumstances but one conclusion is justified which is that thus far on this continent no human bones of undisputed geological antiquity are known. This must not be regarded as equivalent to declaration that there was no early man in this country[;] it means only that if early man did exist in North America convincing proof of the fact from the standpoint of physical anthropology remains to be produced.

His disclaimer notwithstanding, Hrdlička was a tough-minded disbeliever in the repeated and flimsy claims for early humans in the Americas. Ameghino did not, of course, love him for it, and published explosive retorts in any journal that would accept his salvos. Nonetheless, the influence of Hrdlička's hypercritical skepticism has persisted long, literally up until the present day. Years later, the longtime and distinguished professor of physical anthropology at Harvard, Earnest Hooton, gently teased his old friend Hrdlička by describing his role:

> While the scientists have been steadily adding to the number of accredited remains in the Old World, during the past quarter of a century [i.e., since 1911] that formidable and indomitable veteran, Dr. Aleš Hrdlička, has stood like Horatius at the land bridge between Asia and North America, mowing down with deadly precision all would-be geologically ancient invaders of the New World. In fact, the story of alleged fossil man in America is virtually the tale of how well Hrdlička kept the bridge. With penetrating aim and devastating criticism he has annihilated *seriatim* the claims of each successive fossil pretender. Undoubtedly he has preserved science from a credulous acceptance of many spurious Pleistocene Americans.

Hrdlička had arrived at this juncture as self-appointed keeper of the Bering Strait, the location of the onetime bridge between Siberia and Alaska, by an endearingly American path. Born March 29, 1869, in a small textile town nestled in the foothills of the Bohemian highlands, Aleš Hrdlička was the first of seven children born to a Catholic family headed by Maximilian and Karolina Wagner Hrdlička. Maximilian was a successful cabinetmaker and an intensely ambitious man, traits offset

41. Aleš Hrdlička in the 1930s, by then the established physical anthropologist at the Smithsonian Institution. Hrdlička was an ardent debunker of several spuriously ancient skeletons from the Americas yet was one of the few defenders at the time of the Neandertals as modern human ancestors.

by Karolina's calm Bavarian temperament; she also brought to the family considerable musical talent and a love of the dramatic flamboyance of opera.

At the time of Hrdlička's birth, Bohemia was part of the Hapsburg Empire that ruled Austro-Hungary in a sometimes uneasy domination. Shortly thereafter, the Prussian strongman Bismarck began to pursue his notion of a united Germany, attacking France and casting longing eyes on the lands to the south. Economically, things were deteriorating in Bohemia, whose inhabitants wanted neither the Hapsburgs nor the Prussians as rulers. An invitation to join a fellow Bohemian working in New York, in the land of opportunity, proved irresistible to Hrdlička's father.

Thus, in 1881, when Hrdlička was twelve years old, he accompanied his father to New York to prepare the way for the rest of the family to follow. They went to the neighborhoods populated with Slovaks, Bohemians, and the like on the Lower East Side of Manhattan. By that time the bright young boy was fluent in Czech and German—though his antipathy to the Germans was such that he avoided using the language whenever possible—as well as Latin and Greek. He had also excelled in natural history, geography, and music, and was an avid collector of rocks and minerals. After arriving in New York, he soon added fluent English—albeit with a charming and enthusiastic admixture of Central European and New York pronunciation—and in later life expanded his polyglot repertoire to include French, Russian, Italian, and Spanish.

By 1888, the family was well settled and reasonably prosperous.

Hrdlička played out the American dream of the immigrant boy coming to the New World and making his fortune through hard work and perseverance. After a bout of pneumonia, Hrdlička decided to ally himself with the knowledgeable, who had cured him; he was impressed that knowledge imparted power and control, even over life and death. He took as his preceptor for the study of medicine the family doctor, a Hungarian Jew named Meyer Rosenblueth. He enrolled, for his required lectures and demonstrations, at the Eclectic Medical College of the City of New York, graduating first in his class in 1892. He had obviously inherited his father's intensity and ambition and his mother's emotionality, along with a head of thick, dark hair, piercing eyes, and a sensitive, full-lipped face.

His convictions about research and accomplishment were strongly held. A recent biographer of Hrdlička has characterized him neatly:

> Hrdlička was consumed, as he was to be for the rest of his life, by an overwhelming desire to succeed, to be recognized and respected—even loved. While others were to collect money and property, Hrdlička would collect knowledge. . . . Knowledge in Hrdlička's mind was a reflection of human endeavor and its acquisition came only from personal labor; the effort of which seems to be directly proportional to one's character and thus reputation. From the acquisition of knowledge sprang the notion of power and the authority gained by its possession. Never plagued by philosophical doubt, Hrdlička naively assumed . . . that the reality of the human condition would be miraculously revealed after an undetermined amount of data collection.

To improve his professional standing, and to acquire more knowledge, Hrdlička sought—and won—additional medical degrees in homeopathic and allopathic (traditional) medicine. In 1894, he took up his first professional job as a junior physician at the Middletown State Homeopathic Hospital for the Insane, in upstate New York.

There he began the first of a series of large anthropometric surveys that he was to conduct during his professional life. He was hungry for information, for raw data, rather than for chopped and cooked, predigested interpretation. At Middletown, he fought more consistently than successfully to obtain sufficient funds to conduct an extremely ambitious program of anthropometric research on the relationship (if any) between bodily measurements and insanity. It was a perfectly typical Hrdličkian approach: he wanted large sums of money and considerable staff to measure incredible numbers of both patients and "normals" in every way he could think of. Without doubt, the information—the numbers in and of themselves—were valuable and desirable to Hrdlička. He struggled his whole life to collect measurements, to store them up like treasures, hoarding them like secret spells the mere possession of which would protect and empower him.

Of course, he wanted to use the numbers, too. The result of his study would be a database with which he could test assertions that insanity was prevalent among certain genetic types, as well as document the normal range of variation among living humans. Simply understanding the variability among living humans of different races would go a long way to solving a major problem in human evolutionary studies. Despite the fact that this and many other of his research projects had a distinctly statistical bent, Hrdlička retained no fondness for the subject, saying on more than one occasion that "statistics will be the ruin of physical anthropology."

When he left the hospital in January 1896, Hrdlička went to Paris, to the Ecole d'Anthropologie, to work with Léonce-Pierre Manouvrier and to learn the methods of careful measurement pioneered by Manouvrier's mentor, Paul Broca. It was a turning point in Hrdlička's career. The work and the Parisian ambiance were his idea of heaven, save that his fiancée, Marie Strickler—a French refugee and his living symbol of France—was still in the United States, where she received frequent letters written in his tiny, intense scribble.

Professionally, the six-month stint established the close, lifelong friendship between Hrdlička and Manouvrier. Hrdlička absorbed Manouvrier's views, adopting as his own Manouvrier's emphasis on the plasticity of human nature and the tremendous influence that environment and habit wielded over the human body. In particular, Manouvrier reacted strongly against the growing movement of "scientific racism," which daily extolled the virtues of the superior Aryans and the inevitability of disease, insanity, and criminality among other, inferior races. It was a flagrant misuse and misunderstanding of anthropology, in Manouvrier's eyes.

The epitome of the expression of these ideas that Manouvrier detested was Gobineau's classic work, *L'Aryen, son Rôle social* (*The Aryan, His Social Role*), to be published a few years later in 1899. The eugenics movement had started slowly in the late nineteenth century, with books like those by Joseph Galton, who proclaimed his belief that a program of judicious marriages among the most gifted individuals could lead to a superior race.

In 1904, Galton left money in his will to fund a chair in eugenics at University College, London, that was taken up by the mathematician Karl Pearson. A brilliant individual, Pearson virtually founded the field of biostatistics, pioneering the application of probability theory to biological problems. Pearson also attributed so meager an influence to environment in the production of personal traits that he felt the high birthrate of the poor, uneducated, and criminal classes was a threat to civilization. Reproduction at a faster rate by such undesirables meant that their genes would soon overwhelm those of the superior types, he felt. His views thus provided the scientific underpinning to those who blamed, for example, the Jews, the Slavs, or the darker-skinned races for society's ills. Eugenics movements focusing distrust and blame on such groups were growing in England, France, and the United States as well as in Germany. In years to come, these views were put overtly into action in European pogroms attacking the ghettos, to which those believed to be inferior were restricted, and in more subtle but equally virulent ways in other countries. In the early 1900s, immigration quotas to the United States were clearly designed to keep out those of particular national origins. By the 1930s, laws providing for involuntary sterilization of various types of "degenerates," including criminals, epileptics, and the mentally deficient, had been passed in the United States, Denmark, Germany, Switzerland, Norway, and Sweden.

These ideas, so pivotal in the development of World War II, were just sprouts later to bear poisonous fruit when, in 1896, Hrdlička left Paris, returning home to marry Marie Strickler and to follow up his early studies on the insane. In 1903, Hrdlička was appointed to the first job in the United States specifically designated for a physical anthropologist, at the National Museum of Natural History, a division of the Smithsonian Institution in Washington, D.C. He was to build a collection of human skeletons representing different groups, to conduct a "comprehensive biological study of the many and diverse racial elements of the American Nation," and to build a division of physical anthropology within the institution. These studies sprang from the same questions about human variability whose darker, more judgmental side nurtured the eugenics movement.

Over the years, Hrdlička conducted or led several large anthropometric surveys on various ethnic groups, including different North and

South American Indian tribes, native Filipinos, Mongols, ancient Egyptians, Australian aborigines, South African Bushmen, and Eskimos, all focusing on the variability in human form. These surveys were the intellectual foundation for understanding the differences and similarities in human shape and form upon which Hrdlička later built ideas about human evolution. Hrdlička was directly attacking the question that had plagued so many who had studied human fossils: How much does a single species vary in, say, size of the browridges or shape of the teeth and yet remain one species?

He also began assessing all of the evidence for early humans in the Americas, much in the manner that Keith had opened his tenure at the Hunterian Museum with an exhibit and review of early humans in Britain. Unlike Keith, who found or resurrected various British fossils to believe in, Hrdlička settled into a regular round of examining and debunking claim after claim for ancient people in the New World.

The lack of evidence from the Americas fueled Hrdlička's growing conviction that the simple, unilineal schemes showing a European lineage of *Pithecanthropus* evolving through Neandertals to modern humans, put forth by Schwalbe and Manouvrier, were correct. Humans—modern humans—had developed in Europe and then migrated to the Americas, probably via the Bering Strait, Hrdlička asserted. Keith, who had met Hrdlička briefly in 1909, even endorsed Hrdlička's conclusions about the Americas in his 1911 book, *Ancient Types of Men*; this was prior to Keith's puzzling reversal and claims for the tremendous antiquity of the brainy or sapient form of modern humans.

In 1912, Hrdlička traveled overseas, examining many of the important fossils. After talking it over with Keith, Keith's new attitude was flatly incomprehensible to Hrdlička, especially when he had examined for himself the very dubious Galley Hill and Ipswich skeletons as well as the wonderful Neandertal material in Paris, Liège, and Bonn.

In Liège, Julien Fraipont told Hrdlička that Dubois was "going mad" and that he might even have destroyed the *Pithecanthropus* fossils. This sparked a determined attempt to see Dubois and examine the fossils, which unfortunately ended in failure. At the university in Amsterdam, Hrdlička was told Dubois was at home but would not receive him. How could Dubois, who had never seen Hrdlička, turn him away without conversation? He was told that Dubois had set up a mirror above the window on the first floor of his home, so that he could spy on callers undetected and instruct his maid to send away any unwelcome visitors.

So it proved: Hrdlička presented his card; the maid insisted Dubois was not at home; Hrdlička explained who he was and why he had come; the maid insisted that he leave, and closed the door. After some three hours of indecision, Hrdlička tried the door again, only to be told by Madame Dubois that her husband was, indeed, at home but declined to see him. In frustration, Hrdlička scribbled a note on the back of a calling card and left, asking that it be delivered to Dubois. It read:

> The anthropologists of the world owe you a great deal, but it is a *DAMN* shame that it is not possible for scientific purposes to even glance at the specimens.

Extraordinarily, despite this angry first encounter with Dubois, Hrdlička was among the first outsiders whom Dubois finally permitted to view his fossils, but that did not occur until eleven years later, in 1923.

Despite his inability to examine the *Pithecanthropus* remains in 1912, on this trip Hrdlička formed distinct ideas about human evolution. He was skeptical of the Piltdown remains, focusing much of his energy on disputing the association of the jaw with the cranium—a concern in which he was joined by his colleague from the Smithsonian's Department of Mammalogy, Gerrit Miller, Jr., as well as by others at the American Museum of Natural History in New York. Hrdlička's disbelief was, in part, triggered by what he saw in the Neandertal fossils:

> My conviction that the Neanderthal type is merely one phase in the more or less gradual process of evolution of man to his present form, is steadily growing stronger. . . . I find on the one hand, notwithstanding many lapses, nothing but gradual evolution and involution, and on the other hand no substantial break in the line from at least the earliest Neanderthal specimens to the present day. We have today not one but many intermediary forms in both the skull and other bones between the Neanderthal and present man. Take Spy No.2 for instance . . . or take the long bones of the skeletons of Krapina or La Ferrassie. Then take the *Homo aurignacensis*, the Předmost material, and some of the earlier Neolithic crania in Brussels and Warsaw. All of these speak for the continuity of the race.

With his background in large-scale surveys of the variation in skeletons of living humans, Hrdlička had no difficulty seeing continuities among the fossils. Unfortunately, he was sidetracked from these concerns by the outbreak of war in Europe, which made further study of European materials extremely difficult. When the United States joined the war, Hrdlička was called to be a member of a committee to determine ways in which the nation's scientists might help the war effort. He proposed an ambitious scheme to use the occasion to collect a massive database about the American male. He wanted those conducting physicals to participate in an anthropometric survey of all army volunteers and recruits. Unfortunately, most of the committee members were more concerned with furthering their own ambitions and seizing power than with scientific work. In the end, internecine battles over exactly which measurements were to be taken and in what format they were to be recorded led to the study's being aborted.

At the war's close, in 1918, Hrdlička founded the *American Journal of Physical Anthropology*, becoming, as was customary, its (occasionally capricious) editor. By now, Hrdlička had gained an international reputation, albeit of lesser prominence than Keith's or Boule's. He was, undoubtedly, the leading American on matters of human evolution even though he always failed to meet the ultimate criterion: an ancient fossil of his own. The search for yet older and more important fossil humans was now undergoing a subtle shift in emphasis. The expectation was growing that Asia, not Europe or even Africa (Darwin's hypothesis), would prove to be the birthplace of the human species.

This expectation had perhaps arisen with Boule's insistence that European Neandertals had been replaced by *Homo sapiens* who had evolved elsewhere, probably in Central Asia. Fossil apes from the Punjab had been discovered just before the war and seemed to support Boule's contention. Now that the war was over, the time was ripe to follow up on this idea, and more than one scientist was determined to try his luck in Asia.

In 1919, Davidson Black—a promising Canadian student who had received a medical degree from the University of Toronto and then studied under Grafton Elliot Smith—had recently taken up a post as professor of neurology and embryology at the Peking Union Medical College in China. He was a good-looking young man of athletic build and ready smile, with fair hair, round, dark-rimmed glasses, and a pipe clamped firmly between his jaws in almost every extant photograph. In the field, he wore puttees wrapped round his legs and jodhpurs. Black had seen firsthand the excitement of the Piltdown discovery in Elliot Smith's lab, and his interest in the job was largely based on the opportunity to look for evidence that humans had evolved in Asia. Black also had links with Hrdlička, having trained with him at the Smithsonian in anthropometry.

Black began measuring the prehistoric and living races of China enthusiastically, when he was not teaching human anatomy to the medical students. He liked his Chinese co-workers, and they liked him. His experiences were not without culture shock, however. In need of cadavers for dissection, Black turned to the chief of police, who replied that, since prisoners were being executed with regularity, there would be no difficulty in supplying him. To Black's dismay, the first cartload of cadavers arrived, all headless. Decapitated criminals would not suffice, he advised the police. They sent the next contingent over alive and in chains, with a message that Black was to execute them any way he saw fit. Other means of securing cadavers for dissection or skeletons for study were soon worked out.

This interest in anthropology was one of which Black's sponsors and employers, the Rockefeller Foundation, did not approve. Unaware of this fact, Hrdlička applied to the Rockefeller Foundation for money to travel to China to undertake an anthropometric survey in 1919, looking for evidence that the ancestors of American Indians had come from Asia. He was turned down flatly on the grounds that it was not sufficiently medical.

This refusal was the first episode of a twisted, ironical tale. A mere few months later, Black and his colleague Edmund Vincent Cowdry wrote to Hrdlička. Ignorant of his attempts to travel to China, they invited him to come to Beijing—all expenses paid by the Rockefeller Foundation, plus a substantial honorarium—to give a series of lectures that would promote a greater interest in anthropology among the faculty and students. Hrdlička happily accepted, with due haste and considerable glee, only to find that the Rockefeller Foundation had not been informed of the invitation prior to its issuance. The foundation's board then ungraciously withdrew the invitation.

It is difficult to understand the depth of their objection to Hrdlička, who, after all, was medically trained and had been employed by several hospitals, clinics, and medical institutions prior to going to the Smithsonian. Perhaps some of those who had served on committees and with whom he had clashed administratively during the war were at work behind the scenes; Hrdlička never lacked for ideas about spending money and had made many overt moves to seize control of those committees.

On the other hand, perhaps some of the enemies he had earned by rejecting the claims for early human occupation of the New World were retaliating.

Bitterly, Hrdlička protested that arrangements had already been made, that it would shame him to cancel the trip now, and that it would cost him some $4,200 out of his own pocket to pay for it. His emotionality paid off. In the end, the Rockefeller Foundation refused to reinvite him as a lecturer and refused to give him a grant directly to pay for the trip. However, in an outstandingly devious move, the foundation made a special grant of $2,500 to the Smithsonian so that the Smithsonian could pay for Hrdlička's trip. With a fine flair for revenge, Hrdlička made a point of giving a series of unsponsored and unapproved lectures to the Peking Union Medical College, and several more to the Tsing Hua College and the Young Men's Christian Association in Beijing.

Its refusal to fund Hrdlička directly was just the beginning of the Rockefeller Foundation's heartfelt attempts to turn young Professor Black's interests to more medical matters. In 1921, R. M. Pearce was sent out to assess the anatomy department at Beijing and recommend changes. From the United States, he wrote back to Black:

> I know that I have jollied you, threatened you and bullied you, and even cursed you, but you took it well. . . . I realize I have perhaps minimized the importance of anthropology and related subjects because I fear that in China at least it might tend more to ar-cheology than to comparative anatomy. If you think of anatomy for nine months out of the year, it is no one's business what you do in the summer in connection with anthropology, but for the next two years at least give your entire attention to anatomy. Perhaps by that time, you will, with your young son, have other interests which will appear more important than expeditions to mythological caves.

Black blithely ignored the advice, to his everlasting credit. He took a more positive view of human origins research in Asia, and he was not alone. In 1921, the American Museum of Natural History in New York mounted an expensive series of expeditions to the Gobi Desert, led by the dashing Roy Chapman Andrews, to search for human fossils. The president of the American Museum, Henry Fairfield Osborn, was a paleontologist who had declared as long ago as 1900 his conviction that Asia was the birthplace of the human species. Andrews set out to prove it, raising $250,000 for five years of exploration, mostly from private financiers such as J. P. Morgan. In time, Andrews found many extraordinary fossils, including dinosaur eggs, and wrote a charming book, but alas, uncovered no human ancestors.

Africa seemed a less promising frontier, despite Darwin's guess that it was the cradle of the human lineage. In 1913, a German paleontologist named Hans Reck, working in what was then German East Africa, had come across a most interesting find in a large gorge known then as Oldoway (now Olduvai Gorge, Tanzania). It was a skeleton of completely modern aspect, associated with extinct fossils. The debates echoed those over Ipswich and Galley Hill with the exception that Reck did not enjoy Keith's position of authority and power. Most believed, correctly, that he had simply found a modern burial intrusive into much older layers. Africa, and the Oldoway remains were simply disregarded for many years. It was not until many years later that the Cambridge-trained Louis Leakey, who had nonetheless spent enough days in Keith's lab to absorb his views, resurrected the Oldoway skeleton as proof of the early appearance of sapient humans. The ultimate fate of Oldoway Man, like that of Galley Hill and Ipswich, was for it to be discredited as an intrusive burial.

Then Africa yielded up another fossil human that was more enigmatic and harder to ignore. Rhodesian Man, as it was nicknamed, came from a town known as Broken Hill, in Northern Rhodesia (now Kabwe, Zambia), where a limestone hill impregnated with lead and zinc was being mined. On June 17, 1921, in a mine shaft some sixty feet below the surface, a laborer named T. Zwingelaar found an extraordinary skull in a small crevice in the wall. It was large and complete, with massive browridges, a low, sloping forehead, and a long, oval cranial vault. The face was long and heavy, the teeth thoroughly human—even down to the presence of dental caries, or cavities, in many of the teeth. The depth at which it was found bespoke great antiquity.

In many ways, it resembled the Neandertal cranium from Gibraltar or the La Chapelle-aux-Saints skull. Some postcranial bones—three broken femurs, a tibia, two pieces of pelvis, and a sacrum—were recovered as well, and some were assumed to represent the same individual. These bones are disconcerting in appearance. Some resemble those of Neandertals, some are even more archaic than Neandertal bones, and others appear to be rather modern.

A few months after the discovery of these bones, the manager of the mine traveled to London to present the remains to Arthur Smith Woodward, who was delighted to have yet another spectacular fossil fall into his lap. He issued a statement to the press, which appeared in the London

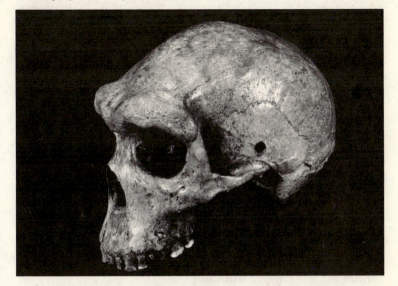

42. The human cranium found in 1921 at Broken Hill (now Kabwe), in Northern Rhodesia (now Zambia). The skull was the first Neandertal-like fossil discovered outside Europe.

Times on November 8, 1921. A brief description followed a week later in the journal *Nature*, in which he proposed to name the fossils *Homo rhodesiensis.*

Keith, the self-designated British expert on fossil humans, was distinctly piqued. How had Smith Woodward managed to corner another treasure? On November 19, in the *Illustrated London News*, Keith had the audacity to publish photographs and a general description of the material, only two days after Smith Woodward's *Nature* paper appeared. In the 1925 edition of *The Antiquity of Man*, Keith sniped bitterly at Smith Woodward:

> It came about, late in the summer of 1921, that Mr W. E. Barren, a mining engineer from New Zealand, was making his round in the mine or quarry, and came across a black labourer thrusting his pick amongst fossil bones which a successful charge had blasted from the deepmost recesses of the ancient cave. Mr Barren intervened, and thus saved the skull of Rhodesian man—the most complete and important document that has yet lain on the anthropologist's table—from being broken into fragments and sent to the melting-pot. Looking around, Mr Barren found other human bones in the confused mass of fossilised remains which lay exposed.
>
> . . . Early in October 1921, the *Sunday Times* of Johannesburg devoted an article to it. . . . Sir Arthur Smith Woodward gave a

preliminary account of him. . . . Professor Eugene Dubois came from Holland, and Professor G. L. Sera from Italy, to see the skull. . . . At the time this chapter was written, (August 1924) no adequate official account of Rhodesian man has been published, but Sir Arthur Smith Woodward very kindly permitted the writer to make a close examination of all the Rhodesian bones, the account given here being founded on what was observed then, and on casts which were withheld from British anatomists [undoubtedly, Keith meant himself] for fully two years after the moulds had been completed.

Keith's sarcastic expression of gratitude to Smith Woodward for permitting an examination of the fossils did not mask his attempt to steal a march on his rival. Following this passage are two full chapters that figure, describe, analyze, and discuss in great detail the Rhodesian fossils that had, after all, been given to Smith Woodward for study. It is an act in flagrant violation of modern scientific ethics that was surely as outrageous then as now.

Keith's conclusions are fascinating:

> His place in this [family] tree [of evolving humanity] . . . is at or near the base of the stem which afterwards branched into all types of modern man—*Homo sapiens*—living and extinct. Herein lies the great importance of the discovery at Broken Hill. It has given us for the first time a glimpse of our ancestral state. . . .
>
> Rhodesian man nearly answers to the common ancestor we have been in search of, but not quite; he has assumed too much of the modern type to serve this purpose. . . .
>
> It is easier to fix the place of Rhodesian man in the scale of human evolution than to estimate his position in geological time. It may be that he was a late survival, an okapi of humanity.

This interesting metaphor, "an okapi of humanity," refers to the discovery in the tropical forests of central Africa of a beautiful striped animal closely related to giraffes. It was with great excitement that live specimens of okapis were reported from the Congo in 1900, eventually being captured and exported to European zoos. Finding new animals such as the strange okapi or the wild gorilla became building blocks in an ill-defined theory that Africa was somehow a lost world or refuge where primitive types had lingered on, surviving long after their extinction elsewhere. Not many years afterwards, Sir Arthur Conan Doyle, an amateur antiquarian and the gifted writer whose works embodied the Edwardian mentality better than any other, used this theme in an adventure book that he entitled *The Lost World*—but his locale was South America, not Africa. Rhodesian Man was a perfect example of a relict from someplace like Doyle's lost world, combining a Neandertal-like skull with modern postcrania.

Keith concludes with a disclaimer:

> We have not yet found the stage which lies between Rhodesian man and modern man. Notwithstanding this blank in our knowledge, the evidence which is ever accumulating makes it more and more difficult to believe that Galley Hill and other examples of modern man [including the Ipswich skeleton] are really of the antiquity assigned to them on geological evidence.

Puzzlingly, the only sapient fossil human Keith continued to support was Piltdown, though no new evidence had come to light about his previous favorites, Galley Hill and Ipswich. His abandonment of Galley Hill and Ipswich seems as inexplicable as his sudden championing of them had been.

Keith also tried to argue that the antiquity of human fossils from Europe could be established by their association with extinct animals but that the same principle couldn't be used in Africa. The Rhodesian material led to some other entertaining mental gymnastics. For example, in 1922 Elliot Smith argued that the specimen was a survival of a "Pre-Neanderthal race" ancestral to the European Neandertals; this would mean that the unusual cranial features of Neandertals had developed first, coupled with a modern body, which had subsequently become less modern and more Neandertaloid.

Not only was the anatomy of the Broken Hill fossil awkward, its discovery turned out to have been somewhat other than as described by Smith Woodward, who accepted the story he was told by the mine manager without qualm. In 1925, Hrdlička—openly unhappy with the fossil—traveled to the mines to question the workmen. Zwingelaar revealed that he had found the cranium and had taken it to the manager, but that no other bones had been found close to it at the time. Only a later search for a jaw to go with the cranium revealed the postcranial bones, but these were not directly associated with the first find. Still other bones had been found at later dates, but not reported. Hrdlička took these and deposited them—very probably reproachfully—with Smith Woodward at the British Museum. Clarifying the way in which the bones were found left Hrdlička comfortable in rejecting the association of cranial and postcranial remains as spurious, a point about which modern opinion largely concurs.

Undaunted, William Plane Pycraft, Smith Woodward's assistant at the

British Museum of Natural History and an expert on birds, wrote a monograph in 1928 on Rhodesian Man, dubbing it *Cyphanthropus rhodesiensis* ("stooping man from Rhodesia"). Pycraft's naïve belief in the functional import of tibial retroversion, combined with his total misunderstanding of the pelvic anatomy of the fossil, led him to surmise that Rhodesian Man could not walk erect. It was a warped but recognizable mimic of Boule's conclusions about European Neandertals.

Rhodesian Man was not the only surprise to come out of Africa around this time. Another of Grafton Elliot Smith's eager students, an Australian named Raymond A. Dart, had caught fossil man fever in Elliot Smith's laboratory, as had Davidson Black before him. Born February 4, 1893, Dart was the fifth of nine children born to Eliza and Samuel Dart, settlers raising cattle on a bush farm. His upbringing was strict and religious.

A bright boy with eager eyes, Dart won a scholarship to become one of the first students at the University of Queensland, where his keenness and hard work won him more scholarships and prizes, which took him on to the University of Sydney for his medical studies. The highlight for the young Dart came in 1914, when the British Association for the Advancement of Science came to Australia, and he was asked to assist S. Arthur Smith, a well-known anatomist and the brother of the still-more-famous Grafton Elliot Smith, in preparing his presentation.

Years later, Dart still remembered the awe and joy with which he listened, spellbound, as world-renowned scientists gave their presentations. Though war intervened, Dart completed his medical studies and was shipped to England with the Australian Army Medical Corps. As the war was drawing to a close, Dart was delighted when his hero, Grafton Elliot Smith, accepted him as an assistant.

Dart worshiped Elliot Smith, regarding him as a "genius, but also one of the most pleasant human beings I had worked for or with."

> Tall, ruddy-complexioned and distinguished, with immaculate white hair, he was the complete antithesis of the woolly-minded, innocent genius of fiction. Elliot Smith was, with all his brilliance, in every sense a man of the world, a great raconteur and popular with his colleagues and assistants who could usually rely on him to attend and enliven their daily tea parties.

Despite Dart's admiration, something somewhere went wrong.

In 1920, Elliot Smith shipped Dart off to the United States for a year to work with R. J. Terry of Washington University in St. Louis. Little more than a year after Dart's return, Elliot Smith sent him off to be professor of anatomy at the brand-new University of the Witwatersrand in Johannesburg, South Africa. It was hardly a plump and juicy opportunity for one of Elliot Smith's most promising students. The whole affair smacks, instead, of exile, of sending a troublemaker to the farthest end of the earth. At the end of his life, Keith wrote of Dart as a "brilliant student" but adds:

> I was one of those who recommended him to the post [at the Witwatersrand], but I did so, I am now free to confess, with a certain degree of trepidation. Of his knowledge, his power of intellect and of imagination there could be no question; what rather frightened me was his flightiness, his scorn for accepted opinion, the unorthodoxy of his outlook.

This from the man who confesses in the same work that his own opinion of the Galley Hill remains "was dead against the accepted authority, but it was one which I was prepared to defend." Unorthodoxy obviously sat better with Keith when it came from his own lips.

Dart's undeniable willingness to fly in the face of the prevailing paradigm became only too apparent a few years after his arrival at Johannesburg. At first, his energies were taken up with a struggle to carry out his job. Conditions at the university were appalling: there were no books save Dart's own; no water taps, compressed air, or electricity graced the labs; there were not even any cloths or body bags to wrap the cadavers in. The walls of the anatomy laboratory were stained and pockmarked where students had practiced their tennis and soccer shots.

Some of the deficits in the physical plant were corrected, but the less concrete problems were harder to fix. In order to build up some kind of comparative skeletal collection, Dart initiated competitions among his students to see who could bring in the most unusual or interesting bones, for a prize of five pounds. This enterprising and unorthodox approach was to lead Dart to his most famous discovery.

His sole female student in 1924, Josephine Salmon, had seen on the mantelpiece at a friend's house a most interesting fossil skull—a baboon, she thought, from the limestone quarries at nearby Taung. As there were almost no fossil primates from Africa, Rhodesian Man being an exception, Dart was surprised and pleased to find her assessment correct. It was but a simple matter then to find a friend who would ask the manager

43. Raymond Dart in 1925, pointing to features on the natural braincase of the Taung *Australopithecus africanus,* shortly after its discovery. For many years his identification of the fossil as hominid was rejected because the specimen was thought to be too apish for a human ancestor.

of the Taung cave to send any bones or fossils the workmen found to Dart.

The first two crates, the contents of which were to usher Dart into a new life, arrived as he was dressing to do much the same for an old friend: serve as best man at his wedding, which was shortly to take place in the Darts' home. Ignoring his wife's pleas to get on with the wedding preparations, Dart wrenched open the boxes, "little guessing," he remembered later, "that from this crate was to emerge a face that would look out on the world after an age-long sleep of nearly a million years." The nervous bridegroom soon interrupted Dart's rapt contemplation of the most extraordinary fossil human yet found: an endocast (a stone replica) of a somewhat humanlike brain that fitted into another lump of stone, where the face might be embedded. Locking the treasures in his wardrobe, Dart reluctantly returned to his social duties, all the while thinking with half his mind of the thing he had discovered.

It was Christmas 1924 before Dart had the stony matrix cleaned off of the fossil, revealing a child's face and jaw, complete with milk teeth, to which the brain belonged. The creature's permanent first molars were about to erupt behind the milk teeth, which—if it were a modern human—would make it almost five years old at the time of death. The skull is small, fitting nicely into Dart's palm, and a beautiful, glowing, mustard brown color with glittering teeth. Like any new father, Dart found the Taung baby, as it came to be called, his pride and joy.

Dart sought no advice or assistance from the experts. He was not about to send his Taung baby off to London all alone. Recognizing that the endocast had many human features and believing that the brain was larger than that of young apes, Dart became convinced he had found the missing link.

On February 3, 1925—a day short of Dart's thirty-second birthday—his paper announcing the find was published by the British journal *Nature*. Dart proposed to call the creature *Australopithecus africanus* ("the southern ape from Africa"). However, he stressed the humanlike aspects of the brain and teeth, saying that "the family typified by this form are the nearest to the prehuman ancestral type that we have." He had the audacity to suggest that an entire new zoological family, the Homo-simiadae or man-apes, should be created since the fossil was a transitional form linking the two.

Congratulations poured in, from Elliot Smith, Hrdlička, and even from General J. C. Smuts, then president of the South African Association for the Advancement of Science. The newspapers announced in the most flamboyant possible terms the discovery of the missing link. The conservative British anthropological establishment gritted their teeth in irritation, but were at first polite. Arthur Keith told the London newspapers that "Professor Dart is not likely to be led astray. If he has thoroughly examined the skull we are prepared to accept his decision"—*for the time being,* he might have added, but didn't.

By February 14, the next issue of *Nature*, Keith, Elliot Smith, Smith Woodward and W. H. L. Duckworth, another London anatomist, had prepared their heartfelt, written attacks. Virchow was dead in fact but not in spirit. They separately argued that Dart had made the fundamental mistake of confusing an immature chimplike creature with a human; he was also criticized for the lack of information about the fossil's antiquity or geological position. Keith, in a turn of phrase hauntingly reminiscent of those "giant gibbon" gibes directed at Dubois years earlier, slathered Dart with bittersweet praise for finding what was merely a new species of ape. Others suggested that Dart had mistaken rather recent material that had simply fallen into the cave for bones of genuine antiquity. About the only reproach that was omitted was the old one from Dubois's trial: that the pieces were not associated with one another. The fit between the endocast and the bones of the forehead, and between the upper and lower jaws, was too precise to be doubted.

While the scientific community erroneously rejected Dart's find as misinterpreted and irrelevant, the public embraced it with a disconcerting fervor. A reconstruction, prepared under the guidance of Grafton Elliot Smith, appeared in the *Illustrated London News*. The name Taung became the subject of music hall and dance tunes, jokes, limericks, and revealing poems, such as:

> *Speechless with half-human leer,*
> *Lies a hidden monster here:*
> *Yet here, read backwards, beauty lies,*
> *And here the wisdom of the wise.*

No blunter statement of the bestiality and savagery associated with the earliest human ancestor—a title now transferred to the Taung baby from *Pithecanthropus*, who had in turn inherited it from the Neandertals—could be made.

44. A reconstruction of the head of the Taung individual, done by the artist A. Forestier under the direction of Grafton Elliot Smith in 1926

Dart, as had Dubois before him, suffered from the near-universal rejection of his ideas. Like Dubois, he had gone to a remote and savage place and had unearthed what was purported to be a human ancestor. Like Dubois's, his description suffered from a serious lack of comparative osteological material, from poor or nonexistent information on geological context, and—most tellingly—from the absence of a champion within the right scientific circles. Dart's hero and onetime adviser,

Elliot Smith, neither attacked him with as much venom as some others nor offered his reputation and expertise as a shield. The affectionate support Elliot Smith was soon to offer to another former student, Davidson Black, was noticeably lacking.

Although Dart prospered in South Africa, becoming dean of the faculty of medicine and widely esteemed, he was regarded as an overenthusiastic fool in the elevated circles of British science he so revered. It left him lonely and hurt. Like Dubois, Dart was judged before he had presented his evidence in any detail. In later years, Dart thought it had been a mistake not to go to London straightaway to enlist support for his ideas, but at the time he was reluctant to travel so far from home and for so long.

The trouble was that only a few renegade scientists bothered to travel to see Dart's material, among them Aleš Hrdlička, who stopped in Johannesburg to see the Taung baby in 1925 after visiting Broken Hill. The affinities of the Taung skull were not clear to Hrdlička who, like so many others, was confused by its immaturity, but he held off from condemning Dart's man-ape as a mere chimpanzee, remarking, "It is undoubtedly a missing link—one of the many still missing links in the realm of primate ancestry."

Almost alone as an unabashed supporter of the lonely Dart was Robert Broom, who burst into Dart's laboratory two weeks after the *Nature* announcement. Striding across the room—and failing to acknowledge either Dart or his startled staff—Broom fell onto his knees "in adoration of our ancestor," the Taung fossil.

Broom, a Scottish vertebrate paleontologist with eccentric habits, had a scientific reputation that never seemed to suffer from his idiosyncrasies. A small man, Broom had been born in 1866 and by the 1920s sported a silver crewcut and wore round, metal-rimmed spectacles that could not hide a perpetual twinkle. He was invariably dressed in a stiff wing collar, dark suit, and vest, unless the fossil-hunting grounds were warm, in which case he stripped naked. Trained in medicine, he was not above experimenting on his patients or, if they died and were of an interesting race, burying them in the garden so that he could later recover their skeletons. He had a reputation as a lady's man late in life and took pains to keep his wife at a safe remove from wherever he was conducting his research. His vertebrate paleontology, focusing mostly on lizards, dinosaurs, and the earliest mammals, was highly regarded, and by 1920 he was a Fellow of the Royal Society.

Although Broom converted immediately to Dart's point of view, few others did. In 1934, Broom gave up his medical practice and undertook full-time work as a paleontologist. He determined to look for more australopithecines; he has been quoted as saying that he already regarded himself as the greatest paleontologist who had ever lived and saw no reason why he shouldn't become the greatest anthropologist as well. Starting in 1936, Broom vindicated Dart's claims that australopithecines were human ancestors, not simply apes, by finding more—and this time adult—australopithecine skulls in the South African caves of Sterkfontein, Swartkrans, and Kromdraai.

By drawing the fire, Dart's discovery had an indirect effect on Neandertal interpretations. During the world tour in which Hrdlička had examined the Taung skull, he also visited many of the prominent scientists, inspected most of the other fossil material that had turned up in recent years, and collected many modern skulls of different races. It was a profitable trip in more ways than one for shortly thereafter, in 1927, Hrdlička was awarded the Huxley Medal. The highest in Great Britain for anthropology, the Huxley Medal had only once before been given to an American. It marked, quite emphatically, Hrdlička's acceptance by the British as a great scholar who had made valuable contributions to his field.

Rather than bask in his success, Hrdlička seized the occasion of the recipient's acceptance lecture to put forward his well-shaped but controversial theory on the fate of the Neandertals. Virtually alone of all of the major figures in paleoanthropology, Hrdlička had come to the conclusion that Neandertals evolved directly into modern humans. In contrast, Keith represented the majority view, referring to Neandertals as "a great step backwards" from modern humans and saying of their fate:

> The most marvellous aspect of the problem raised by the recognition of Neanderthal man as a distinct type [or species] is his apparently sudden disappearance. He is replaced, with the dawn of the Aurignacian period, by men of the same type as now occupy Europe. What happened at the end of the Mousterian period we can only guess, but those who observe the fate of the aboriginal races of America and Australia will have no difficulty in accounting for the disappearance of *Homo neanderthalensis*. A more virile form extinguished him.

Hrdlička would have none of it. Neandertals had not disappeared, they had evolved—into humans. The title of his Huxley Medal lecture was "The Neanderthal Phase of Man." In these few words, he clarified his then-esoteric point of view: Neandertals had been a phase, an evolutionary stage, in the lineage of humankind. He was our own, ourselves, our ancestor. Unlike Breuil, Hrdlička felt that the Aurignacian culture associated with anatomical modern humans was an outgrowth of the Mousterian culture made by Neandertals, even as the toolmakers were an evolutionary development one of the other.

Hrdlička also worked the climatic record into his scheme. He noticed that, through time from the pre-Chellean to Acheulian to Mousterian, the number of living sites in the open decreased and the numbers of rock shelters and cave sites increased. To Hrdlička, this showed that the climatic conditions were worsening and becoming more glacial. But from the Mousterian to the Aurignacian, he found no change in setting, a fact that argued for biological and cultural continuity, Hrdlička felt. No dramatic catastrophe, no fight to the cannibalistic death, no invasion of other humans from the East needed to be invoked to account for the disappearance of the Neandertals: they are still with us, Hrdlička proclaimed.

The scientists present listened quietly, applauded the lecture politely, and went home without a flicker of doubt in their minds that Hrdlička was wrong. No shaft of bright new insight penetrated the gloom of their preconceptions. Hrdlička's theory was nothing more than a dusted-off remake of the old prewar hypothesis put forward by his old mentor, Manouvrier, and by Gustav Schwalbe.

The pre-Sapiens theory, espoused by the defenders of Piltdown and other purportedly ancient, large-brained forms, held the strongest ground. Those who did not like the pre-Sapiens theory could always follow Elliot Smith, who in 1924 had formulated the pre-Neandertal theory. He had argued that modern humans had arisen at several different branching points from the ancestral lineage, with primitive human groups diverging earlier—before Neandertals evolved into a highly specialized cul-de-sac—and with more advanced (read "European") races developing later. The only real difference between Elliot Smith's hypothesis and the mainstream view was that Elliot Smith believed that *Homo sapiens* arose even earlier than the pre-Sapiens crowd thought. As Elliot Smith summed up in *Nature* the response to Hrdlička's lecture:

> In his recent Huxley lecture . . . Dr. Aleš Hrdlička has questioned the validity of the specific distinction of Neanderthal man, an issue which most anatomists imagined to have been definitively settled by the investigation of Schwalbe in 1899, and the corroboration af-

forded by the work of Boule and a host of other anatomists.
. . . The only justification for re-opening the problem of the status
of Neanderthal man would be afforded by new evidence or new
views, either of a destructive or constructive nature. I do not think
Dr. Hrdlička has given any valid reasons for rejecting the view that
Homo neanderthalensis is a species distinct from *sapiens*.

In other words, Hrdlička was flatly dismissed as having offered no new
insights into a dead issue. What a disappointment his Huxley lecture
must have seemed at the time.

Of all of the scholars concerned with human evolution at the time,
only Karl Gorjanović-Kramberger wholeheartedly agreed with Hrdlička's thesis. There was a longstanding empathy between Hrdlička and
Gorjanović, who shared a similar view of the immense importance of
habits and behaviors on the shape of the human skeleton. Gorjanović,
who had retired in 1924, was greatly esteemed as a brilliant scientist in
Yugoslavia. Six months before Hrdlička's lecture, Gorjanović had been
honored with an elaborate celebration marking his seventieth birthday
by the Croatian Natural History Society, the Yugoslav Academy of Arts
and Sciences, and the University of Zagreb. However, Gorjanović's
influence had waned outside Yugoslavia—he was to write only one more
scientific paper before his death in 1936—so his intellectual support of
Hrdlička's ideas did little to sway the general scientific consensus. In fact,
the two were probably written off as an aging pair of foreigners with
outdated ideas.

Though few absorbed his words, Hrdlička had raised several important points. He explicitly linked the unusual Neandertal features with an
adaptation to glacial cold—an idea that, starting in the mid-twentieth
century, was to be resurrected, explored, and elaborated as one of the
most important insights into Neandertal adaptations. He also looked
with a practiced eye at the variability in the Neandertal fossils. With his
background in conducting surveys of the bodies and skeletons of various
races, Hrdlička saw and understood that some Neandertals—such as the
original Neandertal skeleton, the Spy fossils, and those from Le Moustier
and La Chapelle-aux-Saints—were very primitive, heavily built, and
physically extreme, while others—like those from Krapina, La Ferrassie,
and La Quina—more closely approached modern types. A highly variable population subjected to the rigors of glacial conditions would be
strongly shaped by natural selection through time, until the most able to
cope evolved into modern humans and the less fit and more brutish died
out. It was not so much a Neandertal *species*, Hrdlička argued, as a

Neandertal phase. If it had been otherwise, surely there would be traces of very ancient but anatomically modern humans, or their ancestors, in Asia.

At the beginning of 1927 (the year of Hrdlička's Huxley Memorial Lecture) his anthropology mentor, Léonce-Pierre Manouvrier, died of a failing heart at age seventy-six. Active to the end, Manouvrier had had a profound effect on physical anthropology in France and elsewhere, even if Boule and his confreres at the Institut de Paléontologie Humaine had gained domination in human paleontology. At the Société d'Anthropologie de Paris, the Ecole Pratique des Haute Etudes, the Ecole d'Anthropologie and the Collège de France in Paris, the Sociétés des Sciences et des Médicins in his home province of the Creuse, and even at the Washington Academy of Sciences in Washington, D.C., Manouvrier's praises were sung at great length by his grieving colleagues. But at the same time, Verneau, writing as a coeditor of *L'Anthropologie*, could not restrain himself from denigrating virtually every aspect of Manouvrier's scientific work, most particularly his few contributions to human paleontology. Even in death, the successor to Broca and the mentor to Hrdlička played a key role in the controversies over human ancestry.

Manouvrier's death was a blow to Hrdlička, but there were more to come. Little did Hrdlička know at the time, but Elliot Smith's other former student, Davidson Black, was about to announce that he had found ancient material in China. Black's efforts to find human fossils had first been rewarded in 1926, when two lower teeth of a humanlike form from Pleistocene deposits were reported. Apparently, they had been found in 1921 by two Swedish researchers working for the Geological Survey of China: Otto Zdansky and J. Gunnar Anderson. Upon reading their report, Black was so convinced that here was the early human he had been seeking that he prepared manuscripts for the preeminent scientific journals, *Nature* and *Science*—which published them in December 1926—despite the fact that Black had not actually seen the fossils himself. The evidence was transparently skimpy, and Hrdlička expressed his skepticism openly to Black early in 1927.

Black's response was to let Hrdlička's letters lie with their awkward questions unanswered while he began a systematic excavation of the site at Zhoukoudian (then commonly known as Choukoutien). The name of the locality that actually yielded the human fossils means "Dragon Bone Hill" in English. Fossils, especially fossil teeth, were then and are still used as ingredients in traditional Chinese medicine under the general title of "dragon bones."

Black's reputation as a rash publisher was not lessened by a paper that appeared late in 1927, announcing a new species of hominid, *Sinanthropus pekinensis* ("the Chinese man from Peking"), on the basis of the single molar tooth recovered during the first season of excavation. (Much later, this "new" species was shown to be the same as *Pithecanthropus*, and both are now called *Homo erectus*.) Birger Bohlin, then a recent Swedish Ph.D. in paleontology, was working at Zhoukoudian that summer and later recalled:

> I went to China chiefly because I wanted to go somewhere, but I was ordered to find man. You could see from a distance that Davidson Black wanted fossil man. The rest was just by-product. He gave me some directions of how to work at [Zhoukoudian]: he said I should remove the whole deposit in six weeks and take it back to Peking. In the first few days I saw that this was impossible.

So would anyone else; the deposit was about eight hundred meters square and everywhere more than ten meters thick. But, on the third to last day of excavation in 1927, this overzealous approach yielded a single hominid tooth. The 1928 excavations bore out Black's enthusiasm and audacious naming of a new species, however, yielding more teeth, a skull fragment, and part of a jaw, all associated with extinct Pleistocene mammals.

But it was the 1929 season that paid off in full. Pei Wenzhong was an earnest young man who had graduated from Beijing University only a few years before; he had worked as Bohlin's assistant since 1927. On the basis of his experience and talent as a fieldworker, Pei was left solely in charge of the field excavations in 1929, a responsibility he found daunting and melancholy-inducing at first. An easygoing and usually cheerful person, Pei had gained most of his expertise "hands on," and little by formal schooling, but his field notes show the influence of considerable knowledge.

Late in the afternoon of December 2, 1929, Pei and several workmen were digging deep in the cave, in an area so small that standing was impossible. The workers held candles in one hand and dug with the other. By this flickering light, Pei glimpsed a large, rounded fossil: he had discovered a largely complete skullcap of *Sinanthropus*; only the face was missing. He knew what he had found and sent a cable to Davidson Black:

> Found skullcap—perfect—look[s] like man's.

Black could scarcely believe this terse announcement of success, but it was true. It was the first of Pei's many important discoveries over the years. Black wrote to Hrdlička triumphantly:

> The supraorbital [brow] ridges are massive as one expected from the jaw. They are apparently equal in development to those of *Pithecanthropus*. The frontal and parietal development of *Sinanthropus* is much more advanced than the Java type but the frontal development is apparently less than in *Eoanthropus*. *Sinanthropus* is of approximately similar length to *Pithecanthropus* but its shape implies a considerably larger volume than the latter.

The photographs and casts of *Sinanthropus* made a tremendous impact in London, Paris, and Washington, D.C. Hrdlička, seeing the new skull as a contradiction of his Neandertal phase hypothesis, strove in vain to persuade Black and the press that it was, in fact, a Neandertal skull. Black maintained his good humor at first, finding it somewhat amusing to disturb "Dear Old Hrdlička's hypothesis." As Hrdlička's position hardened and his public statements became more critical of Black's ideas, Black became more frosty and less forgiving.

In London, Elliot Smith warmly endorsed Black's new finds, presenting them to the Royal Society in London with his usual élan. Indeed, his presentation coincided with Dart's single visit to present his findings and to persuade the Royal Society to fund publication of his monograph on the Taung skull. As Dart sat through Elliot Smith's spellbinding performance, he knew his case would be completely overshadowed, as it was. The Taung baby was dismissed, overlooked, and largely unpublished. It was even, briefly, lost—left in a taxi by Dart's wife. Besides, Dart remembered later:

> Sir Arthur Keith had already told me that he had written an exhaustive description of the cranial material for his forthcoming book on recent anthropological discoveries, so I took my manuscript back to South Africa in hopes that a more propitious occasion would present itself in the future.

As with the Rhodesian fossil, Keith had beaten to the punch the scientist with the greatest right to analyze the fossils. Keith had acquired a cast of Taung, presumably at Dart's courtesy, and repaid this collegiality by writing a hundred pages on it for his new book before Dart had had time to complete and publish his own analysis. Keith was a master at occupying the limelight, and Dart, for all that he wrote in a flowing prose whose purple hue deepened as he aged, was not.

Dart's fate, and that of his fossil, stood in marked contrast to that of Davidson Black and his new find. While Keith was saying all that was to be said (at the time) about the Taung baby, Elliot Smith was parading *Sinanthropus* before the admiring eyes of English and European anthropologists. In fact, he actually traveled to China to inspect the originals, with funding from the Rockefeller Foundation—who had by now completely reversed their opinion on the value of anthropological research—and Black gave a lecture tour of Europe.

Keith at first openly applauded the discovery as "the most important of all" and declared that "an early pleistocene [*sic*] ancestor of the modern type of man—neanthropic man—has at last come to light." However, when the skull was examined, and did not resemble Piltdown, Keith thought again.

> Thus in the fossil human skulls, found at a depth of 110 feet in deposits which accumulated in a cave at Chou Kou Tien [Zhoukoudian], when the fauna of China was very different from what it is to-day, we find a strange assortment of characters. The greatest number of these link these ancient Chinamen to the Pithecanthropic type of Java; other features link them to the Neanderthal type of Europe; yet others reveal affinities to modern man.

This hazy assessment is clarified only slightly by a diagram, in which the branch representing Peking Man, as Keith and others called it, lies between the branches for *Pithecanthropus* and Neandertals.

Despite some striking similarities of skull shape and size that are evident in various diagrams, few scientists of the day argued against Black's assertion that *Sinanthropus* was distinct from (and more advanced than) Dubois's *Pithecanthropus*. Boule was the rare exception. Today, the scientific establishment accepts without demur that the two are identical in both genus and species. But, once again, the assessment of fossil skulls was hindered by the scientists' tendency to overemphasize the importance of minor variations in shape and size and to ignore the fact that small differences in features might be expected to occur in skulls from different geographic regions.

Black's triumphant assessment of his new species provoked even the aging Eugène Dubois into replying. Dubois had reemerged from his self-imposed isolation a few years before, finally permitting Hrdlička and Hans Weinert, a German anthropologist, to see the *Pithecanthropus* fossils—after pressure was applied through the Royal Dutch Academy of Science. Dubois had written a few papers about Neandertals in the early 1920s, arguing that they were not apish, as Boule maintained. In fact, Dubois pointed out, Neandertals showed a braincase that was both absolutely and relatively larger than that of *Homo sapiens*, no doubt a correlate of their very strongly built, heavily muscled bodies. The bodily peculiarities of Neandertals, Dubois maintained quietly, were due solely to the rigorous exercise they had taken in life.

Dubois did not become truly outspoken until Black began comparing *Sinanthropus* with *Pithecanthropus*. In 1933, Dubois published a paper utterly rejecting Black's idea that the two forms were closely related. *Sinanthropus*, Dubois declared, was fully human, nothing more than a Neandertal. The small cranial capacity for the first known skull—which Dubois estimated at 918 cc—was "certainly very low for a human skull"; ironically, Dubois concluded it must be abnormal or pathological. When a normal male *Sinanthropus* was found, its cranial capacity would be about 1,300 cc, and it would prove to be a Neandertal, Dubois predicted: a view he would eventually retract in face of mounting evidence to the contrary. But he continued, with characteristic stubbornness, to insist on the distinction between *Sinanthropus* and *Pithecanthropus*, the latter of which he, ironically, found more and more gibbonlike as time went on.

Finally, by 1937 Dubois had done almost a complete aboutface. From hotly rejecting Virchow's claims at the turn of the century that *Pithecanthropus* was nought but a giant gibbon, Dubois had now arrived at the point where he could write:

> *Pithecanthropus* was not a man, but a gigantic genus allied to the gibbons, however superior to the gibbons on account of its exceedingly large brain volume and distinguished at the same time by its faculty of assuming an erect attitude and gait. It had the double cephalization [ratio of brain size to body size] of the anthropoid apes in general and half that of man.
>
> It was the surprising volume of the brain—which is very much too large for an anthropoid ape, and which is small compared with the average, though not smaller than the smallest human brain—that led to the now almost general view that the "Ape Man" of Trinil, Java, was really a primitive Man. Morphologically, however, the calvaria [skullcap] closely resembles that of anthropoid apes, especially the gibbon.

That Dubois ever claimed his fossils to be a giant gibbon is denied by some authorities, but his words here are unambiguous.

Yet, in the same paper he continued to defend the "fundamental difference" between *Pithecanthropus* and *Sinanthropus*, especially as regards the shape and size of the brain. To Dubois, these indicated that the giant gibbon *Pithecanthropus*, not *Sinanthropus*, was somehow the more probable human ancestor, especially since it required only a doubling of brain size to transform one into the other. Whatever Dubois thought *Pithecanthropus* was, it wasn't the same as Black's Chinese fossils: of that much he was sure.

Dubois's thoughts were tangled and unclearly expressed. It would seem that few contemporary scientists paid much attention to the ranting of the bitter, eccentric old Dutchman who was to die of a heart attack in 1938. Arthur Keith wrote his obituary, describing Dubois with apt words: "He was an idealist, his ideas being so firmly held that his mind tended to bend facts rather than alter his ideas to fit them."

Black continued working at Zhoukoudian, with great enthusiasm and considerably more support from his sponsors. In 1932, he was elected a Fellow of the Royal Society for his work on *Sinanthropus*, though the detailed analyses of the remains had yet to be published. As was his habit, he attended to his university responsibilities during the afternoon and worked on his fossils at night, starting about midnight—often after a sociable evening with friends—and continuing until the early hours, when he would go home and sleep until noon. In 1934, after one such bout of work, Black was found in his laboratory, dead of heart failure at the age of forty-nine.

His place was taken in part by Pierre Teilhard de Chardin. In 1926, he had been exiled to China by the church for his unorthodox interpretations of original sin in the light of evolutionary theory. Unrepentant, Teilhard was still pursuing his passion for human evolution with the blessing of the Institut de Paléontologie Humaine, working with Boule and Breuil and becoming, in 1928, an adviser to the Chinese Geological Survey. He was involved in the excavations at Zhoukoudian almost from the beginning, and after Black's death, Teilhard assumed overall supervision of them, though the day-to-day work was now directed by Pei Wenzhong.

At the Peking Union Medical College, Davidson Black's successor was Franz Weidenreich, a German anatomist trained by Gustav Schwalbe at the University of Strasbourg, who undertook the job of obtaining funding, keeping track of expenditures (he was a stickler for trying to save money), and eventually writing a monographic description and analysis of the fossils. Weidenreich was an older man, bald, with a courtly demeanor and round glasses; he was a taciturn but articulate scholar. A Jew, Weidenreich had already fled the growing Nazi menace in Europe. After receiving his M.D. from the University of Strasbourg in 1899, he worked there for some years, then took a position as professor of anatomy at the University of Heidelberg in 1919. In 1928, he moved to the University of Frankfurt as a professor of anthropology, where he completed a definitive paleontological study of the Neandertal-like human fossils found in travertine deposits in 1927 at Ehringsdorf, near Weimar. Although he was well known as an anatomist and human paleontologist, Weidenreich was forced to resign his position at Frankfurt in 1935, at the age of sixty-two, because he was Jewish. Forsaking his native land and language, he never again published in German. He insisted on using English even for the foreword to a monograph written otherwise entirely in German, a 1939 work by his colleague G. H. R. von Koenigswald on the subject of additional *Pithecanthropus* fossils from Java.

Age notwithstanding, Weidenreich was not immune to the youthful thrill of discovering totally new and wonderful fossils. His wife reported that when he received a phone call telling him that a new and even more complete skull had been found, Weidenreich put his pants on inside-out in his haste to get dressed and get out to the site. By 1937, Weidenreich had an unparalleled collection to work with. There were fourteen partial skulls, eleven mandibles, assorted teeth that had fallen out of their sockets, and a small selection of limb bones.

But world politics overwhelmed the quest to unravel human origins once again. In 1937, the Sino-Japanese War broke out, clearly signaling Japan's expansionist plans. Japan occupied all of northeastern China; guerrilla fighting infiltrated the hills around Zhoukoudian, and excavations were suspended indefinitely. Three men who stayed to guard the site were captured and killed by the Japanese, who thought they were concealing the whereabouts of Chinese guerrillas.

Weidenreich stayed in his laboratory, making precise drawings, photographs, and casts of the fossils. His work eventually appeared in a series of monographs that were published in the late 1930s and early 1940s, though their impact was felt largely after the war, when attention returned to science.

He had been hounded out of Europe by the Nazis and now he found himself imperiled by expansionist powers once again. The Chinese gov-

45. Farewell photograph at the Peking Union Medical College, as Franz Weidenreich (front row center) was preparing to leave China for the United States in the autumn of 1941. Among other members of the international group, the photograph includes: Claire Taschdjian, Weidenreich's secretary (on his right) and possibly the last European to see the Zhoukoudian fossils before they were lost; Jia Lanpo (in second row, to the left of Weidenreich), now the author of *The Story of Peking Man* and one of the longtime participants in the Zhoukoudian project; and Pei Wenzhong (first row, two to the right of Weidenreich), by this time director of the Cenozoic Research Laboratory of the Geological Survey of China.

ernment had left Beijing but neglected to move the precious fossils. The fossils were being eagerly sought by the Japanese as representing a national treasure, and the Chinese were equally anxious to keep them out of Japanese hands. Weidenreich prepared to flee to the United States but declined to take the fossils with him, fearing they would be seized and confiscated at the border and he might be treated with even less care. Arrangements were made through the U.S. Embassy to send them to the United States for safekeeping. On December 5, 1941, the fossils were packed, lovingly, into two well-padded crates before being turned over to a contingent of U.S. Marines who were going by train to board the SS *President Harrison*.

On December 7, 1941, the Japanese attacked Pearl Harbor, and the Americans were suddenly at war. The train carrying the fossils was intercepted by Japanese troops, who captured the marines. As for the fossils, they have never been seen again, despite considerable publicity and the offer of hefty rewards. Their whereabouts have become the subject of some of the strangest stories in anthropology. Blurry photos of mysterious bones said to be discovered in long-neglected marine footlockers still turn up periodically; anonymous callers make vague appointments to show authorities the bones at peculiar times and places; but nothing tangible has ever come to light. Only Weidenreich's compulsively careful notes, photographs, and casts remain.

Perhaps the looming threat of war gave a dim and eerie significance to all of the fossil humans of the decade. Though discoveries were numerous, their significance was often ambiguous. New material, often of entirely new anatomy, was shoehorned into the theories that had prevailed at the end of World War I, though the fit must have pinched in numerous places.

One of the places yielding fossils that did not fit existing paradigms was Palestine. Throughout the 1930s, it had yielded up confusing profusions of bones, mostly in the excavations run by the American School of Prehistoric Research and the British School of Archaeology, both quartered in Jerusalem. George Grant MacCurdy headed up the American studies, and a remarkable woman, Dorothy Garrod, led the British.

Garrod was the daughter of a renowned medical professor, Sir Archibald Garrod, and had studied many years with the Abbé Henri Breuil at the Institut de Paléontologie Humaine in Paris. Born in 1892, she was in 1929—when the Mount Carmel excavations began—a research fellow of Newnham College, Cambridge, one of the few high-quality women's colleges then in existence in Britain. After years of hard work in the Near East, establishing a broad framework for the prehistoric occupation of this region and describing, analyzing, and naming the new cultures she discovered, Garrod became the first woman to hold a professorship at Cambridge, in 1939. She envisioned the Near East as a "gateway of prehistoric migration into Europe both from the Further East and from Africa."

Her scientific work was no-nonsense and so was her person. Contemporary photographs and recollections paint her as a compact woman, usually wearing a hat, a man's suitcoat over a long skirt, and sensible shoes. Her hair was pulled back, and she wore glasses on occasion. Of course, Garrod spoke Arabic fluently. It is said she would hire only Arab women as workers—not because the men flouted her authority but because the women worked harder. At Mount Carmel, the European staff—including Garrod—was housed in a long, barracks-style building made of mud bricks and roofed with straw, which also served as the expedition's headquarters and working space. Garrod was determined and organized, but her crews also learned a great deal and had fun. The headquarters was known as Tibn (straw) Towers, while the women who washed flint tools were known as the "flint bints"—*bint* being Arabic for woman and an adopted part of British slang.

In an era and a culture in which women rarely commanded, Garrod took full control of the excavations in the region of Mount Carmel, in caves known as Mugharet el-Wad (Cave of the Valley), Mugharet et-Tabun (Cave of the Oven), and Mugharet es-Skhul (Cave of the Kids), all in Palestine (now Israel). Together, the Mount Carmel caves preserved a remarkably complete record, revealing material in ever-deepening layers from the recent Bronze Age steadily back in time to the Aurignacian, Mousterian, and late Acheulian periods.

Her work had been amazingly well rewarded with abundant faunal remains, large quantities of stone tools, and a partial skeleton of a female Neandertal (plus a few extra bones) from the cave at Tabun, and an additional ten partial skeletons, including that of a 2½-year-old child, from the cave at Skhul. By 1932, the finds from Skhul were being referred to as a "Mousterian cemetery"; many appeared to be flexed or crouch burials—individuals interred with their arms and legs tightly drawn up—such as had been recovered in France.

As Garrod's primary interest was in the Paleolithic stone tools, she turned her remarkable human skeletal materials over to Theodore McCown, a young American student who had supervised the digging at Skhul, and Arthur Keith, now retired from the Royal College of Surgeons to an almost nominal supervision at the Buckston Browne Research Farm housed in and around Darwin's former home, Down House in Downe, Kent. Keith had been suffering from ill health for some years, the cause of which proved—in 1932—to be tuberculosis. His position as master of the research farm was intended to supplement his pension and to provide Keith with adequate funds to live on until his death.

Though Keith recovered from his tuberculosis, his stamina was impaired. McCown was faced with a delicate task. The burials from Skhul had been removed in large blocks, which were at first sent to the Royal

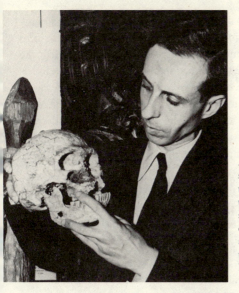

46. Theodore McCown holding the Skhul 5 skull of an early modern human from Palestine (now Israel), when it was presented to the American School of Prehistoric Research in 1946. The fossils from Skhul, including this specimen, are among the most ancient representatives of modern humans; tools like those made by Neandertals in Palestine were also found at Skhul.

College and eventually moved to Downe. Simply removing the bones from the rocky matrix in which they were encased proved a considerable technical challenge. Once that was accomplished, there was the task of measuring, describing, and discerning the significance of the remains— an aspect of the work in which Keith's expertise and experience would be invaluable. But Keith was tired, sometimes ill, and often unable to stand up to the rigors of daily study that he had once enjoyed. In 1934, McCown moved to the farm to help Keith get on with the work.

In that same year, Keith's wife of thirty-six years, Celia, died. Keith, understandably, found it even more difficult to settle down and work after this loss. However, after a few months he developed an "intimate comradeship" with a woman he identifies in his autobiography only as M., and the two undertook several extended trips in the next few years, visiting both vacation spots and sites of archeological or paleontological interest. Keith portrays it as a gentle but delightful romance that endured the rest of his life.

Well earned though these pleasant diversions were, they took much of Keith's time. The energetic McCown simply assumed ever more responsibility for the work and was doubtless pleased to do so. Still, when the resultant monograph, the second volume of *The Stone Age of Mount Carmel*, was published in 1939, it had a distinctly Keithian ring. The problem with the remains was that they were disconcertingly variable.

Even in the field, it was clear that the individuals from Skhul had many features in common with Neandertals from elsewhere: large, thick skulls with heavy browridges; strong limb bones; shin bones showing the retroversion of the tibial plateau that had led Boule to declare Neandertals' gait shuffling. Even the baby had a "massive little mandible."

But the female skeleton from the next-door cave, Tabun, was different, even though it was found in a Lower Mousterian level believed to be contemporaneous with that from which the Skhul fossils had come. In an early report, McCown characterized the situation openly:

> The important contrasts, however, are in the anatomical characters of the bones themselves. . . . There are striking differences between this jaw [from Tabun] and those of several of the Skhul people but the most evident contrasts are with the massive, male mandible discovered in the same layer of the same cave. . . . The limbs of the Tabun skeleton, in comparison with the Skhul bones, are relatively short and slight. The contrast between the massive, lengthy limbs of the Skhul skeletons IV and V and those of the Tabun female are impressive. Even allowing for differences due to sex, they are undeniably very great.

Keith's opinion, added as a note at the end of the report, differs. Young McCown has done an admirable job in extracting the skeletons, he avers; Keith is "entirely satisfied with the manner in which the work is being done under him and with the progress that he is making." However, Keith is not about to let anyone believe McCown's assertion of the great differences within the Mount Carmel skeletons. Sprinkling his remarks with face-saving compliments to McCown, Keith concludes:

> With a wide experience of fossil man to guide me I have to admit that the human beings now being uncovered by Mr. McCown are the most imposing specimens of fossil humanity I have ever seen. . . . Mr. McCown has expressed a suspicion that more than one race of Neandertal Palestinians may be represented by these fossil skeletons. He instances the differences in chin formation and in strength and proportions of the limb bones. This may be so but my own impression, which may have to be modified as further evidence comes to light, is that we are dealing with individuals of one race and that this race is a member of the same genus as that to which the Neandertalians of Europe belong. The Neandertal Palestinians make, I think, a rather nearer approach to the type of modern humanity than do the Neandertal Europeans.

The problem was that the fossils that appeared to be older also appeared to be less Neandertaloid. Could modern humans have preceded

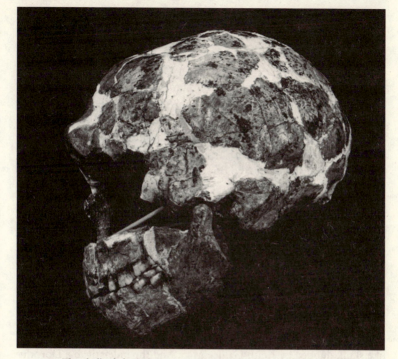

47. The skull of the Tabun 1 Neandertal skeleton, found in Mugharet-et-Tabun in Mount Carmel, Palestine (now Israel). The Tabun fossil documented for the first time the presence of true Neandertals outside Europe.

Neandertals in the region, only to be replaced by migration or evolution with Neandertals? This would be the reverse of the picture seen in Europe and the opposite of what common sense or prevailing prejudice would suggest. And so, in the end, it was Keith's authoritative voice that was heard, and the early modern human skeletons recovered from Skhul were lumped in with the Neandertals from Tabun as a single, highly variable population. What they saw in the Mount Carmel remains was familiar, Keith maintained; the paradigm developed on the basis of the European remains had only to be stretched a little to incorporate a Near Eastern branch of the family rather than be rewritten entirely.

As the interwar era drew to a close, Keith maintained his precarious control over human evolutionary studies in the English-speaking world with difficulty. Neither William Sollas nor Grafton Elliot Smith were inclined to allow Keith to glean all of the credit for new ideas on human evolution and the fossil record that spoke of it. Across the Atlantic, a growing number of Americans—people such as Aleš Hrdlička at the

Smithsonian, Henry Fairfield Osborn and William King Gregory at the American Museum of Natural History, George Grant MacCurdy at Yale, and Earnest Hooton at Harvard (the first American professor of physical anthropology)—felt more than free to comment on new fossil finds and to write popular books on human origins. While few of these American scholars traveled to Europe or Asia to examine the fossils and sites themselves, they were in active contact with their European colleagues. Indeed, they often had as much (or as little) firsthand experience with the material as did Keith or Boule.

During this time, Keith and Boule worked hard to integrate an incredible range of new material into their old, authoritative framework. There was a veritable blizzard of new specimens, most poorly understood at the time and only later to become important, that had been unearthed across the Old World.

In 1924, an enigmatic braincase that might, for once, actually be pathological was found on the west bank of the Blue Nile at Singa, in what was then Anglo-Egyptian Sudan. Arthur Smith Woodward pronounced it an ancestral Bushman. In 1925, a British engineer and amateur archeologist named Francis Turville-Petre excavated the cave of Zuttiyeh, near the Sea of Galilee, finding part of the upper face from a Neandertal-like skull, dubbed by Keith Galilee Man. And the indefatigable Dorothy Garrod, working at the Devil's Tower Cave in Gibraltar in 1926, turned up most of the skull of a juvenile Neandertal. In 1929, the quarry at Saccopastore, a site now within the city limits of Rome, yielded an almost complete cranium; a more fragmentary one followed in 1935. In time, these were studied in detail by the father of modern human paleontology in Italy, Sergio Sergi.

Halfway around the world, two paleontologists, W. F. F. Oppenoorth and G. H. R. von Koenigswald, had been working in central Java since 1931, following up on Dubois's success. They collected portions of the crania of twelve individuals, along with two tibias, from a river terrace overlooking the Solo River at Ngandong. These odd-looking Javanese fossils were poorly dated but were nonetheless given the dubious appellation "tropical Neandertals."

Further confounding attempts to make a single coherent story of the fossil record were two more fossils found in 1933 and 1935–36. One came from a quarry at Steinheim-an-den-Murr near Stuttgart, Germany; the other from archeological excavations at Swanscombe, on a river terrace of the Thames in Kent, England. The Steinheim cranium was small and rounded—probably, it was later shown, due to postmortem warping—yet had a large browridge. Though it was quickly and accurately described by Hans Weinert, the anthropologist responsible for reassembling the Le Moustier skull properly, few scholars were certain of its position in the human family tree. The two fragments of braincase from Swanscombe were equally puzzling, even after a third piece was found in 1955. This later find was little short of a miracle, since the site had been used as a source of ballast during the D-Day landing in Normandy in World War II. Still, the crucial frontal bone, which would show whether or not the skull once boasted a hefty browridge, was missing. Numerous reconstructions of that region were made, but none was convincing.

Most of these numerous new finds were described in detail at the time—some by Keith, none by Boule. But they had little effect on the schemes of human evolution endorsed in Paris and London. The specimens that didn't fit were either denied, like Dart's Taung baby, or misread, like some of the Mount Carmel remains. Others, like the *Sinanthropus* fossils, were allotted new branches on the human evolutionary tree (by Keith) or grafted onto preexisting branches (by Boule, when he argued correctly that *Sinanthropus* was nothing more or less than *Pithecanthropus* in China). Neandertals were eclipsed by the attention being given to all the new and much older fossils. "Neanderthal Man," as the contemporaneous term was, remained a dimly lit, ill-focused figure, easily forgotten but for its troubling resemblances to *Pithecanthropus* and *Sinanthropus*. Piltdown, or something very close to it, was stoutly defended as the true ancestor of modern humans, despite continued unease. Many American scientists were openly skeptical of the association of the Piltdown cranium and mandible into one creature, and as no more Piltdown-like fossils were found, doubts began to grow in Europe as well.

As war again grew ever closer, tempers frayed and optimism grew threadbare. The nature of physical differences among humans paled next to the growing suspicion of deep-rooted psychological ones. Were there no common rules of decency, no species-wide standards of behavior?

Into this climate of bewildered concern came a new fossil, discovered at Monte Circeo, Italy, in the Grotta Guattari. Its story is one of the last of the peaceful days, a charming tale of happenstance discovery that took place only months before the world went to war again.

Some details have blurred, and others have been embroidered with the passage of time. One fact is clear: the day of discovery was February 25, 1939, shortly after the wedding of Alberto Blanc a keen fossil-hunter, though his bride was *not* the young Guattari daughter, as is sometimes stated. The Guattari family owned a large parcel of land and a small, charming hotel in the village of San Felice Circeo, near Monte Circeo, a conspicuous, large limestone promontory that rises above the Pontine plain some one hundred kilometers south of Rome. Monte Circeo is reputed to be the place where the legendary Ulysses met the enchantress Circe, who changed his men into swine.

On this ordinary day in February, workmen employed by the Guattaris were engaged in some mundane task or other—some say it was planting a vineyard or garden, others talk of building a chicken coop—when one of the workers accidentally broke through the roof of a cave no one had known was there. Someone entered the cave and crawled around, exploring. It was known that young Alberto was interested in fossils, so perhaps the intent was to see if the cave would be of interest to him, a sort of prehistoric wedding present.

The cave proved large and dark; no one had brought a light, not anticipating the discovery. The explorer fumbled about, reaching into the darkness with naked hands, peering at objects only dimly apprehended whose shapes seemed distorted and queer. He touched rocks, earth, then bones: finally, a skull covered in the stalagmitic encrustations known as cave coral. Here was a prize for Alberto! Some accounts say he replaced the skull as best he could in its original position, but others assert that it was removed from the cave at the time of discovery. In any case, neither drawing nor photograph was made—indeed, neither could be made in the darkness—of the original position of the skull, a point that was to swell in importance like the proverbial toad eating flies.

In Blanc's hands, the undocumented position of this Neandertal skull from a small town in Italy was to reverse Circe's story, transmuting the brutish, animalistic Neandertal into a sensitive, religious human.

7

Global Thinking for Global Times

1940–1954

When Alberto Blanc arrived at Monte Circeo and inspected the cave, interrupting his honeymoon, he could not have foreseen that his interpretation of its contents would tip the balance, resurrecting Neandertals as human. His source of pleasure was simpler and more immediate. When he wriggled through the cave's constricted entrance, beret on his head and trowel in hand, he found the interior to be dark and large—fifteen meters long and up to twelve meters across—and low: nowhere was the ceiling higher than one and a half meters. But the floor in the main chamber was liberally sprinkled with fossilized animal bones: more than enough material to interest him.

The cranium had been found, according to Blanc's interviews with the discoverer, in an area that was immediately elevated in importance by a grandiose name Antro dell'Uomo ("Chamber of Man"). It was simply one of the smaller chambers that budded off from the main room. What's more, when asked, the discoverer agreed that the skull had been placed bottom up within the center of a roughly circular collection of stones that Blanc had spotted. To be sure, Blanc may well have pointed at the arrangement of stones and asked if that was where the skull had come from—a classic leading question—but there can be no doubt that he believed the answer. Blanc himself had not seen the placement before the cranium was moved—indeed, it is scarcely credible that the discoverer did—nor was he present when the next Neandertal fossil, a mandible that may be from the same individual, turned up a few days later. Blanc himself directed excavations of the cave for a while, and then turned

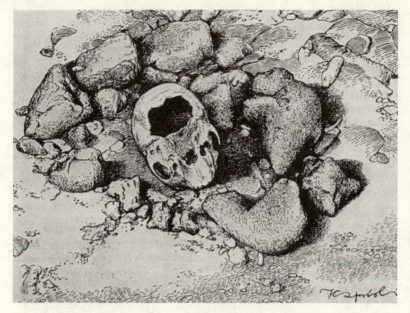

48. Alberto Blanc's reconstruction of the Guattari cranium in the "circle of
stones." It is still not known exactly where the fossil was found on the surface
of the cave, but it is unlikely that humans intentionally placed the skull within
an artificially created circle of stones.

them over to another paleontologist, Luigi Cardini. In 1950, a second
Neandertal mandible was found near one of the cave entrances.

Blanc's interpretation of the skull was to have a profound impact on
human evolutionary studies. Over the next twenty years, he was to weave
the cranium's placement (in what rapidly became a "crown of stones")
and breakage ("to extract the brain") into a theory of Neandertal ritual
behavior so compelling that it became nearly as entrenched as the fossils
themselves. Perhaps Blanc's claims about the Neandertal skull from
Guattari simply reflected the mood that was in the air, rather than
shaped the change, for the evidence itself was not strong. Skeptical
reexaminations of the Monte Circeo material and records in the late
twentieth century offer little support for his theories. Even the "facts"
are in some doubt, and the crown of stones is close to being entirely
fictitious. As archeologist Mary Stiner, who restudied the material in the
late 1980s, observed:

> The arrangement of stones is recreated in an exhibit in the Pigorini
> Museum in Rome, apparently based on Cardini's map made many
> years beforehand. Cardini's map provides excellent documentation

of the bone distributions on the surface, but it only shows stones at the location where the skull was found and excludes all otherwise identical stones. . . . [There was] a pavement of . . . stones on the surface.

Yet despite the stony ground upon which Blanc had sown his intellectual seeds, they grew and flourished. Suddenly Neandertals looked very different to everyone. It was not so much a resurrection, perhaps, as a renaissance—literally, Neandertals' rebirth as humans—that had begun.

It had been known since the early days of the century, at least, that Neandertals buried their dead. Indeed, it was a contentious point initially, probably because the much-despised Otto Hauser was the first to announce a Neandertal burial, and many rivals did not want to lend their support to anything Hauser said. Shortly thereafter, Amédée and Jean Bouyssonie found and described what they called a burial and funeral feast at La Chapelle-aux-Saints. And on August 8, 1912, a commission of some of Europe's most distinguished prehistorians—including Blanc's father, the Abbés Henri Breuil and both Bouyssonnies, and Hugo Obermaier, later of the Institut de Paléontologie Humaine—had produced a sworn document declaring that the remains from La Ferrassie discovered by Louis Capitan and Denis Peyrony had provided "absolute evidence" that Neandertals deliberately buried their dead, "without leaving any doubt."

The evidence grew with the years. By the time excavations were finished at La Ferrassie in 1934, seven individual burials had been found: a man, a woman, two children, and three infants. One of the skeletons, that of a child of about four years of age, was headless; the skull was buried a short distance away, covered with a large stone marked with a series of artificial, cuplike depressions. Placed in the graves with the man and several of the children were flint tools. There were additional pits and trenches—some empty, some containing animal bones. Yet somehow little attention had been paid to the broader implications of burials for Neandertals' beliefs and behaviors.

Now Blanc had found what he took to be evidence not merely of the mechanical act of burial but also of ritual behavior—spirituality, even. The Neandertal man whose skull was found at Monte Circeo showed an ancient, unhealed fracture to the right temple: evidence of the prehistoric murder of an individual struck down from behind. But following the Monte Circeo man's death, the treatment of his body was complex. Blanc believed that the Guattari cranium had been separated from the body and deliberately placed within a crown of stones inside the cave. Then, the

skull had been intentionally broken open and the brain extracted for a
ritual cannibal feast. The empty braincase itself had perhaps been used
as a cup or chalice in a further ritual, involving the sacrifice or consump-
tion of the animals (mostly red deer, fallow deer, and aurochs, a type of
wild ox) whose bones were scattered about the floor. This implied not
simply caring for other individuals to the extent of disposing of their
remains, but a belief in the afterlife and even, perhaps, the concept of
inheriting the qualities of the dead person by consuming his brain.

Aside from the putative positioning of the fossil, Blanc relied on a
somewhat facile analysis of the breakage of the cranium. Working with
Sergio Sergi at the University of Rome, Blanc emphasized the similarity
in the damage found on the Grotta Guattari skull and on skulls in the

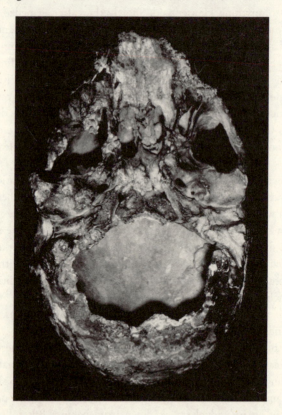

49. Underside of the human skull from the Grotta Guattari in Monte Circeo,
showing the enlarged opening at the base of the braincase. Although interpreted by Alberto Blanc and Sergio Sergi as the product of a cannibalistic
ritual, the hole was probably made by the gnawing of small carnivores, such
as wolves or foxes.

50. Sergio Sergi (left) and Alberto Blanc (right), in April 1939, with the Guattari cranium which they interpreted as evidence of the religious beliefs of Neandertals. The Saccopastore 1 cranium, found earlier in Rome, is on the table behind Sergi, who suggested it was a good example of a Neandertal ancestor.

university's collections from Melanesian headhunters. The haunting resemblances didn't stop there. "It is interesting," Blanc observed, "that Peking Man, living many thousands of years earlier and in another part of the world, is discovered to have mutilated the skull at the base in a similar fashion."

Though Blanc was clearly suggesting a stunning antiquity for head-hunting and ritual cannibalism, he was only seconding a suggestion made about the Zhoukoudian remains by Franz Weidenreich in 1939. Why, Weidenreich asked himself, did the cave produce too many *Sinanthropus* heads for the number of limb bones, when the other animals showed more expected proportions? Why was the face broken away on each and the foramen magnum (the large hole through which the spinal cord passed from the brain to the body) enlarged? Why were there stone tools, hearths, and abundant burnt bones? The answer, he argued, was canni-balism. The accusation reverberated through years of sinister interpreta-tions of Neandertals. It amplified anew the voices that had previously spoken of Neandertal cannibalism, at Krapina or La Naulette, and transformed these suspicions into certainties—yes, Peking Man was a savage, too.

For years, too, the idea of a Paleolithic cult of the skulls had been

growing among paleoanthropologists. Monte Circeo became the epitome, the confirming instance that "proved" the rule. Now paleoanthropologists saw everywhere skulls with no bodies, crania with no jaws.
Excavated remains of early humans at Ngandong, Java, or at Steinheim,
Germany, in the early 1930s were drawn into the cult of the skulls. The
newly discovered Neandertal site of Teshik-Tash, in Uzbekistan, offered
yet another variation: the skeleton of a child was said to be encircled by
pairs of horn cores from wild goats. Mixed into this witches' brew of
vague beliefs was the so-called cult of the cave bears—a notion borrowed
many years later by Jean Auel for her immensely successful novel, *Clan
of the Cave Bear*. Skulls of cave bears—found, not surprisingly, in
caves—were seen as objects involved in ancient rituals, rather than as the
remains of cave-dwelling animals that had died in their dens. The notion
of a cult of the skulls (be they parts of humans, goats, or bears) and of
the ritual behavior of Neandertals became so strong that alternative
explanations simply never occurred to anyone, still less were they explored seriously.

Many anthropologists of the war and postwar years found it almost
self-evident that Neandertals and other primitive humans had attached
a peculiar importance to the skulls of the dead—of a ritual behavior
known under the general term *secondary* or *two-stage burial*. It might
involve cannibalism, but it was cannibalism redeemed by religious beliefs—evidence of a misguided but heartfelt spirituality.

Blanc's impassioned exposition of these ideas led to their widespread
tacit acceptance. Very human ideals, values, and religious beliefs were
projected back into the remote past inhabited by Neandertals and even
earlier human ancestors. Formerly primitive savages, Neandertals were
now nearly human. The discovery and publication a few years before of
numerous skeletons from Mount Carmel—what Theodore McCown
had dubbed a cemetery—simply paved the way for Blanc's humanization
of Neandertals, which transformed them from profane to sacred.

In fact, a striking illustration published by an American anthropologist, Carleton Coon, in the year of the Guattari discovery became the
new and potent symbol of Neandertals' humanity. Coon's 1939 book,
The Races of Europe, was in general a traditional, typological attempt to
divide humanity into racial groups. He drew a map showing seventeen
different racial groups scattered across Europe and adjacent areas of Asia.
One of his main points was that perceived racial differences among living
humans are strongly influenced by superficial characteristics such as hair

color, style of clothing, and so on. To reinforce his assertion, Coon provided an eye-catching sketch of the Old Man from La Chapelle-aux-Saints wearing a natty porkpie hat, coat, white shirt, and discreetly patterned tie; how human he looked. Even with his large nose and strongly projecting face, he would hardly have attracted attention strolling with Coon across Harvard Yard. Although twenty-odd years were to pass before Coon made another major contribution to the study of Neandertals, this reconstruction was vitally important. A generation earlier, Boule's depiction of the very same individual as a stooping, bent-kneed Neandertal had wide influence; now Coon's image of the Neandertal as essentially human infiltrated his readers' minds and stuck.

Another major influence in the abrupt shift in the view of Neandertals was the acceptance of the yet-more-primitive and potentially cannibalistic *Pithecanthropus* and *Sinanthropus* (both today agreed to be *Homo erectus*) fossils. An additional boon was the literally apish *Australopithecus* fossils that Raymond Dart and now Robert Broom kept producing from South Africa. If such almost-chimps were our ancestors, how much more familiar and friendly must the Neandertals have seemed?

The publicity attending Blanc's work at the Grotta Guattari had another effect: San Felice Circeo became a favored resort town, with an establishment called the Hotel Neanderthal that may have been the successor to Signor Guattari's modest hotel. Although Neandertal remains had been found with little fanfare at Saccopastore, Italy, in 1929 and again in 1935, the theories about early religion made the Monte Circeo cranium the first Neandertal from Italy to receive much attention.

While the Monte Circeo skull and its treatment represented an increasingly metaphysical aspect of Neandertal studies, another equally strong trend was an opposing movement toward an ever more scientific and rigorous treatment of fossils. It was all part of a broader resurgence of interest and confidence in science in the postwar years.

By 1945, there was a more than healthy confidence in the ability of modern scientists to attack and solve problems. Human nature and human evolution were but two of these. This era also saw the greatest advance in the understanding of evolution since Darwin, as the new-found information about the mechanisms of inheritance was welded to notions of natural selection and genetic change that had developed in the intervening years. This fusion of old and new information, of process and mechanism, became known as the "evolutionary synthesis" and had an immeasurable effect on all biological sciences.

That traits were passed from parents to offspring had been known for centuries. That the expression of many such traits worked according to fairly simple mathematical principles had been widely known since the pea-plant experiments of the Austrian monk Gregor Mendel had been rediscovered in 1900. Working with simple traits, Mendel showed that one gene for each trait came from the father and one from the mother, with predictable results. But the new synthesis offered the how of inheritance—the combination of genetic information contained in the chromosomes—and of natural selection—a pruning of the frequency of genes within populations—that had been lacking in Darwin's presentation of the theory. The capstone of the new synthesis was the discovery of the structure of DNA (the molecule in which the genetic information is encoded), which was inferred in 1953 by James Watson and Francis Crick. Suddenly, very different sorts of information from different realms interlocked in a wonderfully powerful whole.

Fittingly, there was a Huxley at the forefront of the developing synthesis: Julian Huxley, grandson of Thomas Henry Huxley and one of the many celebrated artists and scientists in the family. The young Huxley was also a gifted scholar, an enthusiastic ornithologist and field biologist, an experimentalist of note, and a writer of appealing clarity. Tall, charming, quick-witted, and eclectic, he was perhaps the best-known biologist of postwar Britain and in a perfect position to fuse information from disparate fields.

Huxley found he had inherited his grandfather's knack for explaining science and its implications in terms that were both lucid and enjoyable. He soon became perhaps the first scientific celebrity, serving as a radio and newspaper commentator on matters biological and writing many popular books on biology, which spread his influence far wider than did his teaching posts at various prestigious universities in the United States and Britain. In 1934, he conceived of and produced the first natural-history film that was a popular success (it was about a colony of seabirds, gannets, on a Welsh island) and was instrumental in winning him the highly visible position as secretary of the London Zoological Society. After leaving the London Zoo, Huxley wrote and broadcast one of the most popular radio shows in wartime Britain. Among his propaganda efforts was an influential pamphlet detailing the flaws in Germany's "scientific" racism.

Huxley was also unafraid to tackle thorny problems and wrote compellingly of his personal philosophy, what he called "evolutionary humanism." It was based, first, on the notion that humans, like other animals, are products of evolution and are not divinely created or guided. But that is not all. This belief, he wrote:

> ... affirms that knowledge and understanding can be increased, that conduct and social organization can be improved, and that more desireable directions for individual and social development can be found. As the overriding aim of evolving man, it is driven to reject power, or mere numbers of people, or efficiency, or material exploitation, and to envisage greater fulfillment and fuller achievement as his true goal.

Through this philosophy, Huxley spoke for many intellectuals and scientists of his day.

With this behind him, Huxley embarked on his masterful overview of the progress in the biological sciences, publishing in 1942 what was probably his most important and enduring work, *Evolution: The Modern Synthesis*. It was neither the only book of the new synthesis, nor even the first, but it was one of the most widely read.

Huxley was able to draw together into a single, comprehensible whole the works of two very disparate groups of biologists who had been separated by a widening gulf since the early twentieth century. On the one hand were the natural-historian types, out of the mold of Darwin, who actually observed species in the wild. Their concerns were to establish the taxonomy, or evolutionary classification, of one species relative to another and also, in many instances, to document a species' anatomy, ecology, and behavior as a means of understanding its evolutionary history. The whole organism and its life were the subject of their studies. It was a biology of ultimate causes.

Since 1900, there were also the geneticists, whose field took a massive bound in popularity with the rediscovery of Mendel's rules of genetics. Their concern was the process of evolution: how genetic information was encoded and passed on; what the connection was between the genetic information (the genotype) and its expression in the individual who carried those genes (the phenotype); and, above all, whether natural selection or mutation drove evolution. They manipulated the mating behavior or environment of short-lived species, carefully recording the outcome, looking for patterns of inheritance, and trying to pair physical traits such as eye color (phenotype) with specific regions of DNA (genotype) that encoded for them. Some worked at a microscopic level, neglecting the organism and studying only the shape, size, and number of its chromosomes. Still others were yet more removed from the organism, preferring to work on a purely theoretical and mathematical level as they tried to identify the rules by which the frequencies of different genes changed within hypothetical populations under imaginary constraints. Thus, the geneticists' was an experiment-based biology of proximate causes. But, as Ernst Mayr characterized the geneticists:

> . . . [They] were only concerned with transformational evolution. Their focus was entirely on genes and characters, and on their changes (transformation) in time. They wrote as if they were unaware that there are taxa, and that they (different populations, species, and so on) are the real actors on the evolutionary stage.

With entirely different data, jargon, and questions, it is little wonder that the practitioners of the two branches of biology rarely spoke to each other. Indeed, if the later remembrances of those who participated in the synthesis are to be believed, practically everyone came to the same conclusions independently—which seems intrinsically unlikely, but these were contagious ideas.

Huxley was one of the few who could and did speak to both camps; so were George Gaylord Simpson, a renowned American paleontologist; Theodosius Dobzhansky, the preeminent expert on fruit flies; and Ernst Mayr, an ornithologist and specialist in taxonomy.

Simpson was almost alone in anchoring his paleontological works explicitly in Darwinian theory—trying to trace and explain the actions of natural selection in the fossil record. It was a time when many other prominent paleontologists either sidestepped the issue (naming and describing a past species without reference to any evolutionary trends) or focused on the transformation of anatomical features through time without reference to mechanisms, selection, or populations. In 1944, Simpson produced his great book, *Tempo and Mode in Evolution*, in which he wrote:

> The attempted synthesis of paleontology and genetics . . . may be particularly surprising and possibly hazardous. Not long ago, paleontologists felt that a geneticist was a person who shut himself in a room, pulled down the shades, watched small flies disporting themselves in milk bottles, and thought that he was studying nature. . . . On the other hand, the geneticists said that paleontology had no further contributions to make to biology, that its only point had been the completed demonstration of the truth of evolution, and that it was a subject too purely descriptive to merit the name

"science." The paleontologist, they believed, is like a man who undertakes to study the principles of the internal combustion engine by standing on a street corner and watching the motor cars whiz by.

That nicely summed up the problem, which Simpson proceeded to dispel by using the fossil record to show that small, incremental changes guided by natural selection led to the adaptation of populations. It was quantitative changes, both in gene frequencies themselves and in the phenotypic expression of genes, that differentiated first one population from another and, ultimately, one species from another. In short, Simpson demonstrated that the fossil record was entirely consistent with both genetic theory as applied to populations, and with the Darwinian notion that natural selection was the primary force at work. With this single book, Simpson was largely responsible for infecting paleontology with both population or statistical concepts and genetic mechanisms.

Simpson's ideas dovetailed nicely with those of Dobzhansky. A geneticist at Columbia University, Dobzhansky worked in both the field and the laboratory on the evolution of fruit flies, those ubiquitous and annoying little insects that make up the genus *Drosophila.* He conducted careful studies of the inherited characteristics of these flies, using laboratory experiments to produce evolutionary changes in various features under specific conditions and then discovering the natural distribution of variable features in the wild. Dobzhansky tried to build the links between the natural histories of populations—their adaptations to changing situations—and the formation of new species. In a sense, he provided the modern experiments and observations that filled in the details of the principles that Simpson was applying to the broader sweep of time seen in the fossil record.

Also essential to the synthesis was a new concept of what a species was, or is. Species were not typological—could not be represented accurately by a single archetypal specimen—they were intermingling and interbreeding groups of populations. Ernst Mayr was particularly effective in putting forth the "biological species concept," as it came to be called. Mayr argued compellingly that geographic isolation was the most common and effective means of producing reproductive isolation: the first step in speciation and one that recalled the words of Alfred Russel Wallace so many years before.

On the genetic side lay great men such as Ronald Fisher, Sewall Wright, and J. B. S. Haldane. These men explored the mathematical and statistical aspects of genetics; they were, to a large extent, theoretical biologists—experts at mathematical modeling rather than keen observers of organisms.

Unlike most of their colleagues, these men became alert to the fascinating problems of *evolutionary* biology. Experimentalists and mathematical geneticists began to show that unnatural (humanly induced) selection acting on even minor differences had considerable power to alter populations, the same point Simpson had made using the fossil record as data. Indeed, though Darwin lacked an understanding of the mechanism, the observations were very similar to his on pigeon breeding and other topics, which he used in *The Origin of Species* to explain the idea of natural selection. The new synthesis offered the mechanism that, coupled with the biological species concept, could empower Darwinian evolution to enter a new era.

For those brought up after the new synthesis, all of these ideas seem tediously self-evident; the fusion of genetics and Darwinian thought, into neo-Darwinism, is a common and dominant paradigm. But for decades between and during the wars, biology was pulling in two separate directions. The true sign that the synthesis had finally occurred, argues Mayr in his reminiscences, was the outcome of a momentous symposium held at Princeton University on January 2–4, 1947. An impressive array of "paleontologists, morphologists, ecologists, ethologists, systematists, and geneticists of various schools" was invited from both the United States and Britain. And miraculously, as Mayr recalled later:

> . . . it was almost impossible to get a controversy going, so far-reaching was the basic agreement among the participants. To test the reliability of my memory, I circulated a questionnaire among the survivors. . . . All of them recalled an essential agreement among all the participants on the gradual mode of evolution, with natural selection as the basic mechanism and only direction-giving force. . . . It was not that the synthesis was hammered out during the Princeton conference—rather, the conference constitutes the most convincing documentation that a synthesis had occurred during the preceding decade. . . . Evolutionary biology was no longer split into two noncommunicating camps.

The impact of the new synthesis on paleoanthropology was ultimately profound and disruptive but seemed infinitely slow in coming. When these ideas struck the field, it was like a cue ball smacking into the rack, sending all the previously tightly ordered tenets ricocheting in entirely new directions.

The delay can be attributed to the character of physical anthropology as a field at the time. Most physical anthropologists in Europe and the United States had been trained mainly as comparative anatomists, studying static physical forms. They were anatomists of the dead, never forced to grapple with living populations in the throes of evolutionary change. The very material they studied led them to tend to think of populations typologically, in terms of an average or ideal form ("the" chimpanzee or "the" Hottentot), rather than appreciating the patterns of variation.

Paul Broca, and after him, Paul Topinard, Léonce-Pierre Manouvrier, Gustav Schwalbe, Aleš Hrdlička, and Earnest Hooton, had led physical anthropology to become one of the most rigorously quantitative of the biological sciences during the first half of the twentieth century. It was virtually the only field then that had a standard reference manual for measurements—a compendium of detailed definitions of measurements and a table of average measurements for various samples of human populations around the world. That book, *Lehrbuch der Anthropologie (Handbook of Anthropology),* had been first published in 1914 by Rudolf Martin, a Swiss-German anthropologist, to be revised and updated three times. In America, one of Hrdlička's last important publications was his own version of such a handbook in 1939, called *Practical Anthropometry*, which was based largely on his own work with Manouvrier. Others were to follow.

Yet, even though so many of the physical anthropologists amassed vast data sets on the physical variability in modern humans, few of them used any statistical techniques to evaluate the significance of the variations they documented. Many, like Hrdlička, openly disdained statistics, and few thought there was anything to be gained from applying to human evolution fancy methods that had been developed in many cases to aid in the breeding of agricultural crops. None seem to have appreciated the scientific strength that a statistical, probabilistic statement can impart.

The mistrust of statistics also sprang from a lingering distaste for the way in which statistics had been used by some geneticists and psychologists to bolster overtly racist plans or to implement eugenics schemes. Some of the major advances in complex statistics during the early twentieth century were made in an attempt to sort different human groups on the basis of their perceived mental and physical characteristics. Those anthropologists who did not dismiss statistics out of hand were usually too ignorant of the techniques to apply them properly. In fact, on the whole, physical anthropologists of this era relied on simple averages (means), occasionally supplemented by a statement of the highest and lowest values of a particular measurement (the range), to express all of the variability they observed. And averages quickly became muddled with the old-fashioned notion of types or ideal forms.

This psychological substitution of averages for ideal types is nowhere shown more clearly than at Harvard University. One of Earnest Hooton's Boston acquaintances, Dr. Dudley Sargent, measured large samples of young adult American men and women, and separately, many male and female undergraduates at Harvard and Radcliffe Colleges. Based on the average values of each measurement, a sculptor then created statues of the "ideal" young American man and woman and the "ideal" Harvard and Radcliffe undergraduate. A tangible expression of the craze for measuring, these nude statues—cast, practically, in plaster but bronzed for effect—stood, until recently, on display at Harvard's Peabody Museum, monuments to the typological thinking of that generation of scientists.

Genetics was little more welcome, at first, but gradually infiltrated and altered the thinking of the major scholars in the field. The change in the teaching emphasis at Harvard between Hooton and one of his most successful students, William Howells, illustrates the more general shift in opinion. Joseph Birdsell, who received his Ph.D. under Hooton in 1941, remembered him as a scholar who "had little use for and no real knowledge of the emerging field of genetics." The Princeton conference had not yet been held when Birdsell was at Harvard, and the new evolutionary synthesis had not yet gelled. By the time Howells took over Hooton's job ten years later, the books and papers of the new evolutionary synthesis were required reading.

Many of the older generation of anthropologists simply found it too painful to adjust to this new, potent current of thought and some, like Hrdlička and Boule, died before it came to fruition. Indeed, Mayr recalls that at the 1950 Cold Spring Harbor conference on human evolution, which was convened to introduce the new synthesis into physical anthropology, Hooton opened a discussion session with the remark, "I hate the word 'population.' " But in general, population thinking—the awareness of the variability within species, especially those spread over large geographic areas—was incorporated into anthropological studies rapidly in the United States and England.

This led to a curious inversion of international relationships. Before World War II, most of the fossils had been found and most of the ideas were generated within Europe; Americans had been mainly on the receiving end. To be blunt, Americans didn't have the goods and had little firsthand knowledge of them; as anthropologists, only a few American scholars were well respected by European scholars. Now, although the fossils continued to be discovered mostly by Europeans, at home or in their colonial outposts, the new ideas and interpretations began to flow from the other side of the Atlantic. Americans were suddenly in the forefront and made their European colleagues look archaic and slow. New approaches to the questions of human evolution began to produce effects that few could have anticipated.

For one thing, the old variability problem took on new aspects. The first tendrils of population biology had been present for years—for example, in the massive anthropometric surveys, such as those Hrdlička was fond of—but now the rapidly maturing ideas promised a fruitful harvest. Variability in human form came to be seen as spread not simply through space but also through time.

As the ideas of the new synthesis infiltrated anthropology a curious sort of reawakening occurred. A strong consensus began to develop about human evolution, spurred in large part by prominent scientists of the new synthesis whose credentials in that intellectual revolution made them seem unimpeachable authorities on any evolutionary question. Starting around 1944 and continuing for ten years or more, Dobzhansky, Mayr, and Simpson independently began looking at the classification of fossil humans with fresh eyes. Although only one of these had any firsthand familiarity with mammalian evolution, a lack of direct experience with the material never stopped anyone from writing about human evolution. Indeed, one of the dominant traits of paleoanthropology as a field is its grand tradition of amateurs and outsiders—some of whom have catalyzed great advances in understanding and some of whom have effectively blocked or hindered productive work for years.

Theodosius Dobzhansky, the fruit-fly geneticist, ventured the opinion that the proliferation of names for fossil humans was probably based on an exaggerated appreciation of geographic variability. Ernst Mayr, the bird taxonomist, and G. G. Simpson, the paleontologist, came to the same conclusion. On biological criteria, they argued, there seemed to be too many different taxa (names) applied to hominids (humans and their fossil relatives). Each specimen seemed to be awarded not only a new species name but also a new genus. In an excess of enthusiasm for simplifying matters, Mayr wanted to place all hominids in the genus

Homo, as did Simpson. A less radical approach was generally adopted, although it was not formally suggested until 1960 and was then put forward by a University of Chicago anthropologist, F. Clark Howell. Howell, articulating what many were already thinking, slashed the number of genera to two: *Australopithecus*, Dart's very primitive, apelike creature; and *Homo*. For their part, *Pithecanthropus* and *Sinanthropus* were recognized as the same sort of creature and were merged into *Homo*, with the trivial name *erectus* since that had been proposed first. Such a revision in names is known, technically and evocatively, as "sinking" taxa—and sink the old names did, with hardly a ripple of protest. With one simple taxonomic revision, the entire pattern of relationships of fossil humans suddenly became clearer.

The Neandertals were already in *Homo*, so they presented no problem on the genus level. However, virtually everyone at the time placed them in their own species, *Homo neanderthalensis*. Similarly, the African fossils from Broken Hill were *Homo rhodesiensis*, and the Ngandong fossils that Oppenoorth and von Koenigswald had discovered in Indonesia were *Homo soloensis*. Clearly, to most paleontologists, these were merely geographical variants of the same human form, and so they could be sunk painlessly into a single species. Dobzhansky and Mayr went one giant step further; they sunk all these forms into *Homo sapiens*, thereby removing any species-level distinction between the Neandertals and ourselves. Even this forcible compression of human taxonomy raised few cries of protest. In the 1950s and 1960s, the anthropological community arrayed itself firmly on the side of minimizing differences and emphasizing the unity of humanity, and the mood carried over to taxonomic decisions.

This revision of the species name applied to the Neandertals was fascinating because it took place without any serious reexamination of the fossils. Whereas once contention and debate had predominated, this very important taxonomic revision was partly a political and social decision—one based largely on consensus and sentiment—partly a theoretical, biological one. Mayr, Dobzhansky, and Simpson had neither gathered new data about the fossils nor thoughtfully reviewed the old information in the light of the new views of variation and geography.

In fact, it was awkward to apply the new synthesis directly to the fossil record. At the heart of the problem was the biological species concept, which is based on the criterion of reproductive isolation of a population from others of similar-appearing organisms. The crucial issue is whether, in the wild, two populations interbreed and produce viable, fertile offspring. If they do, then they are conspecific: one species. If they do not, then they are reproductively isolated from one another: two species.

Unfortunately, this is an unpragmatic definition, difficult to use for living species under field conditions and impossible to apply to the fossil record. Who can tell if fossils would have interbred with each other? How copious a fossil record must be recovered before such a decision can be reached?

Thus, paleontologists were and are forced to use the degree of overall physical similarity between two fossils or two groups of fossils as a proxy for evidence of reproductive isolation. They ask—working with whatever body parts are preserved—whether the two are as different from each another as two known living species are. It usually proves to be a statistical exercise involving minute details of anatomy, often foundering on frustratingly incomplete material.

Neandertals are an exceptional case, for there are a goodly number of largely complete skeletons. But, curiously enough, there had been no overall, statistical evaluation comparing Neandertals and modern *Homo sapiens* since first Schwalbe and then Boule decided that Neandertals were sufficiently different from us to be classified as a separate species. The new synthesis idea of including Neandertals in *Homo sapiens* was perhaps securely based in modern evolutionary theory but—like the original naming of *Homo neanderthalensis* in 1864—it had precious little reference to the features of the fossils themselves.

The revision of hominid classification in the light of the new synthesis effectively solved, or at least shelved, the "Neandertal problem." The only lingering difficulty was *Eoanthropus*, which just wouldn't go away and wouldn't fit in. Piltdown was to lurk in the shadows as a problematic fossil for a few more years yet.

In the meantime, the influence of Julian Huxley and the borrowed ideas of the new synthesis led to another, explicit statement: that all living humans were a single species. The most visible symbol of this view was an official statement put out by UNESCO (the United Nations Educational, Scientific and Cultural Organization), an organization that had been strongly shaped by Huxley as its first director-general between 1946 and 1948. Issued in 1950, this lengthy explanation of the nature of race, as it was understood by modern science, was explicitly designed to "discredit racial doctrines in modern politics" and recalled Huxley's wartime propaganda pamphlet on the same subject. The UNESCO statement—intended to be scientific, liberal, fair-minded, and unify-ing—proved a boomerang, provoking a tidal wave of divisive and self-righteous protests from anthropologists. As one commentator described the situation:

> Anthropologists fell upon this document with such vigor that the English journal, *Man*, was for some months running what amounted to a department of criticism, correction, and amplifica-tion, in the form of letters from Great Britain, France, and the United States. So UNESCO quickly got together another panel in 1951 to do the Statement all over again. This time the draft was circulated widely, so that the rest of the profession could get its comments and abuse in early. By compressing the results UNESCO was able to publish the statement and the gist of the exceptions to it—a sort of minimum anthropological description of race—in a relatively small volume.

Argumentative individuals notwithstanding, what had suddenly come into focus was that humans as a species are *polytypic*, like many species known to biologists. This is a technical term meaning, literally, "many-shaped" but implying that differences in appearance are simply local variants, the way a particular shape of face or nose can ally the people from one region. It was a new, modern, and almost startlingly egalitarian pronouncement. It also made some of the older studies—such as the comparisons of the Mount Carmel skeletons to "a Bushman" and "a Sikh"—look typological and more than a little silly. Appearance and size of anatomical features varied, both within single populations and be-tween one population and the next. A wider range of reference than one or two individuals was obviously needed.

Soon thereafter, the global view anthropologists adopted led to three lasting changes that took place so rapidly and so nearly simultaneously that they are difficult to recount. They began in 1946, with the Harvard anthropologist Earnest Hooton.

Trained in the classics, Hooton nonetheless followed a research trajec-tory similar to that of Hrdlička or Manouvrier. He became one of the foremost somatologists, an expert in the variability in human shape and form, an interesting specialty considering his physical peculiarities. Hoo-ton was so short-necked that one former student remembers him jesting, "If I had a neck, I'd be a reasonably tall man." He also had a heavy jaw, overly long arms, large hands, and eyes sunk beneath a large brow demarcated with dark eyebrows. More than one student quipped that he was the missing link reborn. More to the point, however, Hooton was a consummate lecturer who had picked up an impressive British accent during a stint as a Rhodes scholar at Oxford. He had also adopted the British habit of being overtly polite while making scathingly insulting remarks. He was a fixture at Harvard and had great influence in American anthropology in general.

While the new synthesists were denying the differences among Neandertals, the Ngandong and Broken Hill fossils, and modern humans, Hooton—the expert in racial variation and no respecter of dogma—had looked at the Neandertal record again. He realized that there were real, meaningful, regional differences *within* the group of fossils called Neandertals. He felt that much of the confusion and difficulty arose from a failure to recognize these geographic variants. To Hooton, Neandertals seemed to come in two obvious varieties. There were the strong-featured, massively built, hyperrobust types, like La Chapelle-aux-Saints, which came mostly from western Europe—for which Hooton coined the term "classic Neandertals." Elsewhere, there were the more modern-looking, less extreme Neandertals, like those from central Europe, such as Krapina, or the Near East, as at Mount Carmel. Was this racial variation?

Working along similar lines, Franz Weidenreich was developing a captivating idea: that the regional variations in human form now recognized as racial differences were very ancient indeed, going back to the geographically separated populations of *Homo erectus*. Traditionally, these populations had been called *Sinanthropus pekinensis* in China, *Pithecanthropus erectus* in Java, and—for some very similar skulls discovered by G. H. R. von Koenigswald in Indonesia just before and during the war—*Pithecanthropus modjokertensis*, but all were really the same species.

Ironically, von Koenigswald's fossils were still available for study at the end of the war, while Weidenreich's were not. When the Japanese troops occupying Java threatened to seize the Indonesian fossils, von Koenigswald managed to substitute cunningly authentic-looking plaster casts for some of the originals in the safe at the Geological Survey. He then gave the originals to Swedish friends, who hid the larger pieces and buried others in milk bottles. There they remained until von Koenigswald was released from a prisoner of war camp on Java at the end of the hostilities. Only one of the Indonesian skulls was "looted," taken to Japan as a birthday present for the emperor. But it was found by Walter Fairservis, an American lieutenant who helped take over the Imperial

Palace and was later to become an archeologist working in Egypt and south Asia. Fairservis spotted the skull in a curio cabinet in the palace and by some extraordinary coincidence knew what it was. The fossil was duly returned to von Koenigswald—to his surprise—as he sat in the American Museum of Natural History in New York in September 1946, working with Weidenreich.

Whether he looked at plaster casts or originals, Weidenreich believed that what were being called separate species were actually populations of the same species. In fact, he argued:

> I believe that all primate forms recognized as hominids—no matter whether they lived in the past or live today—represent morphologically a unity when compared with other primate forms, and that they can be regarded as *one species. . . . If all hominid types and their variations, regardless of time and space, are taken into consideration, their arrangement in a continuous evolutionary line, leading from the most primitive state to the most advanced, does not meet with any difficulty. Neither gaps or deviations are recognizable.*

Fusing all hominids into *Homo sapiens* (which, after all, had been suggested by Mayr, Dobzhansky, and Simpson) left Weidenreich with some awkwardness in discussing different types. Therefore, he coined the cumbersome terms Archanthropinae for the *Pithecanthropus-Sinanthropus* group, Paleoanthropinae for the Neandertals, and Neoanthropinae for recent humans. He hoped to emphasize similarities by calling everything *Homo sapiens*, while recognizing regional differences with his new terms, but the proposal was self-defeating. By ending his terms in *-inae,* Weidenreich signaled that they were subfamilies, or groupings of several genera, even while he contradicted himself and asserted that all hominids were generically identical.

To wriggle out of this fix, Weidenreich cited G. G. Simpson, who had suggested, "Perhaps it would be better for the zoological taxonomist to set apart the family Hominidae and to exclude its nomenclature and classification from his studies." It is an astonishing remark that shows clearly the potency of Darwin's basic affront to Victorian sensibilities—his implicit suggestion that humans operated under the same "rules" as other animals—one hundred years later.

Nomenclatural problems aside, Weidenreich's vision was the first even partially successful attempt to provide a global synthesis of the information on human origins. He believed that a single, ancient human species had spread across the Old World into various geographic regions, such as Australia or Asia, in which they had largely remained. The "staying put" pattern gave time for localized characteristics and physical peculiarities to develop, even though he postulated interbreeding between adjacent groups.

There were two key features to Weidenreich's model. First, he believed that the evolution of the genus *Homo* (whether it was comprised of one or more species) was a phenomenon that had occurred across the Old World. This was not a European phenomenon nor even a development particularly centered in Europe. Second, the Neandertals of Europe were just one regional representative of their stage of human evolution, neither more nor less important to later developments than their (presumably) contemporaneous and anatomically similar relatives elsewhere. In fact, Weidenreich was equivocal as to the ultimate fate of the European Neandertals.

His views were neatly laid out in a geometric diagram of human evolution, a checkerboard with diagonals intersecting the corners of all squares. The vertical lines represent regional lineages, each labeled for a part of the Old World. The horizontal lines indicate stages, grades, or phases of human evolutionary development. The diagonal lines show the contact and genetic exchange between neighboring populations, or what would now be called gene flow, caused by interbreeding between adjacent groups. The diagram is precise, but also rather confusing. Weidenreich's stages were arranged with little regard for the fine points of geological time, though, admittedly, these were still poorly known.

In this scheme, each of the geographic lineages represented by a vertical line was evolving through Neandertals toward *Homo sapiens* in parallel, but Weidenreich believed that their progress in humanization proceeded at different rates. Thus, he observed:

> Homo sapiens [by which he meant, in this context, anatomically modern humans] is morphologically without a doubt "a late figure on the human stage." But this really late phase of human evolution may be reached in some regions of the earth earlier than in others and thus give the impression of preceding more primitive forms found in other regions.

This allowance for locally differing rates of evolution neatly swept any contradictions under the rug in a manner thoroughly satisfying to Weidenreich.

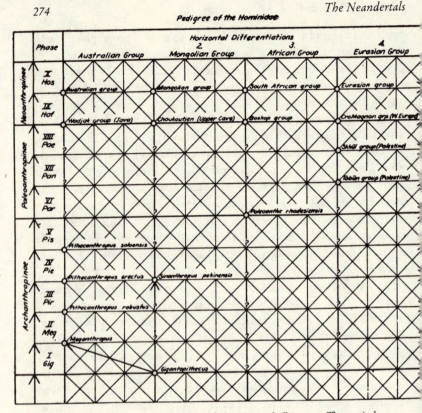

51. Franz Weidenreich's "Pedigree of the Hominidae" in 1947. The vertical lines represent genetic continuities within regions of the Old World, the horizontal lines represent stages of human evolution, and the diagonal lines indicate biological connections (gene flow) between populations living in adjacent regions.

Also, each group retained some of its special characteristics, so that Weidenreich could trace anatomical continuities between, say, *Pithecanthropus* from Java and modern aboriginal Australians or between early Chinese fossils and living Mongoloid peoples. He saw similar resemblances between the Broken Hill fossils and modern southern Africans or between the Mount Carmel remains and recent Europeans. Perhaps because he couldn't decide what to do with them, Weidenreich left the European Neandertals off the diagram completely.

Weidenreich's multiregionalism theory was criticized by some because it was more than reminiscent of the turn-of-the-century ideas of his former professor, Gustav Schwalbe, and of Aleš Hrdlička's more recent Neandertal phase theory. Those unilineal models of human evolution were out of favor and seemed overly simple. Few took the time to see the difference between Weidenreich's multiregionalism hypothesis and Schwalbe's or Hrdlička's Eurocentric schemes.

Another, more central problem was the apparent antiquity of the differences among the human races and the significance Weidenreich allocated to them. In the aftermath of the world wars, physical anthropologists were anxious to classify racial differences as trivial accidents of evolution, small-scale variations that had occurred rapidly and recently. This made it politically unacceptable to trace these differences back to *Homo erectus*.

Carleton Coon, one of the few Weidenreich admirers, later described how Weidenreich's ideas were generally scoffed at or ignored:

> A notable exception [to the rule that many anthropologists were neglecting geography] was Franz Weidenreich. While I was writing *The Races of Europe* in Cambridge, Massachusetts, he was busy in New York, studying the Sinanthropus [*sic*] remains. At that time he concluded that the peculiarities that made Sinanthropus distinct from other fossil men were of two kinds, evolutionary and racial. From the evolutionary point of view, Sinanthropus was more primitive than any known living population. Racially he was Mongoloid.
>
> Like other premature comets of science, Weidenreich's idea flashed across the sky and was gone, obscured by the clouds of incredulity released by his fellow scientists. Most of them believed, as many still do, that the living races of man could have become differentiated from a common ancestor only after the stage of *Homo sapiens* had been reached. Because *Homo sapiens* was believed to have first appeared only 30,000 years ago, in the guise of Cro-Magnon man, the living races could only be that old. Sinanthropus was not *Homo sapiens*. Therefore he could not have belonged to a modern race, the Mongoloid. Q.E.D.

Indeed, Weidenreich was not very happy about the indifferent reception of his great theory. In a paper published posthumously in 1949, he carped:

> Judging from the responses and comments my study of the *Sinanthropus* skull has met with in some circles, . . . there are too many people who do not take pains to check the reported anatomical details from which the conclusions have been drawn but only look over the summaries. Unless these comply with their preconceived opinions or the axioms made sacred by tradition, they refuse acknowledgment. Such an attitude is very characteristic of paleoan-

thropology and has not changed since the first fossil man came to light. It took 50 years before Neanderthal Man was recognized as a special human form and not pushed aside as a pathological variant of modern man, and it took 40 more years before Dubois' *Pithecanthropus erectus*, originally described as a giant ape, was acknowledged as a normal-sized hominid.

Of course, Weidenreich's point was well taken; he described quite perceptively the pattern of skepticism and smugness that hindered progress in paleoanthropology. Like Hrdlička, Weidenreich seemed to project the wrong image: he was a European scientist of the prewar era. When he was espousing his grand multiregionalism theory, Weidenreich was in his mid-seventies; he was old, he was tired, and his ideas seemed out-of-date. About this time, Weidenreich approached Mayr at the American Museum of Natural History and said, "I find this work you young fellows are doing [on the new synthesis] to be very interesting, but I am too old to change." Finally, in 1948, at the age of seventy-five, Weidenreich died, having collected few supporters for his great idea.

While Weidenreich's new view of Neandertals as part of a worldwide evolutionary stage was ignored and forgotten, a seemingly minor change occurred: the spelling of *Neanderthal* was revised to *Neandertal.* It was somehow symbolic of the more global view of biology and politics: a German word ought to be spelled as the Germans spelled it. The idea was suggested in 1952 by Henri Vallois, Weidenreich's chief critic and director of the Musée de l'Homme and the Institut de Paléontologie Humaine, but was more compellingly stated for Anglophones by a former Hooton student, Harvard anthropologist William Howells. Howells noted that the *h* in *Neanderthal* persisted in British and American texts, even though Germans had dropped the *h* from a number of words in which it followed a *t* (including *thal*)—at the turn of the century.

> Although it must be retained, by rules of nomenclature, in *Homo neanderthalensis*, the Germans and the French now use the spelling Neandertal in all other references. It is English-speaking writers only who have retained the "h,"—unfortunately, since unlike French and German, English has a genuine "th" sound for beginning anthropology students to employ in mispronouncing Neanderthal.

Enough said: such deep Anglocentrism was embarrassing. The changed spelling was widely adopted, except in England where *Neanderthal* persists.

52. William W. Howells, the Harvard physical anthropologist whose 1959 book, *Mankind in the Making*, influenced a generation of anthropologists against Weidenreich's theory. Howells was among the first to apply multivariate statistics to the study of human fossil skulls.

Howells, like Carleton Coon, trained under Hooton at Harvard, as did many of the leaders of physical anthropology in the postwar generation. Hooton's influence was due, in part, to the paucity of graduate programs in physical anthropology between and immediately after the wars. But it was also due to his personality. Hooton was an outrageous, outspoken man with a wonderful gift for the surprising turn of phrase. One of the best sources of Hootoniana is a volume *Apes, Men and Morons* that "consists, for the most part, of reluctant addresses publicly delivered at the instigation of persons or organizations whose requests I dared not refuse."

Hooton's summary of anthropology, published just prior to World War II, illuminates both his character and the times.

> In order to survive, an animal must be born into a favoring or at least tolerant environment. Similarly, in order to achieve preservation and recognition, a specimen of fossil man must be discovered in intelligence, attested by scientific knowledge, and interpreted by evolutionary experience. These rigorous prerequisites have undoubtedly caused many still-births in human palaeontology and are partly responsible for the high infant mortality of discoveries of geologically ancient man.

But Hooton could not stop there. He wrote, perceptively if indiscreetly, of the role of national character on scientific research. He lampooned

German anthropology as suffering from "a long and honorable tradition of exhaustive and scrupulous, if somewhat pedestrian, treatment of morphological and metric variation" and from "a tendency to derive man in comparatively late geological times either from a giant anthropoid ape closely related to the existing gorilla, the chimpanzee or the orang-utan, or to a relatively proximate common ancestor of the three." Worse yet was the German tendency to dissociate bones found together, which reflected an unfortunate "predilection for the partitive and microtomic investigation of minutiae, without due consideration of the total problem." The reference to the microtome, a device used in slicing microscopically thin sections of tissues and one of the premiere instruments of pathology, is a clear allusion to Virchow.

In contrast, the British, led by Arthur Keith, are indomitable in their "quest for a sort of Holy Grail in human paleontology, the skeletal remains of *Homo sapiens in situ* in an indubitably Lower Pleistocene or Pliocene deposit." Still, Hooton commended the British for their

> essentially sporting attitude . . . toward the discovery and acceptance of new finds, which may be contrasted with the morbid simian suspicions which obsess the Germans and the cynical detachment of the French. An adventurous spirit in anthropological research and a willingness to take a chance upon being right, have, it seems to me, resulted in many brilliant contributions to our knowledge of human evolution by British scientists. . . . [And], has occasionally promoted some resounding fiascos.

Nor do the French escape Hooton's satire. They are caricatured as

> constricted and noncommittal . . . too rigidly adherent to the idea of an illustrious national past in anthropological research. The myth of a Cro-Magnon race, homogeneous in physical type, gigantic of stature, with an excess of brain size and artistic gifts peculiarly appropriate to France, has been stubbornly perpetuated in the face of all conflicting evidence. It is approximately comparable with the German doctrine of Nordicism [the Aryan race myth].

Little wonder that, with this irreverent attitude and satirical lecturing style, Hooton attracted students like a magnet draws iron filings and they never really lost their Hootonian orientation. Among them, as mentioned earlier, were Carleton Coon (Ph.D. 1928), an expert on race who became the target of scandalous accusations; William W. Howells (Ph.D. 1934), a pioneer in measurement of skulls who became one of the sanest and wittiest observers of the debates in paleoanthropology; and Sherwood L. Washburn (Ph.D. 1940), Coon's antagonist and a visionary of a modern, biology-based physical anthropology.

Indeed, it was these three students—Coon, Howells, and Washburn—who to different degrees actually introduced a new way of thinking into twentieth-century physical anthropology. It was they who began painting human evolution as a process involving populations of organisms changing through time as selection shifted the frequencies of genes within the group.

Coon, the scion of an old New England family, was born in 1904. He attended Harvard as both an undergraduate and graduate student, specializing in racial variability, Middle Eastern culture, archeology, and innumerable languages. He excavated fossil sites, participated in expeditions to measure the physiology and to document the somatotypes

53. Carleton S. Coon, wearing the pith helmet, excavating in Morocco with his wife. In the early 1960s, Coon was attacked for his work on the origin of races. He favored a scheme in which the races initially diverged in the time of *Homo erectus* and evolved, largely independently, toward modern, sapient humans.

(physical proportions) of various peoples around the world, and studied the art, culture, and life-style of many peoples.

Coon was one of Hooton's early students and, in later years, came to share many of his personality traits. Despite his straitlaced family background, Coon was flamboyant, an extraordinary teller of tales—complete with recounted dialogues in multiple obscure languages, accompanied by appropriate gestures and facial expressions—from his equally extraordinary life. Not only had he traveled widely and worked in many areas of the world with people of varied ethnic origins and habits, he had even carried out some espionage work for the Office of Strategic Services during World War II. To hear him talk, he had escaped death, disaster, and mayhem by dint of force of character—or where that failed, by linguistic and physical disguise—over and over again.

One of the best sketches of Coon's character was written by Hooton, in 1930, in an article entitled *An Untamed Anthropologist among the Wilder Whites*:

> I watched Coon getting more and more restless [at Harvard], yearning more and more obviously for the society of the uncivilized and unwashed. I could see it was a case of savages or bust. So we picked out the wildest spot we could find in Europe, with the toughest and least known population of two-gun men. We planned an anthropometric survey of Albania. . . . Coon is quite as energetic in the analysis of his material as in the collecting of it. He goes at it with a kind of divine frenzy, inventing new methods of analysis, improving on old ones, tearing his hair when he gets into difficulties, yet always emerging, disheveled but triumphant. He is a bit like Colonel Lawrence and a great deal like Sir Richard Burton, possibly a little erratic, and with more than a spark of genius.

Tall, lean, and lanky, with a mustache and dark hair that later turned white, Coon was possessed of a patrician self-confidence—what one anthropologist has dubbed that "genteel, Anglo-Saxon sense of superiority"—that seems to run in some families. And many such families have an individual such as Coon: irrepressible, outrageous, and given to escapades such as telling indelicate stories of the sexual practices of exotic tribespeople in a carrying voice, rich with the sound of New England, in the middle of the Harvard Faculty Club dining room.

Coon was one of the last great holistic anthropologists; his interests and research regularly crossed specialty boundaries, wandering freely to "bones (physical anthropology), stones (prehistoric archaeology), and dirty stories (ethnology and ethnography)" and back again. He read everything and had visited almost every site of anthropological significance, a quest that did not lessen as he grew older. Between 1934 and 1948, Coon climbed the academic ladder from assistant to associate to full professor at his beloved alma mater, Harvard. Then, offended by a seemingly offhand proposal by his department chairman to "trade" him to another university that needed a Middle East specialist, Coon decamped Cambridge and accepted a curatorship at the University of Pennsylvania's anthropological museum. After his retirement to Gloucester, Massachusetts, he kept his exhaustive and growing collection of scholarly books and papers in an outbuilding the size of a small-town library.

Throughout his life, as he traveled, as he talked, Coon was always thinking and working on his one deep aim in life: understanding the human races. A prolific writer, Coon produced three great books, all on this subject: *The Races of Europe* (1939), *The Origin of Races* (1962), and *The Living Races of Man* (1965). All the while, the computer in his head ticked off the facial and bodily features of each person he met, classifying and categorizing each individual into a complex and subtle network of pigeonholes of race and ancestry he carried in his mind. "My Portuguese gardener . . ." he would say, starting off on some hilarious tale—but the gardener was thoroughly American in manner, culture, and language, being Portuguese only by descent. It was a characteristic eccentricity of Coon's everyday conversation to refer to people in terms of their racial origin, a habit that led many to believe he attached prejudicial judgments of worth or value to these terms. Indeed, in the 1960s he was to come to grief over this issue.

Far less outrageous than either Hooton or Coon, and several years younger than the latter, William W. Howells was the descendant of another prominent New England family, grandson of the writer William Dean Howells, and son of the noted architect John Mead Howells. Educated at Harvard, Howells became a proper Bostonian through and through, despite being born in New York City, and married into a Boston Brahmin family. He had a dry and literary wit that permeated all of his publications with a notable penchant for ironic understatement. Following in both his grandfather's and professor's literary footsteps, Howells wrote what proved to be a very popular book on human origins: *Mankind So Far,* published in 1944. Rather than update this work too many times, Howells preferred in 1959 to issue "a new book by a revised

282

author," which he called *Mankind in the Making*. It, too, was an immense success, and its anecdotal, readable style passed on to the next generation of anthropologists the stories—as many about the characters who discovered fossils as about the fossils themselves—that would soon be embroidered into the rich legacy of legend and myth that anthropologists hold dear.

He made his career both on his writing skills and, without question, on the new perspective he offered in physical anthropology. Howells was among the first to use a complex statistical procedure known as factor analysis to measure and evaluate the differences and similarities among the skulls of fossil and modern humans. Thus, Howells empowered the "measuring school" of physical anthropology with the modern statistical techniques to understand what their measurements said.

Both Howells and Coon eventually held teaching positions at Harvard, Coon alongside of their mentor, Hooton (then one of the Grand Old Men of Anthropology), and Howells replacing Hooton after Hooton's death. It was in Hooton's later years that they first made the acquaintance of the youngest of the three, Sherwood Washburn. It was also as a Harvard faculty member that Coon unwittingly laid the foundation of a grudge that would add a piquant bitterness to his future confrontation with Washburn.

Sherwood Washburn was born in 1911, the son of yet another old New England family, this time one with a long tradition of clergymen and preachers. His father was a professor of divinity. Perhaps it was this aspect of Washburn's upbringing that lent a moralistic tone to his abundant criticisms of his peers or elders; he certainly had a firm idea of the right and the wrong way to conduct anthropological studies. He was an intense, quick, dark-haired man, but very small, with a head that seemed too large for his body. He believed he represented the new wave of scientific anthropology and, even as a student, was very sure of himself and of the correctness of his ideas.

Not surprisingly, one of the recipients of Washburn's outspoken criticism was Hooton and his old-fashioned, typological approach to human variability. Washburn's biting impatience with Hooton's ways sprang in part from Hooton's signature exercise of teaching, the bone labs. These were long hours during which students learned to identify even the tiniest scrap of a human skeleton, instantly recognizing which bone from which side of the body. The labs were notorious for their exacting precision and merciless tests. Apparently Washburn found them a drudgery of sheer memorization unrelieved by concepts, significance, or analysis. There was always a danger, in Washburn's mind, that typological studies—Hooton's forte—would be misused for racist purposes. "Sherry was always very avid and almost obsessed about anything racist," recalls Lita Osmundsen, a friend of Washburn's and director for many years of the Wenner-Gren Foundation for Anthropological Research. "He was deeply disturbed by the racist overtones of Hooton's work. It left him with a love-hate relationship with the entire Harvard anthropology department at the time." Coon was doubly damned, in Washburn's eyes, as a former Hooton student and a Harvard faculty member.

In contrast with the old typological idea of physical anthropology, Washburn set himself up as the visionary prophet of the "New Physical Anthropology," as he termed it in an influential paper published in 1951. Anatomy was central, but it was the anatomy organized into functioning systems, not the mere "document and describe" anatomy of somatology. He strove to discover the pattern and process of anatomy that would illuminate the nature of humanity and the story of human evolution with meaning. It was the ambitious program of an ambitious man.

After graduating from Harvard, Washburn went to the Columbia College of Physicians and Surgeons, in the anatomy department, where he was strongly influenced by Sam Detweiler, the chairman and an outstanding experimentalist. After eight years, Washburn moved up to a job at the University of Chicago. As the self-proclaimed modern physical anthropologist, he, more than any other individual, brought the architects of the new synthesis in America—Dobzhansky, Simpson, and Mayr—together with his field. It remained for Washburn's students actually to apply the new style of thinking in terms of the evolution of populations to the human fossil record.

One of the first to pay heed to the implications of the new ideas for human evolution was a bright young man from the University of Chicago, F. Clark Howell. He was one of Washburn's earliest and most influential students, one of the first of the new generation to emerge from graduate school deeply imbued with the concepts of modern biology.

Born in 1925, Howell describes himself as a country boy from a farming family who were struggling against hard times brought on by the depression and the Dust Bowl drought. Through fifth grade—about age twelve—Howell attended a one-room schoolhouse near Topeka, Kansas. When the farm failed, the family moved first to Topeka, where Howell found himself painfully behind in his schooling compared with "city

54. F. Clark Howell (left) and François Bordes (right) in France, 1956. During the 1950s, Howell and Bordes greatly modernized approaches to and perceptions of the Neandertals and the Middle Paleolithic period.

kids," a deficiency he managed to remedy after some years. After Topeka came a series of other Midwestern cities as his father sought steady work. In high school, Howell became interested in human evolution and initiated a correspondence with Franz Weidenreich at the American Museum of Natural History.

"Weidenreich was very kind to me," he recalls. "He answered all my letters and pointed out that the Neandertal problem, which he had touched on in his career, was a very interesting one that might be suitable for a bright young man to take up in the future. I suppose I remembered that years later when I started graduate school." In 1943, after graduating from high school, Howell went to work briefly in a factory; World War II further delayed his start at college. But his navy posting in the Pacific gave him ample time to read and to write to various anthropologists whose work interested him. He grew from a raw country boy to a thoughtful, laconic young man, with considerable experience of life and an ever-clearer idea of what he wanted to do. After the war, in 1946, the young Howell spent a week at the American Museum of Natural History, meeting Weidenreich, von Koenigswald, and other luminaries. When he returned to the Midwest, it was to attend the University of Chicago, to work under the anatomist Wilton Marion Krogman.

But Krogman was soon to leave for the University of Pennsylvania. One day before Krogman's departure, Howell walked in to find him deep in conversation with a tiny, dark-haired, intense man, with glasses and an unusually large head. "He was so young and small that I thought he was a student," Howell remembered, "but it was Sherry Washburn. I made some 'bright' remark or other and afterwards Krogman told me that *that* had been Washburn, who was coming to replace him. Of course, I got off on the wrong foot with him."

Washburn was young, quick, feisty, and very critical. But he was a stimulating teacher, full of energy, ideas, and unshakable self-confidence. His vision of how anthropologists should be trained was unyielding; Howell remembers that students who didn't readily follow Washburn's program were often denied his "stamp of approval"—and he, Howell, was more broadly interested in the interplay of human evolution with archeology and ecology than in anatomy per se. Being an older student, Howell simply wouldn't give in. He was also more knowledgeable than many younger students and challenged Washburn when, as Howell describes it, "his theories ran ahead of his knowledge." They argued often, as Washburn did with many of his less malleable students. Although Washburn was willing to let Howell investigate the Neandertal question as a master's thesis, he objected to the research going any further.

When the thesis was finished, Howell was determined to publish it. He remembers that Keith's old collaborator, Theodore McCown, was one of those who subjected his tentative manuscript to rigorous criticism. In 1951, the work became Howell's first professional publication. It was the first of Howell's series of landmark papers about Neandertals that built and elaborated upon one another.

In effect, this work issued his challenge to the status quo, integrating the evolutionary synthesis with the Neandertal fossil record in a new way. The very language he used in the introductory remarks to his 1952 paper made it clear that he was a postwar, new-synthesis anthropologist. Howell began with a classic statement of principles:

> Isolation is one of the most important factors leading to evolutionary change. In nature, a variety of isolating mechanisms are at work . . . geographical and physiological. . . . In one way or another, isolation results in failure of forms of one group to interbreed with those of another, and thereby gives rise to discontinuous variation.

Then he staked claim to his territory: the application of these principles to human evolution. He continued:

> One of the most important barriers to gene flow between potentially interbreeding groups during the Pleistocene was that of climate. . . .

Heretofore, there has been no attempt to examine human evolutionary data for possible evidence as to the influence of climatic factors on hominid distribution and development in the Pleistocene. The reasons for this are perhaps twofold: too few fossils and too much emphasis on morphological evidence with little attention to geography and climatology. . . .

I have suggested elsewhere that one group, designated "classic Neandertals," was most probably an isolated descendant of an earlier and more widespread "Neandertal" type.

A quarter of a century before, Hrdlička had suggested vaguely that the evolution of Neandertals was related to their association with glacial Europe; Howell had, with these few paragraphs, completely changed the tone of the discussion. He was not trying to explain away the Neandertals; he was trying to provide a mechanism whereby the whole phenomenon of Neandertals as an evolutionary group of humans could be understood.

In the process, perhaps inadvertently, Howell brushed into the dustpan the various constructs of human evolution that relied strictly on the morphology or shape of different fossils—the sort of "A turned into B which turned into C" that took no account of climate, geography, populations, or natural selection. These simple schemes had dominated Neandertal studies for most of a century. Even Weidenreich's attempt looked fusty, static, and two-dimensional by comparison. Flying the colors of a new age from the very first paragraph, Howell was making many of the same points as Weidenreich, but in a new vocabulary based more in evolutionary biology and less in the anatomy of dead things.

Howell's synthesis, elaborated in several substantial papers over the next six years, was very persuasive. He provided a simple but insightful model that made sense of the muddled transition from Neandertal to early modern human. He reviewed and compiled the evidence, the key being that he divided Neandertals into groups based both on geography and on differences in details of anatomical shape. The comprehensive, thoughtful compilation was a style of work that Howell was to make peculiarly his own throughout his career.

Howell realized that the type of skeleton everyone thought of as Neandertal—the large-browed, long-headed, squat, and heavy-limbed creature—appeared to be purely a phenomenon of western Europe and of the early part of the last glacial (Würm) period. La Chapelle-aux-Saints, La Ferrassie, Le Moustier, Spy, Gibraltar, Monte Circeo, Feldhofer, and other human fossils were all associated with cold-adapted,

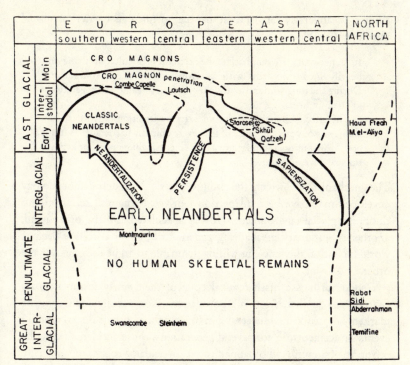

| | | E U R O P E | | | | A S I A | | NORTH |
| | | southern | western | central | eastern | western | central | AFRICA |

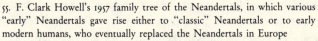

55. F. Clark Howell's 1957 family tree of the Neandertals, in which various "early" Neandertals gave rise either to "classic" Neandertals or to early modern humans, who eventually replaced the Neandertals in Europe

subarctic, glacial-age animals. These were Hooton's classic Neandertals.

The Neandertal specimens that were earlier—dating to the warmer interglacial (Riss-Würm) period that preceded the last glaciation—were more widespread geographically and more generalized anatomically. Into this category, for example, Howell put the Krapina remains; the largely ignored skulls from Saccopastore, Italy; the Tabun fossils from Mount Carmel; and the provocative Teshik-Tash child's skeleton, found (it was said) encircled by horns of wild goats. None of these fossils showed such extreme development of the "typical" Neandertal anatomy. Their brains were smaller, their skulls less long and low, their faces smaller, their limbs less robustly built and straighter, and so on. While noting they were more similar to modern humans, Howell saw these specimens as "incipiently classic Neanderthal."

Considered on its own, Howell concluded, the European record shows increasing "neandertalization" through time. He painted a convincing and shiver-inducing portrait of a small population isolated from similar Neandertals farther east by the formidable barrier of glacial terrain unsuitable for human habitation.

> It is necessary to emphasize the extreme difficulty of living in heavily snowed-in areas without proper clothing and equipment. During the long winter months there is lack of game and vegetation in such an area. . . .
>
> The effects of such a period of extreme isolation (at least some *thousands* of years), because of the severe climatic barriers to continuous distribution and migratory movements, will be peculiar evolutionary developments.

The mechanism by which the unique, classic Neandertal morphology developed may have been adaptation—driven by natural selection—to the harsh glacial environment, Howell speculated. On the other hand, another evolutionary mechanism, genetic drift, could also have been at work. He sat on the fence, unwilling or unable to argue for one over the other.

Genetic drift is a mathematical concept then newly formulated. Its central idea is that, in small populations, some individuals may be markedly more (or less) successful in breeding than others due to random events or accidents. If, for several generations, those accidents favor the offspring of a family who happen to be particularly robust or unusually long-headed or oddly stout of limb, then their genes will become so numerous as to swamp the ones that were originally common and "normal." Dramatic changes in the frequencies of genes in such a population occur not because the favored genes are more advantageous in some way, but by accidental *drift*. Nonetheless, the long-term effect of genetic drift may be as potent as that of strong selective forces. Whatever the mechanism behind the neandertalization in western Europe, Howell recognized an abrupt end to the trend that coincided with the end of the early glacial period. The subsequent, relatively warm period yielded only Cro-Magnon or Aurignacian specimens.

In contrast is the record from a region Howell called "western Asia"—a peculiar term that persists to this day in writing about Neandertals. Howell cannot remember how he coined the term—he suspects he borrowed it from some geography textbook—but it tacitly implies the continuity of the Near East with the vastness of Asia. In fact, it explicitly includes both the areas of the former Soviet Union adjacent to the Middle East, from Uzbekistan (north of the Himalayas) in the east and to the Black Sea in the west, as well as the better-known Levant region of Lebanon and Palestine.

In western Asia as in western Europe, Howell observed, the early Neandertals have a more generalized, less extreme, and hence more modern appearance. But instead of neandertalizing through time, the western Asian Neandertals undergo "sapiensation." The more modern-looking Neandertals from Tabun and Teshik-Tash turn, not into something like La Chapelle-aux-Saints, but into the even more humanlike populations whose remains were found at Skhul.

In a later elaboration of the same hypothesis, Howell drew into the discussion half a dozen skeletons that had been excavated between 1933 and 1935, in a cave known as Jebel Qafzeh near the modern city of Nazareth. The excavator, René Neuville, was an archeologist and also the French consul in Jerusalem. He eventually described the archeological materials from Jebel Qafzeh in 1951, but—as had happened repeatedly in the history of Neandertals—the skeletons languished unremembered in the Institut de Paléontologie Humaine in Paris. Howell realized how closely they resembled the skeletons from Skhul. To him, they were an excellent intermediate that linked the more generalized Neandertals from Tabun, which were presumed to be earlier, to early modern humans. To express this, he chose to call the Qafzeh/Skhul population "Proto–Cro-Magnons."

Howell's synthetic vision accounted for the sudden appearance of modern, Cro-Magnon–type humans in western Europe neatly. The warm break in the middle of the Würm glaciation removed the potent geographical barrier that once isolated western Europe; the progressive and more modern-looking humans could then migrate out of the East (from western Asia into Europe) into classic Neandertal territory. Was there a dramatic confrontation between the two types of humans? Howell asked. His answer sidestepped the question.

> Whether the "classic Neandertals" were already extinct by the time
> of this new peopling, or whether they were extinguished by, or
> hybridized with these invaders, remains a moot point at present.

It was a whole new view of human evolution, and a whole new type of explanation; it made Howell's reputation. It also solved, temporarily, the Neandertal problem.

Howell also changed the way in which paleoanthropology was performed. In the mid-1950s, following the publication of the first few of his series of Neandertal papers, he undertook a "grand tour" in human paleontology, an organized visit to museums and universities across Europe, the Near East, and North America, in order to examine the important fossils firsthand—the first physical anthropologist to do this since Hrdlička. On this trip, he saw the Jebel Qafzeh skeletons as well as other material stored in Europe. In contrast, most European and American scholars had been content to sit at home in their armchairs, pronouncing on the fossils on the basis of what were often poor plaster casts, photographs, or written descriptions provided by others. As the grand tour became de rigueur for any serious student of human evolution, the speed with which information, interpretations, and theories were generated began to accelerate. It became more common to view fossils as representatives of prehistoric populations rather than as isolated specimens to be studied out of context.

The heightened emphasis on firsthand inspection of original fossils was to provoke another momentous change: in 1953, the Piltdown remains were revealed to be a forgery. It was a stunning conclusion to forty years of confusion, unease, and uncertain acceptance. To be sure, no field is immune to forgeries and fraud; much of science is based on the implicit assumption that what another scientist says as a matter of fact is true. But paleoanthropology, especially the reception of *Australopithecus* and the popularity of the pre-Sapiens view, had been forcibly deformed more than a little by Piltdown's shadow.

As time had passed and no new *Eoanthropus* fossils had appeared, Piltdown had slipped ever further from its role as the only true, direct ancestor on the main trunk leading to modern humans. Frequently now, it was banished to various slender twigs on the human evolutionary tree. Initially, the Swanscombe skull, found in Kent in 1935 by an English dentist, Alvan Marston, was taken to be exactly contemporaneous with the Piltdown finds but more primitive. The "skull" was in reality only a few pieces that fitted together to make the back of a cranium; with them were found Acheulian flint implements.

But when geological work showed Piltdown to be much earlier than Swanscombe, Marston was incredulous: there must be something wrong with Piltdown. Never fainthearted, Marston undertook study of the Piltdown remains and in 1936 circulated an announcement that read:

NOTICE OF OPERATION

Eoanthropus dawsoni is about to undergo a major dental operation on Monday, November 23, at the next meeting of the Odontological Society of the Royal Society of Medicine at 8 p.m.

The operation will involve extraction of the right lower canine tooth and the excision of the mandible. The condition of this tooth and of the mandible which has long been a serious problem, has at length been accurately diagnosed.

After excision, it is proposed to offer the removed parts to the British Museum (Natural History) to be placed in the section of fossil anthropoids. *Eoanthropus* has been so heavily doped, that no anaesthetic will be considered necessary. Assistance may be needed, however, in holding the victim down. *Eoanthropus* is expected to make a speedy recovery to convalescence. The prognosis is good. His mental outlook will be more human. He will be less antisocial without a mandible which has prevented him from eating and speaking like a human being.

Dental Surgeon: A. T. Marston, L.D.S.
Assistants: You.

Marston's operation was not a success; Piltdown was still largely unassailable. In fact, in 1938 Arthur Keith unveiled a memorial at Piltdown. Strongly resembling a tombstone, this monolith bore a plaque that read:

Here in the old river gravel Mr Charles Dawson, F.S.A., found the fossil skull of Piltdown, 1912–1913. The discovery was described by Mr Charles Dawson and Sir Arthur Smith Woodward in the Quarterly Journal of the Geological Society.

The establishment's endorsement of Piltdown was literally carved in stone.

Though Marston's anti-Piltdown campaign was interrupted by the war, he resumed publication in 1947, more firmly than ever in the camp of the dualists who believed that Piltdown was a false fusion of an ape and a man. He pushed and crusaded, in professional lectures and papers, for a complete reappraisal of Piltdown.

In the postwar years, the intellectual climate was more receptive. For one thing, the fossil evidence for everything but Piltdown had grown stronger. The discovery of another anomalously modern-looking fossil, a calotte or skullcap from a cave near Fontéchevade, in central France, seemed to reinforce the message of the Swanscombe material. For another, most of the Piltdown men or those influential in its acceptance had died: Charles Dawson, Grafton Elliot Smith, Arthur Smith Woodward, William Sollas, and Marcellin Boule. Arthur Keith was elderly, in retirement. The old guard, who had patrolled the intellectual borders vigilantly and enforced acceptance of the pre–World War I view of human evolution, were either metaphorically toothless or eternally still.

The younger scholars frankly found the Piltdown fossils awkward.

Looking back on the Piltdown revelation, Washburn recalled his struggles with Piltdown when he was a graduate student:

> I remember writing a paper on human evolution in 1944, and I
> simply left Piltdown out. You could make sense of human evolution
> if you didn't try to put Piltdown into it.

Hooton, a firm supporter of Piltdown and a man of strong opinions, was furious and chastised Washburn; it was irresponsible and unprofessional to "leave out" evidence that didn't fit.

Kenneth Oakley, a chemist and paleontologist at the British Museum, now stepped to the fore. Tall and balding, with an aquiline nose and rather noticeable, slightly pointed ears, he was a quiet, soft-spoken man.

Born in 1911, Oakley had been a babe in arms when the Piltdown fossils were found and a chuckling toddler while the debates over its reconstruction raged. He had no preconceived notions about the Piltdown remains. Oakley was one of the new breed of scientists, alive to new techniques and the importance of fair and rigorous—though always gentlemanly—examinations. He saw an innovative way to tackle the Piltdown problem.

In the nineteenth century, it had been observed that the fluorine content of fossils increased over time. Oakley realized this meant that a method of dating fossils could be devised that would be more precise than the vague estimates of antiquity based on faunal "ages" determined by the succession of animals or on estimated rates of sedimentation. Even though fluorine did not accrue in fossils at a steady and constant rate, fluorine content would nonetheless provide a quantitative assessment of the relative ages of fossils from a single deposit.

Fluorine dating was the beginning of a new era in paleoanthropology, in which true radiometric dating would be developed and applied with staggering results. In 1948, Oakley tested the method by comparing the Galley Hill remains with the Swanscombe bones. The results were unequivocal: Galley Hill was obviously a modern burial that had been intruded into much older sediments. When he turned to the Piltdown fossils, Oakley found that the faunal remains were much older than the *Eoanthropus* fossils, which made murkier the atmosphere surrounding the finds. How had fossil animals from a much older period become intermingled with the enigmatic Piltdown remains? What he did not at first appreciate, because of the crudity of his early techniques, was a discrepancy between the fluorine-determined age of the cranium and that of the mandible.

Still, the Piltdown problem had been transformed from a distinctly uncomfortable itch to an implacable irritation. Oakley tried some other approaches, to no avail. He turned his new technique to African fossils, with better luck, and—with funding from a New York–based organization, the Wenner-Gren Foundation for Anthropological Research—he organized an international conference on "Early Man in Africa" that was held in January 1953. As had the Princeton conference in 1947, and as would several other symposia in the next two decades, the London conference left an indelible imprint on human evolutionary studies.

Its primary effect was accidental; the conference provided an opportunity for many to see the original Piltdown remains for the first time. Among the participants was a young South African–born anthropologist, Joseph Weiner. Trained by Raymond Dart at the University of the Witwatersrand, Weiner had cut his anthropological teeth on the meaty ideas of one of the great iconoclasts. Though Dart minded deeply that few agreed with him about the Taung baby—and was pained that for many years the English scientific establishment scorned his work—the loneliness and psychological anguish were never sufficient to make him relent. When the light of intuitive conviction illuminated Dart's eyes and brain, there was no stopping him.

In the late 1940s, Dart had finally been vindicated in part, by the belated recognition of *Australopithecus* as a hominid. This reversal of fortune had come about largely due to the bold support offered to Dart by Wilfrid E. Le Gros Clark, one of the most prominent British anatomists of the mid-twentieth century. Le Gros Clark's endorsement opened the door to other changes of heart. Keith magnanimously retracted his rejection of *Australopithecus*, stating: "I am now convinced . . . that Professor Dart was right and I was wrong." Typically, he was unable to resist adding that the name *Australopithecus* was too cumbersome for colloquial use and wanted to rename the creatures "Dartians."

Not only had Le Gros Clark thrown his considerable prestige and intellectual weight onto Dart's side once he had examined the fossils for himself, he had steadfastly maintained his position in the face of the most bitter opposition by one of his former junior colleagues, Solly Zuckerman. Le Gros Clark had a deep dislike of polemics and unseemly, acrimonious, academic wrangles, which is what this episode became, but he did not abandon Dart once he started championing him. It was Le Gros Clark who gave Dart's assessment of the Taung fossil academic respectability. Perhaps it was no accident that Le Gros Clark, as chairman of anatomy at Oxford, had hired Weiner, one of Dart's own students.

Now that australopithecines were genuine hominids, South African paleoanthropology had a new respectability. Weiner was an outsider with an intellectual heritage of iconoclasty; he was a perfect agent to overturn Piltdown, the hoax that had deprived Dart for so long of his rightful renown.

Dark-haired and prematurely balding, Weiner wore heavy-rimmed glasses and a small mustache. Photographs at the time reveal a no-nonsense look in his steady gaze, which he first turned upon the Piltdown remains at Oakley's Wenner-Gren Conference. He was astonished to learn that the location of the site where the second set of Piltdown fossils had been discovered was unknown. How was such a thing possible? The cranium was, in Weiner's view, rather large-brained and modern; the teeth and mandible were apish and matched nothing else known in the fossil record. The specimen was anatomically puzzling and its history was, to Weiner, literally incredible.

Weiner's exposure to the Piltdown material set him to worrying his way through the entire conundrum once again when he returned to Oxford. In the face of the rest of the fossil record, the Piltdown fossils simply could not be derived from a single animal. Was Piltdown then a chimera of a fossil human and a fossil ape? As he saw it, virtually the sole support for the unity of the jaw and the skull lay in two facts: the flat (hence entirely un-apelike) wear on the molar teeth in the jaw; and the apparent antiquity of the jaw, based on a greater-than-modern amount of fluorine in the bone. But Oakley's reading of 0.3 percent fluorine in the jaw incorporated an error factor of plus or minus 0.2 percent, based on the precision of the measurements of fluorine. Weiner suddenly realized that the true reading could be as low as 0.1 percent—a reasonable figure for a modern bone—or as high as 0.5 percent.

If the jaw were modern, then the only remaining peculiarities to be explained were how a modern ape jaw came to be placed in a fossil deposit and how it came to acquire the flat wear on its teeth. But there was another oddity: how remains of a modern ape came to be placed in a fossil deposit in association with a fossil human, *twice*, with the exact locality lost once. Uncertainty grew to unease; unease to suspicion; suspicion to conviction. Piltdown was a hoax. Weiner was convinced, but knew the hypothesis of a forgery to be outrageous. He turned to his superior at Oxford, Le Gros Clark, for advice.

From Weiner's point of view, Le Gros Clark was the obvious man to consult about his precarious theory. Weiner was young and not particularly well connected, having carried with him some of the "taint" that still clung to Dart. Le Gros Clark was just the opposite. He was the professor of anatomy at Oxford, esteemed and universally respected. He could judge the anatomy, listen to Weiner's evidence, and—if the notion seemed sound—figure out how to proceed with a minimum of fuss.

Together, Weiner and Le Gros Clark examined the cast of Piltdown kept in the department of anatomy at Oxford. They found the teeth were not only "worn" flat but that the plane of "wear" included an impossible step: the adjacent first and second molars were planed off at different heights. Because the upper teeth that would have produced the wear must have moved back and forth across the first and second molars in a continuous motion, it is mechanically inconceivable that such a step had been produced by a living, chewing creature. Under the microscope, the wear on the original teeth looked remarkably coarse, as if it had been created by a metal file or rasp, and quite different from the normal wear on other ape teeth. At one point—to show the Piltdown jaw was from an ape, not a human—the aggrieved dentist Marston had actually repeated the hoaxer's actions, filing down an orangutan's teeth to match the Piltdown molars, yet he never suspected foul play.

Now that the pair were convinced the tooth wear was phony, it remained only to approach Oakley, to see if he would run the fluorine dates again with this new hypothesis in mind. Weiner feared it would be a touchy phone call to make. Oakley was the consummate scientist, precise and exacting in the lab. No good would come of insulting him by implying his original work was sloppy; it would make an enemy and block their chances of gaining Oakley's cooperation. Le Gros Clark, ever gentle, tactful, and respectful, made the call to Oakley—a man from a very similar social background who would understand exactly what Le Gros Clark meant even if it were not stated overtly. He obviously struck the right note; Oakley was entirely open to applying a new fluorine test, with the improved methodology he had worked out in the intervening years, plus a number of other physical and chemical tests. The outcome was transparently clear.

On November 21, 1953, the trio published their conclusions in five history-making pages:

> From the evidence which we have obtained, it is now clear that the distinguished palaeontologists and archaeologists who took part in the excavations at Piltdown were the victims of a most elaborate and carefully prepared hoax. Let it be said, however, in exoneration

of those who have assumed the Piltdown fragments to belong to a single individual, or who, having examined the original specimens, either regarded the mandible and canine as those of a fossil ape or else assumed (tacitly, or explicitly) that the problem was not capable of solution on the available evidence, that the faking of the mandible and canine is so extraordinarily skillful, and the perpetration of the hoax appears to have been so entirely unscrupulous and inexplicable, as to find no parallel in the history of palaeontological discovery.

Both the eoliths (the dubious stone tools) and the animal fossils had also been fraudulently planted at the site.

The London *Times* led the world's press in publicizing the discovered hoax. At the November 25, 1953, meeting of the Geological Society, Oakley and Weiner presented their evidence to a large audience including the incredulous and openly skeptical Alvan Marston, who objected most vigorously to the implication that Dawson had carried out the hoax. On the same day, a motion was presented in Parliament to express a vote of "no confidence" in the British Museum, whose scientists had been so thoroughly misled. It became the occasion for clever quips about skeletons in the closet and old bones, and the motion was withdrawn to laughter.

Weiner, Oakley, and Le Gros Clark tried, discreetly, to track down the hoaxer, talking carefully with Keith, Teilhard, and others who were still alive. They agreed privately that Dawson was probably involved, and Oakley, for one, thought Teilhard knew much more than he was letting on. Le Gros Clark summed it up later:

> It is a story which has a number of different aspects, depending on the way in which you look at it. It has a tragic aspect when you consider it in the light of human frailty and the intentions behind the deliberate deception, and when you consider the unhappy controversies and personal estrangements to which the "discoveries" gave rise. It gives one a furious sense of anger when one thinks of the hours and weeks and months of wasted time spent on the study of these bogus fossils. It has (let us admit it) a distinctly humorous aspect, for there is undoubtedly something that titillates our sense of the ridiculous in the idea of learned men being, so to speak, "led up the garden path" by the skill and cunning of a hoaxer. It has a melancholy aspect when one remembers that the late Sir Arthur Smith Woodward, on his retirement, went to live near Piltdown in order to continue excavations there, which he did for a number of years until failing health prevented him from continuing his search. Of course, he did not find anything, for the fact is (and you may

put any construction you like on it, though your construction on this fact alone will not necessarily be the right one) that after Charles Dawson's illness and death in 1916, that is to say, after Dawson ceased to play any part in the excavations at Piltdown, no fossils have ever been found in the gravel deposits there—the latter are apparently quite unfossiliferous. But the story of Piltdown also has a positive aspect. For the detection of the forgery has led to the development and perfection of a whole battery of techniques which will in future be of the greatest use in estimating the antiquity of genuine fossils. They will also make it virtually impossible for anyone ever to repeat a similar deception again.

Attempts to identify the perpetrator of this clever hoax have continued ever since. Weiner, in his 1955 book, *The Piltdown Forgery*, pointed at Charles Dawson, the solicitor and amateur antiquarian who enthusiastically "discovered" most of the Piltdown specimens himself. Opportunity was certainly his and motivation might have been his desire for acceptance by the scientific community and for an enhanced reputation among his fellow eolith-hunters. His status as an outsider certainly made it less repugnant for professional anthropologists to accuse him. In any case, it is difficult to see how Dawson could have been manipulated into digging in just the right spots to find the material if someone else planted it—but it is said that Dawson was suggestible, if not downright gullible. It has always been questionable, however, whether Dawson had the means and the requisite technical knowledge.

Dawson may have been a scapegoat or a willing but ignorant accomplice in this scientific embarrassment; it is difficult to paint him convincingly as the mastermind. In the years that have passed since the exposure, virtually everyone who was in any way involved with human origins and who could have possibly been in Sussex in 1912 has been accused, though Frank Spencer, an anthropologist who has recently reviewed the matter in detail, notes that "few of these cases have stood up to scrutiny. Some are little more than embroidered gossip."

The list of accused includes among its more noteworthy members William Sollas, the geologist who hated Smith Woodward bitterly; Martin Alistair Campbell Hinton, a volunteer at the British Museum (Natural History) who presumably wanted to embarrass the martinet Smith Woodward; Grafton Elliot Smith, the neuroanatomist who found that the Piltdown skull conveniently supported his theory that the early development of the brain was of preeminent importance in human evolution; Arthur Keith, who seemed to know more than he should and whose pre-Sapiens theory of human evolution required Piltdown-like evidence; Pierre Teilhard de Chardin, for the misfortunes of finding the crucial canine tooth, of being suspiciously reluctant to discuss Piltdown, and of being a French Jesuit, which in British eyes gave him an obvious motivation for wanting to make British scientists look incompetent; and even Sir Arthur Conan Doyle, the creator of Sherlock Holmes, whose motivation would be to get back at E. Ray Lankester, director of the British Museum (Natural History), for attacking spiritualism, in which Doyle believed strongly. It has even been suggested, in a spoof, that Smith Woodward, Keith, Elliot Smith, Sollas, and others were part of a British Secret Service conspiracy featuring Dawson as the hitman. The supposed motivation was to create positive, pro-British propaganda on the eve of World War I, because Germany and France already had their early humans and Belgium even had its "Spys."

The real lesson in this episode lies in its revelation of the dangerous power of theory over fact. Good scientists in paleontology—competent anatomists, incisive thinkers—were taken in by a forgery that neatly matched their preconceived ideas, that embodied their pet theories. Even the doubting Thomases of the early twentieth century frequently accepted some of the Piltdown specimens as valid. Quite simply, the physical facts were apparently less persuasive than the mental constructs of the examiners. Theory became a distorting lens through which all—bone shape or size, evidence of antiquity, even association with tools or bones of other animals—were transformed. As in a kaleidoscope, the truth lay somewhere within, obscured by false patterns created by the intensity and number of reflected ideas.

For the most part, the scientific community simply breathed a sigh of relief: they no longer had to search to find a plausible and innocuous spot for Piltdown on their family trees. At Harvard's Peabody Museum, some curator simply opened a display case and pried off the lettering *"Eoanthropus dawsoni"* from the diagram of human ancestry. Fittingly, the unfaded letter shapes left on the cloth backing of the exhibit were still legible decades later. Piltdown was dead, but not forgotten; its influence still lingered.

With Piltdown a dim spectral figure, the next great change of the decade was in store. Neandertals had already been resurrected spiritually; they were about to be transubstantiated.

8

Race and Unreason

1955–1970

The transubstantiation started with a pain in the neck suffered by Camille Arambourg. A French paleontologist, Arambourg was a small, neat, mustachioed man of sixty-two years. He was still vigorous, used to physical activity, and he resented the ache. He couldn't know it was about to trigger a sweeping reevaluation of Neandertals' physical appearance.

If Arambourg had entered the family vineyard business in Algeria, as his parents had intended him to, it all would never have happened. Born in 1885, he had dutifully studied agronomy as a young man. Fortunately for the field of human evolution, it was a short-lived career. When his father asked him to find a more effective way to irrigate, young Arambourg took up geology, which had the unanticipated effect of exposing him to fossils. He was captivated by this record of past life and soon developed what a colleague later called a "veritable passion for paleontology"; grapes and viniculture were left behind. Arambourg's passion was diverted temporarily by World War I, in which he served his country with distinction. When he returned in 1920, he took a job as professor of geology at l'Institut agricole d'Alger (Agricultural Institute of Algiers). Then, in 1936, in mid-career, he ascended to the powerful position of professor at the Muséum National d'Histoire Naturelle, replacing Marcellin Boule.

Most of Arambourg's research was concerned with the evolution of African species of fish, reptiles, and mammals. He collected the specimens himself, organizing successful field projects in remote areas of

Ethiopia and eastern Africa in the 1930s. It was a distinguished career, from its beginning to his death in 1970, crowned with innumerable honors and awards. His colleagues praised him as a warm, modest, courteous man—and a most energetic and tireless fieldworker.

The fossils had led him, during the winter of 1947–48, into a ridiculous accident. Arambourg was prospecting a new region in the Sahara for possible fossil sites, being flown from place to place in a small airplane. At each stop, a postal service vehicle was to meet him, but the logistics of such maneuvers were inevitably fragile. He and the pilot had to wait for a long time at one stop and soon retreated from the relentless glare of the desert sun to the only shade available: that cast by the plane's wing. When the extreme temperature burst the tire on that side of the plane with a sudden bang, the plane tilted sideways. The lowered wing cracked Arambourg sharply on the head.

It was only one of many trials of fieldwork in remote desert regions, but the pain persisted. When he returned to Paris, Arambourg had an X ray taken of his aching neck. Being thoroughly familiar with anatomy, he asked to inspect the radiograph himself. Much to his surprise, it was hauntingly familiar. The vertebrae in his lower neck had long spines that stuck straight out horizontally rather than the short, downward-sloping ones usually depicted as normal in human beings. He had seen other vertebrae with the same distinctive shape as his own . . . but the other specimen was the La Chapelle-aux-Saints Neandertal.

Arambourg's famous predecessor at the museum, Boule, had called La Chapelle's neck vertebrae simian, the cause of Neandertals' rigid spine, inhuman posture, and forwardly thrust head. Boule was obviously, blatantly mistaken. Arambourg published an article to this effect, comparing Boule's famous tracing of the La Chapelle vertebrae with those of a chimpanzee and his own, labeled discreetly "a modern Frenchman."

It was not the first time a scientist had observed that the vertebrae of La Chapelle-aux-Saints were not really very simian. In 1938, in a largely unnoticed publication, a German biologist named Otto Kleinschmidt had begun chipping away at this aspect of Boule's reconstruction. Kleinschmidt simply followed along after the anatomist Daniel J. Cunningham, who as early as 1886 had pointed out how variable the neck vertebrae were among the different races, to no avail. Thus, the change in opinion that resulted from Arambourg's publication cannot be attributed to the newness of the observations so much as to the difference in intellectual climate. The new reassessment of Neandertal spirituality made it easier to believe that Neandertals were physically more human; so, too, did Boule's death in 1942, which meant that a direct confrontation with the foremost proponent of Neandertal-as-beast could be avoided.

Following rapidly upon the heels of Arambourg's work, and reinforcing its theme, were other studies by scientists from various parts of the world. It was a classic case of several researchers converging on the same points. Soon Etienne Patte, a paleontologist at the University of Poitiers, published an impressive book entitled *Les Néandertaliens*. It appeared in 1956 with a publication date of 1955. This voluminous and meticulous compendium compared measurements of various parts of the Neandertal skeleton to those of modern humans from around the world. Like Arambourg, Patte was forced to abandon Boule's simian reconstruction of La Chapelle-aux-Saints as badly flawed; measurement after measurement placed Neandertals within or near the range of modern humans. But Patte, unlike Arambourg, was a provincial—albeit one with a good record of studies of vertebrate paleontology and archeology to his credit—so his criticism came from outside the centralized power structure of French science. Similar challenges, though less sweeping, came from others' research.

For the English-speaking world, the decisive work was that of William Straus, Jr., an anthropologist and anatomist at Johns Hopkins University, and A. J. E. Cave, an anatomist from St. Bartholomew's Hospital Medical College in London. The two were interested in human fossils and, while attending the Sixth International Anatomical Congress in Paris, took advantage of the occasion to visit the Musée de l'Homme to try to see some of the originals stored there. As they recalled in their article published in 1957:

> On July 26, 1955, we visited the Musée de l'Homme in Paris. The prime purpose of our visit was, admittedly, an examination of the controversial Fontéchevade skulls. . . . We soon turned our attention to the skeleton of La Chapelle-aux-Saints and to other additional Neanderthal skeletons which were housed in the Museum. . . . At the time we were entirely unaware of Arambourg's (1955) study, which came to our attention some months later. Familiar only with the published descriptions and illustrations of the La Chapelle remains and with casts of the skull, we were somewhat unprepared for the fragmentary nature of the skeleton itself and for the consequent extent of restoration required. Nor were we prepared for

the severity of the osteoarthritis deformans affecting the vertebral column.

What they saw, with their anatomists' eyes, was the skeleton of a man who could no longer stand straight or walk freely because he was arthritic, not because his posture or gait was normal for his species. In case any of their readers were in danger of missing the point, or of overlooking the role played by the early twentieth-century view of Neandertal mental capacity in Boule's assessment, they quoted Boule at length. Boule had written:

> It is probable, therefore, that Neanderthal Man must have possessed only a rudimentary psychic nature, superior certainly to that of the anthropoid apes, but markedly inferior to that of any modern race whatever. He had doubtless only the most rudimentary language. . . . It is important to note that the physical characters of the Neanderthal type are quite in agreement with what archaeology teaches us as to his bodily capacity, his psychology, and his habits. . . . There is hardly a more rudimentary or degraded form of industry than that of our Mousterian Man. . . . [There is] a probable absence of all traces of any pre-occupation of an aesthetic or of a moral kind . . . quite in agreement with the brutish appearance of this energetic and clumsy body, of the heavy-jawed skull, which itself still declares the predominance of functions of a purely vegetative or bestial kind over the functions of the mind.

They then reproduced Boule's remarks about Cro-Magnon:

> What contrast with the men of the next geological and archaeological period, with the men of the Cro-Magnon type, who had a more elegant body, a finer head, an upright and spacious brow, and who have left, in the caves which they inhabited, so much evidence of their manual skill, artistic and religious preoccupations, of their abstract faculties, and who were the first to merit the glorious title of *Homo sapiens*!

Next to their matter-of-fact, medically oriented prose and deadpan delivery, Boule's hyperbole looked foolish. Straus and Cave commented, calmly but unforgivingly:

> It is unnecessary to detail the respective roles of fact, fancy, and, perhaps, even emotion in Boule's estimation. . . . There is thus no valid reason for the assumption that the posture of Neanderthal man of the fourth glacial period differed significantly from that of

present-day men. This is not to deny that his limbs, as well as his skull, exhibit distinctive features—features which collectively distinguish him from all groups of modern men.... It may well be that the arthritic "old man" of La Chapelle-aux-Saints, the postural prototype of Neanderthal man, did actually stand and walk with something of a pathological kyphosis [curvature of the spine]; but, if so, he has his counterparts in modern men similarly affected with spinal osteoarthritis.

But it was a brief metaphor, a small aside, that captured the imagination of their fellow scientists and became the new, enduring image of the Neandertal. With an unerring instinct for the striking image, Straus and Cave remarked: "Notwithstanding, if he could be reincarnated and placed in a New York subway—provided that he were bathed, shaved, and dressed in modern clothing—it is doubtful whether he would attract any more attention than some of its other denizens." This comment was picked up in many popular texts, illustrated neatly with Coon's drawing of a Neandertal in hat, coat, and tie done in 1939.

Straus and Cave made some concessions to saving Boule's face—arguing that Boule's work "must be placed in its proper historical setting" and allowing that "it seems unlikely, moreover, that we are free from similar [biasing] influences at the present time." But, in the end, they effectively dismantled Boule's credibility on the matter of Neandertal anatomy, at least for the next generation of Anglophone anthropologists.

Perhaps inadvertently—or perhaps in an attempt to afford Boule an excuse, however thin—Straus and Cave left the impression that Boule's postural reconstruction was wrong simply because he had failed to recognize the arthritic condition of the specimen. Their article engendered a new myth: that Boule, under the influence of his prejudice that Neandertals were primitive and beastly, had mistaken a pathological Neandertal specimen for a normal one. But careful reading of Boule's work shows that he was well aware that the La Chapelle-aux-Saints vertebrae were arthritic and abnormal, and that he "corrected" for this problem. Apparently, Boule's prejudices were so strong that he was perfectly capable of creating a stooped posture and shuffling gait for the Old Man based on the normal bones from the skeleton (and on those from the Neandertal, La Ferrassie, and Spy specimens, which he also consulted). Attempting to dispel one myth, Straus and Cave created a new one: that of the paleontologist who couldn't recognize arthritis.

56. Henri Vallois, student of Marcellin Boule and director of the Institut de Paléontologie Humaine. He was one of the last to argue vigorously for the pre-Sapiens hypothesis—the view that modern-appearing humans had great antiquity, long preceding the Neandertals.

Although the edifice of Boule's interpretation of Neandertals was crumbling, bulldozed by the accelerating bulk of hard evidence produced by several scholars, it had not yet been razed. Only Franz Weidenreich was promoting Neandertals as closely related to modern humans, and this idea won few converts. Among them, however, was Arthur Keith, who in 1948 declared for Weidenreich and abandoned his long-held belief that humans had been big-brained—sapient—in very ancient times.

Chief among the skeptics of Weidenreich's work was Henri Vallois, Boule's onetime student who had succeeded him as head of the Institut de Paléontologie Humaine in Paris. After Boule's death in 1942, his three protégés—Vallois, Pierre Teilhard de Chardin, and Jean Piveteau—were left "in charge" of paleontology in France. Teilhard was by then occupied with metaphysics and philosophy more than human evolution. Piveteau was the senior vertebrate paleontologist at the Sorbonne in Paris, interested more in the anatomy of fossil frogs than that of fossil Frenchmen. Only Vallois valiantly guarded the sacred flame, revising and re-revising Boule's textbook *Les Hommes Fossiles* (*Fossil Men*) with only minor changes for years. In addition to succeeding Boule at the Institut de Paléontologie Humaine, Vallois also managed to appropriate the directorship of the Musée de l'Homme during World War II. Its only previous director had been Paul Rivet, an ethnologist with strong socialist leanings; the Musée de l'Homme had actually been built for him during the 1930s. When the Germans occupied France, Rivet fled to the United States rather than work under the hated invaders, but Vallois agreed to take over the directorship.

This dual position gave Vallois considerable power if not universal respect. In 1958, at the conclusion of his monograph on the Fontéchevade fossils, he published a critique of the three main theories of the Neandertals' place in human evolution. This work rapidly became a classic, recognized for its clarity and directness. Vallois wrote:

> Without going into the details of a historical survey such as may be found in the majority of studies of human paleontology, the many conceptions suggested by writers . . . may be classed under three headings:
>
> I. *H. sapiens* derives directly from Neanderthal man;
> II. *H. sapiens* derives from the Preneanderthals;
> III. *H. sapiens* derives from a special trunk, independent from that of the Neanderthals and Preneanderthals, the trunk of Presapiens.

For Vallois, the first theory—which he dubbed the Neandertal hypothesis—subsumed a variety of late-nineteenth-century views as well as the early twentieth-century schemes of Aleš Hrdlička and Franz Weidenreich. Hrdlička had undoubtedly provided the clearest exposition of the Neandertal hypothesis in his Huxley Memorial Lecture in 1927. Vallois grouped his ideas with Weidenreich's multiregionalism hypothesis, because both fundamentally believed in a "Neandertal phase" spread across the Old World. Vallois ignored the fact that Weidenreich had set the classic Neandertals of Europe on a side-branch, deriving modern Europeans from late archaic humans in the Near East. To Vallois, "the theory of a Neandertal origin . . . presents gross defects."

Vallois felt that Boule's monograph had demonstrated for all time that Neandertals were too specialized to lie on the path from *Pithecanthropus* to *Homo sapiens*. Vallois devised various anatomical indices, such as the humeroradial index, which reflects the proportion of the forearm to the upper arm. If apes, Neandertals, early *Homo sapiens,* and modern humans were an evolutionary series, Vallois flatly expected to find a gradient from long to short in the values of these indices. Instead, Neandertals fell out of their expected place in the sequence, being either like modern humans or even "more human" than humans—that is, having shorter lower limbs than humans do.

Vallois's second objection was that he could see no intergradation or morphological continuity between European Neandertals and the Cro-Magnon modern humans, makers of the Aurignacian industry, who succeeded them. The classic Neandertals who lived in Europe during the Würm glaciation are remarkably similar to one another, Vallois asserted. But the oldest skeletons associated with Aurignacian culture, Combe Capelle and the purportedly Negroid skeletons from Grimaldi, are markedly different and obviously human. The two are separated by at most a "few thousand" years, not long enough for such a dramatic change in morphology. "The thesis which derives men of the Upper Paleolithic from the classic Neanderthals of that continent cannot be sustained," Vallois concluded.

As for the pre-Neandertal theory, developed and explained most clearly by Sergio Sergi, Blanc's collaborator, it too had problems. The essence of the theory was the belief that a more generalized form of hominid—the pre-Neandertal—gave rise to two divergent branches, one of which evolved into modern humans, and the other of which become more and more specialized, eventually culminating in the dead-end Neandertals.

In 1944, 1948, and 1953, Sergi elaborated his ideas, which were based on his research on the Saccopastore material and its resemblances to the fragmentary remains from Fontéchevade, Steinheim, Swanscombe, and Ehringsdorf. To Sergi's eyes, these few fossils attested to the presence in Europe of a less specialized type of human living before the Neandertals developed their extreme morphology. He created a large cluster of fossils with Swanscombe and Steinheim at the base, leading to Krapina, Ehringsdorf, and Saccopastore on the one hand and then to the Neandertals—and their approximate contemporary, Fontéchevade, on the other—leading to modern humans. Sergi believed that this pre-Neandertal cluster looked more like modern humans than the Neandertals did. The feature that was pointed to over and over was their lack of prominent browridges, the very same feature that had always made Neandertals seem brutish, savage, and uncivilized. Sergi painted Neandertals as a deviant offshoot, destined for extinction, from the anatomically more modern pre-Neandertals.

F. Clark Howell, in his influential papers in the early 1950s, had expressed a similar view using slightly different terms. Howell's "progressive Neandertals" were a group containing the same fossils that held the same position as Sergi's pre-Neandertals: they were the source population from which both classic Neandertals and modern humans sprang.

The pre-Neandertal theory was "most seductive," according to Vallois, but "is marked by a fundamental contradiction." That contradiction, to Vallois, was the artificiality of the group, the lack of coherency in the physical structure, or morphology, of the different fossils clustered together as pre-Neandertals. He emphasized, for example, the impossibility of grouping "Fontéchevade man, with a voluminous cranium and no frontal torus [browridge], and Steinheim, whose dimensions are much smaller but whose torus is even more developed than in Neandertals proper."

For Vallois, and many others, the Fontéchevade fossils were the crux of the issue. It was unfortunate indeed that they were so fragmentary and that there appeared to be some confusion about their positions in the deposits prior to excavation. A detailed account of the discovery was published after ten years had passed, which perhaps encouraged skeptics to wonder whether or not the excavation had been properly documented at the time. But Vallois himself suffered no doubts. In 1949, two years after the Fontéchevade fossils were found, he proclaimed in suitably magisterial prose:

> In contrast to earlier finds of human remains we have here, in effect, a specimen which is well dated and found in a stratigraphic context which allows of no dispute: *this is the first time that man, certainly not Neanderthal although earlier than the Neanderthals, has been found in Europe under such conditions.*

What is even more amazing than Vallois's overall confidence was the authoritative tone with which he wrote of the lack of browridge, or torus, on Fontéchevade. This "fact" relied upon a hefty degree of reconstruction. The better specimen, known as the Fontéchevade II cranium, is broken off above the orbits: there is simply no way to tell if a torus was there or not. The Fontéchevade I fragment preserves only a small portion of the forehead region, and it does not show a browridge. However, its vault bones are so much thinner than those of Fontéchevade II that most believe either this was an immature individual, too young to have developed a marked browridge, or else it was an intrusive specimen from more recent levels.

Not content to base his far-reaching conclusions on only the incomplete Fontéchevade fossils, Vallois also invoked the evidence of the skull fragments found at Swanscombe in the 1930s. The Swanscombe specimen includes only the occipital and parietal bones (the back and top of the braincase); there is no trace of the all-important frontal bone, the one which bears the brow and forehead region. Clearly, the state of the brow of the Swanscombe fossil was at least as ambiguous as that of the Fontéchevade remains, but two poor cases seemed more convincing than one.

Evidence—or lack of it—notwithstanding, Vallois himself greatly preferred the third hypothesis: the pre-Sapiens theory. Like Boule and Keith before him, Vallois liked the idea of a very ancient, sapient ancestor of modern humans that long predated (and was well removed from) either the pre-Neandertals or their descendants, the brutish Neandertals, both of which were destined for extinction.

The pre-Sapiens theory was based originally on the existence of various putatively ancient fossils with the morphology of modern humans; it was propped up by Boule's expulsion of Neandertals from our family tree; and it was glorified into apparent truth by the forged fossils from Piltdown. As formulated by Keith and Boule, the pre-Sapiens theory argued that large-brained, modern-skulled humans were so distinctive that they must have had a long (and honorable) evolutionary history. Besides, anything as special as ourselves must have taken a long time to evolve—a rather exalted view of modern humans. Boule and Keith were distinctly uncomfortable with any suggestion that we might have been descended, relatively recently, from anything less human than ourselves. They preferred to believe that pre-Sapiens humans existed far back into the Pliocene, the geological epoch preceding the Pleistocene, relegating all known fossil hominids to aberrant side-branches on the family tree. In this way, although Boule, Keith, and Vallois never denied that human evolution had occurred, they were more than content to see the known record of human fossils as a series of "corpses left on the road along which humanity has differentiated."

Of course, the unmasking of the Piltdown fraud was a bitter blow to the pre-Sapiens theorists. Other candidates for pre-Sapiens status—fossils such as Moulin Quignon, Galley Hill or Ipswich—had been discredited in less dramatic style. As Vallois conceded, tactfully, "The discovery of Piltdown has now lost all its significance but, more than compensating for this, that of Fontéchevade has at last provided the crucial proof that should bring conviction." There is more than a subtle

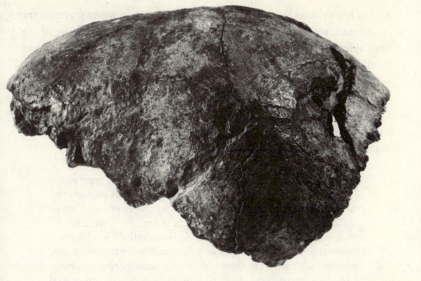

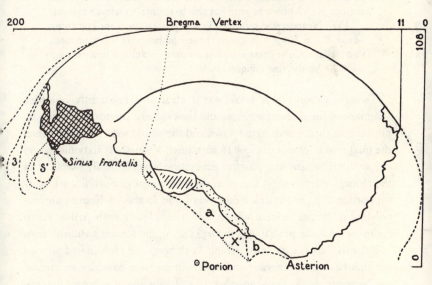

57. The incomplete Fontéchevade 2 skullcap (above) and Vallois's reconstruction of the missing brow region (below). Vallois's preferred reconstruction was no. 3, without a browridge, but the specimen is fragmentary, and a reconstruction with a large browridge (no. 1) would actually fit the fossil better. With a smooth brow, the Fontéchevade fossil became the proof of Vallois's belief that anatomically modern humans were very ancient.

hint in his writings that any modern-looking fossil, however fragmentary or dubious, would have been embraced as preventing the collapse of the pre-Sapiens theory after the exposure of Piltdown. Swanscombe and Fontéchevade appeared suitably modern—in the few parts preserved —and sufficiently ancient to qualify for the rescuer's role.

From *where* did Vallois's pre-Sapiens heroes migrate into Europe? As did so many during this period, Vallois pointed to the conveniently sketchy fossil record of the ever-mysterious East and constructed a dramatic and plausible tale of exploration and conquest.

> Somewhere in the east, doubtless in Western Asia, and prior to the Würm [glaciation], there must have existed Presapiens men who by gradual development became sapiens proper. We have seen that, in parallel fashion in Europe, the Preneanderthals were likewise becoming transformed into the classic Neanderthals. Under these circumstances one may suppose . . . that the Swanscombe and Fontéchevade men were emissaries of an Asiatic stock [of humans of modern appearance], coming into Europe during interglacial periods, which however were not able to maintain themselves there. . . . [The Neandertals] remained in sole possession at the beginning of the Würm. Reappearing with the second period of this glaciation, descendants of the Presapiens lost no time in taking a final revenge on their Mousterian conquerors.

Though Vallois's 1958 book was a clear and apparently objective summary of the three hypotheses and the evidence supporting them, the pre-Sapiens theory was on the wane, and the words were little more than the final charge of troops close to surrender. Vallois was sixty-nine years old at the time, and the postwar generation was ruthlessly skeptical of their elders. After Vallois's demise, the only remaining scholar seriously supporting the pre-Sapiens model was Louis Leakey, a Kenyan anthropologist of British descent who had worked closely with Arthur Keith (proponent of the pre-Sapiens theory) during the former's student days.

Prior to Vallois's 1958 monograph, both Sergi and Howell had pointed out that both Fontéchevade and Swanscombe were basically archaic, or pre-Neandertal–like, in shape. A series of subsequent scholars reexamined these enigmatic fossils seriously and agreed that they were good Neandertal ancestors, belonging in the same lineage as the Steinheim, Saccopastore, and Ehringsdorf fossils. Vallois's last-ditch effort to rescue and resurrect a moribund approach to human ancestry failed. The pre-Neandertal theory predominated, leaving classic Neandertals on a side-branch with no descendants. It was once again respectable to include anatomically archaic humans among our ancestors.

While the Italians and Americans were supporting pre-Neandertals, and the French were nurturing pre-Sapiens, the Germans were simply in disarray—hardly surprising given the devastation of postwar Germany. Physical anthropology was in severe disrepute because it had been perverted to support the racist policies of Nazi Germany. Several decades would pass before paleoanthropology would reemerge as a significant science east of the Rhine.

Belgium was beginning to resurface as an important force in physical anthropology, resuming the crucial role it had played in the nineteenth century. In the intervening years, the only significant Belgian publication on Neandertals had been a monograph by Charles Fraipont—the son of Julien Fraipont, who found and described the Spy Neandertals—in 1936, on the child's cranium from Engis. Though the fossil had been found in 1829 by Schmerling, it was only belatedly recognized as a Neandertal. Unfortunately, Fraipont was personally discredited for his pro-German sympathies in World War II.

Fraipont's loss of credibility left the field largely to François Twiesselmann. A medical doctor, Twiesselmann studied the development of the chicken embryo, yet he was asked to apply for the position of physical anthropologist at the newly created Institut royal des Sciences naturelles de Belgique (the Belgian Royal Institute of Natural Sciences) in the mid-1930s. Twiesselmann confesses now that he had to look up *anthropology* in the dictionary to figure out what he might be expected to do in this job, but he applied nonetheless. Neither he nor any of his colleagues were in a position to turn down a firm job during the depression, however far that job might seem to deviate from what he had trained to do.

Perhaps Twiesselmann felt himself ill qualified for a few years. But when the new synthesis highlighted the relevance of population studies to physical anthropology, Twiesselmann was both intellectually sympathetic and practically well equipped. As a physician, he had collaborated closely with statisticians on problems of epidemiology and public health. He appreciated, deeply, the power that statistical analyses had to enhance understanding. In 1961, he was among the first to employ statistical analyses in a metrical study of a human fossil: a Neandertal femur, originally found in 1895 in the small cave of Fond-de-Forêt, which had long lain unappreciated in the Musée de la Cinquantenaire (the Museum of the Fiftieth Anniversary of the Belgian State) in Brussels. It was an unimpressive specimen, but the study was ground-breaking. Twiesselmann was part of the new order, the new generation of scholars who were shaping the future of the field.

In contrast, the aging New Englander Carleton Coon was about to experience an unhappy fate somewhat similar to Vallois's. Coon must have expected his 1962 book, *The Origin of Races*, to be the triumphant culmination of his life's work on race—and race, as ever, was intimately entwined with the Neandertals. Coon picked up the flag that Weidenreich had dropped, subtly altering the multiregionalism hypothesis.

When Weidenreich proposed the existence of multiple human lineages developing in parallel, he had emphasized the existence of gene flow among these lines. In fact, the classic diagram with which Weidenreich illustrated his hypothesis was so criss-crossed with interconnections that the naïve reader might easily have been bewildered into overlooking the vertical continuity of the lines representing each geographic population evolving through time.

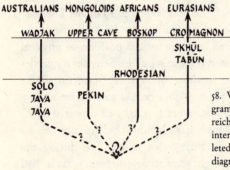

58. William Howells's "candelabra" diagram was a simplification of Franz Weidenreich's model of human evolution, with the interconnections between the regions deleted—a point overlooked by some. This diagram appeared in *Mankind in the Making* in 1959.

But the popular perception of Weidenreich's ideas had shifted. In 1959, the Harvard anthropologist William Howells published his popular textbook *Mankind in the Making*. In it, he reproduced diagrams illustrating various authors' schemes of human evolution, side by side. Weidenreich's confusing, criss-crossing diagram was simplified and shown as a candelabra. All of the interbreeding and genetic exchange so important to Weidenreich's formulation of the theory disappeared. To be fair, Howells made no attempt to deceive: the caption to the diagram read, "Left, above, the Polyphyletic or Candelabra School, modified (and exaggerated) from Weidenreich."

The alterations in Weidenreich's diagram, though openly acknowledged in the caption, went unnoticed by many who turned to Howells's authoritative book. His representation was taken as accurate. That being so, then it seemed most unlikely that the lineages representing the different human races had separated genetically and geographically well before *Homo erectus* and yet continued to evolve in parallel for so long a period. Many discarded Weidenreich's theory without ever consulting the original and thus without ever discovering that Weidenreich "solved" the problem by proposing a continued intermixing and interbreeding among the different lineages.

Coon offered another view. He masterfully summarized evidence from ethnology, linguistics, and paleontology, concluding that the human races had separated long ago, as Weidenreich had believed. He knew that Weidenreich's views were unpopular, but Coon was never one to be pressured to follow the crowd. "To me, there was something very pat, dogmatic, and wrong about the anti-Weidenreich point of view," Coon wrote in the introduction to *The Origin of Races*.

> For years I mulled it over in my mind, and then I decided to collect every scrap of existing information about every single fossil-man bone and tooth in the world. Once I had acquired as much information as I could, I concentrated on the dimension of space and tried to see how many racial lines, including the mongoloid, could be traced back to the first instance that any kind of man had appeared on the earth. In the end I succeeded in tracing back five, each as old as man himself.
>
> Realizing the enormity of my discovery in terms of its divergence from accepted dogma, I knew that I must provide a theoretical foundation for the facts I had unearthed. The possibility that races can be older than species had to be explored. I soon found, by reading and through conversation with [Ernst] Mayr, [G. G.] Simpson, and other biologists, that what I had thought a revolutionary concept was so common an event in nature that others rarely bothered to mention it; to wit, that a species which is divided into geographical races can evolve into a daughter species while retaining the same geographical races.

Coon believed, quite rightly, that he was integrating modern population biology with the fossil record; his grand synthesis would offer an up-to-date treatment of a nineteenth-century problem. He wrote of the evolution of a polytypic species—the new term used to describe a species broken up into a series of geographic populations that vary from one another in appearance. Each of the geographic variants in a polytypic species can be thought of as species-in-the-making, or potential species, for—if the geographic barriers prove formidable enough—no individuals will cross them, and gene flow between adjacent populations cease. Through generations, the adjacent but separate populations will become increasingly distinct genetically. Thus, polytypic species have a better than average chance to give rise to one or more daughter species. Coon felt that the human lineage provided a perfect example of a species separated into geographic groups—subspecies or races—that evolved through time.

In effect, Coon was suggesting the candelabra model—Weidenreich's multiregionalism hypothesis but without the genetic connections between geographic populations—that was already in disrepute.

> My thesis is, in essence, that at the beginning of our record, over half a million years ago, man was a single species, *Homo erectus*, perhaps already divided into five geographic races or subspecies. *Homo erectus* then evolved into *Homo sapiens* not once but five times, as each subspecies, living in its own territory, passed a critical threshold from a more brutal to a more *sapient* state.

The dangerous and highly inflammatory part of his synthesis was the observation that each subspecies not only crossed the threshold from *Homo erectus* to *Homo sapiens* independently, but they also seemed to cross it at different times. Coon considered a complex of features discernible from fossils, but the Rubicon was based on brain size (greater than 1,250–1,300 cc being considered sapient). And as he reviewed the fossil evidence from each region, following what he believed to be racial lineages, his data suggested that Caucasoids and Mongoloids had crossed the Rubicon first, with Congoids ("the Negroes and Pygmies of Africa"), Capoids ("the Bushmen and Hottentots and other relict tribes"), and Australoids trailing behind.

The troublesome implication was that some of the darker-skinned, living races of humankind are evolutionarily backward. Alert to this potential landmine in his work, Coon actually attempted to defuse it in a long and revealing passage at the end of his book:

> Once a race has become established as the principal population of a region, it has a tendency to stay there and to resist the genetic influences swept in by later invasions. . . .
> When two races come into contact and mixture occurs, one race

tends to dominate the other. The local advantage that the geneti-cally superior group (superior for its time and place) possesses may be primarily cultural or primarily physiological, or a combination of both. For example, the dominance of the Europeans over the native peoples of North America, Australia, and New Zealand is primarily cultural; that of the Negroes in the tropical lowlands of the New World and of the Indians in the Andes is primarily physiological.

There is, however, a third kind of dominance, expressed by the resistance of a population to the intrusion of large numbers of outsiders into its social and genetic structure. Call it xenophobia, prejudice, or whatever, people do not ordinarily welcome masses of strangers in their midst, particularly if the strangers come with women and children and settle down to stay. Social mechanisms arise automatically to isolate the newcomers as much as possible and to keep them genetically separate. . . .

The above is the behavioral aspect of race relations. The genetic aspect operates in a comparable way. Genes that form part of a cell nucleus possess an internal equilibrium as a group, just as do the members of social institutions. Genes in a population are in equilib-rium if the population is living a healthy life as a corporate entity. Racial intermixture can upset the genetic as well as the social equilibrium of a group.

I am making these statements not for any political or social purpose but merely to show that, were it not for the mechanisms cited above, men would not be black, white, yellow, or brown. We would all be light khaki, for there has been enough gene flow over the . . . regions of the world during the last half million years to have homogenized us all had that been the evolutionary scheme of things, and had it not been advantageous to each of the geographic races for it to retain, for the most part, the adaptive elements in its genetic *status quo.* . . .

Caucasoids and Mongoloids who live in their homelands and in recently colonized regions, such as North America, did not rise to their present population levels and positions of cultural dominance by accident. They achieved all this because their ancestors occupied the most favorable of the earth's zoological regions. . . . These regions had challenging climates and ample breeding grounds and were centrally located within continental land masses. There general adaptation was more important than special adaptation. Any other subspecies that had evolved in these regions would probably have been just as successful.

Read carefully, Coon was suggesting a sort of ecological determinism. He attributed the apparent superiority of Mongoloids and Caucasoids simply to fortuitous geography: being in the right place at the right time. But in trying to avert charges of racism, he had introduced a new and still more incendiary idea. Acknowledging openly that races resist homogenization, he suggested both a mechanism and an evolutionary explanation for the fact, in a way that seemed to condone racial prejudice as correct, "natural," or even evolutionarily advantageous.

Coon's words can be read in a variety of ways, and those who knew him are divided on the question of whether he was or was not a racist. He commonly used racial or ethnic labels in describing people, a habit strongly associated with unfavorable, prejudicial judgments about the qualities of various ethnic groups. A more generous interpretation of Coon's habit was that it simply reflected his mental processes and the lifelong practice of observing, noting, and collecting information about the physical expression of racial forms.

The full truth of what he felt in his heart about the people he classified, and sometimes worked with, may never be known. He was obviously happy among and truly fond of many of the non-Western peoples he lived with on his field trips, respecting deeply those who were brave, honest, and intelligent. Did he believe them his equal? *Equal* in such a context can be interpreted so many ways that this is almost a meaningless question. Did he believe they were no different from himself? Obviously not; he acknowledged, examined, documented, and sometimes relished the differences. In the end, perhaps Coon's innermost feelings were irrelevant. Others' interpretations of his words were shortly to become far more important than anything Coon actually did, thought, or said.

Aside from his controversial views on racial issues, Coon managed to put an insightful new twist on the understanding of Neandertals. By taking a broad view of the effect of geography on all mammals, Coon realized that what had often been left out of human evolutionary schemes was any real grappling with adaptation. Animals, it was well known, were strongly influenced by their environment, with desert species evolving mechanisms to conserve water and avoid heat, or forest animals evolving highly maneuverable, grasping hands and feet for climbing. The same principles would apply to the perceptible differences among humans, Coon asserted boldly. "By comparing man with other animals," he wrote, "we shall see, in particular, how adaptation to the external, nonhuman environment helped shape the living races of man."

Not only did Coon seek to explain the differences among the living human races—a formidable task in itself that would have daunted a scholar less sure of his own abilities—but he looked for evidence of adaptation in the fossil record, too. To understand how these adaptations might manifest themselves, Coon turned to two nineteenth-century "rules" of biology, generally known as Bergmann's and Allen's rules. These state that, in order to conserve heat in cold climates, animals will tend to have greater body bulk and shorter extremities than similar species living in warmer climates. Coon observed that humans fit the predictions perfectly. Eskimos, living under Arctic conditions, tend to have shorter necks, stubbier arms and legs, and stockier builds than, say, Maasai or other equatorial peoples, whose adaptation to heat stress shows in their elongate, slender body build and longer-than-average limbs. These were interesting, if uninspiring, observations.

Where Coon surpassed what had gone before was in trying to apply this same knowledge to the fossil record. It was a breathtaking insight, for no one had tried seriously to integrate the concepts of adaptation and selection with a thorough treatment of the fossil record before. When Coon turned to the Neandertals, he saw everywhere in their anatomy the telltale signs of adaptations to a cold, glacial climate. The stocky build and short limbs were reminiscent of Eskimos' features.

But, as ever, the head of Neandertals drew the greatest amount of comment. Coon saw the nose as "the prime architect of the Neanderthal face." By this phrase he referred to three dominant features that typified the Neandertal face: the large opening in the cranium for the nose, or the nasal aperture; the prominent bridge of the nose, as judged from the shape of the nasal bones; and the overall forward thrust of the middle region of the face—an arrangement described by a later scholar, Erik Trinkaus, as looking as if a modern human face, made of rubber, had been grabbed by the nose and pulled forward.

What Coon proposed came to be known as the radiator theory of Neandertal noses.

> The western Neanderthals, and particularly the French ones, must have needed big noses for some reason. The nose serves the purpose, among others, of warming and moistening the inhaled air on the way to the lungs. . . . [But] it is not so much the lungs . . . [as] the brain that is in danger of chilling by inhaled air. . . . In ordinary human heads and necks the nasal passages are quite close to the arteries that feed blood to the brain. In a flat-headed, short-necked individual exposed to intense cold the proximity of nasal passages

to these blood vessels could be critical, for the brain must be kept at a constant temperature.

Coon argued that the peculiar facial architecture of the western Neandertals served to buffer the brain from "extreme cold without adequate headgear or protection for the neck." He added:

> As the climate grew colder, Neanderthal men may have increasingly needed a large, projecting nasal "radiator," particularly as there is no archaeological evidence of cultural improvement that would help mitigate the severity of the climate.

In other words, the size and prominence of Neandertal noses allowed the frigid air to be warmed, preventing it from refrigerating the brain stem. The presumed mechanism relied on the fact that the nasal mucosa are capillary-rich and thus capable of heating the incoming air. This was a major step forward in the history of attempts to explain Neandertal morphology and place it within the modern evolutionary framework, even though later scholars would have much new to say on the subject of Neandertal noses.

When Coon completed his magnum opus, synthesizing the latest information on evolutionary theory with all that was known of modern human variability *and* with the entire fossil record of primates in general and hominids in particular, he must have felt an unparalleled sense of satisfaction. It was, and remains—without question—an extraordinary piece of scholarship.

Coon had chosen to ignore the warning signs that his work was headed for trouble. In 1961, the year before *The Origin of Races* was published, Coon had been elected president of the American Association of Physical Anthropologists, a sign of the esteem and respect with which his peers regarded him. But at the first annual meeting over which he presided, in May 1962, Coon ran afoul of an attempt to politicize the academic organization. Some of the younger men demanded an extra session be held to present (and pass) important resolutions.

With his vice president, T. Dale Stewart of the Smithsonian Institution, Coon managed to derail a motion to vote on whether all races were equal in intelligence. Their objection was that this was a point about which there was precious little evidence; only brain *size* was well documented, but it has little to do with intelligence, at least within a species. To call for a vote on a matter of fact, without knowing the facts, seemed ludicrous to Coon and Stewart.

Though they kept that motion from the floor, they could not forestall the next resolution, which was for an official censure of a small book called *Race and Reason: A Yankee View*, just published by Carleton Putnam.

Though endorsed by the American Bar Association and the chairman of the Senate's Armed Services Committee, the book was widely reputed to be racist (and is). Its author was no flyweight, either. He was an "ex-chairman of the board of Delta Airlines, biographer of Theodore Roosevelt, and a son of a New York Federal judge" and was, to boot, a distant relation of Coon. The issue was further complicated by the fact that a widely circulated pamphlet written by Putnam said that Coon's data supported his ideas.

When the resolution to condemn Putnam's book finally arose, Coon challenged the membership to raise their hands if they had actually read the book, as Coon had; one person raised his hand. Asked what he thought of it, that man replied, "Not much." Coon was incensed that his friends and colleagues were prepared to condemn a book they had not even bothered to read; what sort of scientific responsibility was that? He used his presidential status to chastise the membership for their disgraceful cowardice and all-around idiotic behavior. He then offered his resignation—"I told my fellow members that I would no longer preside over such a craven lot"—and left them to vote on their resolution. The next day he resigned his curatorship at the University of Pennsylvania, taking early retirement following a terminal sabbatical of one year. It was some time before he learned that his resignation as president of the American Association of Physical Anthropologists had been refused, and that the resolution was passed—meaning that it appeared in print over his signature, a point that infuriated Coon still more.

Soon it was rumored falsely that Coon had given Putnam as-yet-unpublished data from his forthcoming *The Origin of Races* so that Putnam could voice the racist beliefs Coon had too little courage to espouse openly. Some, struck by the similarity in their names, apparently believed that "Carleton Putnam" was none other than Carleton Coon in disguise. Given Coon's lifelong penchant for outspokenness, consequences be damned, this seems a particularly flimsy and baseless accusation. It was also rumored, equally incorrectly, that Coon had been fired from the University of Pennsylvania for writing and speaking about race.

Then, on October 25, 1962, Coon's *The Origin of Races* was published, the cover decorated with high praise from such luminaries of the new synthesis as Julian Huxley, G. G. Simpson, and Ernst Mayr, and such prominent anthropologists as William Howells from Harvard; William Straus, Jr., who had recognized arthritis in the La Chapelle-aux-Saints skeleton; Lawrence Angel at the Smithsonian; and W. M. Krogman of the University of Pennsylvania. But not every member of the new synthesis crowd was enchanted. Theodosius Dobzhansky, the fruit-fly man at Columbia, wrote a blistering review for the *Saturday Review*, accusing Coon of both racism and misunderstanding evolutionary biology. The review was so defamatory that the *Saturday Review* chose not to publish it, although it later appeared in *Scientific American* and *Current Anthropology*. Morton Fried, a professor of anthropology also at Columbia, attempted to organize an abortive advertising campaign to reject Coon's book publicly, and M. F. Ashley Montagu, another anthropologist, disparaged Coon at length on a television talk show.

The subsequent argument in the journals and at meetings rapidly devolved into blazing exchanges about the sizes of the brain in different races, with the comparison of the brain of Turgenev (a large brain) and Anatole France (an unusually small one) being made repeatedly. On November 16, 1962, less than a month after *The Origin of Races* was published, Sherwood Washburn sided with his former colleague and close friend Dobzhansky in incendiary fashion. Now president of the American Anthropological Association, a powerful, middle-aged leader of the field, Washburn had been urged by the Executive Board to make clear that responsible anthropologists did not condone Putnam's racist views. He turned the full force of his formidable verbal and intellectual skills to humiliating and castigating Coon, his former Harvard professor and racial expert, the symbol of everything old-fashioned that needed eradicating in physical anthropology now that Hooton was dead.

Washburn started off his polemic slowly:

> The Executive Board has asked me to give my address on the subject of race, and, reluctantly and diffidently, I have agreed to do so. I am not a specialist on the subject. I have never done research on race, but I have taught it for a number of years.
>
> Discussion of the races of man seems to generate endless emotion and confusion. I am under no illusion that this paper can do much to dispel the confusion; it may add to the emotion. The latest information available supports the traditional findings of anthropologists and other social scientists—that there is no scientific basis of any kind for racial discrimination.

Washburn then mentioned by name Dobzhansky's then-recent book, *Mankind Evolving*—of which he approved most strongly—contrasting it with Coon's *The Origin of Races*. Though he infrequently mentioned Coon by name thereafter, at least in the printed version of his speech, Washburn proceeded to criticize (thoroughly), misrepresent (occasionally), and insult (frequently) Coon throughout the rest of his talk. No one in the audience was in doubt that Coon was Washburn's target. Neither Putnam's name nor his work was ever mentioned.

Washburn lectured on the modern view of evolution, contrasting it with the typological thinking about race that he felt Coon's work represented: "Those of you who have read *Current Anthropology* [which had published Dobzhansky's critical review of Coon's book] will realize that this kind of anthropology is still alive, amazingly, and in full force in some countries; relics of it are still alive in our teaching today." Washburn parodied Coon's attempts to trace the origin of races and, more cruelly, declared the touchy issue of race, the subject of Coon's life work, to be nonexistent: "Race isn't very important biologically."

Washburn also ridiculed Coon's nasal radiator—an idea that, although not entirely correct in the eyes of modern scholars, was nonetheless a credible and useful first attempt at understanding Neandertal anatomy as a function of an environmental adaptation. He also flatly accused Coon of professional incompetency.

> I should like to speak for a moment on the notion that the Mongoloids are a race which are adapted to live in the cold, that these are arctic-adapted people.
>
> In the first place ... large numbers of Mongoloids are living in the hot, moist tropics. ... Actually, there is no correlation, that is, none that has been well worked out, to support the notion that any of these racial groups is cold-adapted. ... If one follows the form of the nose, in Europe, as one moves north, narrow noses are correlated with cold climate; in eastern Asia low noses are correlated with cold climate. In neither case is there the slightest evidence that the difference in the form of the nose has anything whatsoever to do with warming the air that comes into the face. ...
>
> The point I wish to stress is that those who have spoken of the cold-adaptation of the Mongoloid face and of the Neanderthal face do not know the structure of the human face. We have people writing about human faces who are anatomically illiterate.

Coming from a former student—one who, in all probability, was taught some of the anatomy he now bragged about by Coon himself—this was insufferable.

Though Washburn's open attacks diminished fairly rapidly, Dobzhansky continued to throw vitriol at Coon until 1968, when he published an article called "Bogus Science" in *Journal of Heredity*. Coon's reply provides an interesting view of the whole affair:

> You published a review of Carleton Putnam's [second] book, *Race and Reality*, by Theodosius Dobzhansky. The latter devoted one fifth of his space to reiterating for the nth time his denunciation of my book . . . following which he castigates me, also for the nth time, for not having repudiated Mr. Putnam's quotation of one brief statement in my book. . . . Dobzhansky stated that "It is the duty of a scientist to prevent misuse and prostitution of his findings." I disagree with him. It is the duty of a scientist to do his work conscientiously and to the best of his ability, which is exactly what I have done and shall continue to do, and to reject publicly only the writings of those persons who, influenced by one cause or another, have misquoted him, as Dobzhansky repeatedly has done with my work, for reasons best known unto himself.
>
> Were the evolution of fruit flies a prime social and political issue, Dobzhansky might easily find himself in the same situation in which he and his followers have tried to place me.

With that exchange, the controversy cooled off. Coon and Dobzhansky, each approaching the end of his career, largely retreated from the stage, leaving it to Washburn whose "new physical anthropology" program soon came to dominate the field. Yet, all in all, it was one of the most acrimonious and shameful conflicts between social concern and scientific discussion that anthropology has ever endured. No doubt Washburn, Dobzhansky, and others intended to offer strong support for the burgeoning, liberal, civil rights movement—for which they should be applauded—and to overthrow those whom they perceived as representing the establishment that had permitted if not actually fostered racism and repression. It was, after all, the beginning of the 1960s, the era of flower children, peace marches, and new, more egalitarian, and sometimes highly disruptive social roles.

But beneath the benign, gentle ambiance of the 1960s was an outspoken moralizing and merciless judgmental quality as inflexible as the attitudes of the reactionary establishment against which the liberals of the 1960s were reacting. The behavior of Dobzhansky and Washburn over the matter of Coon's *The Origin of Races*, while ostensibly fighting prejudice and stereotype, had a stony undertone of political correctness that shows how fully they were synchronized with the times. Anthropology was being transformed from an arcane study of exotic tribes, bits and pieces of potsherd or stone, and dusty bones, to a science of humankind that was asked tacitly to provide a better, more natural way of living. Scholars and laypeople alike generalized with breathtakingly casual abandon from the social organization of baboons or the details of daily life among the Bushmen of the Kalahari Desert, for example, to how modern, industrial societies should be structured.

In 1966, two of Washburn's former students—Irven DeVore and Richard Lee—organized a conference called "Man the Hunter" that was to crystallize the dominant paradigm of anthropological studies for years to come. The impressive array of participants, and the highly influential book, *Man the Hunter*, which was published two years later, represented a new consensus on the purpose and principles of physical anthropology. DeVore and Lee gathered together primate behaviorists, ethnologists, and ethnographers who had worked with living hunter-gatherers, and paleoanthropologists to share information on the evolution of human behavior. That hunting as a way of life had shaped human society, human psychology, and human anatomy was clearly and unquestioningly agreed. What remained was to triangulate from the habits of living primates and of living "primitive" peoples to deduce what the ancient behaviors of the human lineage had been. The manly occupation of hunting was glorified and ennobled, as it is in the eyes of the hunter-gatherers that the participants eagerly discussed, even though the data kept indicating, awkwardly, that survival depended upon the decidedly unromantic roots, fruits, and berries that the women gathered. Yet hunting seemed to provide the evolutionary explanation for virtually all human traits: upright, bipedal walking; toolmaking and culture; language; the nuclear family; the division of labor along lines of age and sex; the control of society by male groups. It was even proposed by William Laughlin, a former student of Hooton's who had studied Eskimos, that hunting was the "integrating schedule" of the human nervous system.

In short, the Noble Savage of whom Rousseau had written in the eighteenth century was recycled, this time with an evolutionary and political overtone. The Bushmen of the Kalahari, everyone's favorite example of "the" hunter-gatherer, were popularized as a peaceful, whole, contented, untroubled group in a classic book entitled fittingly *The Harmless People*. In an age of social turmoil like the 1960s, it was almost impossible to resist the temptation to draw morals for modern life from such studies. And if some anthropologists were eager to tell others how to live based on their interpretation of the fossil record, others were just as anxious to tell them how to interpret the fossil record based on the way they thought humans ought to live.

This was a distortion of the goals and insights of anthropology that in retrospect is disturbing. But there was another unanticipated effect that is even more troublesome. The public attacks on Coon impressed an entire generation of anthropologists with the notion that any discussion or even acknowledgment of racial differences would call similar censure down on their heads. Washburn and Dobzhansky together were the gatekeepers; they declared race off-limits, verboten, taboo in the fullest sense of the word for anthropologists. Race was not only not a fit subject to study, *it didn't even exist.*

The specter that had haunted Neandertal studies since their inception—the problem of dealing with modern races—became abruptly more powerful and more amorphous. Like a pagan oracle in the nineteenth century, or a terrorist organization in the twentieth, race went underground. By becoming unseeable, unknowable, and intangible, race became a threatening and all-powerful issue. With Coon publicly humiliated and race both amplified and hidden, even Coon's insights into Neandertal adaptations lay dormant for years.

The only thing that could divert the attention of a gossipy field like anthropology from Coon and Washburn's public brawl was another controversy. And another New Englander, a bright young man by the name of C. Loring Brace IV, jumped up to draw the fire.

Brace was an iconoclast. To some extent, Brace's family background and personal history do much to explain his later, independent views. He was born in 1930 into an old New England family, on both his mother's and father's side; there are family stories that some of his ancestors had settled in New England before the Mayflower voyage. "There were," Brace says, "schoolteachers and clergymen in quantity, generations and generations of them . . . with strong ties to nineteenth-century, liberal Protestantism." Even by the time of Brace's birth, there persisted a deep, tacit emphasis in the family on the importance of being educated, articulate, literate, and above all humane. There was also a long-standing concern with evolution: Brace's great-grandfather, Charles Loring Brace, was a friend and correspondent of Darwin's and helped introduce Darwinism to America.

By the time of Charles Loring Brace IV, evolutionary biology was taking a new twist. Brace attributes his interest in human evolution to two books. One was his mother's college biology text, which he perused from the time he was a small boy. The book was full of fascinating anatomical illustrations with see-through overlays that could be peeled

59. C. Loring Brace IV in the early 1960s, when he launched his campaign to give the Neandertals a place in modern human ancestry

away to reveal still deeper layers in the body. The other was Roy Chapman Andrews's book, *Meet Your Ancestors*, published in 1945 when Brace was an impressionable fifteen years old. Andrews was the bold explorer in jodhpurs and Canadian Mountie–style hat who had led the Central Asiatic Expedition in 1927 to try to find early human fossils in the Gobi Desert, a dramatic tale recounted in *On the Trail of Ancient Man*. His later book (the one given to young Brace) was a romantic, thrilling epic summarizing human ancestry and evolution and retelling the stirring tales of fossil discoveries in exotic locales. It persuaded Brace that he wanted to become an anthropologist, even though his father—a Boston University English professor—gently expressed some skepticism at his chances of making a living at it.

As an undergraduate, Brace avoided the family tradition—attending Yale—and went to Williams College, where he began his academic career as he continued it: by having an utterly divergent view from everyone around him. To him, at the time, Williams's mission was "to try to add a veneer of civilization to people who are at bottom pretty crass and greedy": in other words to educate, but only mildly, the "sons of industrialists and pampered rich." As the son of an English teacher and the descendant of those who had spoken out against slavery, exploitation, and injustice since colonial days, Brace was in anything but his element.

Because there was no major in anthropology, he tried to design his own major, combining geology—mostly vertebrate paleontology—with courses in biology that made up most of the premedical curriculum. When he began to look for a graduate school to attend, he remembered the fascinating lectures of Earnest Hooton, who had come to Williams to speak, using his elegant voice and peculiar physical appearance to its fullest. Hooton headed up the most visible, and almost the only, program in physical anthropology in the country. Like a salmon returning to its birthplace, Brace was drawn to Harvard in 1952.

During Brace's graduate career, he experienced the changing of the guard in anthropology. He spent his first two years under Hooton, taking courses and absorbing knowledge. Drafted in 1954, shortly after Hooton's death, Brace managed to spend his military service working as an anthropometrist or old-style physical anthropologist. His task was to design a system of measurements—and then to take them—that would ensure that gas masks would fit the servicemen who needed to wear them. Combining Hooton's emphasis on rigorous measurement with some of the new statistical techniques that were beginning to infiltrate anthropology, Brace worked out exactly how many of the permanent army staff—and who—would have to be measured to make sure the masks fit.

When he returned to Harvard, a substantial change had occurred. Hooton's former student William Howells had replaced him as the senior physical anthropologist. Many believed that Coon had yearned for Hooton's professorship himself; in any case, Coon had left for the University of Pennsylvania. In his autobiography, Coon says only, "One of his [Hooton's] last expressed wishes was that he should not be succeeded by Sherwood L. Washburn, who had oedipally criticized him. William W. Howells got the job and held it most competently until his retirement in 1974."

Howells was widely known for using the new technique of factor analysis to classify skulls into racial groups or species. It was the same procedure Brace had used on the gas mask project, giving the two some common interests. Because Brace was basically an inherited student and an unproven quantity in Howells's eyes, Howells asked him to repeat a year of courses, which he did. It was to have a major—perhaps even *the* major—influence on Brace's later career. Howells demanded that his students read and argue through all of the important books and papers of the new synthesis, which had hardly been in evidence when Brace was first at Harvard. Brace quickly adopted the evolutionary paradigm as his own.

Howells then steered Brace into an innovative but highly unusual thesis project. For the previous ten or fifteen years, with consultation from Hooton, the Jackson Laboratory in Bar Harbor, Maine, had been measuring and observing the dogs in their breeding colonies to explore the relationship between physique and behavior. They had meticulous records, perfect scientific controls, veritable mounds of information, and no one who knew how to analyze it. It was an opportunity to conduct an innovative study, analyzing the anatomical variability in a large data set. Brace was duly dispatched to Maine, where he copied the data and transferred it onto punch cards. His project became one of the first "guinea pigs" for the new computer system just being set up at Harvard. To see if their hardware and software were functioning properly, the computer experts needed a real problem, a massive data set needing analysis. Brace desperately needed computerized help in his analysis. The first step of his study, calculating simple correlation coefficients that would tell him whether one anatomical feature varied in size with another, had taken Brace a year by hand—and took twenty minutes to repeat using the huge, room-filling computer in the basement of the Littauer Building.

Brace delayed his final writing up of the canine information because he had received two fellowships to travel to Europe and study the human fossils, especially the Neandertal remains that were his true interest. It was Brace's chance to undertake the grand tour, in the same way that F. Clark Howell had done just a few years before, and he leapt at the chance. His base abroad in 1959–60 was Niko Tinbergen's animal behavior lab at Oxford, but the highlight of his trip was going to Zagreb to crawl through Gorjanović's collections—the first person to do so, he believed, since Gorjanović's death.

By the time he returned home, thesis still not quite finished, Brace took a teaching position at the University of Wisconsin at Milwaukee, moving next to the University of California at Santa Barbara and delaying completion of his thesis until fall of 1961, just as Carleton Coon's troubles were brewing. In the meantime, young Brace had been thinking hard about the Neandertal bones he had seen and had come to some startling conclusions.

While at Milwaukee, Brace had found the time to write and submit a paper called "Refocusing on the Neanderthal Problem" to *American Anthropologist*; it was published in 1962. It was but a few years after the publication of Vallois's purportedly objective summary of the three views of Neandertals' place in human evolution. At the time, many anthropologists had been swayed by Vallois's argument that Neandertals were too specialized and too close in time to anatomically modern humans to be the latter's ancestors, although few were convinced that the pre-Sapiens theory had much validity.

Brace galloped straight at these ideas like Don Quixote, lance at the ready. Vallois's interpretation was fundamentally erroneous and was based on two fallacies. First, according to Brace, was an erroneous supposition that the small, early populations of humans would be prone to inbreeding and hence would show very little anatomical variation.

> Second, only one fairly complete specimen of pre-Upper Paleolithic man was well known. . . .
>
> With the expectation of relatively uniform populations, the picture presented by a single fairly complete skeleton has been sufficient to satisfy many authors that the characteristics of the human populations immediately prior to the Upper Paleolithic were well known and that they corresponded to a single, easily recognizable "type". . . . It has apparently been repugnant to many authors to regard this as the population from which later forms of man have arisen.

Reviewing the material from western Europe, central Europe (mostly Krapina), and western Asia (the Mount Carmel remains), Brace demonstrated that the *size* of certain anatomical features differed markedly among Neandertals, though he made no attempt to deal with the thorny problem of variability in *shape.*

On these grounds, Brace counterargued that Neandertals were highly variable, not uniformly specialized at all; indeed, "conformity to rigid type was not one of the characteristics of early man." Those who claimed it was were either unfamiliar with the material or—and this became the battle hymn of Brace's entire career—were not integrating modern evolutionary thought with the fossil record.

As for the second part of Vallois's argument—the sudden replacement of Neandertals by Cro-Magnons—Brace suggested that it, too, relied upon a badly flawed reading of the evidence.

> If the relationships of pre-Upper Paleolithic peoples with subsequent, preceding, and contemporary peoples is not to be simply discovered from published morphological evidence, one might expect some help from archeology since archeological material, being less perishable than skeletal remains, is preserved and known in far greater quantity and detail. Recently many physical anthropologists

have been clinging to the old view of a sudden migration into Europe of Upper Paleolithic [anatomically modern] peoples, although they have been unconvinced by the skeletal evidence. According to them the proof is mainly archeological. On the other hand, archeologists have continued paying lip service to the sudden migration view with the feeling that the justification was largely based upon the supposedly clear-cut morphological distinctions made by the physical anthropologists.

This Alphonse and Gaston situation has been notably broken by the French archeologist François Bordes who sees a relatively gradual transition from an essentially Mousterian to an essentially Upper Paleolithic status marked by a gradual change in the number and variety of tools made on blades. . . .

The enduring reluctance to see a development of Upper Paleolithic tool-making tradition from some sort of Mousterian base is compared by Bordes to those who claim Hamlet was not written by William Shakespeare but by a contemporary of the same name. . . . It would appear that . . . we have been looking for the ancestors of modern man in populations that are not supposed to be termed Neanderthals, although they look like them.

Brace continued to confront the establishment's views in his next paper, called "The Fate of the 'Classic' Neanderthals: A Consideration of Hominid Catastrophism" and published in 1964. Ironically, the article was submitted on the same day Washburn attacked Coon in his presidential address to the American Anthropological Association.

Brace's article appeared in *Current Anthropology* and, in accordance with that journal's policy, was sent to fifty scholars who were invited to submit comments for publication in what is called CA star treatment. Brace's is a long, meandering piece that openly criticizes or at least sidewipes almost all previous work in the field. Still, it was vibrant with ideas, an audacious challenge issued by a young man starting on his professional career. The replies and comments range from "gentle reproof to angry indignation," with a heavy dose of the latter. The entire correspondence makes fascinating reading for its juicy exchanges of thinly veiled insults and its generous doses of misunderstanding and misinterpretation of meaning.

Brace began with an unquestionably accurate statement, one of the most important observations of the entire paper—although it was neither universally admired nor admitted: "Interpretation of the hominid fossil record has inevitably been colored by the climate of opinion prevalent at the time of the discovery of the major pieces of evidence."

He proceeded to argue that the widespread rejection of Neandertals as human ancestors could be traced to Boule's work, which, Brace maintained, simply reflected Boule's rejection of the paradigm of Darwinian evolution in favor of a Cuvier-flavored notion of catastrophism. No "brutish" Neandertals could possibly transform themselves into the " 'noble,' 'handsome,' 'clean-limbed,' fully modern men of superior form and culture." There must have been a complete decimation of the lower forms and a sudden replacement by the higher, similar to successive creations separated by catastrophes.

But, he pointed out, since 1908 when Boule started publishing on La Chapelle-aux-Saints,

> the evidence has undergone a complete change while the argument has remained substantially the same. . . . The aim [of many studies] was to prove that these non-modern hominids could not be the forerunners of truly modern men.
>
> Despite this clearly anti-evolutionary bias . . . no modern work goes so far as to deny that human evolution occurred (although Boule and Vallois [in] 1957 would deny almost all of the fossil evidence for it). It would seem to be rather a case of "out of sight, out of mind" since the crucial events in the development of *sapiens* morphology are generally pushed back in time to a point where "the fossil record dwindles into obscurity" . . . and people are not likely to be disturbed by the sight of a human ancestor who looks rather less than human.

Many of Brace's verbal arrows were palpable hits—for example, he clearly saw the disjunction between changes in evidence and theory. Vallois for one was unwilling to revise Boule's interpretations substantially, as expressed in later editions of *Les Hommes Fossiles*, despite substantive changes in the record itself. Brace appreciated, too, the resonant similarities of the Boulean pre-Sapiens view, sustained by Vallois in France, and the Keithian conviction "which sails on without him," nurtured in Kenya by Louis Leakey and in America by Hooton and later T. Dale Stewart of the Smithsonian.

In opposition to what he labeled as antievolutionary, pre-Sapiens views, Brace placed those of Weidenreich and Hrdlička, noting—as had Coon, independently—that they had never been evaluated seriously. At least Hrdlička had offered a concise definition of Neandertals, "the only one offered in conjunction with clear evolutionary principles," according to Brace. Hrdlička had written: "The only workable definition of the

Neanderthal man and period seems, for the time being, to be, *the man and period of the Mousterian culture.*"

The real anatomical differences between Neandertals and modern humans, in Brace's view, were primarily in the dimensions of their faces and teeth. Downplaying the evidence from the rest of the skeleton, and neglecting the changes in the *shape* of the face, Brace declared that reducing the *size* of the face and teeth was not such an unreasonable task for evolution to accomplish. The important issue, he felt, was that physical evolution had been largely replaced by cultural evolution; culture had become the fundamental, nongenetic specialization of our lineage, easing the selective pressures operating on our anatomy. For example, specialized tools apparently took over the tasks formerly performed by the teeth, especially the front teeth, leading to significant reduction of facial dimensions. Thus, Brace offered a revision of Hrdlička's definition: *"Neanderthal man is the man of the Mousterian culture prior to the reduction in form and dimension of the Middle Pleistocene face."*

Finally, boldly, Brace addressed in closing the question inherently implied in his title:

> I suggest that it was the fate of the Neanderthal to give rise to modern man, and, as has frequently happened to members of the older generation in this changing world, to have been perceived in caricature, rejected, and disavowed by their own offspring, *Homo sapiens.*

There was no denying Brace's clever way with words and the startlingly new effect of his iconoclastic view of the field. But Brace's accusations of antievolutionary thinking, his bald-faced and sometimes hardhearted criticism of others, set many against him. Fewer scholars criticized him for his ideas than for his language and ungentlemanly allegations of bad faith or of deliberately ignoring the evidence. Not only did he criticize with vigor, but he also failed to offer any substitutes in place of that which he deplored. His ideas about the links among evolution, culture, and the face were important but as yet vague, poorly formulated, and difficult to test. Even Brace's former adviser at Harvard, Howells, who admitted to favoring the Neandertals as potential ancestors, remarked:

> A study like Brace's is useful in testing opposing hypotheses against the demands of sound evolutionary theory and new developments

of fact. I wish he had stuck to the point; one gets the feeling he is more interested in analyzing *Homo oldguardensis* than having a close look at *Homo neanderthalensis*.

The politics of science—in essence, the real subject of Brace's diatribe—had not escaped Howells's attention, either.

The critics were bluntly outspoken, referring to some of Brace's ideas as "polemic and tendentious . . . sheer nonsense," "aggressive slang . . . quite out of place in 'a World Journal of the Sciences of Man,'" and calling his accusations of antievolutionary bias among the French "far-fetched."

Among the most revealing of replies on this point were those from the French, whose responses were somewhat delayed and appeared in a later issue published in 1966. François Bordes's remarks read in their entirety:

> I was shocked by Brace's contention that French anthropologists have consistently been anti-evolutionists. I would like to point out, 1st, that Lamarck proposed an evolutionary theory almost before Darwin was born; that his mechanism was wrong is another matter. After all, posterity always proves that precursors are wrong on 1 point or another.
>
> From Brace's reply it is clear that he equates Evolutionism with Neo-Darwinism. This strikes me as a most totalitarian point of view. One can be an evolutionist—that is, believe that all present living forms are derived from other forms—and still not accept the entire Neo-Darwinist position. Certainly Neo-Darwinism has been a most important step; if, however, it should prove to be 100% correct, it would be the only such case in the history of science.

In short, Bordes resented strongly Brace's unfounded accusations that a belief in Cuvier-flavored catastrophism persisted among French anthropologists. Yet, Bordes remained skeptical of the tenets of Neo-Darwinian evolution that Brace implicitly accepted as the only evolutionary theory that counted. It was a magnificent case of two scholars trained in contrasting traditions, differing so fundamentally in their basic premises that they can talk only past each other—a problem that was greatly exacerbated by the accusatory, name-calling tone of Brace's article.

Vallois, rather hotly defending his point of view from Brace's equally warm attacks, contested a number of issues and stood firmly by his pre-Sapiens theory. Like many others, he attacked Brace on style, not substance. Vallois suggested haughtily that works meant to draw together, criticize, and synthesize large amounts of complex material were best attempted by "those who, having read and seen much, are better able to reflect on the problems that this science poses" instead of "those who are beginners in science"—a harrumph from Howells's *Homo oldguardensis* directed straight at *Homo newguardensis*.

The turmoil over Brace's ideas served to distract attention from the Coon controversy and to refocus it on the Neandertal problem. Without question, Brace achieved his stated aim of "jarring a complacent discipline. . . ." But nearly thirty years later, Brace is amazed at the lack (in his mind) of long-term effect of these papers.

> I expected fuss and furor but I never expected the whole thing to relapse as if it had never happened. No, I expected that when I pointed out the non-Darwinian paradigm on which biological anthropology was operating, that they would look at it—not gratefully perhaps—but nonetheless, at least make an effort to incorporate the orthodox point of view of evolutionary biology into dealing with the data of anthropology. That never happened and it hasn't happened yet.

In some minds Brace, not Neandertals, became the "problem," a position he found uncomfortable. Yet through the years, Brace has continued in his iconoclastic ways. Shortly after "The Fate of the Neanderthals" appeared, he grew a mustache, beard, and ponytail, through which he used to wear a chicken bone. In the mid-sixties, this was an outré but not outrageous fashion for a professor—particularly one of anthropology, a field that has always tolerated or even encouraged eccentricities in dress or behavior. But thirty years later, although the vogue for hippie hairdos on academics has faded, Brace still sports the beard, ponytail, and mustache—long since turned snow-white. His papers remain provocative and often challenge prevailing opinion in his field, reiterating the themes he first developed in the 1960s. His acknowledgments often report the work as having been done despite rejections by this or that funding agency.

Yet some of Brace's points became influential, even if he is disappointed that others have been ignored. His was the first clear statement that the major changes in human behavior in the Middle Pleistocene were ultimately and dramatically responsible for changes in the anatomy of Neandertals, who were driven by natural selection (or genetic drift) in the direction of modern humans. In these papers, he began articulating a view of culture as a major part of the human evolutionary and adaptive mechanism that has been widely incorporated into anthropological thinking. In his many subsequent studies of the dentition and facial structure of different populations, prehistoric and recent, Brace has emphasized the evolutionary trends and changes that he could document and the necessary and powerful interaction of anatomy and culture.

"We live in a cultural milieu," Brace asserts. "The idea that culture is our ecological niche is still applicable. The impact and force of natural selection on the human physique are conditioned by the dimensions of culture." It is an argument he makes forcefully now and made equally forcefully in the 1960s.

Whether or not it was consciously derived from Brace's polemics, the evidence of Neandertal culture and behavior was about to become a potent force in anthropological thinking. Now that the field's understanding of Neandertal anatomy had changed, the stage was set for a new appreciation of the less tangible role of Neandertals.

Act One had occurred many years before. In 1953, a young archeologist, Ralph Solecki, with assistance from his anthropologist wife, Rose, had started excavating a promising cave known as Shanidar in Iraqi Kurdistan. It was the big break of Solecki's very young career.

Solecki's undergraduate and graduate degrees from Columbia were taken later than is usually the case now, but he had considerably more field experience in archeology than is usual now by the time he entered graduate school in 1956. Some of that experience had been acquired in the Near East. In 1950 and 1951, Solecki had been taken on as camp manager and archeologist for an expedition to investigate a village dated to about 800 B.C. in Kurdistan. Solecki was himself most interested in older material, so he stayed behind after the second field season was completed to make a horseback survey of the area, seeking caves likely to have been inhabited in the distant past. He was accompanied by two or three policemen, a representative of the National Museum, and a local government official. Luck must have been riding with them, for they found and explored some forty caves in the area. (Caves were all the rage in paleoanthropology. Carleton Coon, still at the University of Pennsylvania then, was busily excavating caves just across the border in Iran, with good results, and the remarkable Dorothy Garrod was finding promising material in caves in the nearby Levant.) Solecki returned to Iraq within the year and, with a young man's confidence, approached the government in the person of the head of antiquities, asking for permission to excavate for prehistoric material. The success experienced in neighboring, rival countries may have had some influence; so, too, may his claim that he had found a spectacular cave.

It was indeed a wonderful cave—large and spacious, with a command-ing view overlooking the Greater Zab River. It was also intermittently inhabited by Kurdish tribesmen, their families, and their herds, the cave easily accommodating seven families (about forty-five people), a hundred goats, forty chickens, ten horses, and ten cows. There was ample room within the cave's arching vault—about fifty meters wide by forty-five meters deep—for the herders to build a series of small rooms around the edges (for privacy), a large penning area to the rear, and still leave the central area largely open for communal fires that were shared by several families. As far as Solecki could tell, Shanidar was such a prime piece of real estate that it must have been occupied on and off for the last 100,000 years, with each set of tenants leaving their telltale housekeeping rubbish behind. It was just too good to ignore, he argued.

Luckily, the government official agreed with him. Even more miracu-lously, the official parted with one-third of his annual budget to provide a car, equipment, food, and workmen. This was enough to let Solecki sink a test trench that yielded numerous ancient hearths, potsherds, and flints. Ever mindful of those around him, especially when "those" were Kurds—a tribe with a well-deserved reputation for ferocity—Solecki dug his trench in the common area in the center of the cave, so that he wouldn't disturb anyone's house. Throughout the four seasons of excava-tion at Shanidar, between 1953 and 1960, the modern Kurds were present, in spirit or flesh, a living example of cave dwellers in that region. Their habits inevitably influenced Solecki's view of the past and gave him clues to interpreting the archeological record he was accumulating.

In the lowest level, about 5.5 meters down, the team began finding unmistakably Mousterian tools, the signature of Neandertals. Later, radiocarbon dates told Solecki the top of this level was older than 45,000 years, while the bottom was estimated to be about 100,000 years old. Shanidar was to prove one of the richest caches of Neandertal remains yet found. During the first full field season, on June 22, 1953, they excavated a skeleton of an infant, buried lying on its right side with its arms and legs folded up in a tightly flexed position. Although crushed to a thickness of a few inches, the skeleton had obviously once been complete. A Turkish anthropologist trained at Harvard by Coon, Muz-zafir Şenyürek, was given the remains—known for years simply as "the

Shanidar child"—for study, while Solecki concentrated on the abundant stone tools. That the child was some sort of human was apparent, but the crushing and distortion of the bones and the sheer youth of the individual (it was about nine months old at death) meant that the Neandertal aspects of its features were very subtle.

Despite the obvious success of the first field season, Solecki did not return until 1956, when he had been awarded one of the first Fulbright scholarships for study abroad. That year, the excavation focused mainly on the more recent layers, with mundane results. But in April and May 1957, as the field season was winding up, the team recovered three adult Neandertal skeletons (known as Shanidar 1, 2, and 3). Shanidar 3 was excavated first, but because it was fragmentary, the bones were initially identified as nonhuman. This meant that it was not until April 27, 1957, the day on which they excavated Shanidar 1—an extraordinarily well-preserved Neandertal adult male—that Solecki knew he had found what were truly Neandertal burials.

Then, in the closing week of the work, one of his team, Philip Smith,

60. The Shanidar 1 Neandertal skull as it was exposed during excavation. It was the first adult skeleton out of nine Neandertals found at the site, all of which led to a kinder, gentler view of these prehistoric humans.

61. Ralph S. Solecki (left) and T. Dale Stewart (middle) in 1960 during the excavations at Shanidar Cave that produced many Neandertal skeletons

discovered Shanidar 2 by accident. As archeologists do at the end of a season, Smith was "tidying up" the walls of the excavation, smoothing them off and taking some soil samples for analysis. Carving back the wall's surface by a minuscule amount, he ran his trowel across the nose of the cranium of Shanidar 2. The team hastily removed the skull, rather than leave it in a vulnerable state, but left the rest of the skeleton in place until the next season. They returned to the United States, delighted at having found two Neandertal burials, many animal bones, and lots of stone tools with the promise of more to come.

In the meantime, Şenyürek had died in a tragic small plane crash, so Solecki turned to his senior colleague in physical anthropology at the Smithsonian Institution, T. Dale Stewart. Stewart was an expert on the skeletons of American Indians, having just completed a research project on the then oldest-known prehistoric human remains from North America, the Midland skull from western Texas. Because Aleš Hrdlička had been until his death in 1943 the Smithsonian's "fossil man" man, Stewart had always stayed well away from fossils. But now Stewart was pleased to accept Solecki's invitation to reconstruct and study the Neandertals found at Shanidar in 1957. Stewart recognized Shanidar 3 as a Neandertal and enthusiastically departed for Baghdad in 1957 and again in 1958 to reconstruct the Shanidar 1 skeleton. He quickly published a preliminary report about it.

From the beginning, the Shanidar fossils seemed destined to overturn existing ideas. The Shanidar 1 skull was clearly not a progressive Neandertal, as F. Clark Howell's recent synthesis led everyone to expect. Far from being like the Tabun fossils from the Levant, Shanidar 1 closely resembled the Classic Neandertals of Europe. More work—and more thought—was needed.

The next season at Shanidar proved to be 1960—Solecki had been busy writing his Ph.D. thesis on the early Upper Paleolithic stone tools from Shanidar in the interim. Stewart came along and spent most of that season in the Iraq Museum, in Baghdad, struggling with the crushed remains of Shanidar 2, which had been soaked in preservative while still partially embedded in its surrounding earth and rock. But he was at the cave in August when an isolated adult skeleton, Shanidar 5, was found as well as a remarkable series of superimposed burials, yielding individuals who were eventually numbered 4, 6, 8, and 9. By the time the season ended, Solecki's team had documented nine different rockfalls in the cave, accounting for the deaths of four of the Neandertals, while the other five seem to have been intentionally buried.

It was a rich haul, a cemetery comparable to those on Mount Carmel. In fact, Solecki believes there are more Neandertals to be recovered from the cave, and he may well be correct because only a small part of the cave's floor has been excavated. Political exigencies have made it impossible to work in the area; Solecki was given a military escort out of the area in 1978, when he tried to resume excavation. Since then, the continual battles between the Kurds and the central Iraqi government, between the Iraqis and the Iranians, and between the Iraqis and the U.N. forces have kept Solecki and other scholars at bay. It remains to be seen if the Neandertal skeletons stored in Baghdad survived the extensive bombing in 1991 or if they met the fate of the Zhoukoudian fossils destroyed during World War II. It may be that only Shanidar 3, which has remained in the United States since its recognition, still survives.

The Shanidar remains quickly became central to a new understanding of Neandertals. Solecki first published a series of scholarly papers, some in the Iraq Museum journal, *Sumer*, selected no doubt for political reasons. Solecki then wrote a popular book summarizing his findings and placing them before the public. What he, or his editors, chose to emphasize was a small detail, a perfectly amazing bit of information that seemed to illuminate Neandertal life and times with startling clarity.

It was not a point that most excavators would even have noticed. From the first, Solecki had taken soil samples almost compulsively,

62. The "Flower Burial" in Shanidar Cave at the time of its discovery. The skeleton most visible is an older man, Shanidar 4, whose body was apparently covered in flowers. The arm bones of Shanidar 6, a young woman, can be seen in front of those of Shanidar 4, and fragments of a young adult (Shanidar 8), and an infant (Shanidar 9), were found below Shanidar 4 and 6. The presence of large quantities of flower pollen in this burial became the basis of the view that Neandertals were "flower children" with religious beliefs and sensitivities.

collecting dirt for analysis that might yield clues about the environment. Not many archeologists would have done this, for the archeology of the time was focused almost exclusively on studying the frequencies of different types of stone tools and the techniques by which they had been manufactured. Perhaps Solecki simply demanded a fuller, richer understanding of the past he was excavating. In 1968, expert palynologist (pollen analyst) Arlette Leroi-Gourhan published a scientific article in her native French on the results of her study of the sample taken from the immediate vicinity of the burial of Shanidar 4. She found wildflower pollen, lots of it, much more than she believed could have been blown in on the wind or carried in on people's or animals' feet.

Solecki thought about this finding and realized that there was a stunning implication: perhaps the Neandertals of Shanidar Cave had buried this individual, this elderly male, with offerings of flowers. So, in 1971, he called his popular book simply *Shanidar, The First Flower People*. It was an effective and captivating title, one that—before the reader even opened the book—convinced him or her that Neandertals were behaviorally very, very human. As Solecki remarked in a later paper, "The death had occurred approximately 60,000 years ago . . . yet the evidence of flowers in the grave brings Neanderthals closer to us in spirit than we have ever before suspected. . . . The association of flowers with Neanderthals adds a whole new dimension to our knowledge of his humanness, indicating that he had 'soul.' "

Added to the flower burial was another compelling piece of evidence of Neandertals' humanity that emerged more slowly as analysis of the fossils proceeded. Shanidar 1, one of the best-preserved burials, was another male, aged somewhere between thirty and forty-five at death. This was a ripe old age for a prehistoric human, since few Neandertals lived into their forties and almost none lived beyond the age of fifty. Yet Shanidar 1 had lived a brutally hard life by anyone's standards.

Careful study of his bones revealed a plethora of serious but healed fractures. There had been a crushing blow to the left side of the head, fracturing the eye socket, displacing the left eye, and probably causing blindness on that side. He also sustained a massive blow to the right side of the body that so badly damaged the right arm that it became withered and useless; the bones of the shoulder blade, collar bone, and upper arm are much smaller and thinner than those on the left. The right lower arm and hand are missing, probably not because of poor preservation as fossils but because they either atrophied and dropped off or because they were amputated. The right foot and lower right leg were also damaged, possibly at the same time. There is a healed fracture of one of the bones in the arch of the foot associated with advanced degenerative disease of various bones of the ankle and big toe. These problems would have left the foot with little, and very painful, mobility. The right knee and various parts of the left leg also show signs of pathological damage; these may have been either further consequences of the same traumatic injury or lesions that developed in reaction to the abnormal limping gait that must have resulted from the damage to the right leg and foot.

As Solecki argued, someone so devastatingly injured could not possibly have survived without care and sustenance. Whether the right arm was severed intentionally, accidentally, or as a result of physical deterioration, a one-armed, partially blind, crippled man could have made no pretense of hunting or gathering his own food. That he survived for years after his trauma was a testament to Neandertal compassion and humanity. In fact, Solecki argued in later papers, some of the wildflowers included in the Shanidar 4 burial had medicinal value and might have been used in healing. Years later, Jean Auel, author of *Clan of the Cave Bear*, would pick up this information and transform Shanidar 1 into a Neandertal shaman or magician.

Coming as it did on the heels of the destruction of Boule's apish Neandertal and the construction of a new, improved, and more human Neandertal anatomy, Solecki's view of Neandertals as human, humane, compassionate, and caring was accepted widely and with remarkably little demur. Following Brace's lead, Solecki had shifted the focus of Neandertal studies from the anatomical pre-Sapiens to the behavioral pre-Sapiens. This view suggested that, although modern humans were descended from anatomically primitive ancestors, we could comfort ourselves with the knowledge that they were just as human *behaviorally* as we think ourselves to be. Neandertals were simply flower children under the skin. The skepticism came later.

9

Welcome to Hard Times

1971–1983

The new vision of behaviorally modern Neandertals did little to solve the Neandertal problem. Theoretically, Solecki's ideas made Neandertals more palatable as close human relatives or ancestors, but, practically, few scientists were ready to adopt this point of view.

Still, Brace had done much to shake the status quo ("not my ancestor") regarding the Neandertals, especially among the young who had little invested in the establishment view or who, like Brace in 1962, felt a need to challenge it. Young scholars had the advantage—and the disadvantage—of not yet understanding how difficult it is to make progress in science, or how easy it is to err in interpretation. Brace's work revived interest in the Neandertals; it showed there were significant problems yet to be solved even after Howell's brilliant synthesis of the late 1950s.

The hot topics in paleoanthropology of the 1960s and 1970s tended to cluster around the australopithecines and other very early hominids whose fossil remains and stone tools were being uncovered in Africa, and especially in eastern Africa by the Leakey family. But at least two fledgling professors—David Brose and Milford Wolpoff—thought there was a chance to make an important contribution by reexamining the Neandertal problem.

The two were both at Case Western Reserve University and decided to teach a course together, Brose contributing his knowledge of archeology and Wolpoff covering physical anthropology. In years to come, Brose would play no further role in Neandertal studies, but for Wolpoff, it was the beginning of a prominent career.

Milford Wolpoff's is a classic American story of the bright son of a working-class family making good. He was a war baby, born in October 1942 in Chicago, the first of two sons to Ruth and Benjamin Wolpoff. Though Benjamin Wolpoff had always wanted to be an aeronautical engineer, there was no money for him to attend college. After the war, he worked in the family's dry-cleaning business and drove a taxi. Thus, while Wolpoff's parents gave their children a respect for learning and encouraged them to aim for college, they could provide little money with which to finance it.

When Milford Wolpoff was in fifth grade, about ten years old, he happened upon Roy Chapman Andrews's book *Meet Your Ancestors*— the very one that had so inspired Brace. Wolpoff was fascinated by cavemen and human evolution, writing an enthusiastic report for his science class, but, Wolpoff recalls, he "didn't think 'fossil stuff' was something you could do for a living." Besides, he was interested in all types of science.

When he applied to college, Wolpoff was offered a full-tuition scholarship by the University of Illinois at Urbana; summer jobs and student loans covered the rest. He plunged into physics, a difficult major that left time for few electives. Still, in his second year Wolpoff noticed an irresistible entry in the course catalog: a graduate seminar on the fossil evidence for human evolution, offered by a well-known, Harvard-trained archeologist, Donald Lathrap. Wolpoff persuaded Lathrap to let him enroll despite his being an undergraduate. The textbooks, Wolpoff remembers, clearly showed the orientation of the course. They were Mayr's new synthesis treatise, *Systematics and the Origin of Species*, and Le Gros Clark's careful summary, *The Fossil Evidence for Human Evolution*. Thus, Wolpoff's very first exposure to paleoanthropology, aside from Roy Chapman Andrews, was a course that placed human evolution squarely in the context of the new synthesis.

Wolpoff loved the course and did well, but he didn't decide to make anthropology his major until the next year. When Lathrap asked Wolpoff to give three lectures in his stead while he would be out of town, the young man was enormously flattered. As a result, Wolpoff tried to assess his chances in the two fields as realistically as he could. He believed he could either become a mediocre physicist or a good anthropologist, and so turned toward the field where his chances of success seemed higher.

He soon took a course in the philosophy of science that was to mold his thinking in important ways. It was the first time Wolpoff was exposed to the Popperian (after the philosopher Karl Popper) or hypothetico-

63. A celebration in 1988 of the publication of a new monograph about the Krapina Neandertal fossils by the Hrvatski Priodoslovni Muzej (Croatian Natural History Museum). From left to right: Jakov Radovčić of the Hrvatski Priodoslovni Muzej; Milford Wolpoff of the University of Michigan; Drazen Polmykalo, also of the Hrvatski Priodoslovni Muzej; a stand-in for Erik Trinkaus of the University of New Mexico; and Fred H. Smith of Northern Illinois University. Radovčić, Smith, and Wolpoff have argued vigorously that the Neandertals in central Europe evolved into modern humans.

deductive approach. Much simplified, Popper's philosophy states that scientific knowledge progresses in a series of stages. First, a specific hypothesis is formulated about a subject; then predictions that are logical consequences of the hypothesis are generated. Next, data that are capable of refuting (or agreeing with) those predictions are gathered. The hypothesis is thus tested against the data and deduced to be false or—and here is the catch—not-yet-falsified. If it is not-yet-falsified, then either more testable predictions are generated or the hypothesis is modified, in the light of the additional knowledge, and the process begins again.

The two most important issues in Popperian science are that hypotheses can never be proven to be true and that hypotheses must be tested. Science is seen as an ongoing process, a restless dialectic between ideas and evidence that narrows the realm of possible truths ever further. Data are never gathered without a specific question in mind; they never "speak for themselves" or reveal the truth by some sort of intuitive leap of understanding. Wolpoff internalized these procedures and this view of science completely; even those who have disagreed with some of his views later in his career would agree that he has been an unusually fertile source of testable hypotheses.

After graduation, Wolpoff gladly accepted a teaching assistantship in order to stay at the University of Illinois and study under Eugene Giles, who had trained with Howells at Harvard. In his second year as a graduate student, Wolpoff applied for, and received, a lucrative scholarship from the National Institutes of Mental Health that paid for the rest of his education.

Giles provided Wolpoff with guidance and direction. Wolpoff already knew a good deal about computer programming from his days as a physics major; now Giles pushed him to study population genetics at the Agricultural School and human anatomy, a subject the University of Illinois didn't offer at the Urbana campus because its medical school is located in Chicago. But the University of Illinois was part of a consortium of midwestern universities, so Wolpoff was able to cross-register at the University of Wisconsin at Madison for his anatomy studies. The choice was doubtless influenced by the presence of John Robinson, a South African anthropologist who was deeply involved with the exciting, new, early hominid fossils being found in South and East Africa. Wolpoff spent the fall of 1966 taking a reading course with Robinson and the winter taking anatomy.

It was Robinson who first forced Wolpoff to deal with the particular, detailed anatomy of the fossil specimens rather than generating grandiose, abstract theories based on what somebody else had said about the fossils. Prior to his exposure to Robinson, Wolpoff's graduate school education had been heavily theoretical, pure book-learning. Robinson would hand him a fossil and ask him to describe what he saw.

Wolpoff credits Robinson with being a dedicated empiricist who had a major influence on his career:

> Robinson was a real no-nonsense character. He didn't want to hear about theories about the mutual feedback on culture and physical evolution. . . . He wanted to know what there was about these specimens that made them the same as each other or different from each other. . . . He made me look at things *as things*, not as representations of a theory about how they should be. . . . It was the first time that I *looked* at the physical objects.

Inspired by Robinson, Wolpoff applied—fruitlessly—for funding to do his doctoral dissertation on dental evolution in the South and East

African fossils. As a fallback, he decided to write a dissertation reviewing the literature on the dentition of these fossils, comparing their variability in tooth size with that which he would document (or could find in the literature) for large samples from various modern human populations. While it was useful as a thorough review of the literature and as an exercise in writing computer programs for large-scale data analysis, the work was plagued by differences in the way various scholars measured teeth. Wolpoff was bitterly disappointed that he couldn't work on the original fossils that had sparked his interest.

Before he finished his dissertation in 1969, Wolpoff accepted a job at Case Western Reserve University, which was just starting up an anthropology program. He and Brose decided to offer their joint course in Pleistocene human evolution—because both were new to the job and team-teaching seemed easier—not expecting that the process of teaching would lead them to a new understanding of Neandertals. But the give and take of the classroom and the interaction of perspectives led to something new.

In 1971, they published their synthesis in *American Anthropologist*, in a now-classic paper with an unpromising title: "Early Upper Paleolithic Man and Late Middle Paleolithic Tools." Translated into colloquial speech, their title suggested that the biological transition from Neandertals to anatomically modern humans was somehow uncoupled in time from the archeological transition from Middle Paleolithic to Upper Paleolithic tool industries. In other words, knowing which tools you had did not tell you which people you had.

Determining precisely the distinction between Middle and Upper Paleolithic was difficult, but not for want of trying. John Lubbock, back in 1865, had first coined the term "Paleolithic," meaning Old Stone Age, to refer to the period of human history when tools were made of chipped stone. Shortly thereafter, the Paleolithic was subdivided into Lower (older) and Upper (more recent), in recognition of a fundamental difference among the types and sophistication of stone tools that were known. Lower Paleolithic industries were seen as cruder as well as simpler technologically; tools were made by striking one stone, the core, with another, the hammerstone, to remove flakes from the core and produce the desired shape. Later in the Lower Paleolithic, and on into what became known as the Middle Paleolithic, the working of stone became more sophisticated; cores were prepared more carefully and hammers were more likely to be made from "soft" materials—wood, bone, and antler. The tools themselves remained simple and were mostly designed to be held in the hand, not hafted.

Upper Paleolithic tools were made by more careful and precise flaking techniques, and long blades were struck, or "punched," off cores using pressure rather than an abrupt blow. The blades were then worked further to make specialized types of tools, including projectile points and engraving tools. The former were used with an object known as an atlatl or spear-thrower, which made it possible to throw a spear farther and harder. Stone was no longer the predominant raw material used in tool manufacture; significant numbers of bone and antler tools are found in Upper Paleolithic assemblages. There were also fabulous artworks—paintings, sculptures, and carvings—and the dead were buried elaborately with beads, necklaces, and other grave goods.

Within these broad periods, archeologists strove to establish the sequence of local industries or successive, distinctive assemblages of tools. These were commonly named after the site where they were first recognized, such as the Mousterian industry from Le Moustier or the Solutrean industry from Le Solutré, both in France. It was tacitly assumed that tools evolved—the metaphors of evolution and descent were and still are exceptionally common in archeology—in a more or less constant pattern around the world. There the matter rested for many years. But, starting in the early 1950s, the French geologist/archeologist François Bordes began struggling with the need to provide more scientific and precise definitions of periods. Confusingly, the term Middle Paleolithic was now often used synonymously with Mousterian in western Europe.

Bordes was a native of the cave-rich Périgord region of southwestern France and, during World War II, a member of the French Resistance. He was a crusty, demanding individual, rigidly organized and precise. He decided that the only way to make sense of the whole mess was to systematize and standardize the classification of stone tools. He factored in the shapes of tools, the techniques by which they had been produced, and the percentages of various tool forms found in the different assemblages. Bordes was unusual in that he was one of the first to indulge in flint knapping, learning by experimentation which techniques were used by prehistoric humans in making their tools. Thus, he was more able than most to consider both form and manufacturing technique in his classificatory system.

Although various tool classifications had been suggested previously, there was little agreement on which one to use. A common flaw in other systems was the reliance on a technique borrowed from paleontology, in which a *"fossile directeur"* (a single fossil species) was taken to indicate the age of a deposit. Applied to stone tool assemblages, *fossiles directeurs* techniques were sometimes misleading. A single tool out of hundreds in an assemblage could dictate its equivalency to another assemblage, again on the basis of one out of many specimens. At its worst, the approach simply sacrificed much of the information present in those assemblages in the interest of producing a neat sequence of assemblages.

Once Bordes had established his basic type list of sixty-three forms and categories of tools, he began to compile data on the cumulative frequencies of various tool types within each stratigraphic level of a site. These frequencies became standards, providing a simple framework of expectations into which any archeologist could enter information on an unknown site or level. Though a very typological and mechanistic approach, it offered rigor and consistency to an area of study that had grown increasingly idiosyncratic and haphazard. Just as important, he treated each object as a part of an assemblage, rather than as an isolated entity.

In 1953, Bordes began publishing his new approach in a series of articles, which culminated in his grand synthesis in 1961: *Typologie du Paléolithique Ancien et Moyen (Typology of the Lower and Middle Paleolithic).* This work rapidly became the bible for Paleolithic archeologists, for it illustrated the standard types for every Lower or Middle Paleolithic tool form known anywhere in Europe, the Near East, or North Africa at the time. Simultaneously, Bordes's formidable wife, Denise de Sonneville-Bordes, and a younger colleague, Jean Perrot, published a parallel series of articles that showed a set of standard types for the Upper Paleolithic. Although de Sonneville-Bordes and Perrot relied more heavily on *fossiles directeurs*, the two lists of types were sufficiently complementary that all Paleolithic archeologists could use them to find out exactly where their site fit into the scheme. If the approach was unabashedly Eurocentric, so, too, were most of the scholars.

Furthermore, Bordes's system was deeply rooted in the belief that the various industries of Paleolithic tools represented stylistic differences among ancient ethnic groups. This was a reasonable deduction for the Upper Paleolithic. Tool types that were functionally equivalent but stylistically different could be shown to have complementary distributions in time and space, as if different cultural groups had had the same tasks to perform but had manufactured the tools with which to carry out those tasks along slightly different lines. Extending this notion to the Middle Paleolithic was more problematic. Bordes, undaunted, divided the Middle Paleolithic into a series of "facies," borrowing a geological term that refers to stratigraphic deposits formed under particular conditions. Each of Bordes's archeological facies was implicitly assumed to have been formed by a particular ethnic lineage as it migrated or evolved.

In its original, nineteenth-century form, the ethnicity argument had used the presence of stone tool types to trace racial migrations and origins. Updated by Bordes in 1960, this idea proved almost as durable as the tools upon which it was based. The argument succumbed only recently in favor of more sophisticated models that relate the differing behaviors of Paleolithic humans to the exploitation of different ecological zones.

Though long-lasting, Bordes's idea was challenged almost immediately by scholars who argued that the differences among these facies reflected different tasks. In short, they said that Bordes's facies were no more and no less than different tool-kits—collections of tools for a specific set of activities—rather than objects made by different ethnic groups. It was later suggested that the sequence of facies represented technical progress through the Middle Paleolithic, a sort of series of directional changes toward the Upper Paleolithic. If, indeed, a series of directional steps occurred, it was more probably caused by progressive ecological changes rather than by any pattern of technological advance.

Although the meaning and significance of the variations in tool form and assemblage composition have remained hotly debated, Bordes's typology meant that at least the various contingents could recognize exactly what was under discussion.

Understood in this context, Brose and Wolpoff's contention that tool industries were not necessarily linked to evolutionary transitions in the toolmaker was particularly crucial. All of the threads of Wolpoff's training and education were clearly visible: his theoretical interest in the integration of archeology (material culture) and physical anthropology (anatomical evolution); his Popperian penchant for testing hypotheses; his grounding in population genetics and modern evolutionary theory; and his Robinsonian emphasis on detail and specifics.

The two started their analysis by constructing a dichotomy: "The appearance of anatomically modern *Homo sapiens* in Europe, the Near East, and Africa must represent either an *in situ* evolution of Neandertals or a migration. Those who suggest the latter claim a sudden replacement of Neandertals by anatomically modern *Homo sapiens*." They then proceeded to test the sudden replacement hypothesis by examining the archeological and physical evidence, harking back to Brace's quip that it was virtually an Alphonse and Gaston farce. They assumed, tacitly, that the two hypotheses were mutually exclusive; that is, if migration were refuted, then the evolution of Neandertals into modern humans was by default supported. While they did not explicitly list the testable predictions of the hypotheses, their modus operandi was unquestionably Popperian: "This work seeks to examine one hypothesis concerning the origin of anatomically modern *Homo sapiens*, and to test this hypothesis against the archaeological and palaeontological record."

First, they summarized evidence about the dating of Neandertal and modern human fossils, observing that *Homo sapiens* was never contemporary with or older than Neandertals "as would have to be the case if the former evolved somewhere separately and then 'suddenly replaced' Neandertals all over the world." Turning to the archeological record, they observed:

> Wherever continuous archaeological sequences spanning this period are clear there seems to be no overlap or obviously rapid replacement, but rather a gradual transition from late Middle Paleolithic [Mousterian] to early Upper Paleolithic [Aurignacian] industries. ... Most of the tool types which are considered characteristic of the Upper Paleolithic are present (albeit in lower frequencies) in Late Middle Paleolithic assemblages.

Their contention was supported by a table of types of Upper Paleolithic tools accompanied by lists of Neandertal or Mousterian sites in which such tools were found. Brose and Wolpoff concluded that the traditional distinction between Middle and Upper Paleolithic industries was artificial, being based on "arbitrary cut-off points in relative frequencies of particular types of stone tools present in both, or upon the purported presence or absence of worked bone tools." Their criticism was well taken, but it did not seem to deter even one archeologist from subsequently using Bordes's handy system.

Finally, they focused on anatomy. Wolpoff compiled long tables of cranial dimensions from the literature, using his computer programs to generate simple statistical measures of variability. As had Brace, they found Neandertals to be as highly variable in the size of their physical features as recent human samples, which they took to be a sign of morphological continuity, or evidence of evolution within one lineage.

To them, the distinction between classic and nonclassic Neandertals was meaningless, at least in evolutionary terms. The exaggerated, classic Neandertal physique was simply a result of grafting the cold adaptations that Coon had recognized onto a more generalized Neandertal body. The Neandertals who looked more modern, they argued, were simply those who hadn't been forced to cope with glacial cold. Thus, classic Neandertal anatomy was explained away—rendered relatively insignificant—and the emphasis was on the extent to which Neandertal anatomy overlapped with that of modern humans (while not being identical).

One of the more interesting contentions in the paper dealt with Wolpoff's old fascination with culture and biology. It followed up directly on Brace's idea that the Neandertal face and dentition became smaller over time as tools were developed that took over the gripping, viselike, or "third hand" role formerly played by teeth and jaws.

"We propose," Brose and Wolpoff said, "that transitions in hominid morphology precede the established changes in hominid industries. . . . Thus, the earliest anatomically modern *H. sapiens* should be found with Middle Paleolithic [Mousterian] material." In other words, if new tools triggered the reduction of the Neandertal face and the transition to *Homo sapiens*, then the tools in question must be Middle Paleolithic ones. It was the transition from Lower to Middle Paleolithic that ought to be examined, not the Middle-to-Upper transition. The key idea in their "adaptive model" of Neandertal facial reduction was that the Middle Paleolithic tools were designed for more specific functions than were Lower Paleolithic tools.

These ideas of Brose and Wolpoff were firmly embedded in an evolutionary milieu. By then, it was widely recognized that subtle shifts in behavior (within the range of capabilities of a population) could cause significant, gradual changes in anatomy by altering the direction or intensity of natural selection. Over generations, such changes in natural selection can alter first gene frequencies and, finally, the expression of gene frequencies as anatomical features.

The ideas of Solecki, Brose, and Wolpoff reflected a common attitude of the time: the conviction that Neandertals were, after all, just like us. The vision was one of behaviorally modern humans trapped in archaic bodies, waiting for biological evolution to catch up. A hidden corollary of this premise was that evolution had produced only changes in physical appearance, and not any significant ones in *behavior*, between Neandertals and modern humans.

Indeed, this view of early humans was clearly evident in a pair of articles that appeared in the early 1970s, one by Wolpoff and the other by Alan Mann, a new Ph.D. who had studied under Washburn at the University of California at Berkeley. Both Wolpoff and Mann were writing about the earliest members of the human lineage, the australopithecines. Both agreed that culture—or complex, socially learned behaviors combined with a dependence on tools for survival—had been fundamental to the human lineage from the outset. Culture *was* the human evolutionary niche. If the primitive, small-brained australopithecines were human enough to have culture, then by implication the much later and larger-brained Neandertals must have been fully human in their overall behavior patterns. Taken to the extreme, this behavioral pre-Sapiens scheme transformed human evolution into a sort of Russian comedy, in which everyone dies, but dies happy. Neandertals, despite their sad fate, could rest eternally happy in the honor of being fully human.

Although Brose and Wolpoff were confident they had so clearly proven an hypothesis false that they might turn the field around, they were soon disappointed. The reception to the paper was reasonably agreeable, but no one changed his or her mind. However, Brace had been following Wolpoff's work and was delighted that someone had picked up the torch; he soon persuaded his department at the University of Michigan to hire Wolpoff away from Case Western Reserve.

William Howells, at Harvard, responded to Brose and Wolpoff's paper in a long, gently critical discussion in 1974. He pointed out that their hypothesis was so global and pooled so many samples from so many regions and time periods as to be virtually untestable (or untenable) in itself. "Here we are back at the essential faults of the hypothesis [they propose]: it is so broad and assertive that it fudges the distinctions it should be examining, and leads to a dubious method of morphological analysis and a mistaken view of population differences and their meaning." He also suggested that perhaps they had exaggerated the suddenness in the sudden replacement hypothesis to make their argument appear stronger.

Wolpoff's hyperbole, if such it was, was born of the deep frustration felt by this energetic and eager young scholar unable to get a grant to examine the material for himself. Wolpoff remembers feeling that he was being deliberately kept out of the museums abroad during this period, denied funding and access—and hence, also, publications—because his conclusions might be unwelcome. This was more than a scholarly issue.

Wolpoff's Eastern European heritage, and his intolerance for incompetents, sometimes translated into intimidating performances at professional meetings. He is a large and tall man, with dark curly hair, a loud voice, and an incorrigible habit of playing the devil's advocate. He acquired a reputation for being impatient, bombastic, and unvaryingly argumentative. The Brose and Wolpoff article echoed Wolpoff's personal style.

In the same year, 1971, another fascinating problem concerning Neandertal behavior was raised. A new and otherwise obscure journal, *Linguistic Inquiry*, published an article by two nonanthropologists, Phillip Lieberman and Edmund Crelin. It was modestly entitled "On the Speech of Neanderthal Man."

Lieberman was a speech analyst at Brown University who specialized in predicting the linguistic capabilities of children with congenital defects of the vocal tract. Using computer models, he tried to determine the range of sounds a child would be able to make from the three-dimensional shape of his or her vocal tract. Crelin, a popular teacher of human gross anatomy at Yale Medical School, was an expert on the anatomy of the newborn. Though many anthropologists missed the article in *Linguistic Inquiry*, a follow-up paper published the next year in *American Anthropologist* produced immediate reactions from the anthropological community—almost all of them negative.

Crelin reconstructed the vocal tract of the Old Man of La Chapelle-aux-Saints, using a cast of the skull in which Boule had freely restored the missing teeth and the broken-away portions of the base of the skull. Using those anatomical reference points that were at least partly preserved, Crelin positioned the larynx high in the throat, much higher than in modern human adults and even slightly higher than in chimpanzees or newborn humans. Then Lieberman entered the shape of this reconstructed vocal tract into his computer-modeling program and found that the resonating chamber at the back of the mouth was all but eliminated. They concluded that Neandertals lacked the ability to produce a full range of vowels that normal humans can, suggesting that /u/, /i/, and /a/ were beyond Neandertal capabilities.

Their work was scrutinized, especially because spoken language had long been accorded tremendous importance in academic circles. For example, nineteenth-century anatomists believed that spoken language depended upon particular tongue muscles that attach on the inside of the lower jaw to small bony tubercles, or bumps. When it was first asked whether Neandertals could speak, and these tubercles were found to be insufficiently developed in the La Naulette mandible, the reply was: "The La Naulette mandible says 'no'!"

Marcellin Boule had made a similar, if less cleverly phrased, assessment of the La Chapelle-aux-Saints skeleton. He felt, incorrectly, that the skull showed only a poor development of a region of the brain known as Broca's area. As discussed earlier, the function of these areas had been discovered by the nineteenth-century French anatomist, Paul Broca, when he performed an autopsy on a mute but otherwise normal individual. Finding a lesion, or defect, in Broca's area, the anatomist deduced that this region was crucial for the integration of the muscular activity needed for articulate speech, although very recent research suggests this interpretation is simplistic. Position emission tomography, or PET, scans of human volunteers show that Broca's area is involved in various activities, including making hand gestures or *thinking* of making hand gestures. Certainly monkeys and apes also possess Broca's areas, though they are far less developed than in modern humans. Its supposedly poor development in Neandertals was thus believed to attest to poor or nonexistent capacities for speech. Lieberman and Crelin were following along an already-established path of trying to put words into—or take them out of—the mouths of Neandertals.

Various anatomists and anthropologists were quick to criticize Lieberman and Crelin. Their first error lay in accepting Boule's reconstruction of the base of the skull, which was abnormally flat. How faulty Boule's effort was came to light in 1983, when a horrified graduate student examining the La Chapelle-aux-Saints skull found that Boule's old glue joins came apart in her hands. When she recovered from the shock, the student consulted the museum authorities. Jean-Louis Heim, a paleoanthropologist at the Musée de l'Homme, took the opportunity to clean off all the antique glue and to reassemble the fragments anew. The result was a much less flat, and much more human, configuration. Crelin also made a serious mistake in positioning the larynx. This is at best a difficult task because even normal, modern, articulate humans show a lot of variation in exactly where the different muscles attach to the skull.

But the largest problem with the reconstruction by Crelin and Lieberman lay in the position of the hyoid, a small bone lying above the larynx to which the tongue muscles attach. As reconstructed, Neandertals were not only unable to talk, various anthropologists and anatomists observed, they were also unable to swallow or open their mouths. These minor problems were jestingly suggested to account very neatly for Neandertals' extinction as well as their inarticulateness.

But Crelin and Lieberman's work, though it was heavily disparaged, raised some important issues. How much language is required to make "language"? Do all articulate humans express themselves with the same range of sounds? The answer, obviously, is no, because many languages possess sounds not shared by others. What's more, the status of the crucial neurological component of speech—the fine controls over muscular complexes and the sophisticated processing centers in the brain—in Neandertals remains unknown and, at this time, unknowable. *If* Neandertals could have learned to sing a Verdi opera, their large noses, sinuses, and mouths would have made resonating chambers to rival the best operatic basses today.

Like that by Brose and Wolpoff, the research by Lieberman and Crelin was focused essentially on the behavioral capabilities of Neandertals. While capabilities are, at best, hard to estimate, what was actually and habitually done remains even more enigmatic. In retrospect, this problematic attempt to assess Neandertals' capacity for speech was a timely if nettlesome effort, one of several bids to document the anatomical differences between humans and Neandertals and to try to explain them in evolutionary or behavioral terms.

Criticisms aside, Crelin and Lieberman, Brose and Wolpoff—and before them, Brace—had reminded the field that there were many absorbing problems about Neandertals as yet unsolved. And there was a cohort of young anthropologists, those in graduate school in the early 1970s, who were both attracted to the opportunity to explore open questions about Neandertals and repelled by the rancorous debates that were beginning to typify the hot topics associated with the earliest hominids in Africa. To them, both the problems and the specimens of the earliest hominids seemed to be the domain of an older, intensely territorial, and well-funded group of scholars.

Four major issues about Neandertals were now raised to the point of urgency: How can differences in size and shape be measured and compared? What functions had shaped Neandertal anatomy (or, less eloquently, what were Neandertals *doing*)? Were Neandertals our ancestors or an evolutionary dead end? And who made which tools during the Middle and Upper Paleolithic? The research on these questions was to flourish in the 1970s and 1980s.

One such analysis had been completed: a doctoral dissertation awarded in 1970 at Cambridge University. It was written by Jonathan Musgrave, a young Englishman with a penchant for brightly colored waistcoats and red socks, a mildly eccentric fellow whose previous claim to fame was the translation of Beatrix Potter's *The Tale of Mrs. Tiggy-winkle* into Latin.

Musgrave studied under John Napier, an anatomist at the Royal Free Hospital in London. Napier had been grappling with the problem of analyzing some of the earliest known hominid hand bones, so he steered Musgrave toward a comparative study of hand bones of Neandertals and early modern humans. Through detailed measurements and statistical analysis, Musgrave was able to show that Neandertals had neither short thumbs—contrary to Boule's statements—nor any particular limitations on manual dexterity. He did notice, and puzzle over, some of the anatomical oddities and the extreme muscularity of Neandertal hands.

At the time, Musgrave's work caused hardly a ripple of interest, even when he published a review article in 1971. Anthropologists were still reeling from Brose and Wolpoff's paper and from Lieberman and Crelin's work. But Musgrave's was, in a sense, exactly the type of study that Brose and Wolpoff had called for, and it was the first of a new wave of studies.

Simultaneously, there was another clarification of the Neandertal sample. In 1972, Jean-Louis Heim published the first scientific description of the adult Neandertal skeletons from La Ferrassie, which had been found a mere sixty-three years earlier. The work was perfectly competent, but held no surprises, and Heim continued to work on the other remains from La Ferrassie over the next ten years. At long last, these skeletons were added to the growing sample that revealed Neandertal shape and size. It was another small sign that the field had gone far beyond Boule's high-water mark.

Along with Heim was another young scholar, Bernard Vandermeersch, who helped disentangle the confused Neandertal–modern human sample in the 1970s. Vandermeersch was born in the late 1930s in a village that spanned the French-Belgian border. He remembers standing open-mouthed as a child in his quiet village and watching the Allied bombers fly overhead en route to Germany. As his fascination with war machines faded, his interest turned to prehistory; eventually, he enrolled at the University of Paris, where he was to study Paleolithic archeology and human paleontology. He became a student of Jean Piveteau, then the preeminent paleontologist at the University of Paris,

64. European paleoanthropologists producing new views of Neandertals. From left to right: Anne-Marie Tillier, Bernard Vandermeersch, and Jean-Jacques Hublin. Work by Tillier and Vandermeersch has clarified modern human origins in the Near East; Hublin's research has helped to sort out the origins of European Neandertals and the evolution of their North African relatives.

spending his vacations as a field assistant at various excavations of French Paleolithic sites. The young Vandermeersch gradually gained the reputation of being a solid student of the two fields. His Thèse du Troisième Cycle—roughly the equivalent of a master's thesis in the United States—was a hefty summary of the evidence about the dating of Middle Paleolithic sites in southwestern France.

This work brought Vandermeersch to the attention of Jean Perrot, the archeologist who had collaborated with Denise de Sonneville-Bordes on the typology of the Upper Paleolithic. Perrot had since been excavating in Israel and used his excellent connections there to obtain for Vandermeersch an incomparable opportunity: the permission of the Israeli Department of Antiquities to reexcavate the Jebel Qafzeh cave outside Nazareth. In 1964, Vandermeersch traveled briefly to Israel, establishing his priority at the site in the nick of time; a young and subsequently famous American archeologist, Lewis Binford, was preparing to apply for a permit to excavate Qafzeh as well.

As the forestalled Binford knew, the Qafzeh cave was a likely prospect for good material. In the 1930s, René Neuville had excavated there; he had concentrated mostly on the interior, finding parts of seven skeletons, five of which were from Middle Paleolithic levels. Those were already in residence at the Institut de Paléontologie Humaine in Paris, under Vallois's guard. Few in the scientific community had seen or studied them, but F. Clark Howell had brought them into his synthesis, noting the similarities between the best Qafzeh skull and those from Skhul.

Vandermeersch's success exceeded any reasonable expectations. Between 1965 and 1980, Qafzeh yielded eight more partial skeletons of adults and children and fragments of others, for a total of about twenty-four individuals. It was an impressive sample that even included a double burial, a young adult female and a child known as Qafzeh 9 and 10.

Vandermeersch still shudders over his memories of the removal of this burial from the site and the disasters that might have—but didn't—occur. The two skeletons, and a block of surrounding sediments, were carefully jacketed in plaster bandages, a standard but not simple procedure. Then the entire massive bundle was airlifted out by an Israeli Air Force helicopter made available through the intervention of Moshe Dayan, who had long been interested in prehistory. During the lift, the helicopter's blades stirred up so much dust that visibility was near zero. Vandermeersch watched and worried, as loss of human lives and precious fossils was narrowly averted by the pilot's uncanny ability to sense exactly how far from the limestone cliffs the helicopter's blades were spinning.

Understandably, with this treasure in hand, Vandermeersch's attention veered away from the archeological remains and came to focus on the human fossils. The more strictly archeological side of the work at Qafzeh was turned over to his Israeli colleague, Ofer Bar-Yosef. In 1977, Vandermeersch finished his Thèse d'Etat, describing and comparing all of the then known adults from the Middle Paleolithic levels at Qafzeh.

His important conclusion was the culmination of a whole series of hints, suspicions, and reassessments. What Vandermeersch showed, conclusively, was that the remains of Skhul and Qafzeh were not Neandertals. Even the Neandertal-like fossils from Israel, found in nearby sites including Tabun, Amud Cave near the Sea of Galilee, and Kebara Cave, were different from those at Skhul and Qafzeh. Because the remains from Skhul and Qafzeh were anatomically modern, Vandermeersch revived F. Clark Howell's term "Proto–Cro-Magnon" for them, implying that they were probably ancestral to the Cro-Magnons of Europe.

This meant that Brose, Wolpoff, and others had contaminated their samples when they included Skhul and Qafzeh as Neandertals. It also meant that both Neandertals and anatomically modern humans were making Middle Paleolithic tools and leaving them behind in the same areas of the Near East. Awkwardly, no one was able to find any good evidence for two different cultural traditions, which threw into question many of the interpretations in Europe that had relied on an equation of particular tool assemblages with particular toolmakers. The Near Eastern story of Neandertals and modern humans was becoming daily more complicated and enigmatic.

While Vandermeersch was finding more fossils at Qafzeh, Musgrave began supervising a doctoral student who was to become a major figure in Neandertal studies: Christopher Stringer. Born to a Cockney, working-class couple, Stringer was partly raised by foster parents. He had none of the advantages of accent, manner, or prestigious schooling enjoyed by most successful academics in England. He had, however, a bright and independent mind, a keen ear for nonsense, and a willingness to work hard.

From the age of about ten, Stringer was fascinated with human evolution, disconcerting his parents by spending hours drawing skulls and staring at exhibits at the Natural History Museum. Though he was inspired by a teacher with training in geology, no one ever suggested to Stringer that there was such a thing as a career in anthropology. He dutifully prepared to go to medical school. When, at the eleventh hour, Stringer discovered it was possible to take a degree in anthropology, he promptly headed straight for University College, London, where he met visiting lecturers Don Brothwell, a prominent archeologist and physical anthropologist, and Michael Day, an anatomist.

After graduation, Stringer obtained a part-time job at the British Museum (Natural History), while Day and Brothwell tried to find funding for his graduate studies. It seemed hopeless. Stringer was on the verge of quitting to become a teacher, when—miraculously—Musgrave phoned Brothwell to say there was a spare graduate student grant at Bristol: did he know of any promising young students? Indeed he did— and for a student interested in Neandertals and hoping to use multivariate statistics, Musgrave was a thoroughly appropriate adviser.

Stringer had already determined that it was time to attack the Neandertal problem with new tools and new energy, an approach that was to become a trademark of his career. A neatly built man with fair hair and beard and a blunt accent that openly bespeaks his modest origins,

65. Christopher Stringer of the Natural History Museum in London, one of the major proponents of the idea that the Neandertals were completely replaced by modern humans

Stringer is the very antithesis of the drawling, lackadaisical, elegant, upper-class Englishman for whom appearing to work too hard is "bad form." To Stringer, bad form is doing sloppy science or being too lazy or mentally hidebound to get at the truth. Thus, he was almost constitutionally unable to accept the prevailing wisdom about Neandertals without a closer look.

"I thought they were getting a raw deal," Stringer says of Neandertals. Perhaps the casual dismissal of Neandertals on the basis of their appearance smacked too much of the class distinctions in British society with which he was undoubtedly familiar. Certainly Stringer was a member of one of the first few generations of working-class Britons to rise to positions of academic prominence, positions that were once tacitly reserved for the elite products of the better public schools.

Though he refused to dismiss the Neandertals as ancestors out of hand, neither was Stringer committed to proving that they *were* human ancestors; he feels he embarked on his study with an open mind. Traveling across Europe from museum to museum in his rusty, ancient car, Stringer pondered over, photographed, and measured all the skulls he could. By 1974, he had completed his study of cranial form among Neandertals and had developed a new, quantitative way to evaluate the resemblances and differences among Neandertals and early modern humans.

From his perspective, the solution to the Neandertal problem was clear: Neandertals were far too different from modern humans to have been their ancestors. In time, Stringer became one of the most articulate and staunchest advocates of the replacement hypothesis.

The weak point of the replacement hypothesis was always the lack of evidence of an early, modern human population that could have migrated into Europe and replaced the Neandertals. Without a "replacer" the whole concept seemed specious. But one of Stringer's next projects provided a vital clue. He was asked to work with Day on some new skulls from Ethiopia known as Omo 1 and 2. These were puzzling and enigmatic fossils, for the two Omo skulls showed different morphology. Omo 2 displays a mixture of archaic and modern features, while Omo 1 is anatomically modern, if robust.

Omo 1 was found *in situ* in the rock, where it was dated to more than 40,000 years ago and perhaps as many as 130,000; it was associated with stone tools identified as being Middle Stone Age, the African equivalent of Mousterian. These facts would tend to suggest that the Omo 1 skull is an extremely early modern human, one of the first in Africa. They are reinforced by what Stringer sees as recognizably African characteristics. In short, his work neatly provided a complete inversion of what Coon's data had suggested; Africans were the first, not the last, to become sapient. "We are all Africans under the skin," Stringer says emphatically.

Unfortunately, the Omo 2 skull has a less certain story. Omo 2 was found on the surface, weathered out of the rock, but all indications were that it came from the same stratigraphic level as Omo 1. If they were even approximately contemporaneous, then two hypotheses can be entertained. There could have been two very distinct populations present in Ethiopia, one archaic and one modern, or perhaps there was a single population with an unusual degree of variability of cranial shape. Stringer and Day preferred the former interpretation and suggested that Omo 2 could be older than and ancestral to Omo 1.

At almost the same time, two Americans were pulling at the threads of the knotty Neandertal problem from their own perspectives. One was Fred Smith, the other was Erik Trinkaus, one of the authors of this book.

The two, though friends and colleagues in later years, made a striking contrast. Smith was a sturdy, dark-haired, young anthropologist from the hills of Tennessee; Trinkaus was a tall, lanky, fair-haired youth from Connecticut. Smith spent his boyhood in his hometown, Lenoir City, absorbed in "basketball, baseball, and band"; Trinkaus grew up in a cosmopolitan environment in Connecticut and even lived in Paris for a year while his professor-father took a sabbatical there. Smith was only the second in his family to go to college, while academia was the family business for Trinkaus. Smith has retained the slow, charming drawl of his natal area, coupled with an infectious grin; the bespectacled Trinkaus speaks quickly, with an occasional mild stammer and a delight in word-play.

Born in 1948, Smith was first attracted to anthropology by reading *National Geographic* in high school. The Leakey family's exciting discoveries in Africa enthralled him, but it never occurred to him that a "mountain boy" like him could make a living as an anthropologist. He attended the University of Tennessee, courtesy of an Army Reserve Officers Training Corps scholarship. Like Stringer, he aimed at a medical career until he found out that a career in anthropology was possible.

One of the turning points in Smith's life came when his anthropology professor invited him and a few fellow undergraduates to go along on a dig in what was then Yugoslavia. He loved Yugoslavia, and when someone told him that there were Neandertals from Yugoslavia stored in the museum in Zagreb, he took a quick side trip to see them. He remembers standing in the exhibit area, staring through the glass, overwhelmed by the sheer volume of the material: "There were *boxes* full of temporal bones," he marvels, referring to the region of the skull that houses the ear bones. "It was incredible."

When he returned home, still dazzled by the Krapina Neandertals, he checked the library to see what had been published on the site. He found nothing in English that did justice to the material and set his sights on returning to Yugoslavia and studying it for himself. By sheer chance, he had already started learning German, the only foreign language class that fit his schedule and coincidentally the only language (other than Croatian, which he learned later) that would be useful to his future work in Yugoslavia.

After graduating from the University of Tennessee, Smith managed to postpone his military obligations until after graduate school. He set out for Case Western Reserve, where he came into contact with Wolpoff, who was in the process of writing his seminal paper with Brose. Few young professors can have had the good fortune to have such a student walk in the door: one who was directed, knowledgeable, and determined. For his part, Smith found the young Wolpoff inspiring for his tremendous energy and his analytical perspective on human evolution. Wolpoff encouraged Smith to attack the central European fossil record, which had been largely neglected by English-speaking scientists.

By the end of Smith's first year of graduate school, he had secured a grant from the Wenner-Gren Foundation to go to Zagreb and study the Krapina material. It was an almost unheard-of accomplishment for a first-year student.

Smith wrote eagerly to the director of the Zagreb Museum, asking for permission to come, but there was no reply. The date for departure crept closer and still there was no word. Sensing there might be some lingering anti-American sentiment in Yugoslavia—and, equally, betting that no one could resist Smith's charm and sincerity—Wolpoff told his young student, "Go. Just go." It was good advice, for a few days after Smith's departure, the long-awaited letter came, refusing Smith permission to come.

Smith, blissfully ignorant of this denial, turned up at the museum, thrilled and delighted to fulfill his boyhood dream. He walked into the museum and introduced himself to the receptionist who, he remembers, "looked at me like I was the devil incarnate." Only slightly perturbed, he asked to see the director, Ivan Crnolatac, who arrived and told him sternly that he could not see the Krapina material. Dragutin Gorjanović, the greatest of Croatian paleontologists, had already done every study that could be done and the fossils were a national treasure. Had Smith not received the letter denying him permission?

Smith's grin disappeared, and his face fell: no, he had not. His genuine disappointment must have been palpable. He had come so far and studied so hard to see for himself the wonderful material that Gorjanović had excavated. And what was he going to tell the granting agency—that he went to Yugoslavia, spent their money, and did nothing? "I saw my career completely destroyed before it even started," he recalls, "and I began to think maybe working in the family grocery store wouldn't be so bad after all."

Despite the director's firm words, he had a soft heart. Smith was so visibly crestfallen that the director offered a compromise: if Smith returned the next day, perhaps the director would show him a few bones and they would see. Fortunately for Smith, he had been well trained and was able to make intelligent comments about the bones. Crnolatac showed him a few more, and then a few more. Smith did exactly and only what the director suggested would be permitted, trying to be careful not to offend.

After two weeks, the director agreed to give him free access to the material; by now, the museum staff were all charmed and treating him like family anyway, he remembers. The day after he had been given permission, Smith was photographing some of the skull bones and the flash attachment fell off his camera and dropped on the specimens. One of them broke; Smith was horrified. He called the director in to show him what had happened, expecting that he might be thrown out.

"Never mind," the director said, handing him a tube of glue, "we won't tell anyone this happened."

Smith continued to work under some restrictions, for Gorjanović's office and lab were maintained more or less as a shrine. Smith was given access to only one precious boxful of fossils at a time, and sometimes the logic behind the content of any particular box was mystifying. He was prohibited from setting all of the specimens from one region of the body out on the table at once, which kept him from fitting together some of the fragments that later scholars were able to conjoin once the box-by-box procedure had been abandoned.

After two prolonged visits to Zagreb, Smith completed his doctoral dissertation in 1976, later published as a monograph by the University of Tennessee. This work was the first modern study of anything approaching a population of Neandertals—and, at that, the population was one relatively unknown to western Europeans and Americans.

Smith summarized for the non–Croatian-speakers of the world many of Gorjanović's original publications on the fauna, geological age, and stone tools. This cleared up some of the confusions about Gorjanović's excavation procedures and documentation. He also gave a detailed anatomical description, complete with photographs, drawings, measurements, and comparisons, of the Krapina Neandertals, literally from head to toe. He estimated the number of individuals preserved at Krapina (somewhere between twelve and twenty-eight) and the time span involved (perhaps fifty thousand years). This information provided a sobering look at what a "population" of Neandertals actually entailed: fewer than one individual per thousand years. Somewhat reluctantly, for it smacked of melodrama rather than science, Smith also reexamined the dark question of cannibalism and concluded that there were indeed points suggestive of cannibalistic practices.

The real aim of Smith's study, and for him the most important conclusion, dealt with the problem of the Neandertal's relationship to modern humans. Using Vallois's famous paper as a framework, Smith carefully restated and reevaluated the different hypotheses.

About the pre-Sapiens scheme, Smith's conclusions are unequivocal:

> There is absolutely no evidence in the Krapina sample of a hominid form more advanced than Neandertals inhabiting the site or the area at a time contemporaneous with the Neandertals. . . . While it cannot be proven on the basis of Krapina alone that pre-sapiens do not exist at this time, it is definitely not possible to use any data from Krapina to support it.

The pre-Neandertal scheme fared equally poorly. The Krapina human fossils spanned the hypothetical pre-Neandertal and Neandertal eras, yet all were Neandertal in morphology. There was simply no support for the idea that the earlier remains were more anatomically modern or could be more readily linked to modern humans. Instead, Smith came out obliquely in favor of the Neandertal scheme or unilineal hypothesis, a position he has supported strongly through the years. He wrote:

> The Krapina data cannot conclusively demonstrate the *in situ* evolution from Neandertals to early modern man in Europe, because a complete sequence of hominid remains spanning this period is not available at Krapina. . . . The fact that the largest sample of European Neandertals [i.e., Krapina], spanning probably the longest time period of any series of Neandertal skeletal remains, shows no indication of the presence of more advanced hominids, must be considered at least indirect support for the Unilineal scheme; . . . it seems most likely to consider Neandertals of Europe direct ancestors to the modern populations of the area.

Here, then, was the second recent Ph.D. thesis focusing on the Neandertals, yet he and Stringer had come to diametrically opposed conclusions. Stringer argued forcefully for the replacement of Neandertals by modern humans; Smith was equally convinced that the opposite was true, that Neandertals showed a continuity with modern humans that indicated Neandertals had actually evolved into modern humans. Both scholars relied on measurements and both had similar samples; they had inspected and measured the very same specimens, in many cases. It was a puzzling turn of events.

As the polarity of opinions developed and hardened in the field, a fascinating fact slowly became evident: those who worked first or primarily on the western European Neandertals opted for replacement, while those whose ideas were formed by an initial exposure to the central European fossils embraced continuity.

In the material from France and Italy, the discrepancy between the Neandertal fossils and the subsequent modern humans, and the apparent rapidity of the changeover, convinced anthropologists that here was a genuine evolutionary discontinuity. Neandertals were one species or subspecies and modern humans, *Homo sapiens sapiens*, were quite another. But, in what was then Yugoslavia and nearby Czechoslovakia, the specimens seemed to tell a different story, one of greater initial variability in size and shape among Neandertals that gave way gradually to modern humans. It was not until the late 1980s that it became generally appreciated that the evidence, not simply its interpretation, seemed to be different in the two geographic regions.

While Stringer and Smith wanted to settle the phylogenetic question about Neandertals' descendants, Trinkaus embarked on a study of Neandertals from an entirely different point of view: he wanted to know about Neandertal biology rather than Neandertal phylogeny. Never mind to whom Neandertals did or did not give rise; Trinkaus wanted to know how they *lived*. Of course, he was aware that this, in turn, might reveal why they either were replaced by or evolved into modern humans.

Trinkaus was an unlikely prospect for such a viewpoint. Born in 1948—only a few months later than Fred Smith—Trinkaus had spent many years of his education avoiding biology, his father's field. He admits that he managed to get through a physics and an art history degree at the University of Wisconsin untainted by any formal exposure to biology. Initially, he hoped to attend graduate school to look at how art reflected the organization of society in ancient Peru. But when Trinkaus arrived at the University of Pennsylvania, he found it impossible to work with the professor he had been planning to study under.

Casting about for a new direction, he took a seminar with Alan Mann in physical anthropology, focusing on Neandertals and *Homo erectus*. That course dragged him into biological anthropology, with an unanticipated bonus. Because Trinkaus had become fluent in French as a child—he had spent the sixth grade in France—he could read the abundant French literature that was only indirectly available to many Americans at the time. For Mann's course, Trinkaus studied Vallois's original monograph on the Fontéchevade fossils; his command of French was sufficient to convince him that Vallois's conclusions didn't follow logically from the evidence. His critique of the work, written for the seminar, eventually became Trinkaus's first publication. It was the first of a series of papers during this era that dismissed Vallois's fervent attempts to champion the pre-Sapiens view.

Although the seminar was focused largely on phylogenetic issues—the Neandertal problem—Mann was enthusiastic about the possibility of examining the interplay of biology and behavior in the fossil record, as his own doctoral dissertation had done for the australopithecines. For Trinkaus, human paleontology was a way to combine his interests in culture and physics into a promising career.

The question was which group in human evolution to tackle. Like many graduate students at the time, Trinkaus was not anxious to join Mann and others in the endless controversies over the australopithecines or *Homo habilis,* a recently discovered, early species, whose anatomy and dating was (and still is) highly problematic. But why not specialize in Neandertals, where his linguistic abilities would be an asset? He liked the idea and reasoned that the fairly large numbers of associated skeletons of Neandertals might yield behavioral answers to carefully formulated questions. A nonconfrontational person, Trinkaus consciously or unconsciously selected the strategy of identifying a vacant academic niche and making it his own.

In 1973–74, Trinkaus obtained funding for his first grand tour to try to test Coon's hypothesis. The question was: Did Neandertals really have short limbs, like the cold-adapted Lapps and Eskimos, as Coon had suggested? Once in Europe, however, he soon saw that the topic was too big to handle if he wanted to get out of graduate school before his hair turned gray.

He was in a quandary. Trinkaus's firsthand examination of the fossils, especially those from La Chapelle-aux-Saints and La Ferrassie in the Musée de l'Homme in Paris, had impressed upon him how massive and robust Neandertal legs and feet were. Nothing in the literature had prepared him for what he saw. But a detailed study of the anatomy of this region and its implications for Neandertal adaptations or gait would be too large and unfocused a topic for a good thesis. In the end, because there were lots of foot bones and a number of almost complete foot skeletons, Trinkaus embarked on what a fellow student called "one of the more pedestrian theses in human paleontology." He tried simply to document how Neandertal feet resembled and differed from modern ones and what this implied.

Because the emphasis in almost every previous study had been on Neandertal cranial anatomy—Musgrave's hand research excepted—Trinkaus knew his project would step on no metaphorical toes along the way. Underlying his work was the conviction that major morphological differences must reflect significant differences in behavior and evolutionary adaptations: if they were built differently from us, Neandertals were not and could not behave just like us.

When Trinkaus finished his dissertation, in 1975, he had shown that Boule's reconstruction of Neandertals as having divergent big toes, like apes, was quite simply fictitious. Without physically altering the joint surfaces in the bones of Neandertal big toes, it was impossible to set the big toe off at an apish angle from the other toes. Instead, like humans, their big toe was aligned closely with the other toes. In fact, sometimes the big toe slanted strongly toward the other toes, in a condition called hallux valgus by physicians who often treat bunion problems in modern humans caused by this rather pinched arrangement of the toes.

He also found that Neandertals had fully developed arches and short toes, like modern humans and unlike apes. In short, he confirmed in detail what had been stated by Patte and Straus and Cave: there was no reason whatsoever to believe that Neandertals walked differently from us and every reason to think the contrary. The specter of the shuffling, bent-kneed Neandertal faded undramatically away under Trinkaus's calm assessment.

However, Neandertals had exceptionally wide and robust toes, with strong muscle markings: "fat toes." Fat toes seemed to be an adaptation for something akin to broken-field running while barefoot, in which the toes must grip the rugged terrain. Could Neandertals have spent most of their time scrambling around on the landscape, rather than strolling or even walking briskly from place to place? If so, then their daily quest for food, through hunting and gathering, was probably not much like what modern hunter-gatherers do.

Trinkaus's research topic also provided him with a singular opportunity, one of those strokes of good fortune that sometimes befall the diligent. In the course of his foot studies, Trinkaus had contacted T. Dale Stewart, the physical anthropologist at the Smithsonian who was responsible for all of the Shanidar Neandertals except for the child found in 1953. Here, Trinkaus's strategy of selecting a focus that had been ignored previously paid off lavishly. Because Stewart had done little with the foot bones, he was glad to let Trinkaus examine his collection of casts and originals of Shanidar foot bones. Here was no selfish scholar, jealously hoarding material for himself and hiding it away from others. Indeed, Stewart was exceptionally kind to the young man.

Looking at the remains, and talking with Stewart, Trinkaus quickly realized that full analysis of the Shanidar material was vital to an improved understanding of Neandertals. It was a daunting task; no wonder fifteen years had passed since the last of the bones had come out of the ground. Not only were there nine partial skeletons, consisting of anywhere from a few to a hundred bones each, but Stewart—born in 1901—was, by his own admission, aging. He had been almost sixty when he went to Shanidar and tackled the enormous job of cleaning, restoring, describing, and analyzing the abundant specimens. By the mid-1970s, even the indefatigable Stewart was beginning to slow down.

Hoping the older man would let him collaborate—in effect, offering his youth and energy to complement Stewart's vast experience—Trinkaus wrote a carefully worded letter to Stewart in the summer of 1975, hesitantly but politely offering his assistance. Stewart's reply was long in coming, fueling Trinkaus's worst fears that he had insulted the esteemed scholar and ruined his own reputation. Finally, in September 1975, the letter arrived, complete with an apology for the delay in answering caused by Stewart's absence from the United States.

Stewart did not agree to the collaboration. Instead, "to my surprise," Trinkaus recalls, "he suggested that I assume full responsibility for the completion of the reconstruction, study, and eventual publication of the Shanidar Neandertal sample. He was at the time completing a summary of his own work on the Iraqi fossils and planned only to finish the description of the fragmentary Shanidar 3 remains, then in Washington."

That was in 1975. At Stewart's and Solecki's suggestion, Trinkaus decided to begin by reconstructing and studying the Shanidar 5 skeleton. Although Shanidar 5 had been found in 1960, the tremendous attention paid to Shanidar 4 (the "Flower Burial") had meant that Shanidar 5 had been simply wrapped in burlap and plaster and sent to gather dust in the Iraq Museum in Baghdad.

It was a challenging experience. Day after day during the summer of 1976, Trinkaus worked in a dimly lit room, wrestling with an unwieldy bundle of plaster and dirt in temperatures hovering around 100 degrees. He was far from home and his new fiancée, alone in a strange country with limited funds and a difficult task to perform. By the end of his visit, he had cleaned off most of the face and the front half of the braincase of the largest known Neandertal skull. Impressed, the Iraqi authorities agreed to give Trinkaus access to as much of the Shanidar material as he wished henceforth.

The following autumn, Stewart relinquished the Shanidar 3 remains to Trinkaus's care as well, "because of the good personal relationship we developed and the good research reports he produced." Thus, Trinkaus was in the enviable position of having exclusive rights to study a poorly known and large sample of Neandertals. The opportunity was well worth a few uncomfortable summer visits to Baghdad, which was not the romantic garden spot of the Arabian Nights even before Operation Desert Storm took its toll.

The skeletons were as complete as those from western Europe—many were, after all, deliberate burials—and almost as numerous as the much more fragmentary remains from Krapina. They became the impeccable foundation of Trinkaus's rising young career.

Trinkaus was never very interested in resolving the question of Neandertals' place in our ancestry, and initially, he paid little attention to the problem. But he, like Stringer, thought it was all-important to compare Neandertal morphology to that of the earliest, anatomically modern humans. Even after humans first became "anatomically modern," there seemed to be more significant changes yet to come—a fact that was implicit in the nineteenth-century assessments of many of the fossils but which had somehow been forgotten along the way.

Wolpoff developed this idea in a different way, returning to Neandertal studies by embarking on a study of the 281 isolated teeth from Krapina. Although some specimens were broken and fragmentary, others simply suffered from no longer being emplaced in bony jaws. Wolpoff spent months estimating the age of each individual represented by a tooth and trying to reassociate the teeth that had once belonged in the same head, with some success. Because in the previous years he had amassed a huge set of data on the measurements of fossil human teeth, Wolpoff could now plug in the Krapina data.

Wolpoff found a long-term, evolutionary trend for the cheek teeth (molars) to get smaller while the anterior teeth (incisors) enlarged, with much of the change in tooth size happening after anatomically modern humans had first evolved. He hypothesized that this progressive change reflected improvements in food preparation, such as processing of dietary items with tools or by cooking—a suggestion that evoked some of Brace's ideas and that elaborated upon those in the seminal Brose and Wolpoff paper.

Wolpoff, even more than Smith, now became a vocal advocate of the hypothesis that Neandertals were the direct ancestors of modern humans, a predictable outcome because his most pivotal experience with Neandertals occurred at Krapina. But Wolpoff put a special twist on it. At first, he was simply prodded and provoked by Australian anthropologist Alan Thorne; later, the two became active collaborators in reviving some of Weidenreich's ideas, updating them in terms of the evolutionary synthesis, and promulgating what was called the multiregionalism hypothesis. As had Weidenreich, and later Coon, Wolpoff and Thorne saw clear signs of evolutionary continuity within broad geographic regions— central European Neandertals looked like modern central Europeans, Asian specimens of *Homo erectus* resembled Asian late archaic humans, which in turn evoked modern Asian features, and so on. This would mean that the development of each race's distinctive constellation of physical characteristics could be traced back to *Homo erectus* times.

Since then, Wolpoff believed, there had been both migration of human populations into new areas and limited genetic exchange between populations. Gene flow had been rather like that which occurs between neighboring groups, with populations basically staying where they were, while some individuals move back and forth as they intermarry. Regional groups were thus sufficiently isolated from one another that local patterns of physical traits began to develop, some in response to climatic factors and other simply through the random accumulation of traits with little adaptive significance. According to this scenario, distinct anatomical patterns persisted over long periods of time despite the indirect genetic contact between populations in separate regions. Simultaneously, traits that promoted better or more proficient cultural behavior spread unimpeded from group to group.

This was a true updating of Weidenreich's model that incorporated concepts from the evolutionary synthesis. Metaphorically, Wolpoff's work restored the criss-crossing lines that had originally connected different lineages in Weidenreich's model—the lines that had been eliminated by Howells and Coon in transforming Weidenreich's diagram from a grid into a candlelabra. It also transformed Europe from *the* place where Neandertals evolved into humans into one periphery (the other being Australia) of total area inhabited by the evolving human lineage. It was an abrupt about-face from the Eurocentrism that had prevailed for generations.

Eventually, this global, unilineal scheme for the origin of modern humans put Wolpoff at the opposite end of the spectrum from Stringer. The two became arguing partners, each swinging from excitement at his own sense of new understanding to despair at the possibility of ever convincing the other.

Comparing Neandertals to the group that was now being called early anatomically modern humans also appealed to a young Frenchwoman, Anne-Marie Tillier. Tillier was a member of the same academic generation as Stringer, Smith, and Trinkaus, having studied under Vandermeersch at the University of Paris. She cut her paleontological teeth at the excavation at Qafzeh with Vandermeersch.

One of the special things about the Qafzeh sample was the large number of immature individuals, who ranged in age from infants to early adolescents. Although fossils of immature Neandertals and modern humans had been known since the 1829 discovery of the Engis child, juvenile material had generally been dismissed as too difficult to analyze.

But the intrepid Tillier set out to take the issue of development even further by comparing the process in Neandertals to that in modern humans. She did not want to use immature individuals simply to establish the primacy of different traits, as Charles Fraipont had done when he spoke of the bestial characters that turned up in the two- or three-year-old Neandertal toddler from Engis. Tillier hoped to discover which traits appeared earliest so she could understand what features were most fundamental to Neandertal (or modern human) anatomy. Knowing the developmental basis of the Neandertal physique and biology would, Tillier believed, help her decide which adult traits were the most important to consider in attempting to trace or refute Neandertals' evolution into modern human.

She started by focusing on the children from Qafzeh, but soon expanded her purview to encompass most of the immature specimens from the entire Middle Paleolithic, whether they were Neandertals or anatomically modern humans. Neandertal development was compared thoughtfully with that of anatomically modern humans.

Following a few years after Tillier was another Vandermeersch student—a European Frenchman from Algeria—by the name of Jean-Jacques Hublin. At an early age, Hublin lost his father. His mother and he subsequently moved to the region near Paris where he grew up, an enthusiastic leader of school geology clubs and an avid participant in paleontological field trips. When he went to the University of Paris as an undergraduate, he specialized in geology. For his graduate degree, however, he wanted to shift gears and work with Vandermeersch on human evolution—even though his geology-student friends scoffed that it was "unscientific stuff." In 1978, Hublin completed a Thèse de Troisième Cycle on the anatomy of the back and base of human skulls from the Pleistocene.

Early in the century, the German Hermann Klaatsch, among others, had noticed that this region of the skull bore features linking Neandertal specimens from different regions, such as those from Spy in Belgium with those from Krapina in Croatia. Would these features prove helpful in sorting out the relationships among a wider group of prehistoric human groups? Hublin's thesis, though conservative in its immediate conclusions, showed that they would.

Hublin found that the pre-Neandertal fossils in Europe all showed incipiently Neandertal-like features in this part of the skull—all, that is, except the very oldest fossils. This meant that enigmatic specimens like

Swanscombe now fit neatly into a lineage leading toward Neandertals, causing the last evidence for any European pre-Sapiens fossils to evaporate. As he was to say emphatically at a conference years later, "The pre-Sapiens theory is dead. Period." These same traits that demarcated an ancient Neandertal lineage in Europe essentially disappeared with the advent of early modern humans in the region.

More recently, Hublin has specialized in fossil humans from North Africa and the Iberian peninsula—a concentration that he freely admits might be seen as searching for his own roots in some psychological sense. More obviously, he has tried to incorporate new specimens into the biogeographic clusters postulated by F. Clark Howell back in the 1950s.

Hublin's research seemed to confirm Stringer's ideas, for at every turn, Hublin found evidence of a large morphological difference between Neandertals and the early, anatomically modern humans who followed Neandertals chronologically in Europe. Prior to Neandertals, the European story seemed relatively clear-cut. The morphology of fossils could be traced continuously from *erectus*-like forms through the archaic forms like Swanscombe, to classic Neandertals, and then . . . then there seemed to be an abrupt shift in physical form. If modern humans hadn't evolved from Neandertals, then they had evolved somewhere outside Europe. Stringer, among others, felt that Africa might yield the answers.

Now another young European scholar spoke up, a newly minted German Ph.D. by the name of Günter Bräuer, whose work would help fill in the gaps in the African fossil story. Although paleoanthropology had been in the doldrums in postwar Germany, with few active and internationally respected scientists, Bräuer came out of a different mold from the generation before him.

Capitalizing on the long-standing ties between Germany and Tanzania (formerly German East Africa), Bräuer began his Ph.D. by studying some fossil human remains from the Mumba Rockshelter in northern Tanzania. While in Tanzania, he made a fateful trip to visit Olduvai Gorge, site of the Leakeys' famous discoveries, and Lake Eyasi, where another archaic human fossil had been found. He decided to try to unravel the confused evidence for the evolution of *Homo sapiens*, modern humans, in Africa. His strategy was to begin with the recent, Late Stone Age skeletons from Africa and work backward in time, trying to establish continuity in anatomical features.

Once again, it was a largely vacant research niche. Few scholars had looked at all of the specimens, which were scattered in several museums,

66. Günter Bräuer shown working with a fossil cranium of an East African relative of the Neandertals. Bräuer is known for his emphasis on Africa as a homeland of modern humans.

and no one had attempted a rigorous, analytical synthesis. If anyone were going to understand where either modern Africans or Europeans had come from, Bräuer reasoned, they needed to stop overlooking the African material—which was as neglected as the central European material had been when Smith started working on it.

He also recognized that there was an ill-defined collection of fossils older than Neandertals that seemed to represent a real biological group. These were the late archaic humans from Africa—the earliest members of our species on the continent, such as the Broken Hill remains from Northern Rhodesia (now Zambia) or various specimens from South Africa, Tanzania, and Ethiopia. Bräuer's advantage was that he took a modern African perspective, not a Eurocentric one. The next logical step was to inspect the European fossils from a more tropical perspective.

While the African specimens had received little attention, their antiquity had been recently revised, with important results. Up until the early 1970s, it was generally assumed that the tools found with these remains in Africa (a culture known as the Middle Stone Age) were more recent than the Mousterian tools associated with Neandertals. They were believed to be only about twenty to thirty thousand years old, making them contemporaneous with the Upper Paleolithic in Europe. But new radiocarbon dates from South African and other sites, published in 1972, suddenly shifted the Middle Stone Age backward in time, until this culture overlapped with the Mousterian. As the 1970s and 1980s proceeded, more and more dates suggested a formidable antiquity for these late archaic humans in Africa, in some places 200,000 years or more.

The fact that late archaic humans in Africa were suddenly discovered to be older only made Bräuer's intuition and measurements more valuable. By 1976, when he completed his Ph.D., he had begun articulating his "out of Africa" hypothesis. He argued that modern *Homo sapiens* had arisen initially in Africa and migrated outward to populate the rest of the world. Humans must have moved northward into Europe and westward across that continent, until they encountered and hybridized with Neandertals, Bräuer postulated.

Consequently, he believed that Neandertals were not replaced *entirely* by modern humans, for they had left some genetic contribution to future generations. He emphasized the interbreeding between the modern humans who had migrated into Europe from Africa and the Neandertals they met along the way, over a period that might have covered several millennia, yet his was basically a modified replacement model. Because of Bräuer's conviction that Africa was the site of the origin of modern human characteristics, he found a firm ally in Stringer.

Bräuer's expertise and his appreciation of the importance of the African record brought him national and international attention. In 1985, he was promoted to professor of anthropology at Hamburg University and was awarded the Rudolf Martin Prize by the German Society of Anthropology and Human Genetics—the only such prize for anthropology in Germany—for his "out of Africa" hypothesis.

The batch of young scholars from England, France, Germany, and the United States who shaped the Neandertal studies of the 1970s shared several traits. They were all born within a few years of each other, and many were influenced by the works of Brace, Brose, and Wolpoff. As a result, many perceived the most burning issue to be the question of whether or not Neandertals were the ancestors of modern humans.

Many—if not all—consciously gravitated toward this neglected question and opted for new approaches, seeking what would be called, in an evolutionary metaphor, an empty niche. At the time, the glare of popular and scientific attention was very much focused on Africa, on the earliest part of the hominid record and on the new discoveries of ever-yet-older australopithecines. That was a realm into which only the especially thick-skinned and competitive of this generation ventured. Ironically, of

course, after ten years of study and publication by such a gifted generation, the origin of modern humans and the fate of Neandertals have now
superseded the australopithecines as the hottest topic. Seeking to avoid
the controversy and jealous scrutiny that always characterize the biggest
questions in paleoanthropology, this group has inadvertently induced
vehement debate in their own topic by making evident the importance
and fascination of the work.

Their views were also colored by the new evolutionary synthesis of the
postwar period and population thinking, which was tied directly to a new
appreciation of the power of statistical studies. As a result, this group
attacked the problem from a new perspective. They wanted, if possible,
to study an approximation of a true biological sample—at the least, a
group of individuals from a restricted geographic region and time period.
And they hoped to be able to characterize those fossils using newer and
more sophisticated measurements and analyses, which would give them
a feeling for the variability in size and shape, or morphology, that was
represented in the anatomy of that group. Simple, descriptive anatomy
would no longer suffice.

The debate about the solution to the Neandertal problem rapidly
reached an impasse, with Wolpoff at one extreme and Stringer at the
other, and the other scholars arrayed somewhere between the two. The
radical difference in their perceptions was abruptly illuminated in 1979
by a seemingly trivial note in the "News" column of the *Bulletin de la
Société Préhistorique Française*. The note was signed by François
Lévêque, conservator of archeological excavations for the Poitou-Cha-
rentes region, and Bernard Vandermeersch, by then director of antiquities for the region and *maître assistant* (the equivalent of an associate
professor in the United States or a senior lecturer in England) at the
University of Paris.

The note repeated information that had been presented at the meeting
of the Société Préhistorique Française (the French Prehistoric Society) on
February 7, 1980. A site had been found near the village of Saint-Césaire.

> A few preliminary observations concerning the stratigraphy and the
> cultural material in the levels allowed us to place the remains of a
> human skeleton unequivocally in the Châtelperronian level [the
> cultural level which is, in that region, the earliest Upper Paleo-
> lithic]. The first results of the paleontological analysis of the skele-
> ton, made difficult by the fragmentary state of the remains, are in
> complete agreement with the conclusion that the individual was a
> classic Neandertal.

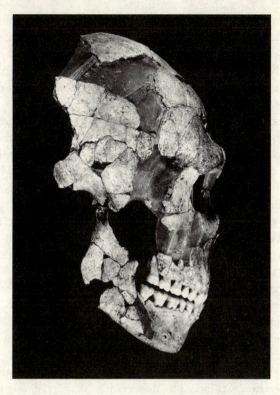

67. The skull of the Saint-Césaire Neandertal, found in 1979 in western France. Most Neandertals are found with Mousterian tools. The association of this Neandertal skeleton with Châtelperronian tools—one of the early Upper Paleolithic industries long believed to be a signature of anatomically modern humans—polarized the debate about the Neandertals' place in human ancestry.

It was an amusingly serendipitous find. Near the village of Saint-Césaire was a series of old limestone quarries, lying along a cliff known as La Roche à Pierrot; they were being used to grow mushrooms. In 1979, the owner of the mushroomery decided to enlarge the turnaround area for trucks and brought in front-loaders to clear away some of the earth. Unknowingly, they dug into an archeological site, exposing stone tools that were noticed by a local amateur who notified Lévêque. The owner of the quarry was less than pleased when Lévêque and Vandermeersch turned up to persuade him to stop work. But when they explained the possible significance of the site, leaving him several books on human evolution to peruse, his annoyance turned to cooperation. In the end, he funded the building of a local exhibit near the site.

Lévêque then started a salvage operation designed to retrieve the archeological material swiftly but with appropriate care and adequate scientific documentation. On July 27, 1979, a badly crushed skeleton of an adult Neandertal was uncovered in a layer bearing Châtelperronian tools. The skeleton was in such a tightly flexed position that it occupied an oval of only about one meter in diameter.

Had the skeleton been found in a Mousterian level, this find would have aroused only moderate interest. But the Châtelperronian industry had long been assumed to have been made by early modern humans, not Neandertals. But, in fact, only one diagnostic skeleton had ever been found with Châtelperronian tools before—the obviously modern Combe Capelle skeleton discovered by Otto Hauser—and that one probably was intrusive from a higher (more recent) Aurignacian level.

The facts stated in the initial publication, that a Neandertal skeleton was found in a Châtelperronian level, have never been seriously questioned by a paleontologist. Indeed, the Saint-Césaire skeleton was readily accepted as "the last Neanderthal in France." Yet none of the participants in the ensuing debate had actually seen either the fossil or the site.

If the find startled Lévêque, the response from the field at large was even more astonishing, for both camps—those favoring replacement and those favoring *in situ* evolution—deftly incorporated this find into their scenarios. To Stringer, Vandermeersch, Tillier, and Hublin, the Saint-Césaire skeleton was indeed a late-surviving Neandertal, one that was demonstrably contemporaneous with early modern humans from other sites. Stringer had been arguing for years that equating different types of humans with different types of tools was likely to be misleading. If Neandertals and anatomically modern humans occupied the same area, the Neandertals might well have learned new stone-working techniques from the modern humans.

To Wolpoff, the Saint-Césaire Neandertal was simply an individual from a population that was evolving toward modern humans; it was a case where the tools had "evolved" faster than the individual's skeleton. No find could have been much closer to fulfilling the prediction he and Brose had made almost a decade earlier. No better proof of the continuity between Neandertals and their successors could be asked for, he felt.

And to Bräuer, the Saint-Césaire Neandertal was "an individual from a population of the hybridization and replacement period."

Ironically, the only person unhappy with Saint-Césaire was the archeologist François Bordes; he openly questioned the association of the skeleton with the Châtelperronian. Yet Bordes had long maintained that some form of pre-Sapiens had been responsible for manufacturing what he called the Mousterian of Acheulian Tradition in France while Neandertals were responsible for the other facies of the Mousterian. Bordes had gone to great lengths to argue that the Le Moustier and Spy fossils, while obviously Neandertals, could not have come from the levels that included tools he classified as Mousterian of Acheulian Tradition. The root of the problem with the Saint-Césaire fossil was that Bordes believed the Châtelperronian had evolved out of the Mousterian of Acheulian Tradition, which by definition made it an industry produced by modern humans. A Neandertal with Châtelperronian tools at Saint-Césaire simply did not fit, and Bordes would not accept it to his dying day. That day arrived sooner than expected, when Bordes died prematurely of a heart attack the following year. Symbolically, his death was also the demise of the last serious vestige of the pre-Sapiens hypothesis.

In short, the Saint-Césaire fossil was a perfect mirror, reflecting back into each viewer's eyes the convictions brought to it. Indeed, it didn't even have to be viewed in a photograph or "in the flesh," so to speak, in order to perform this valuable function. Ironically, by polarizing the debate and by being so very malleable, the Saint-Césaire fossil made a serious contribution to the Neandertal problem. While it by no means produced a consensus, it did reveal to the participants that they were constructing their hypotheses so flexibly that no evidence could possibly disprove them.

Stringer issued a plea for a new approach and more rational discussion. As the 1980s began, the group of scholars working on Neandertals began to respond to two new thrusts in research.

The first was an increasingly global perspective on the question of Neandertals' phylogenetic position. It was no longer possible to discuss the European evidence without reference to the Asian fossils, or to make scenarios based on the Asian or Near Eastern material without considering the African data. Wolpoff and Thorne were arguing fervently that they saw evolutionary continuity when they reviewed the fossil record in eastern Asia and in the islands scattered from southeast Asia to Australia. They were later joined in this position by Wu Xin-zhi of the People's Republic of China. Smith was documenting morphological continuity and evolution from early to late Neandertals, comparing the Krapina material with fossils from another Croatian Neandertal site, Vindija, that he, Wolpoff, and others had been studying. Jean-Jacques Hublin saw a similar pattern in the fossils from northwest Africa, while Bräuer and Stringer championed sub-Saharan Africa as the place where modern human origins began. The Neandertals from Europe and western Asia, once the focus of attention, remained important but no longer played the only leading role.

The other thrust was epitomized by Trinkaus's work. Unlike the others, Trinkaus had little interest in the evolutionary fate of the Neandertals; his emphasis was on understanding Neandertals in their own terms. For the first time, Neandertals began to be studied as a species or subspecies with its own behavior, life-style, ecology, and anatomy—not as either a transient stop along the way to becoming human, or a dead-end, failed human. It was a subtle but extremely powerful shift in purpose. No longer did Neandertal anatomy need to be explained away as significantly (or not so significantly) different from that of modern humans. Trinkaus forged the way for asking, and answering, the question: What differences in *function*, in habitual use, are revealed by the peculiarities of Neandertal anatomy?

With Trinkaus's influence, the relationship of Neandertals to the earliest humans could be examined by trying to discover what changes would be needed for a Neandertal to become anatomically modern. Whether replacement or *in situ* evolution had occurred, in some very real sense modern humans were more successful than Neandertals; they had, after all, lived on while Neandertals had died out. Now attention could be focused on exploring the evidence of culture, biology, and ecological adaptation to see if these explained the evolutionary advantage enjoyed by modern humans.

It is a realm of exploration that has yet to be exhausted, though many laudable initial attempts have been made by the new cohort of Neandertal experts. Perhaps fittingly, it was the Shanidar Neandertals that, once again, led the way to a fresh understanding. At the time of their discovery, the Shanidar fossils had provoked a rehumanization of Neandertals as a group. Now, as their detailed analysis proceeded, a stunning image of Neandertal life and adaptations began to emerge.

The Shanidar Neandertals were now in the hands of Trinkaus, who published paper after paper on their anatomy, but these were primarily descriptive in content. Conservative by nature, Trinkaus worked until 1983 before publishing a monograph, *The Shanidar Neandertals*, which overflowed with factual data supporting a plethora of genuinely new and provocative hypotheses.

In some senses, the Shanidar monograph paralleled Boule's on the La Chapelle-aux-Saints Neandertal. Boule's monograph, which had appeared in installments between 1911 and 1913, set the paradigm within which Neandertals were interpreted for the next forty-odd years: Neandertals were brutish, apish, and physically (as well as morally) primitive. Trinkaus's vision of Neandertals was diametrically different from Boule's, but as had the earlier monograph, it set the tone for much of the work that followed it.

Trinkaus was exceptionally fortunate in the quality of the Shanidar sample. Like Smith, he had the rare opportunity to study something approaching a population sample; like Boule, he could also look at the proportions and relationships within a single individual's skeleton; like Vandermeersch and Tillier, who together analyzed the Qafzeh fossils, he had representatives of both sexes and a wide range of ages.

In his monograph, Trinkaus repeated and elaborated upon Stewart's observations on the shudder-inducing set of traumatic injuries the Neandertals at Shanidar had experienced, discussing their possible causes and interpretation. Without question, life was neither gentle nor easy at Shanidar. Tremendous strength, endurance, and fortitude exceeding those of any modern human life-style were required on a daily basis.

Trinkaus also set forth his ideas about the functional significance of Neandertal anatomy. For example, he picked up Brace's idea that Neandertals had used their front teeth as a "third hand" or vise for clamping or holding items that were being worked. Trinkaus documented patterns of extreme wear and rounding of the front teeth that suggested that materials—perhaps hides or fibers—were pulled through the teeth and stripped. He also noticed that several Neandertal specimens, including one from Shanidar, showed horizontal grooves on the front of their incisors that probably came from cutting meat or some other material while it was being held between the teeth.

Similarly, Trinkaus showed that various features of the upper arm bones that are typical of Neandertals would all serve to increase the mechanical advantage, or leverage, of different muscles. Not only were the bones of the Shanidar Neandertals exceptionally stout and robust, he argued, but the locations at which muscles were attached to those bones enhanced the power with which the biceps muscle could bend the elbow or with which the forearm muscles rotated the hand into a supine (palm-up) or prone (palm-down) position—important maneuvers in thrusting with a spear, for example.

The most fascinating of all of Trinkaus's hypotheses—and the one that attracted the most attention—involved the pelvis. Although there was not one complete pelvis among the Shanidar remains (or in any set of Neandertal bones known at the time), there were substantial portions of the pelves of three individuals. There were also some pelvic remains from La Ferrassie, Krapina, and Tabun, which had long been known but had been little studied. Together, they indicated that the segments of bone known as the pubic rami, which run from the hips to meet at the midline at the front of the body, were unusually long. Because the main difference between the larger pelvis of modern women and the narrower one of modern men lies in the dimensions of the pubic rami, the logical deduction was that Neandertal pelves of both genders were broader side to side than human pelves. For female Neandertals, this would provide a very wide birth canal indeed. Trinkaus suggested that this anatomical fact might reflect an important reproductive difference between Neandertals and modern humans.

What was that difference? Trinkaus's reasoning was based on the well-known fact that modern human babies are premature in terms of brain development. Judged by the rules that apply to all other mammals, humans ought to have a gestation period of about twelve months in order to allow the fetal brain to develop. It is a simple matter of "economics." Growing a brain is metabolically expensive, so it is accomplished most efficiently while the baby is still in the womb—while the baby is still effectively a part of its mother. Once the baby is born, the mother must take in food, process it through her own system (thus expending most of the energy she has taken in), transform it into milk, and then suckle the baby. For this reason, in all other mammals, the rate of brain growth slows down markedly soon after birth.

In contrast, humans have acquired a unique evolutionary "trick": we give birth to an infant after only nine months, instead of twelve, and provide such excellent care and nourishment to the nursing mother that the baby's brain continues to grow at the rapid fetal rate for a full year after birth. This enables humans to have exceptionally large-brained offspring while maintaining a pelvis that is narrow enough to make two-legged locomotion reasonably efficient. It is a teetering compromise at best, but one which has worked for our species so far.

Trinkaus proposed that Neandertals had not yet evolved this evolutionary solution to the big-brained-baby problem. By his estimate, a Neandertal woman would have been able to give birth to a baby with a head 15 to 25 percent bigger than that of modern babies without obstetrical difficulties. This might mean that Neandertals kept their babies in the womb for the full eleven to twelve months, as their brain size would predict.

The idea invokes, to some, a comic image of a monstrously pregnant Neandertal woman, lumbering along looking and feeling as if she had swallowed a bison. Clearly, in the later months of pregnancy, she must have been assisted and cared for by her relatives and friends, for obtaining her own food or keeping up on long treks would have been almost impossible. The advantage would have been a more mature, less dependent baby—a distinct plus considering the extraordinarily rugged, rough-and-tumble life Neandertals lived.

On the other hand, if anatomically modern humans were the first to develop the knack of giving birth "early," then they would have faced formidable challenges. Substantial increases in the support and care given to nursing mothers and their infants would be required if the premature infants were to survive. Although modern human mothers are pregnant for a shorter period of time, their overall nutritional requirements are much higher because the metabolically costly period of suckling and infant brain growth is prolonged.

What social or economic changes could be envisioned that would support such a novel and serious demand? How could they be deciphered from the fossil and archeological record? And did the diminished gestation of modern humans—the ability to have babies more frequently, with closer spacing—provide the key to their greater evolutionary success? In other words, did anatomically modern humans "replace" Neandertals simply by breeding faster? These questions were challenges to paleoanthropologists' ingenuity, to their ability to put biology back into the fossil record. And, of course, Trinkaus soon heard from those who thought his notion of a year-long gestation must be wrong, however interesting it appeared to be.

Altercations notwithstanding, Trinkaus's work exemplified what a modern approach to the old field of functional anatomy might provide. His was a clear voice reminding the field that "who is related to whom?" is not the only question; he softened some of the acrimonious debates over phylogeny with his intriguing hypotheses about how Neandertals lived. Concern shifted gradually to the origin of modern humans in a broadly biological and behavioral sense, rather than focusing on the fate of the Neandertals alone.

This time, as before, it was not the discoveries themselves that compelled a change of paradigm, but their interpretation. A new era in Neandertal studies had been ushered in.

10

Created in Our Own Image

1984–1991

With Trinkaus's novel suggestion about Neandertal gestation lengths, Neandertal studies took on not only a new direction but a new texture. His hypothesis epitomized the growing concern for Neandertal *biology* that now flavored the debate. Even arguments about Neandertals' place in human ancestry began to deal more overtly with Neandertal behavior and adaptation rather than simply with abstract phylogenetic questions.

Trinkaus's idea was by no means accepted without demur. His original statement of the hypothesis was tucked into his Shanidar monograph, but it was followed by a longer and more explicit paper that appeared in 1984, in the journal *Current Anthropology*. Subsequent issues of that journal and others featured various rebuttals and alternative interpretations of the significance of the peculiar pelvis of Neandertals. Ironically, none of the commentators disagreed with Trinkaus's preliminary assumption: that the unusual length of the pubis, the anterior portion of the pelvis, implied a larger birth canal. What seemed to invoke the sharpest labor pains in the birth of Trinkaus's theory was the notion of a year-long pregnancy. Nine months seemed an inviolable duration.

Two other theories were put forward and received significant attention. One, formulated by a team including Christopher Stringer, suggested that Neandertals had a schedule of growth and development that was accelerated relative to that of modern humans. In other words, Neandertals grew faster—matured more rapidly—before as well as after birth, making their heads (and brains) larger at birth without gestation taking any longer.

The other, put forward by Karen Rosenberg, a student of Milford Wolpoff, suggested that the Neandertal pelvis was large but not particularly unusual. If a human mother is heavy, so, too, is her baby, and large babies have large heads, Rosenberg argued. In large mothers, with large babies, the opening of the pelvic inlet (birth canal) has to be larger, too, or the babies could never be born. Therefore, Rosenberg reasoned, the relatively short and heavily built Neandertals had both large-headed babies and proportionately capacious pelves. In essence, Rosenberg suggested that Neandertal anatomy did not reflect a distinctly different biology or adaptation from that of modern humans; the large pelvic inlet of Neandertals was exactly what would be expected from a human of exceptionally short and stout build.

She and Trinkaus found themselves at odds because they had such divergent views of the meaning of Neandertal morphology. Trinkaus believed, deeply, that Neandertals looked different because they were biologically and behaviorally different from modern humans; the point of his career was to understand and unravel what Neandertal anatomy meant. On her part, Rosenberg was convinced, equally sincerely, that Neandertals were simply funny-looking humans—the extreme case that proves the rule. Neandertals were stoutly built, unusually strong, and robust, but they were nonetheless fundamentally human. Compromise between the two was simply unobtainable.

In the midst of the debate—during which papers, comments, and replies to comments flew back and forth in the published literature and at professional conferences—the participants were abruptly confronted with new evidence from the fossil record itself that froze the argument in mid-sentence.

The telling bones came from a joint Israeli-French expedition that had been excavating at Kebara Cave, in Israel, for several years. In 1983, the year in which Trinkaus's monograph was published, the team discovered an adult male Neandertal in a burial; it took several years to analyze and publish the remains fully. Though missing its cranium and most of the leg and foot bones, the Kebara skeleton included the one anatomical element that had the most to say about reproduction: the first Neandertal pelvis so complete that only trivial reconstruction was needed.

To everyone's surprise, its pelvic aperture was no larger than that of a modern human's, strong evidence that female Neanderthals had modern-size birth canals. Yoel Rak and Baruch Arensburg, of the University of Tel Aviv, wrote up the remains for publication. "It was most surprising," they deadpanned, "to find that the elongated superior pubic ramus (which has long been noted in Neanderthals) has no bearing upon the size of the Neanderthal pelvic inlet, as previously speculated." This rendered false the fundamental assumption upon which all of the previous theories were based. Trinkaus soon retracted the gestation length hypothesis, and the others gradually fell silent. For once, a theoretical discussion of Neandertals had been resolved by actual, not interpretative, evidence from the fossil record. Somehow, no one was very satisfied.

But another controversy was to rise up and overshadow the Neandertal pelvis argument, putting another bizarre twist on the study of human evolution. The contribution came from a group of total outsiders, scientists of the post–new-synthesis revolution in molecular biology who knew very little about fossil humans. But what they believed they had discovered was to polarize the field of modern human origins more completely than ever before. The first hints of what was to come had begun circulating in the early 1980s, at meetings and informal talks and in preliminary publications. Viewed with the acuity of hindsight, these were clearly the signposts to a new highway. As they emerged, however, only a few anthropologists realized the importance of what was being said; others overlooked these ideas, either out of misunderstanding or stubbornness.

In 1987, the molecular biologists issued their challenge so clearly that it could no longer be ignored. In a pivotal paper, two young biochemists, Rebecca Cann and Mark Stoneking, and their former adviser, Allan Wilson, published an article claiming evidence for a recent, common origin for all modern humans. The data were derived from studies of a small segment of DNA that resides not in the nucleus of the cell, but in its mitochondria, the organelles that are the energy warehouses of the cell.

What Cann, Stoneking, and Wilson had done was capitalize on a discovery made some years before by others. Since 1964, it had been known that DNA, the molecule that encodes all of the body's genetic information, is present both in the cell's nucleus and in the mitochondria found in the cell's cytoplasm. Nuclear DNA is the type that condenses into chromosomes that are reassorted each time a mother's egg or a father's sperm is formed; nuclear DNA from each parent is thus contributed to the new offspring, as egg and sperm fuse. So far as anyone knows, nuclear DNA is the control center for inheritance. But the fact that there is also DNA within mitochondria is fascinating. The sperm is little more than nucleus with a tail and contributes only its nuclear contents to the new offspring, while the egg is a complete cell. This means that mito-chondrial DNA (mtDNA), residing in the cytoplasm, must be passed to the fertilized egg only from the mother. There is no recombination and reassortment in mtDNA, so any mutations that occur in mtDNA will be recorded in generation after generation. In other words, mtDNA is a wondrous record of matrilineal evolution.

Back in 1974, a young scientist named Wesley Brown had found effective techniques for comparing mtDNA from different individuals and for mapping the resemblances. As a source of mtDNA he used the placenta, a large quantity of tissue from a female that can be obtained without performing any invasive procedure. By 1979, Brown had pub-lished a study based on mtDNA from twenty-one placentas taken from mothers of diverse racial backgrounds. True, the number of individuals was small. Nonetheless, Brown's results looked promising.

He borrowed an approach that had been developed by the late Allan Wilson and his collaborator, Vincent Sarich at Berkeley. In their previous studies of rates of molecular evolution, they had argued that—because mutations are believed to accumulate randomly—the number of muta-tions distinguishing two species from each other was proportional to the amount of time since their divergence. In effect, they proposed that the accumulation of mutations approximated the ticking of a molecular clock; if this were true, then the number of mutations could be used to estimate the timing of evolutionary divergences.

Brown found that the number of mutations distinguishing the mtDNA of different racial groups in his sample was very small, implying that the various human races separated relatively recently. If substan-tiated by further work, these data would be powerful evidence against the multiregionalism hypothesis. Brown went further. He suggested that the surprising homogeneity of the mtDNA in his samples might mean that all of the individuals were descended from a single ancestral popula-tion—one not only recent but also small in size. In short, he proposed that perhaps all modern humans were descended from an ancestral group that had gone through a severe reduction in size, or a bottleneck.

It was while this work was still being published that Brown joined Wilson's lab at Berkeley, where Cann, then a young student, learned his techniques. It was her Ph.D. project to explore further the implications of mtDNA for racial origins, by collecting much larger and better samples and by trying to calculate the time of the evolutionary bottle-neck at whose existence Brown's work had hinted.

The results were published in a 1987 paper in *Nature*, with Cann as first author. They had samples from 147 individuals representing Asians, aboriginal Australians, aboriginal New Guineans, Caucasians, and "Africans." A point upon which the team was to be criticized later was that all but two of their "Africans" were actually black Americans and were therefore likely to have an unknown admixture of Caucasian and quite possibly American Indian mtDNA.

Their analysis of the results reinforced Brown's preliminary work and took it several steps farther. First, they established that there were 133 different types of mtDNA represented by the 147 specimens. Then they clustered the specimens, using a mathematical procedure that paired each specimen with the one most similar to it, then added in the next most similar, and so on, until an evolutionary tree or phylogeny was deduced. This is a common procedure in such analyses.

They believed that simplest evolutionary tree that could be constructed from the mtDNA data—that is, the one that required the fewest mutations to produce the modern situation—made the African specimens the starting point, although, there were a number of trees that were about equally as simple. The mtDNA data seemed clear and unequivocal on this point: anatomically modern humans arose first in Africa and then, apparently, migrated out to populate the rest of the world. The hypothetical, original mother on this migration was immediately nicknamed "Eve," a term that captured considerable media attention and publicity. Cann is at pains to point out that Eve may actually have been a population with a number of females who shared a common mtDNA type rather than a single woman.

Stringer rejoiced at this unexpected confirmation of his ideas, coming from a technique that could not have been more different from his own. Modern Caucasians may have developed lighter skin, Asians may have evolved epicanthic folds that give them "slanting" eyes, and so on, but the first, original, and basic human was a woman living in Africa. If the Garden of Eden—Eve's home—could be found, it was on the African continent. It all had that satisfactory ring produced by the merging of science and mythology.

The most problematic issue came with the attempt by Cann and her colleagues to set a time scale on their data. They relied on the timing of the first migrations of *Homo sapiens* to Australia and New Guinea, which was reasonably well documented by the archeological and fossil record. By dividing the number of mutations in those lineages by the estimated number of years since migration, they could derive a rate of mutations per year. This computation gave an answer entirely congruent with similar calculations for other species: in mtDNA, there were changes in 2 to 4 percent of the genes per million years. Using this calibration method, the mtDNA data suggested that modern humans first originated in Africa somewhere between 142,500 and 285,000 years ago. The team compromised on a nice, round figure: 200,000 years ago.

But, exclaimed many paleoanthropologists, *a 200,000-year-old date for the origin of modern humans in Africa would mean that neither* Homo erectus (which was spread around the Old World by about 700,000 years ago) *nor Neandertals* (which appeared all over Europe and western Asia between about 100,000 and 35,000 years ago) *had anything to do with our ancestry.* Replacement of Neandertals, and of all other Eurasian archaic humans, would be total and absolute. The hypothesized bottleneck would be the migration episode itself, in which only a small group left Africa (or a more sizable group, or even several groups, left, but only the offspring of a small group survived in the long term).

Yes, exactly, replied the biochemists, with perhaps a bit of self-satisfaction. *Not a chance,* countered the paleoanthropologists. *What were all those fossils that look just like good human ancestors doing if not evolving into humans?* It is a valid and troubling question that has provoked much discussion.

One of the most persistent voices of protest has been that of Milford Wolpoff, whose multiregional hypothesis would be severely undercut if the biochemical data, and its interpretation by Cann, Stoneking, and Wilson, were maintained. His observations of the fossils has convinced him that the bones showed clear signs of regional continuity and evolution, with racial distinctions appearing as long ago as *Homo erectus*; if this evidence cannot be reconciled with the mtDNA data, then there must be some flaw in the mtDNA, either in technique or analysis.

Wolpoff came to represent one extreme in this debate, but many other anthropologists sided with him in reacting against the extreme "no admixture whatsoever" stance of the biochemists. While Bräuer, Hublin, Tillier, Vandermeersch, and Trinkaus, among others, were willing to accept that the European and Near Eastern Neandertals might not have been human ancestors, they found it difficult to swallow that none of the late archaic humans from North Africa, eastern Asia, or Indonesia were related to modern human populations. Yet this was exactly the interpretation the mitochondrial team put on their data: *none* of the late archaic humans, except for a small founding population from sub-Saharan Africa, had *anything* to do with modern human ancestry.

Wolpoff led the tireless charge to examine the assumptions and methodology of mtDNA analysis to uncover the errors. His opposite, Stringer, accepted the mtDNA data wholeheartedly and worked to integrate it into his hypothesis. What is uncanny—and disheartening—is the way in which each side can muster the fossil record into seemingly convincing and yet utterly different syntheses of the course of human evolution. Reading their review papers side by side gives the reader a distinct feeling of having awakened in a Kafka novel. What Wolpoff discounts, Stringer credits, and vice versa.

Though criticism has been torrential, Cann and the other biochemists undertook to refine their techniques and improve their samples substantially over the last few years in response. As a result of their work, and Stringer's defenses, many paleoanthropologists began accepting the evidence for an important African contribution to the origin of modern humans. Few upheld the extreme position of an absolute, complete replacement, without admixture, of all other groups by a single, sub-Saharan African population and its descendants.

The more global approach to Neandertals' position in human phylogeny, while illuminating, has been unsuccessful in ending debate over the Neandertal problem. However, the perspective is markedly more evolutionary, and most scholars take less polarized positions than in the earlier parallel debate featuring "Neandertal phase" Hrdlička versus the "ancient sapiens" advocates, Boule and Keith, for example. The popular press has, of course, fostered extreme positions in the interests of good stories and has encouraged confrontations between Wolpoff and Stringer, though both have grown somewhat more flexible in their positions since the revelation of the Saint-Césaire material. Most paleoanthropologists have come to occupy a more intermediate position, accepting the validity of the genetic data but according its interpretation the same skepticism that they would direct at a paleoanthropological interpretation.

Wilson stuck closely to his original beliefs and embroidered yet another design on the colorful quilt of Neandertal interpretations. Until his death in 1991, his was an inventive, inquisitive, and original mind that generated ideas—good, bad, and nondescript—at a remarkable speed. That some of them fell outside of his area of competency was both a boon and a curse, for his I-wonder-if's were initially unencumbered by either prevailing wisdom or detailed factual knowledge; some have even been called scientifically embarrassing. When anthropologists challenged him to account for the overwhelming success Eve and her progeny must have had if they marched out of Africa and conquered the world genetically, Wilson listened. As he thought about it, he formulated an hypothesis that owed something to the image of the inarticulate Neandertal painted by the anatomist Crelin and the language specialist Lieberman: only Eve and her progeny had language. The mutation responsible must lie in the mtDNA.

Lieberman had argued that "the extinction of Neanderthal hominids was due to the competition of modern human beings who were better adapted for speech and language." Even he had never gone so far as to suggest that Neandertals had been entirely speechless or that the acquisition of language was the result of a single mutation. In fact, Lieberman maintained strongly that language was extremely complex, that it had evolved over a long period of time, and that it was the degree of linguistic complexity rather than the presence or absence of language that made modern humans selectively superior to Neandertals.

Wilson was out on a limb. Anthropologists, even those who were generally receptive to the mtDNA data, were almost united in pointing to what they regard as hard evidence contradicting Wilson's hypothesis.

In particular, the same Kebara skeleton that produced the first complete Neandertal pelvis also yielded a hyoid bone, which anchors the muscles of the tongue and forms a link between the muscles of the lower jaw and those of the neck. All of these are crucial components in producing the sounds of articulate speech.

The Kebara hyoid and Wilson's provocative statements reopened the whole question of Neandertal linguistic capabilities. Although no one had explicitly predicted what a Neandertal hyoid would look like, few were really surprised when it turned out to be a slightly enlarged version of a human hyoid and nothing like an ape hyoid. Lieberman and his colleagues reacted negatively to the news, suggesting facetiously that, because the measurements of the Kebara hyoid could distinguish it neither from human hyoids nor from pig hyoids, perhaps Neandertals oinked rather than spoke.

Curiously, it was not the hyoid itself but rather the clear restatement of many of the anatomical arguments arrayed a decade earlier against Lieberman and Crelin that were persuasive. Many anthropologists came to believe that Neandertals could have spoken any modern human language, whatever their accent may have been.

Faced with these arguments, Wilson smiled and nodded thoughtfully, before suggesting that perhaps there was a quantum leap within language-possessing hominids. Perhaps Neandertals had poor, rudimentary speech and anatomically modern humans had something much more efficient, much better. Skepticism remains strong in most quarters, and Wilson's much-regretted death means that he will never be able to articulate more convincingly what this quantum difference might entail or what mtDNA might have to do with it.

Data of ambiguous interpretation were not confined to the molecular realm. The late 1980s saw yet another reshuffling of the Neandertals and early modern humans in the Near East, this time caused by new dates for some of the sites. Once Qafzeh and Shanidar had been analyzed by Vandermeersch, Tillier, and Trinkaus, it was almost universally recognized by anthropologists that there were two groups of humans in the Near East during the Middle Paleolithic period. One was Neandertal or Neandertal-like, late archaic humans at such sites as Amud, Tabun, Shanidar, and Kebara. The other was an early, modern human population whose remains were found at Qafzeh and Skhul. Though McCown and Keith had placed Skhul and Tabun into one rather puzzling sample, a host of later scholars from many countries had demonstrated how contrasting these two groups of humans were.

The problem was to establish their chronological relationship to each other, which underwent so many revisions that Neandertals and modern humans seemed to come and go like characters in a Restoration comedy.

Initially, rather tenuous correlations of stratigraphy, stone tools, and fauna suggested that Skhul and Qafzeh, the modern human sites, were more recent than the others. Then, in 1981, Eitan Tchernov, an Israeli paleontologist working with Vandermeersch and Bar-Yosef, did a careful and detailed comparison of the rodents and other small mammals at the sites. Based on Tchernov's work, and adding in some preliminary radiometric dates, Vandermeersch and Bar-Yosef began to suspect that Qafzeh was older than the Near Eastern sites from which the Neandertals had come. If this were true, then the Near East was the only area of the world in which modern human fossils preceded those of Neandertals.

The implications were important, so the team began using two newly refined dating techniques to test their ideas: thermoluminescence (TL) and electron spin resonance (ESR). Both measure, in different ways, the amount of energy from background radiation in the sediments that has been absorbed by crystalline materials. In this case, the "crystalline materials" were stone tools and tooth enamel from Kebara, Skhul, and Qafzeh. The first TL dates, published in 1987, were unsurprising. They gave dates for Neandertal levels at Kebara of around sixty thousand years ago, which would be the middle of the last glacial period from which Neandertals derive. But the TL dates for the modern humans at Qafzeh, published the next year, were about ninety thousand years ago, which supported Tchernov, Vandermeersch, and Bar-Yosef in their claim that early modern humans preceded Neandertals in the Near East. ESR dates from the Qafzeh material confirmed the story of the TL dates. Subsequently, the modern humans from Skhul were dated by ESR to about eighty thousand years ago, clustering them with the modern humans at Qafzeh.

This evidence suggested that the original inhabitants of the Near East in the Upper Pleistocene were early modern humans. Neandertals were late arrivals, driven southward from Europe as the climate deteriorated during the early part of the last glacial period. Trinkaus countered that there were evolutionary changes through time in the Near Eastern Neandertals—changes that paralleled those seen between 100,000 and 40,000 years ago in Europe. Therefore, he contended that the Near Eastern Neandertals had had a long period of residency in the region.

A new series of ESR dates for Tabun, published in 1991, caused further complications. They showed Neandertals from Tabun to be approximately the same age as the modern humans from Skhul and Qafzeh. This new twist pointed up a fundamental problem that had been there all along, overshadowed by the problems of chronology and phylogeny. It was awkward, if not downright contorted, to try to explain how two groups of humans occupied the same region—either alternately or simultaneously—using the same set of tools to exploit the same plants and animals over a period of fifty thousand years and yet remained anatomically and genetically separate.

Trinkaus and his students are attacking this issue from the point of view of human biology, using functional analyses of the fossils to try to determine how the two groups lived and for what they were adapted. Bar-Yosef and his students and colleagues are addressing the same problem from an archeological point of view, examining the tools and technology to try to understand cultural adaptations and life-style. As the 1990s proceed, the focus of research has shifted from the issue of pure phylogeny or pure morphology to one questioning the fundamental nature of the differences and similiarities between Neandertals and modern humans.

Wolpoff, never one to let an issue die suddenly, has suggested a third resolution to the problem. He has revived McCown and Keith's old proposal that Skhul and Tabun simply represent a single, highly variable population, adding in Amud, Kebara, Qafzeh, and Shanidar. Only Wolpoff's approach offers an immediate resolution, for by redefining the groups as a single group, he conveniently eliminates the problem altogether. In the past, as in the present, the Near East seems destined to be a major continental crossroads and a center of confrontation, confusion, and strongly held opinion.

While arguments were exchanged over the Near Eastern Neandertals and their relatives from Qafzeh and Skhul, the spotlight again illuminated the mtDNA research. Stoneking and Linda Vigilant, another former student of Wilson's, increased the number of individuals whose mtDNA had been studied in an attempt to derive more reliable information about branching patterns and relationships among various modern human groups. In September 1991, they and their associates published their results in the journal *Science.* Their expanded analysis of the mtDNA in living humans confirmed the earlier conclusions: their family tree showed that all modern humans were descended from an ancestral African group, as Stringer and Bräuer had argued from the fossil record. Their estimated time of origin for this group, however, remained disconcertingly recent: between 166,000 and 249,000 years ago. Feeling secure in the reliability of their data, the authors boldly issued an explicit challenge to the paleontological community to provide as secure a statistical analysis of the fossil material as this paper had offered for the molecular information. Not six months passed before their pride in their statistical work began to look like hubris.

In February 1992, two more papers appeared in *Science* on the subject as well as another in a more technical journal. But, instead of a paleontological response, Vigilant and Stoneking received an unexpected reply from other quarters. One paper was by Alan Templeton, a geneticist at Washington University, Saint Louis; another came from a team at Harvard; and the third was written by three biologists at Pennsylvania State University and their cross-campus colleague, Stoneking himself. All three papers concurred that there were fundamental errors in the procedures being used to build genetic trees from mtDNA data.

To be sure, the process of taking genetic information, such as that derived from human mtDNA, and creating not just *a* family tree, but also the most probable tree, is no simple matter. Complex calculations based on elaborate computer programs are used to create trees, or branching patterns with a single root, by tallying and comparing the genetic similarities and differences among individuals. The difficulty is that any one data set can provide a large number of possible trees; indeed, the larger the data set, the more possible trees there are. It has been estimated that the available mtDNA set, based on 189 individuals, can produce more than 10^{250} different trees.

The problem is to identify the best or most probable tree out of the forest of possibilities, a task complicated by evolutionary reversals and parallelisms. An evolutionary reversal happens when a specific mutation occurs, followed by its opposite; in short, the genetic information is altered and then re-altered at some later time back to its original state. There is no net change, so this segment of the evolutionary process is invisible in the molecular record. A parallelism is the independent evolution of the same genetic changes in two different lineages; instead of showing similar mutations because the lineages were one at the time that the mutation occurred, the lineages have evolved in the same direction (in parallel) by accident. Both reversals and parallelisms will cause a divergence time to be underestimated, because there appear to be fewer evolutionary changes since divergence than actually occurred. But both reversals and parallelisms are believed to occur infrequently, so the most probable or most parsimonious tree is the one that involves the fewest such unlikely events, as determined by yet more computer calculations.

What the authors of these three papers showed was that the analysts of the mtDNA data had failed to examine enough trees out of the vast number that can be generated. There were, in fact, several highly parsimonious trees—some with African roots, some with Eurasian roots, and some with roots all over the Old World (implying simultaneous evolution to modern humans in many different regions). This finding does not refute the African-origin hypothesis, but it does remove the support for that hypothesis which it was believed the mtDNA data provided. Such data simply cannot be analyzed in such a way as to provide evidence for any specific homeland. The statistical difficulty of determining a geographic origin for modern humans from mtDNA data had been seriously underestimated.

Templeton also challenged the calibration of the molecular clock used by the mtDNA researchers. Instead of trying to pinpoint a specific *date* at which the mtDNA in all modern human groups separated evolutionarily, Templeton estimated the 95 percent confidence limits on that time. In other words, he defined a divergence *period* by picking the most recent likely date and the most ancient likely date, between which there was a period when the divergence actually occurred, with 95 percent certainty. Basing his work on conservative assumptions, Templeton showed that the mtDNA divergence lay not in the relatively narrow band of time between 166,000 and 249,000 years ago, as had previously been estimated, but in a broad swath sometime between 191,000 and 772,000 years ago. This time interval embraces the period in which *Homo erectus* was spreading out of Africa and across Eurasia—meaning that the divergence in mtDNA might well have occurred long before the appearance of modern humans.

Templeton's work raised the serious question: does the mtDNA data tell us anything about modern human origins? Some anthropologists, eager to throw out the troublesome data, gleefully concluded that the answer was "no." But, undaunted by the ambiguities in their findings, Stoneking and Vigilant defended the value of their work at joint meetings of the Royal Society and the CIBA Foundation in London in late February 1992. Although Stoneking, especially, was acutely aware of previous errors in the tree-building procedures, he and Vigilant took the opportunity to defend the African origin of the mtDNA tree, drawing attention to other evidence supporting their claim, including fossil remains. The duo also tried to establish a better calibration of the molecular clock. In good anthropological tradition, they stuck to their convictions even as the evidential foundations of those convictions showed serious cracks, believing themselves right, albeit for the wrong reasons.

In contrast, Stringer—the principal proponent of the extreme "out-of-Africa," total replacement hypothesis among the paleontologists—had a different response at the Royal Society–CIBA meetings. He backed off from his former vehemence, admitting that there were greater possibilities for genetic admixture between African and non-African groups of late archaic humans than he had previously accepted. And, at the same meeting, Smith and Trinkaus presented a new examination of the African fossils most often cited as the earliest anatomically modern humans. Their work challenged the supposed modernity of these remains, casting further doubts on the "out-of-Africa" model.

By the meeting's end, few would any longer espouse Africa as the geographic region with the sole claim to have given rise to all modern humans. As well, the total replacement hypothesis had been succeeded by a more moderate view of the past in which replacement of some populations, in some regions, may have been balanced by genetic admixture between adjacent populations in others. The extreme, polarized positions of the late 1980s were dying out, overwhelmed by a more mature appreciation of the complexity of reconstructing family trees from either skulls or mtDNA. The evolutionary process no longer seemed so clear-cut or simple. Sobered, the field turned toward a more realistic view of the complex process of the evolutionary and geographic origins of modern humans. As a result, the possibility of sorting out what really happened to the Neandertals and our other ancestors has been reopened. Their fates are no longer pawns to be rearranged or sacrificed in support of one or another rigid models of reality.

And there the matter rests, tossing and turning in its lumpy and ill-fitting bed. The past decade has seen the focusing and refocusing of attention on a variety of questions about phylogeny, behavior, anatomy and molecular biology as we come to know Neandertals and their kin better. Tellingly, the issue is no longer simply what happened to Neandertals, but how and why they disappeared and modern humans appeared. Neandertals thus have become just one critical element in a broader and more general problem of understanding ourselves and our origins.

The more optimistic in the field say we have come a long way, because we now know what the relevant questions are. The more pessimistic point gloomily to the recycling, under new labels, of old arguments about Neandertals' identity and descendants. The challenge will be to integrate the evidence, to bring together the molecular, archeological, and fossil evidence into a unified and sensible whole. All of the evidence is speaking, urgently and insistently, of our past. What is needed now is a Rosetta Stone that will enable us to translate the various languages of evidence into a single tongue that we can speak.

Looking back on the history of Neandertal discoveries is at once an exhilarating and a frightening task. So much work has been done on Neandertals, so many fossils have been found, so many lives expended, so many new types of analyses have been applied since 1856 . . . and what has been learned?

For Thomas Henry Huxley, the question of questions was our place in nature, our relationship to the apes and other primates. And that, surely, has been settled. There can be little doubt that humans and apes share a common ancestry, that apes are our cousins rather than our ancestors. This is not to say there are none who contest this undoubted fact, as the ongoing challenges to the teaching of evolution in our schools show. But those who continue to question the existence of evolution are those who wrap the simple fact up in a tissue paper of morality or ethics that makes it impossible for them to accept the ape within ourselves. They feel an essential conflict between evolution and religious beliefs and, unable to resolve the dichotomy, choose perceived righteousness. Others are unequipped by their educational background to cope with the evidence of evolution; they are confused by half-understood principles or misstated half-facts and reject what makes little sense to them. Still, among those points that have been established must be counted that humans, like all organisms, evolved and that Neandertals record a segment of that evolution.

Exactly where Neandertals belong in our family tree remains the subject of debate. In almost 140 years, Neandertals have been cast in virtually every imaginable relationship to ourselves. They have been subsumed under our own modern species by some and thrust far out on the most remote branch of our family tree by others.

Perhaps the most suggestive, graphic portrayal—one that combined effectiveness with ambiguity—was part of the opening sequence of a brief and ill-fated television series on human evolution that appeared in the 1970s. The show opened with a homey scene of Neandertal life, an extended family talking cozily if unintelligibly around the fireside in a cave somewhere in Europe. They were muscular, hairy, somewhat ugly, but nonetheless clearly a family. The music deepened, then grew ominous, as footsteps were heard outside the cave. Suddenly, there in the doorway, stood a tall, slender, blond, and blue-eyed Cro-Magnon, spear in hand. The family members looked up, surprised. The music swelled to a crescendo as the point of view shifted to outside the cave, so that the Cro-Magnon was outlined against the firelight. As the camera drew nearer, his dark silhouette obscured and then blotted out the fire—and then eliminated the figures babbling in alarm within, leaving only the shape of humans to come on the screen.

These differing ideas about Neandertal phylogeny hinge upon two factors: the interpretation of Neandertal anatomy and Neandertal behavior. Anatomically, much has been established and much more remains to be done. We now know that Neandertals are distinctly and recognizably different from modern humans in almost every part of their body and yet they are not particularly chimpanzee-ish. What, exactly, these differences *mean*, what they signify about Neandertal adaptations, remains undetermined.

68. An anonymous reconstruction of a Neandertal domestic scene that appeared in an 1873 issue of *Harper's Weekly*

Behaviorally, Neandertals have vacillated—in scientists' views—from brutish, glowering fiends to religious, gentle, and caring family members and back again. Where does the truth lie?

Infuriatingly, the fossils do not speak for themselves. It is the examining scientists who bring them to life, often endowing them with their own best or worst characteristics. Each generation projects onto Neandertals its own fears, culture, and sometimes even personal history. They are a mute repository for our own nature, though we flatter ourselves that we are uncovering theirs rather than displaying ours.

This is especially evident in one of the more fascinating aspects of the twisting tale of Neandertals and their interpretation: the creation of full-flesh reconstructions, sometimes in the form of drawings or paintings and at other times in stone, plaster, or metal. While it is commonplace now to "flesh out" a fossil human and bring it "to life" for purposes of display or illustration, this practice was invented for Neandertals.

And how revealing those reconstructions have been. The earliest known is a sketch that appeared in *Harper's Weekly* in 1873. It features a Neandertal couple and their humble cave—complete with what appear to be domestic dogs. The dogs lend a homey air to the setting, which otherwise reads as a tragedy of sorts. (Since dogs were domesticated only about ten thousand years ago, they have no business in a respectable Neandertal cave and may, in fact, have been meant to be tame wolves.)

Pets aside, the sketch shows a cave strewn with bones of wild animals. In the shadowed recesses of the cave, a long-haired Neandertal woman—racily naked to the waist—lies face down on a bear skin, face buried in her arms. It is a posture more suggestive of post-quarrel tears than sleep. At the other side, a crude-faced man clad in skins stands upright, his right hand clutching a stone axe hafted to a stick, his left holding something indistinguishable. He is near the cave opening, light streaming in. It is his eyes that give power to the drawing; he stands looking in surprise—or is it hope?—out of the opening of the cave. One of the dogs looks alertly in the same direction. What is coming?

It is almost irresistible to see this drawing as a metaphor for the Victorian view of gender roles, especially because it appeared in a popular rather than a scientific magazine. The sketch was made during an era in which the feminine ideal, as expressed in art, was passive, innocent, and home-oriented. Women, if not portrayed as asleep, were often shown as fainting or collapsing invalids; activity, robustness, worldliness in women were not admired. In this reading, the man is far-sighted, preparing for the future, dealing with the outside world, while the woman —emotional, sheltered—reclines in the dim light, facing backward.

Some sketches by Lohest, from his notes on the Spy fossils, show a more dutiful attempt to grapple with the evidence. Faced with the responsibility of analyzing an almost complete skeleton, it was Lohest and Fraipont who first began struggling with the significance of tibial retroversion—the backward-sloping head of the shin bone—for Neandertal posture. The drawings show a male Neandertal with a pleasant expression: chunky of build, short, heavy-browed, and sporting unmistakably bent knees. Here, clearly, is one of the earliest representations of the shuffling, apish gait that Boule later promulgated, despite evidence that perfectly normal, modern humans also show tibial retroversion. Although this reconstruction is less embroidered than some, it still shows the physical manifestation of the amoral, bestial habits that led so quickly to accusations of cannibalism among Neandertals.

A bit later in time, some popular reconstructions appeared flatly menacing. Along with the 1908 announcement of the La Chapelle-aux-Saints discovery, the popular press offered up another Neandertal recon-

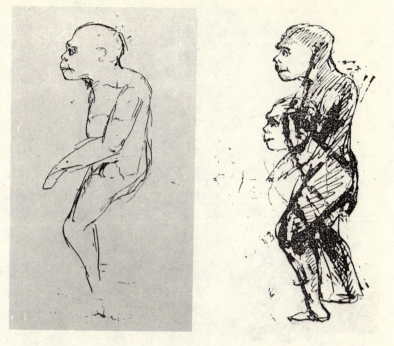

69. Sketch reconstructions of a Spy Neandertal, done about 1886 by Maximin Lohest, when Neandertals were first winning acceptance as non-modern human ancestors

struction, male again and poised to strike, resentful, hairy, and powerful of build. His shadow, even more horrible and savage than his person, blackens the rockface behind him. His teeth are bared, his eyes glare out from beneath his hefty browridges. Here is Neandertal prepared to kill and destroy, perhaps metaphorically guarding his secrets. Here, brought back to life, are our own vicious past and worst inclinations. What an unwelcome relative he must have seemed.

Boule's skeletal reconstruction of 1913 marks a return to a more scientific consideration. His openly avowed aim was to make paleoanthropology a respectable science, like vertebrate paleontology. He wanted no emotional, dramatic, moral-laden drawings. Here, in skeletal profile, is Neandertal compared with modern human. Point by point, the reader can observe Boule's beliefs about Neandertals: the large browridge and heavy face; the forwardly thrust head and stiff spine; the bent knees and inability to stride properly. All that is lacking—it is a fault of the view

70. A glowering, bestial reconstruction of the La Chapelle-aux-Saints Neandertal by the artist František Kupka published in *L'Illustration* in 1909

which was chosen—is the divergent, apish big toe, in which Boule also believed implicitly. This was the reconstruction that threw the weight of measured, scientific study against a physically brutish view of Neandertals, even though Boule repeatedly ignored solid anatomical evidence to the contrary.

Another reconstruction, this time dating to the years between the world wars, is the statue that still stands at the Musée National de Préhistoire in Les Eyzies-de-Tayac, France. Monolithic, hulking, and solid, it emphasizes the sheer physical power and bulk of Neandertals. The shoulders are massive, the arms long and muscled like a weightlifter's. All but gone are the bent knees and stooping posture, but the divergent big toe clearly persists. The face suggests little intelligence, only mute stolidity and endurance. It is an image of the Neandertal who withstood the glacial cold stoically, who succeeded with crude tools and little knowledge, who survived by virtue of brute strength and perseverance. It is a symbol of endurance. And he, too, looks off into the distance,

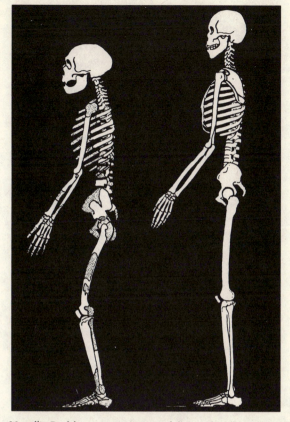

71. Marcellin Boule's 1913 reconstruction of the La Chapelle-aux-Saints skeleton (left) compared to that of a modern Australian, emphasizing the primitiveness of the Neandertal. Many of Boule's conclusions were based on a faulty understanding of human functional anatomy.

into the future, with only the faintest glimmering of hope. The statue is an image created by a world that had survived—but only just—a great and terrible world war.

How different, then, is Coon's 1939 representation of Neandertal as a modern man, the picture that later became the incarnation of Straus and Cave's Neandertal in the New York subway. He is heavy-jawed, crude-faced, but by no means more brutish than men met every day in any civilized country. He looks like a businessman, dressed for work in hat, coat, and tie. More than any previous reconstruction, Coon's drawing brought Neandertals into our family, into our household, even. It was the era of Monte Circeo, of the resurrection of Neandertals as

72. Statue of a Neandertal in front of the Musée National de Préhistoire, Les Eyzies-de-Tayac, France, sculpted in 1931 by Paul Darde. This image suggests the brute strength and endurance that enabled Neandertals to live in Ice Age Europe.

behaviorally human, and this drawing epitomizes those beliefs. Whatever the physical brutishness of Neandertals, this picture argues, they were humans like ourselves.

One side of the postwar experience is shown in the 1953 poster for a lurid B movie called *The Neanderthal Man.* Without a doubt, the screaming, wide-eyed, partially clad women are in imminent danger of sexual assault from the chimplike Neandertal. His appearance is far less explicit—but also far less human—than in any of the previous reconstructions. The evolutionary primitiveness of the Neandertal has been translated directly into unrestrained sexuality. Of course, part of what is portrayed is the generic delight of the horror movie, the delicious plea-

73. A 1939 drawing of a Neandertal by Carleton Coon, illustrating the effects of clothing and cleanliness on the Neandertal's appearance. This image signaled the changing views of the Neandertals on the eve of World War II.

sure of being frightened by a fantasy that is yet utterly safe. And in that regard, the poster reveals a postwar fear of sexual liberation, perhaps of men returned from the front who had forgotten how to behave—or of women left behind, who, unguarded, lost their demure modesty.

But this was also an era of horror movies, of giant ants or dragons or Mother Nature run riot because of scientists' meddling. The public's unease at the scientific breakthroughs that ended the war was made manifest in dozens of these films. The plot of *The Neanderthal Man* followed the rules of the genre to a T. A scientist experimenting with a mysterious serum injects both himself—transforming himself into a Neandertal—and his housecat—who becomes a ravening saber-toothed cat. Thus the scientist, the scholar who goes beyond the bounds of decency or knowledge, is to blame for re-creating these beasts from the past, for revealing the unbridled danger lurking within the seemingly tame and familiar, and in the end, he dies for it. Coincident with the flowering of the new evolutionary synthesis, this movie's theme echoes both the exhilarating excitement of scientific progress as well as its vaguely disturbing and threatening aspects.

In contrast with this sensationalized view of Neandertals is another reconstruction of the early 1950s, created by a Czech artist. The emphasis is once again on Neandertal as family man and cave dweller, complete with bones scattered about the place. The painting rings with visual echoes of the 1873 drawing, down to the skin garments and the cave bear skull with which the child is playing. Despite the wealth of anatomical analysis intervening between the two reconstructions, there is more than a hint of divergent big toes and bent knees in the more recent painting. Indeed, the subtext of this picture would appear to be that Neandertals behave in familiar ways—have spouses, suckle babes, and play with children—although their physical representation is decidedly hairy and apish. It is the age of the physically brutish and psychologically human Neandertal. This image, like Coon's and the lurid movie poster, reflects a deep ambivalence about Neandertals. They testify to an ongoing struggle between our willingness to accept Neandertals as close relatives and

74. Lurid poster for the 1953 movie *The Neanderthal Man,* showing fear of the rampant sexuality that was equated with physical primitiveness

75. Painting of a Neandertal family by the Czech artist Zdeuck Burian done in 1950, contrasting their physical primitiveness with their warm, human, family nature

yet our abhorrence at having anything so potentially inhuman so close at hand. It is the age-old struggle between the godlike and the bestial in humans restated.

This very contrast was the subject of a 1986 cartoon that spoofs the physical transformation proposed by Coon as effected by "Evo-Lotion." Aside from the pun, the joke is that only the superficial appearance changes from the "before" picture to the "after." It is an appropriate commentary on the academic debates over the fate of the Neandertal that erupted in the early 1980s, an era in which superficial appearance assumed tremendous importance to the consuming American public.

The last portrayal of the Neandertals, in this case a statue made under the direction of Erik Trinkaus for an exhibit at the Maxwell Museum of the University of New Mexico in 1990, reflects the increasing attention to representing anatomical detail accurately and to maintaining emotional neutrality in reconstructing Neandertals. It is but one of several such statues made recently for museum exhibitions that represent the current emphasis on seeing Neandertals as who they were, rather than as projections of our fears or worst traits. And yet, in this case, not judged likelihood but public propriety overruled scientific certainty, and the male Neandertal is shown without genitalia. Inevitably, subtle beliefs and judgments about what "seems likely" creep into a hundred decisions that must be made in the process of creating such an image.

What has characterized the whole record of Neandertal studies has been malleability—of opinion, of analysis, of Neandertals' physical features or inferred psychological status. Because a Neandertal was the first fossil human ever known, because their very discovery provoked the painful growth of a new field, Neandertals have led a tortured "life after fossilization." Neandertals were commandeered as one of the major battlegrounds of the war for acceptance of evolutionary theory. Discov-

76. A 1986 postcard illustrating the Neandertal's dilemma: no amount of evolution can change his essential nature

77. A Neandertal statue made by Michael Anderson under the direction of Erik Trinkaus for an exhibit in the Maxwell Museum, University of New Mexico, in 1990. This recent statue represents the results of careful anatomical study of the Neandertals, building up muscle and face from the underlying bony structure. The aim was to produce a Neandertal based more on biological facts and less on prejudices.

ered and first recognized in the shadow of *The Origin of Species,* Neandertals were not freed of that role until the end of the nineteenth century.

These mute fossils shouldered the burden as anthropology—in the person of professional and amateur scientists of every stripe—underwent its birth struggles. Neandertals were the fossil upon which so many new techniques and approaches were tried; was this measurement, that ratio, the other statistical test the right one? Try it on Neandertals and see.

Indeed, Neandertals were the mirrorlike fossils to which everyone looked for evidence of human nature—and found it. What they have revealed, more than their own lives, is the lives of those who have gazed at them and pronounced. It has been, for humans, a journey of revelation and self-discovery, an exercise in ogling the fun-house mirror. It has been a story of humans learning how to study themselves, building a scientific consensus, establishing scientific procedures. There has been plenty of room for human vanity, competition, prejudice, and pride to flourish, while careers have been constructed and dismantled along the way.

As the world turned to anthropology, searching for the truth about human nature, anthropology has always obliged by providing an answer. The problem is that the answer has rarely stayed the same for more than ten years at a time. In fact, as a saying from a Chinese fortune cookie declares: "We do not see things the way they are; we see them the way we are."

Perhaps Neandertals have been little more than the unseen, the unknowable, the endlessly provocative guide on a stumbling quest for a greater and deeper understanding of ourselves. Neandertals have been a mute set of fossils onto which we can project our own characteristics, creating them in our own image.

And yet, progress has been made. The same old questions may be wrestled with, but these are struggles waged under new rules, with new and more sophisticated procedures. We have found out more about the complexity and subtlety of those questions and about the dangerous resonances that are set up by potential answers. Testable hypotheses have come to be important factors in Neandertal studies although, even yet, it is disconcerting to all when a fossil tests and shatters a carefully built theory. Still, genuinely new questions have arisen and new emphases give hope that we may yet be able to see Neandertals as they were, neither as we are nor through the distorting lens of our ideas of how they should have been.

Perhaps the greatest truth in this twisting tale is that we cannot understand Neandertals until we first understand ourselves. We still struggle in confusion— bitterly, poignantly—to recognize and evaluate the differences and resemblances among humans. What does it mean that this group is richly dark-skinned, that one translucently fair? Does it mean something fundamental, something inescapable, that humans are always warring, always fighting over territory? Are turmoil and restlessness, social upheaval and maladjustment, signs that we are denying our basic nature—or is it the legacy of hundreds of thousands of years of migration, of catch-as-catch-can adjustment to new lands, new resources, new climates? And what of compassion, kindness, altruism?

Are we yet a god, or beast?

Epilogue
The Current View

Despite decades of controversy about the Neandertals, despite our tendency either to embrace them as immediate family or to exile them to the fringes of the human lineage, despite our irresistible impulse to imbue them with our most (or least) desirable characteristics, we have come to know a lot about the Neandertals. Scholars who work actively on these issues, handling Neandertals' fossil remains both physically and metaphorically, now agree on many aspects of their biology and their meaning in the web of human ancestry.

Of course, controversies continue as we probe deeper into the nature of Neandertals, learning ever more about ourselves in the process. But the level of detail in our inquiries becomes increasingly finer, more closely focused on interpreting this aspect of their anatomy or that sequence of human populations in one small region of the Old World, while the broad picture becomes clearer.

All of the modern debates were born of the three big questions that have dominated studies of prehistoric human groups like Neandertals since Marcel de Puydt, Max Lohest, and Julien Fraipont first demonstrated conclusively that archaic, pre-modern humans existed, by finding their skeletons at Spy in 1886. Once it was clear that humans, like other creatures, had an evolutionary history and that it involved Neandertals, the issues revolved around their *identity*, their *kinship*, and their *nature*.

Neandertals are delimited biologically as a distinct group of humans (whether they are called part of our own species, *Homo sapiens*, or members of an extinct species, *Homo neanderthalensis*, is largely a matter of scientific style, not substance) who lived from approximately 100,000 years ago until between 50,000 and 35,000 years ago in different geographic regions. They are known to have spread over a huge region, the northwestern Old World, that stretches across Europe from the Strait of Gibraltar and the Mediterranean north to Belgium, across the Near East from the Levant to the Zagros Mountains, and around the Black and Caspian Seas east to Uzbekistan. Their appearance, as they emerged out of still-more-archaic ancestors, seems to have been a more slow and gradual process than their disappearance—or evolution—into modern humans.

Anatomically, the Neandertals are quite similar to ourselves, having a skeletal arrangement identical to ours, brains as large as ours, and—to the best of our knowledge—the capability to perform any act normally within the ability of a modern human. Although Carleton Coon's famous 1939 drawing may have exaggerated the physical resemblance between Neandertals and ourselves, he was correct in showing that they probably had the same behavioral capabilities as modern humans.

Yet neither the physical similarities nor the behavioral capabilities constitute identity. Rare individuals among modern humans may share one, or even a few, of the anatomical characteristics of Neandertals, but not one human—much less any population—can be found that possesses the entire constellation of traits that define Neandertals. Indeed, Neandertals more closely resembled their predecessor species, *Homo erectus* (or the odd, difficult-to-classify and poorly known archaic humans that intervened between *Homo erectus* and Neandertals), than ourselves. These resemblances take the form of exceptional physical robustness, a skeletal and muscular massiveness that enabled them to accomplish through sheer bodily effort tasks beyond our physical capabilities. Other characteristics—the shape of the face, details of the back of the skull, the overall proportions of the trunk and limbs—are regional features of the Neandertals, analogous to the patterns of facial shape or bodily proportions that differ among living human populations.

We can now identify reasonably complete fossils, and even some isolated bones, as Neandertals on the basis of these detailed aspects of robustness, facial shape, and cranial minutiae. If the specimens are sufficiently complete, Neandertals can be confused neither with their predecessors in Europe and western Asia nor with early modern humans. They are most similar to their contemporaries, the late archaic humans in Africa and the Far East who have sometimes been referred to loosely as

"African Neandertals" or "Asian Neandertals," although the current consensus is to restrict the term *Neandertal* to the groups that inhabited the northwestern Old World. It is reassuring that we have finally come to agree about what is a Neandertal.

Once defining characteristics have been delineated, sorting fossils into piles based on the shapes of their bones and teeth is a relatively straight-forward task—one that can be reviewed and re-reviewed as the number of specimens increases. Problematic specimens can be set aside as being too incomplete in crucial areas or may be assigned with lesser confidence to one sample or another. However, kinship and nature are matters of interpretation, much more dependent upon the interpreter's assumptions, preconceptions, and goals.

We want to close this book with our personal view of Neandertals. While it is based on intimate familiarity with the fossils and on the latest evidence, we do not doubt it is irrevocably stained with our prejudices and convictions. The strongest of these is that human evolution indeed occurred and that this process is reflected both in the changing anatomy and in the shifting patterns of behavior, twin witnesses to the adaptability of the human organism. Historically, some have argued that our ancestors could not have looked substantially less human than ourselves, while others have maintained that, however different their appearance, Neandertal behavior must have been effectively human. To us, such views are by their nature anathema to any genuine inquiry into human origins; the outcome cannot be known in advance.

So who were these much-maligned and little-appreciated people, the Neandertals? We believe that they evolved gradually out of more archaic human ancestors across Europe and western Asia. What occurred was a process, not an event, in which Neandertal characteristics steadily in-creased in frequency in populations that lived in these regions between about 400,000 and 100,000 years ago. This process of neandertalization is currently better documented in western Europe than elsewhere, but more skimpy evidence from central and eastern Europe and the Near East suggests a similar, gradual emergence of the Neandertal anatomical pattern across those regions, too.

Given the immense geographic distance from the Atlantic shores to the Hindu Kush, it is not surprising that there are also subtle differences in the degrees of expression of these Neandertal traits among samples of fossils from different regions. But the scale of these differences was damped by the genetic contact among these ancient subgroups, for there were similar trends of major evolutionary change across this group of humans as a whole. Regional groups were isolated enough to develop some local peculiarities, but not so isolated that they failed to evolve in concert.

The evolution of *Homo erectus* into Neandertals (or into very similar forms of late archaic humans that differ from Neandertals mostly in the shapes of their faces) was also happening at about the same time in eastern Asia. We do not know if there were some geographic or biological barrier between the Neandertals of the northwestern Old World and the late archaic peoples of eastern Asia—and thus cannot tell whether the two interbred—because there are virtually no fossils from the crucial time period in the enormous area lying between Uzbekistan and eastern China. In another huge region—northern, eastern, and southern Africa—late archaic humans followed their own evolutionary trajectory parallel to and apparently separate from Neandertals.

The most difficult—and eternal—question is therefore this: did Neandertals from the northwestern Old World evolve into modern humans? Emerging from almost a century and a half of debate is an answer: a qualified yes, since only some of the Neandertals belong in the family album.

To us, the fossils indicate that the earliest modern humans evolved out of Neandertals (or out of late archaic peoples very like them) soon after Neandertals had themselves appeared, about 100,000 years ago. This was not an evolutionary event that happened simultaneously across the entire Neandertal range. Africa has been a popular choice for the birthplace of early modern humans, but new dates on fossil sites from the Levant show that early modern humans were there as early as in Africa; the same has been suggested for some eastern Asian sites. It will be impossible to discover exactly where (one region or several regions?) and when early modern humans arose without additional, well-dated fossil sites.

But the first appearance of modern humans is not the same thing as the end of the Neandertals, at least in the Levant. After modern humans appeared there, within the geographic range already inhabited by Neandertals, Neandertals persisted. This complex situation suggests that the modern humans of the Levant did not evolve out of the local Neandertal population. Either these modern humans evolved somewhere else or they evolved locally but simultaneously and in parallel to Neandertals from the same parent stock. If they migrated into the Levant from outside, where was this "somewhere else"? We don't yet know. We do know that, after they appeared, modern humans were a restless lot, migrating *out* of the Levant, spreading into central Europe by about 36,000 years ago and reaching the Atlantic coast of Europe within a few millennia more.

While these migrations were occurring, some Neandertals and modern humans stayed in the Levant, making the same kinds of tools, hunting the same animals in similar ways, and occupying similar shelters. We are unable, as yet, to find convincing evidence for two distinctive life-styles or ways of exploiting the resources of the region, and yet Neandertals and modern humans appear to remain physically distinct in the Levant even though there is good evidence for their interbreeding elsewhere. This paradox begs for explanation and there are two alternative hypotheses. First, the two types of humans may have remained distinct because of nonphysical barriers to interbreeding, such as linguistic differences or different cultural traditions that are invisible in the archeological record. This is an awkward hypothesis because it rests on nonexistent evidence, though such data may be forthcoming. Alternatively, we find it easier to envision that modern humans and Neandertals remained morphologically distinctive—and that they avoided coming into direct competition for resources—if the region were a fluctuating contact zone or boundary, with first one and then the other type of human occupying the area alternately. This interpretation argues that the two groups appear to overlap in time and space only because of the familiar problems of the sparseness of the fossil record and the crudeness of our dating techniques.

A different picture comes from central Europe, where there is abundant evidence of continuous evolution, genetic admixture and interbreeding between the resident Neandertals and the early modern humans who were filtering in slowly from the Levant and possibly elsewhere. Specific details in the shape of the nose and brows, and particular features of the back of the skull and the femur that are shared by Neandertals and modern humans in central Europe, all indicate genetic continuity during the long period over which a major anatomical change from fully Neandertal to fully modern human occurred.

If any portion of the geographic area inhabited by Neandertals indicates their simple replacement by modern humans, it is western Europe—a region that is the periphery, the cul-de-sac, the last region to be occupied by early modern humans. There, apparently, Neandertals lingered on in relative isolation until about 35,000 years ago. The enigmatic Saint-Césaire material (a Neandertal skeleton buried with an early,

Upper Paleolithic tool-kit of the type formerly believed to be made only by modern humans) may record a late Neandertal population facing competition from early modern humans. Does this preserve evidence of Neandertals' attempt to achieve a comparable efficiency in exploiting resources by adopting the superior technology of modern humans?

Though the evidence in different regions of the Old World records genuinely different events, nowhere is there evidence for violent confrontations between Neandertals and modern humans (myths notwithstanding). The mosaic of local evolution, migration, admixture, absorption, or local extinction of Neandertals was a complex process that occurred over at least 10,000 years. This is a long time for modern humans to spread from the Levant to the Atlantic coast of Europe, whether or not Neandertals were "in the way." Slowly, the populations expanded, absorbed or displaced local inhabitants, developed new genetic and behavioral adaptations to new circumstances, retaining the best of the Neandertals and combining it with the emerging features of the newcomers who more closely resembled ourselves. This same intricate pattern of change, varying in rate and degree, occurred across the entire Old World and gave rise both to modern humanity and to the geographical clusters of traits—many superficial—that are now recognized as racial characteristics. Only humans from the Near East and parts of Europe can claim Neandertals per se in their direct ancestry. Still, every modern human group surely arose from a Neandertal-like, archaic human population, even if all these ancestors would not fit our precise and restricted definition of "Neandertal."

The nature of Neandertals has been intimately linked to issues of kinship ever since early in this century, when Keith and Boule argued that Neandertals were too brutally apish to be a part of our own ancestry. This is an unfortunate and unnecessary coupling. We must examine Neandertals and infer their behavioral patterns separate from considerations of whether they belong in our own personal ancestries, because what they did is not a function of how they were related to us. Indeed, because all humans today are a single species, if Neandertals are ancestral to some of us, they are in some sense ancestral to all. More important, Neandertals were a curious mix of archaic and modern features, reflecting the dynamic evolutionary process of which they were—and we are—a part.

Both through their biology and through the tangible, archeological remains their behaviors left behind, we know that Neandertals continued behavioral trends that were well established among their predecessors. The aspects of their anatomy that are most telling of their behavior are their tremendous strength and endurance. From the robust dimensions of their limb bones, which had massive shafts and large joints, to the pronounced bony crests and sturdy ridges where brawny muscles attached—on their necks, backs, shoulders, arms, hands, legs, and feet— the primary message bespoken by Neandertal anatomy is "power." No Olympic athlete of today has a comparable overall robustness.

Although they were in some sense hunter-gatherers, like some living peoples today, this category covers a diverse range of options that was wider still in the past. The evidence suggests that the elaborateness and the efficacy of Neandertal technology was apparently much poorer than that of modern hunter-gatherers, leaving Neandertals no choice but to accomplish the tasks of daily life through brute strength, incredible stamina, and dogged perseverance.

In addition, there is poignant testimony to their life-style in the high frequency of lesions on Neandertal skeletons, some caused by traumatic bone breakage and others simply by the stress of malnutrition, disease, or both during crucial periods of growth. It was a hard life, from infancy to death, yet one which Neandertals endured and survived—we know this because many of these traumatic lesions healed during life. Still, few Neandertals reached old age; most adults died in their twenties and thirties.

Not only the life-style but also the habitat was harsh. Climatic reconstructions based on many types of evidence speak repeatedly of cold. Neandertals' body proportions echo this evidence. Their bulky trunks and relatively short limbs and digits are designed for conserving metabolic heat in near-arctic conditions. Once again, we see a *bodily* adaptation to a fact of life rather than a technological one; somehow, their ability to keep warm through efficient use of fire, shelter, and clothing— all of which we know Neandertals possessed—was inadequate when compared with that of later humans. In fact, it was not simply the need to keep from freezing that shaped Neandertal bodies. Their broad, projecting, and sharply angled noses probably reflect both the urgent problem of conserving moisture under cold and arid conditions and the equally compelling need to dissipate excess body heat that was sometimes generated by vigorous activity.

While in these ways Neandertals may appear inept, they were also the first humans to exhibit a number of important behaviors. Difficult though the task may have been, Neandertals succeeded in occupying the cold, glacial climates of Eurasia—no paltry accomplishment. They spread much farther under worse conditions than any previous human group and were stopped only by the incredibly harsh, truly arctic zones of Eurasia. A major factor in this success was, without doubt, intelligence. Neandertals had brains as large and apparently as complex as ours; they were the culmination of a period of rapid increase in relative brain size over the previous half million years.

Neandertals were also remarkable in other ways. They were among the first to bury their dead intentionally, if in rather plain graves, and they made simple body ornaments, though these are rare. Both these behaviors—mortuary customs and bodily adornment—indicate that their social roles were complex. Seemingly, the social role or status of an individual could be modified or signified through voluntary changes in personal appearance. In some sense, the ornaments an individual wore gave the message, "this is who or what I am"—meaning that not everyone was the same. What's more, an individual's standing continued to exist after death, long enough for his or her social group to bury the body. And burial often occurred in a specific, unnatural posture, showing that the corpse was not simply dropped into some convenient depression in the earth without preparation. A dead Neandertal was more than a dead animal or an inert lump: he or she was a specific person, about whom others cared. Individuality—the specialness of one person from any other—took on a meaning that it did not seem to have previously existed in human evolution.

Another indicator of strong social ties and social complexity is the survival of individuals with severe, sometimes crippling injuries; an individual's value was not solely based on his or her ability to obtain food or carry out physical work effectively. This fact again suggests that there was an elaboration of different roles within Neandertal society: different individuals did different things. Those who did not or could not procure food must have been supported by the rest of the group who valued their other contributions. Just what those contributions may have been—knowledge? art? music? linguistic gifts?—remains elusive.

Overall, the image of Neandertals is one of humans who had made several major adaptive advances over their predecessors, developments that allowed them to exploit previously uninhabitable regions and climates. These new facets of their behavior probably fell into the social and organizational spheres, perhaps in the more efficient sharing of knowledge and division of labor. Yet they had not reached a level of behavioral adaptation that made those massive bodies redundant or that lowered the extraordinary levels of stress that they endured in their brief lives. While on the one hand Neandertals can be seen as the culmination of two million years of evolution since the earliest appearance of *Homo erectus*, on the other hand they were also heralds of a new human biology—one that would be enhanced and exaggerated in millennia to come by the further advances in technology, foraging behavior, social organization, and information transmission that occurred with the rise of modern humans.

Seeing Neandertals in context, in the broad sweep of human evolution, is a valuable perspective. But we must not forget that they were neither "new and improved" versions of *Homo erectus* nor crude prototypes of modern *Homo sapiens*. They were themselves; they were Neandertals—one of the more distinctive, successful, and intriguing groups of humans that ever enriched our family history.

Notes

Prologue.

PAGE 4 — "Know then thyself" Alexander Pope "An Essay on Man." Epistle 2.1.1. In John Bartlett, comp., and Emily Morison Beck, ed., *Familiar Quotations*, 15th ed. (Boston: Little, Brown, 1980), 337.

Chapter 1: God or Beast?

PAGE 10 — "How extremely stupid" Gavin de Beer, ed., *Charles Darwin and T. H. Huxley: Autobiographies* (London: Oxford University Press, 1974), xv.

PAGE 11 — "new Adam" Loren Eiseley, *Darwin's Century* (Garden City: Anchor Books, 1961), 19.

— "most systematical genius" D. H. Stoever, *The Life of Sir Charles Linnaeus*, trans. Joseph Trapp (London, 1794). Quoted in Lynn Barber, *The Heyday of Natural History: 1820–1870* (Garden City: Doubleday, 1980), 48.

PAGE 12 — "The first step" James Edward Smith, *A Selection of the Correspondence of Linnaeus and Other Naturalists from the Original Manuscripts*, vol 2. (London, 1821), 460. Quoted in Eiseley, *Darwin's Century*, 15.

PAGE 18 — "cosmological romances" A–L Millin, 1792. Full reference not given. Quoted in Martin J. S. Rudwick, *The Meaning of Fossils: Episodes in the History of Palaeontology* (New York: Neale Watson Academic Publications, 1972), 103.

PAGE 19 — "One must believe" J. B. Lamarck, *Système des animaux sans vertèbres* (Paris, 1801), 403–411. Quoted in Rudwick, *Meaning of Fossils*, 119.

PAGE 22 — "There is, philosophically speaking" Etienne Geoffroy Saint-Hilaire, *Philosophie anatomique*, 2 vols. (Paris, 1818–22). Quoted in Eiseley, *Darwin's Century*, 118.

— "A system resting" Georges Cuvier, "Eloge de M. de Lamarck." Full reference not given. Quoted in Barber, *Heyday*, 213.

PAGE 24 — "By use of fossils" William Smith, "The Stratigraphical System of Organized Fossils" (London, 1817), vi. Quoted in Eiseley, *Darwin's Century*, 79.

— "Each layer of these fossil" F. J. North, "Deductions from Established Facts in Geology, by William Smith: Notes on a Recently Discovered Broadsheet" *Geological Magazine* 64 (1927): 534. Quoted in Eiseley, *Darwin's Century,* 79.

PAGE 25 — "on the Power" Full reference not given. Quoted in Eiseley, *Darwin's Century,* 177.

PAGE 27 — "keep-moving" Archibald Geikie, *Life of Sir Roderick Impey Murchison,* vol. 1 (London, 1875), 129. Quoted in Barber, *Heyday,* 189.

— "My work" K. Lyell, *Life and Letters of Sir Charles Lyell,* vol. 1 (London, 1881), 253. Quoted in Barber, *Heyday,* 221.

PAGE 28 — "a total want" Geikie, *Murchison,* 316. Quoted in Barber, *Heyday,* 191.

PAGE 30 — "During the early part" de Beer, *Darwin,* 44, 58–9.

PAGE 31 — "Take Lyell's new book" John W. Judd, *The Coming of Evolution* (Cambridge: Cambridge University Press, 1911), 72.

— "The very first place" de Beer, *Darwin,* 44.

PAGE 32 — "so as not" Ibid., 29.

PAGE 33 — "Exposition is not" Leslie Stephen, "Appreciation," in Brander Matthews, ed., *Autobiography and Essays by Thomas Henry Huxley* (New York: Gregg Publishing Company, 1919), 266.

— "What can a man" Henrietta Litchfield, ed., *Emma Darwin, Wife of Charles Darwin: A Century of Family Letters,* vol. 2. (London: John Murray & Sons, 1915), 15.

— "But where" Judd, *Coming of Evolution,* 125.

PAGE 34 — "evidently weapons" John Frere, "An account of flint weapons discovered at Hoxne in Suffolk," *Archaeologia* 13 (1800): 204–5.

PAGE 35 — "It consists" William Buckland, *Reliquiae Diluvianae; or, Observations on the organic remains contained in caves, fissures and diluvial gravel, and on other geological phenomena, attesting to the action of an Universal Deluge* (London, 1823), 82.

— "together with a large part" Ibid., 83.

— "whatever may have been" Ibid., 90.

PAGE 36 — "a portion of the scapula" Ibid., 87.

PAGE 37 — "candle stuck" Quoted in John Powe, *Kents Cavern.* (Privately published in Torquay, England, n.d.), 4.

— "I must therefore" Robert Godwin-Austen, *Transactions of the Geological Society,* 2nd ser., 4 (1840): 433. Quoted in John Lubbock, *Pre-historic Times, as Illustrated by Ancient Remains and the Manners and Customs of Modern Savages,* 2nd ed. (New York, 1872), 316.

PAGE 38 — "Notwithstanding the high authority" Lubbock, *Pre-historic Times,* 316.

PAGE 39 — "when I expressed" Charles Lyell, *The Geological Evidences of the Antiquity of Man with Remarks on Theories of the Origin of Species by Variation* (London, 1863), 59–74. Reprinted in Theodore D. McCown and Kenneth A. R. Kennedy, eds., *Climbing Man's Family Tree* (Englewood Cliffs, N.J.: Prentice-Hall, 1972), 113.

— "I can only plead" Lyell, *Geological Evidences.* Reprinted in McCown and Kennedy, *Climbing,* 113.

PAGE 42 — "Imbecile" C. Cohen and J.-J. Hublin, *Boucher de Perthes: Les Origines romantiques de la préhistoire* (Paris: Editions Belin, 1989), 72.

PAGE 44 — "We abstain" Anonymous, *Anthropological Review* 2 (1864): 222.

— "For seven years" Lubbock, *Pre-historic Times,* 343.

PAGE 45 — "presented a human skull" Anonymous, "Minutes of meeting of the Gibraltar

Scientific Society, 3 March, 1848" (1848). Quoted in John Reader, *Missing Links* (Boston: Little, Brown, 1981), 30.

Chapter 2. Not My Ancestor: *1856–1865*

PAGE 47 — "Physical, mental and moral" T. H. Huxley, "A lecture on January 9, 1870," *Pall Mall Gazette*, 10 Jan. 1870. Reprinted in T. H. Huxley, *Man's Place in Nature and Other Anthropological Essays* (New York: D. Appleton, 1900), 280–1.

PAGE 49 — "to whom" Hermann Schaaffhausen, "Zur Kentniss der ältesten Rassenschädel," *Archiv Verbindung Mehreren Gelehrten* (1858): 453–88. Reprinted as D. Schaaffhausen [*sic*], "On the Crania of the Most Ancient Races of Man," trans. George Busk, *Natural History Review* (Apr. 1, No. 2 1861): 155.

— "covered to a thickness" and "Of this I was assured" Schaaffhausen, "On the Crania," 156.

PAGE 50 — "The conclusions" Ibid., 156.

PAGE 52 — "presents no sign" and "Giant's-bones" Ibid., p. 158.

PAGE 54 — "Virchow was born" Information about Virchow from Erwin H. Ackernecht, *Rudolf Virchow: Doctor, Statesman, Anthropologist* (Madison: University of Wisconsin Press, 1953).

PAGE 55 — "socially inferior" Marie Rabl, ed., *Rudolf Virchow: Letters to His Parents 1839 to 1864* (Canton, Mass.: Science History Publications/U.S.A., 1990), 17.

PAGE 57 — "most minute and most careful" Ernst Haeckel, *The Story of the Development of a Youth; Letters to his Parents 1852–56,* trans. G. Barry Gifford (New York: Harper & Brothers, 1923), 184.

— *Omnis cellula* Ackerknecht, *Virchow*, 23.

PAGE 58 — "This flexure" A. F. Mayer, "Ueber die fossilen Ueberreste eines Menschlichen Schädels und Skeletes in einer Felsenhohle des Düssel-oder Neanderthales." *Muller's Archiv* 1 (1864). Quoted and translated in T. H. Huxley, "Further Remarks upon the Human Remains from the Neanderthal," *Natural History Review* 1 (1864): 429–46; 435.

— "The prominence" Huxley, "Further Remarks," 436–7.

— "Given a rickety child" Ibid., 436.

PAGE 59 — "an uncommon thickness" Schaaffhausen, "On the Crania," 162.

PAGE 60 — "full and unlimited" Ackerknecht, *Virchow*, 15.

— "a playground" and "the second" Rabl, *Virchow*, 110.

PAGE 62 — "Light will be shed" Charles Darwin, *The Origin of Species* (London, 1859). In later editions, Darwin boldly amended this statement—his only reference to human evolution—to read: "*Much* light will be shed . . ." [italics added]. In the 1958 Mentor edition, this quotation appears on page 449.

PAGE 63 — "Born in January 1823" Much of the information on Wallace's life is taken from Arnold Brackman, *A Delicate Arrangement: The Strange Case of Charles Darwin and Alfred Russel Wallace* (New York: Times Books, 1980).

PAGE 66 — "absolutely independent" Brackman, *Delicate Arrangement*, 145.

— "There can hardly be a doubt" Charles Darwin, *The Descent of Man*, 2nd American ed. (New York, 1871), 707.

PAGE 67 — "*Every species*" Alfred Russel Wallace, "On the Law Regulating the Introduction of New Species," *Annals and Magazine of Natural History*, 2nd ser., 16 (1855): 184–96. Quoted in Rudwick, *Meaning of Fossils*, 226.

PAGE 68 – "With Darwin" Brackman, *Delicate Arrangement*, 32.

– "best mode of representing" Wallace, "On the Law." Reprinted in Brackman, *Delicate Arrangement*, 320.

– "Can this be true?" Brackman, *Delicate Arrangement*, 30.

– "On February 12" Information on Darwin taken from Barber, *Heyday*; John Bowlby, *Charles Darwin: A New Life* (New York: Norton, 1990); de Beer, *Darwin*; William Irvine, *Apes, Angels and Victorians* (London: McGraw-Hill, 1955).

– "deep mortification" and "You care for nothing" de Beer, *Darwin*, 12.

– "As [he] was doing" Ibid., 24.

PAGE 69 – "my time" Ibid., 33.

PAGE 70 – "If you can find" and "I should be" and "But they all" Ibid., 40–1.

– "write up his ideas" Ibid., 72.

PAGE 71 – "With respect" F. Darwin, ed., *Life and Letters of Charles Darwin*, vol 1. (New York, 1891), 426–7.

– "I very much want" Ibid., 428.

PAGE 72 – "I have been" Brackman, *Delicate Arrangement*, 49.

– "He may save me" Ibid., 50.

– "[Wallace] has to-day" Darwin, *Life and Letters*, 473.

PAGE 73 – "I am quite" Ibid., 476.

– "Some have argued" See, for example, Brackman, *Delicate Arrangement*, or C. D. Darlington, *Darwin's Place in History* (Oxford: Blackwell, 1959).

– "a delicate arrangement" Leonard Huxley, ed., *The Life and Letters of Sir Joseph Dalton Hooker.* (London: John Murray, 1918). Quoted in Brackman, *Delicate Arrangement*, 1.

PAGE 74 – "If I can convert" Darwin, *Life and Letters* 17–20.

– "Huxley was not" Information about Huxley's life taken from sources including: C. Bibby, *T. H. Huxley, Scientist, Humanist and Educator* (London: Watts, 1959); C. Bibby, *Scientist Extraordinary: The Life and Scientific Work of Thomas Henry Huxley, 1825–95* (New York: Pergamon Press, 1972); Ronald W. Clark, *The Huxleys* (Toronto: McGraw-Hill, 1968); Irvine, *Apes.*

– "Autobiographies are" de Beer, *Darwin*, ix.

PAGE 75 – "the society I fell into" Ibid., 101–2.

PAGE 77 – "Well, six months or not" Clark, *The Huxleys*, 36.

– "I always think" Henry Fairfield Osborn, *Impressions of Great Naturalists* (New York: Charles Scribner's Sons, 1924), 80.

PAGE 78 – "Your letter to Wallace" Darwin, *Life and Letters*, 484.

– "what they thought" Ibid., 501.

PAGE 79 – "sharpening up his claws" Darwin, *Life and Letters*, 27.

– "detestation" Ibid., 91–2.

– "meeting of the British Association" Ibid., 114–16.

– "dulcet tones" Ibid., 114.

PAGE 80 – "I asserted" Leonard Huxley, ed., *Life and Letters of Thomas Huxley* (New York: D. Appleton, 1900), 199.

– "The publication" T. H. Huxley, "On the reception of the 'Origin of Species'," in Darwin, *Life and Letters*, 550, 557–8.

PAGE 81 – "the ruin" Ronald Millar, 1974. *The Piltdown Men* (St. Albans, Eng.: Granada, 1974), 32.

– "The fact" George Busk, "With Remarks, and original Figures, taken from a

Cast of the Neanderthal Cranium." *Natural History Review* 1, 2 (Apr. 1861): 155–75; 172.

PAGE 82 — "A very savage type" Ibid., 173.
— "not cerebrally inferior" and "none of the other" C. Carter Blake, "On the Occurrence of Human Remains Contemporaneous with those of Extinct Animals," *Geologist,* Sept. 1861, 365. Quoted in C. Carter Blake, "On the alleged peculiar characters and assumed antiquity of the Human Cranium from the Neanderthal," *Journal of the Anthropological Society,* 2 (1864): 139–57; cxli.
— "The apparent ape-like" C. Carter Blake, "On the cranium of the most ancient races of man," *Geologist,* June 1862, 206. Quoted in Blake, "On the alleged," clii–cxliii.

PAGE 83 — "A theory" Anonymous, *Medical Times and Gazette,* 28 June 1862. Quoted in Blake, "On the alleged," cxliv.
— "The whole" Paul Broca, "Response to paper by Pruner-Bey" (1864). Quoted in Blake, "On the alleged," cliii.

PAGE 84 — "Ethnologists regard" Robert A. Fletcher, "Paul Broca and the French School of Anthropology," *The Saturday Lectures* (Anthropological and Biological Societies of Washington; Washington, D.C., Judd and Detweiller, 1882), 113–42; 118.
— "Broca's struggle" Information taken from Fletcher, "Paul Broca," and Michael Hammond, "Anthropology as a weapon of social combat in late-nineteenth-century France," *Journal of the History of the Behavioral Sciences* 16 (1980): 118–32.
— "one of the most powerful" Fletcher, "Paul Broca," 116.

PAGE 86 — "It is not I" T. H. Huxley, *Man's Place in Nature and Other Collected Essays* (New York: D. Appleton, 1900), 152.

PAGE 87 — "a fair average" Ibid., 205.
— "And indeed" Ibid., 206–9.

PAGE 88 — "The distinctive faculties" William King, "The Reputed Fossil Man of the Neanderthal," *Quarterly Journal of Science* 1 (1864): 96.

PAGE 89 — "A paper advocating" Ibid., 96.
— "If you hear" Hugh Falconer, *Paleontological Memoirs and Notes,* vol 2. (London, 1868), 561.

PAGE 90 — "Vous m'avez tué" Grace Ann Prestwich, ed., *Life and Letters of Sir Joseph Prestwich* (London, 1899), 119.

Chapter 3. *L'Affaire Moulin Quignon: 1865–1885*

PAGE 91 — "He showed me" Ibid., 143–4.
PAGE 92 — "I am making" Cohen and Hublin, *Boucher de Perthes,* 140.
PAGE 93 — "We were" Prestwich, *Life and Letters,* 180.
PAGE 94 — "Thus, in the period" E. Lartet, "On the Ancient Migrations of Mammals of the Present Period" ("Sur les migrations anciennes des Mammifères de l'époque actuelle") (Paris, 1858). Quoted in Marcellin Boule, *Fossil Men* (Edinburgh: Oliver & Boyd, 1923), 19.
PAGE 95 — "it proved to be quite" Prestwich, *Life and Letters,* 179.
PAGE 96 — "The jaw in question" Ibid., 185–6.
PAGE 98 — "the principles of" Lubbock, *Pre-historic Times,* vi.
— "In order to prevent" Ibid., 8.
PAGE 99 — "Although our knowledge" Ibid., 424–8.

PAGE IOI   — "the right to live" Gabriel de Mortillet, *Politique et Socialisme à la portée de tous* (Paris, 1849), 49–50. Quoted in Michael Hammond, "Anthropology as a weapon of social combat in late-nineteenth-century France," *Journal of the History of the Behavioral Sciences* 16 (1980): 118–32, 119.

PAGE IO3   — "This mandible" Paul Broca, "Discours de M. Broca sur l'ensemble de la question," *Congrès International d'Anthropologie et d'Archéologie Préhistoriques* (Paris, 1868), 367–402; 396.

— "the first fact" Paul Broca, "Discussion sur la machoire humaine de la Naulette (Belgique)," *Bulletin de la Société d'Anthropologie de Paris,* 2nd ser., 1 (1866): 584–603; 595.

— "As for me" Paul Broca, "Sur le Transformisme; Remarques Générales." *Bulletin de la Société d'Anthropologie de Paris,* 2nd ser., 5 (1870): 169–239; 169–70.

PAGE IO5   — "As the twentieth-century anthropologist" William Arens, *The Man-Eating Myth* (Oxford: Oxford University Press, 1979).

— "Pruner-Bey, and his English friend" Darwin, *Descent of Man,* 46.

— "It's [the La Naulette jaw's] C. Carter Blake, "On a human jaw from the cave of La Naulette near Dinant, Belgium," *Anthropological Review,* July and October (1867), 295-395: 302–3.

PAGE IO8   — "Yet, however divided the views" Anonymous, "The Neanderthal Man," *Harper's Weekly,* 18, no. 864 (1873): 618.

PAGE II3   — "Full of warm" Anonymous introduction to Haeckel, *Story of the Development,* xi–xii.

PAGE II4   — "sum of the functions" and "the chief point" Ibid., 167–8.

— "this rationalistic" Ibid., 145.

PAGE II5   — "magnificent trees," "the most delightful," "most magnificent starfish," and "deep, calm" Ibid., 243–5.

PAGE II6   — "concentrated on" and "Your letter" Darwin, *Life and Letters,* 68–9.

PAGE II8   — "For Haeckel's confused" See Daniel Gasman, *The Scientific Origins of National Socialism* (London: MacDonald & Co., 1971), for a thoughtful and well-documented summary of Haeckel's pivotal place in Nazi doctrine.

PAGE I2O   — "At last" Much of this information is derived from Hammond, "Anthropology," and Fletcher, "Paul Broca."

PAGE I2I   — "They would not have thought" Fletcher, "Paul Broca," 132.

PAGE I23   — "Therefore, Virchow asserted" Rudolf Virchow, "Der keifer aus der Schipka-Höhle under der Kiefer von La Naulette," *Zeitschrift für Ethnologie* 14 (1882): 277–95.

PAGE I25   — "The wisest course" Paul Topinard, "Les caractères simiens de la Machoire de la Naulette," *Revue d'Anthropologie,* 2nd ser., 9 (1886): 395–431; 431.

Chapter 4. Shuffling into the Light: 1886–1905

PAGE I26   "In July 1886" Marcel de Puydt and Maximin Lohest, "L'homme contemporain du Mammouth à Spy (Namur)," *Annales de la Féderation Archéologique et Historique de Belgique* 2 (1887): 207–240.

PAGE I28   — "eminently Neanderthaloid" and "brutal depth" Julien Fraipont and Max Lohest, "La Race humaine de Néanderthal ou de Cannstadt en Beligique— Recherches ethnographiques sur des ossements humains découverts dans les dépôts quaternaires d'une grotte à Spy et détermination de leur âge géologique," *Archives de Biologie* 7 (1887): 587-57. Quoted in Frank Spencer, "The Neandertals and Their Evolutionary Significance: A Brief Historical Survey," in F. H. Smith and F. Spencer, eds., *The Origin of Modern Humans: a World Survey of the Fossil Evidence* (New York: Alan R. Liss, 1984), 1–49; 13.

PAGE 129 — "The men of Spy" Julien Fraipont and Max Lohest, "La Race humaine de Néanderthal ou de Cannstadt en Belgique—Recherches ethnographiques sur des ossements humains découverts dans les dépôts quaternaires d'une grotte à Spy et détermination de leur âge géologique," *Archives de Biologie* 7 (1887): 587–757. Quoted in Julien Fraipont, "Le tibia dans la race de Néanderthal; Etude comparative de l'incurvation de la tête du tibia, dans ses rapports avec la station verticale chez l'homme et les anthropoides," *Revue d'Anthropologie*, 3rd ser., 3, no. 2 (1888): 145–58; 145.

PAGE 132 — "The man of the Neander valley" O. C. Marsh, "On the *Pithecanthropus erectus* from the Tertiary of Java," *American Journal of Science* 1 (1896): 475–83, 476.

PAGE 133 — "Marie Eugène François Thomas Dubois" Information about Dubois taken from Bert Theunissen, *Eugène Dubois and the Ape-Man from Java* (Dordrecht: Kluwer Academic Publishers, 1989).

PAGE 137 — "And will the Netherlands" Eugène Dubois, "Over de wenschelijkheid van een onderzoek naar de diluviale fauna van Ned. Indië, in het bijzonder van Sumatra," *Natuurkundig tijdschrift voor Nederlandisch-Indië* 48 (1889): 148–65; 165. Quoted in Theunissen, *Eugène Dubois*, 39.

PAGE 138 — "first representative" Eugène Dubois, "Uit een schrijven van den heer Dubois te Pajacombo naar aanleiding van den aan dien heer toegezonden schedel, door den heer can Rietschoten in zijn marmergroeven in het Kedirische opgegraven," *Natuurkundig tijdschrift voor Nederlandisch-Indië* 49 (1890): 209–210. Quoted in Theunissen, *Eugène Dubois*, 42.

PAGE 139 — "This being was" Eugène Dubois, "Paleontologische onderzoekingen op Java," *Verslag van het Mijnwezen. Extra bijvoegsel der Javasche courant*, 3rd quarter report, 10 (1892): 10–14; 12–13. Quoted in Theunissen, *Eugène Dubois*, 58.

PAGE 140 — "From a study" Eugène Dubois, *"Pithecanthropus erectus*, eine Menschenähnliche Uebergangsform aus Java,"* (1894) Batavia. Quoted in Henry Fairfield Osborn, *Men of the Old Stone Age* (New York: Charles Scribner's Sons, 1914), 74–5.

PAGE 141 — "This last conclusion" J. A. C. A. Timmerman, "Belangrijke palaeontologische vondsten" (1893), 312. Quoted in Theunissen, *Eugène Dubois*, 80.

— "airy speculative constructions" Rudolf Martin, "Kritische Bedenken gegen den Pithecanthropus erectus Dubois." *Globus* 67 (1895): 213–17; 217. Quoted in Theunissen, *Eugène Dubois*, 87.

— "By then, Manouvrier" Information on Manouvrier from: R. Anthony, G. Papillaut, M. Weisgerber, E. Gley, L. Lacroq, Dr. Dumont, A. Hrdlička, J. W. Fewkes, and W. Hough, "Discours prononcés aux obsèques de M. L. Manouvrier, le 20 janvier 1927," *Bulletin et Mémoires de la Société d'Anthropologie de Paris*, 7th ser., 8 (1927): 2–13; René Verneau, "Nécrologie—Léonce-Pierre Manouvrier," *L'Anthropologie* 37 (1927): 220–2; and Frank Spencer, *Aleš Hrdlička, M.D., 1869–1943: A Chronicle of the Life and Work of an American Physical Anthropologist* (Ann Arbor, Mich.: University Microfilms, 1979).

PAGE 144 — "Unhappily, the tooth" Léonce Manouvrier, "Discussion du 'Pithecanthropus erectus' comme précurseur présumé de l'homme," *Bulletin de la Société d'Anthropologie de Paris*, 4th ser., 6 (1895): 12–47; 14.

PAGE 145 – "in river banks" Wilhelm Krause, "Discussion of Dubois' Pithecanthropus erectus, eine Menschenähnliche Uebergangsform aus Java," *Zeitschrift für Ethnologie* 27 (1895): 78–81; 80. Quoted in Theunissen, *Eugène Dubois*, 82.

PAGE 147 – "Lydekker" Theunissen, *Eugène Dubois*, discusses the reception of Dubois's monograph thoroughly, see 79–117.

– "At this particular talk" Information on Keith here and later is from Arthur Keith, *An Autobiography* (London: Watts, 1950).

PAGE 148 – "It seems to me" Arthur Keith, "Pithecanthropus erectus—a brief review of human fossil remains," *Science Progress* 3 (1895): 348–69; 368–89.

PAGE 150 – "In a paper" William Turner, "On M. Dubois' description of remains recently found in Java, named by him *Pithecanthropus erectus*. With remarks on so-called transitional forms between apes and man," *Journal of Anatomy and Physiology* 29 (1895): 424–45; 425, 428–89.

PAGE 151 – "to be an anatomist" and "he has proved" O. C. Marsh, "On the *Pithecanthropus erectus*, from the Tertiary of Java," *American Journal of Science* 1 (1896): 475–83; 475–6.

PAGE 153 – "mistaking individual" Rudolf Virchow, "Commentary on Dubois' 'Pithecanthropus erectus betrachtet als eine wirkliche Uebergangsform und als Stammform des Menschen,'" *Zeitschrift für Ethnologie* 27 (1895): 744–7, 748–79; 744. Quoted in Theunissen, *Eugène Dubois*, 102.

PAGE 154 – "To maintain an apelike" The precise ratios and estimates used by Dubois changed slightly over time; this example is given as illustrative, not exact. See Theunissen, *Eugène Dubois*, 132–3 for details.

PAGE 156 – "A zoology of mammals" Gustav Schwalbe, "Ziele und Wege einer vergleichenden physischen Anthropologie," *Zeitschrift für Morphologie und Anthropologie* 1 (1899): 1–15; 3. Quoted in Fred Smith, "Gustav Schwalbe: Neandertal Morphology and Systematics 1899–1916," *Physical Anthropology News* 6, no. 1 (1987): 1–5; 2.

PAGE 157 – "I lay little value" Gustav Schwalbe, "Studien zur Vorgeschichte des Menschen" (Stuttgart: E. Schweizerbartche, 1906), 14. Quoted in Smith, "Schwalbe," 3.

Chapter 5. The Proper Study of Mankind: 1906–1918

PAGE 159 "Dragutin Gorjanović-Kramberger" Information on Gorjanović-Kramberger throughout is largely taken from Jakov Radovčić, *Dragutin Gorjanović-Kramberger i krapinski pračovjek: počeci suvremene paleoantropologije (Dragutin Gorjanović-Kramberger and Krapina Early Man; The Foundations of Modern Paleoanthropology*, trans. Ellen Elias-Bursać (Zagreb: Hrvatski Prirodoslovni Muzej, 1988).

PAGE 160 – "exemplary diligence" Ibid., 61–2.

PAGE 161 – "There are a lot" Ibid., 64.

PAGE 162 – "At quite some distance" Ibid., 21.

PAGE 165 – "And so" and "The limited perimeter" D. Gorjanović-Kramberger, "Paleolitički ostaci čovjeka i njegovih suvremenika iz diluvija u Krapini," *Ljetopis Jugoslavenske akademije znanosti i umjetnosti*, 14 (1899): 90–8. Quoted in Radovčić, *Gorjanović* 30–1.

PAGE 167 – "arrogant wind-bag" Spencer, *Aleš Hrdlička*, 422.

– "the vigorous body and mind" Keith, *An Autobiography*, 339.

PAGE 168 – "Due to the great" Radovčić, *Gorjanović*, 85.

PAGE 168 — "I was delighted" Ibid., 90.

PAGE 169 — "Your book shows" Ibid., 90.

PAGE 170 — "He appears to be" Karl Gorjanović-Kramberger, *Pračovjek iz Krapine* (Zagreb: Hrvatsko prirodoslovno društvo [preštampano iz Prirode], 1918). Quoted in Radovčić, *Gorjanović* 121–3.

PAGE 174 — "That the lower jaws" George Grant MacCurdy, no title, *Smithsonian Report* (1900). Quoted in Paul Carus, *The Rise of Man; A Sketch of the Origin of the Human Race* (Chicago: Open Court, 1900), 100.

PAGE 175 — "Dordogne district" Boule, *Fossil Men,* 189.

PAGE 176 — "An unsympathetic appearance" Maurice Barres, *L'Echo de Paris* (Paris: 1915). Quoted in M. Boule, "M. Hauser et les Eyzies," *L'Anthropologie* 26 (1915): 176–82; 178–9.

— "dilettanti, sensation-mongers" Wendt, *I Looked,* 402.

PAGE 177 — "that had been buried" Otto Hauser, "Découverte d'un Squelette du Type du Néandertal sous l'Abri Inférieur de Moustier," *L'Homme Préhistorique* 7, no. 1 (1909): 1–9; 5–7.

PAGE 179 — "Even Hauser" Wendt, *I Looked,* 410.

PAGE 180 — "a servant of German science" Marcellin Boule, "La guerre et M. Hauser," *L'Anthropologie* 26 (1915): 169–82; 171.

— "It is said" Wendt, *I Looked,* 411.

— "The scientific value" Boule, *Fossil Men* 189–90.

— "An attempt" Ibid., 281.

PAGE 183 — "disciple" Michael Hammond, "The Expulsion of the Neanderthals from Human Ancestry; Marcellin Boule and the Social Context of Scientific Research," *Social Studies in Science* 12 (1982): 1–36. Much of the analysis concerning Boule and his position on the La Chapelle-aux-Saints Neandertal is taken from Hammond's insightful article.

— "widening the path" and "agonizing problem" Marcellin Boule, "Résponse pour le Jubilee de M. Marcellin Boule," *L'Anthropologie* 47 (1937): 611. Quoted in Hammond, "Expulsion," 10.

PAGE 184 — "under his protection" Marcellin Boule, "The Anthropological Work of Prince Albert I of Monaco and the Recent Progress of Human Paleontology in France," *Smithsonian Report for 1923* (1925): 495–507; 502.

PAGE 185 — "In time" Bruno Albarello, "L'Affaire de l'Homme de la Chapelle-aux-Saints, 1905–1908" (Treignac: Editions "Les Monédières," 1987), 40.

PAGE 186 — "Thus, it was Josef" Mme. Bouyt (granddaughter of M. Bonneval), personal communication to E.T., 1990.

— "The man that" A. Bouyssonie, J. Bouyssonie, and L. Bardon, "Découverte d'un squelette humain mousterien à la bouffia de la Chapelle-aux-Saints (Corrèze)," *L'Anthropologie* 19 (1908): 513–19; 516. Quoted in Marcellin Boule, "L'Homme Fossile de la Chapelle-aux-Saints," *Annales de Paléontologie* 6 (1911): 1–64, 7 (1912): 65–208, 8: 209–279; 12–14. Italics in original.

PAGE 187 — "He also had some ideas" Interpretation taken from Michael Hammond, "Expulsion."

PAGE 190 — "the science of paleontology" Boule, "L'Homme Fossile," 270.

PAGE 191 — "From the perspective" See discussion of Boule's interpretation in Erik Trinkaus, "Pathology and Posture of the La Chapelle-aux-Saints Neandertal," *American Journal of Physical Anthropology* 67 (1985): 19–41.

PAGE 194 — "mirage of doctrines" Marcellin Boule, "Mortillet, (G. de), Evolution quaternaire de la Pierre," *L'Anthropologie* 8 (1897): 344, and "Gabriel et Adrien de Mortillet, 'Le Préhistorique,' " ibid., 12 (1901): 428. Quoted in Hammond, "Expulsion," 20.

PAGE 194   – "prepare for him" Boule, "Anthropological Work," 504.

PAGE 196   – "Keith had espoused" In 1911 (Arthur Keith, *Ancient Types of Man* [New York: Harper, 1911]), Keith presented a unilineal scheme with the Neandertals directly ancestral to modern humans. By 1912 (second edition of the same book and Arthur Keith, "The relationship of Neanderthal man and Pithecanthropus to modern man," *Nature* 89 [1912]: 155–6), he had excluded them from the ancestry of modern humans, strongly emphasizing his rogue's gallery of supposedly ancient but really modern fossils, such as Moulin Quignon.

– "came to the conclusion" Keith, "The relationship," 155.

PAGE 197   – "It was on one" Arthur Keith, *The Antiquity of Man* (Philadelphia: J. B. Lippincott, 1928), 252–3.

– "To my utter" and "The man or animal" Ibid., 255–6.

PAGE 198   – "modern aeroplane" Keith, *Ancient Types,* 143.

PAGE 199   – *"Eoanthropus dawsoni"* The most thorough and recent review of the entire Piltdown affair is Frank Spencer, *Piltdown: A Scientific Forgery* (New York: Oxford University Press, 1990); and Frank Spencer, ed., *The Piltdown Papers* (New York: Oxford University Press, 1990). Other discussions can be found in S. J. Gould, "The Piltdown conspiracy," *Natural History* 89 (1980):8–28; L. B. Halstead, "New light on the Piltdown hoax?" *Nature* 276 (1978): 11–13; Millar, *Piltdown Men;* and Joseph Weiner, *The Piltdown Forgery* (London: Oxford University Press, 1955).

PAGE 200   – "Visiting a local" Millar, *Piltdown Men,* 116.

PAGE 203   – "the best student" and "externally rather cold" Ibid., 119.

– "There seems to be" Anonymous, "The Earliest Man?" [Manchester] *Guardian,* 21 Nov. 1912. Quoted in Spencer, *Piltdown: A Scientific Forgery,* 47–8.

PAGE 205   – "an amusing heresy" Keith, *An Autobiography,* 324.

– "Of all the 'dualists,' " See Aleš Hrdlička, "The Piltdown Jaw," *American Journal of Physical Anthropology* 5 (1922): 337–47; and Aleš Hrdlička, "The Skeletal Remains of Early Man." *Smithsonian Miscellaneous Collections,* vol. 83 (Washington, D.C.: Smithsonian, 1930).

PAGE 206   – "He even argued" Boule, *Fossil Men,* 171–2.

PAGE 207   – "had, indeed, been long previously" William Sollas, *Ancient Hunters and their Modern Representatives* (New York: Macmillan, 1915), 54–5.

– "Providentially" Michael Hammond, "A Framework for Plausibility for an Anthropological Forgery" *Anthropology* 3 (1979): 47–58; 55.

PAGE 208   – "The events of the year" Arthur Keith, "Additional note to Preface of First Edition," in Arthur Keith, *The Antiquity of Man* (Philadelphia: J. B. Lippincott, 1928), xxiii.

Chapter 6. An Okapi of Humanity: 1918–1939

PAGE 213   – "Ancestor of the Monkeys" F. Ameghino, "Les formations sédimentaires du crétace supérieur et du tertière de Patagonie," *Annales del Museo Nacional de Buenos Aires* 15 (1906): 416–50. Quoted in Spencer, *Aleš Hrdlička,* 331.

– "It proved at every point" Aleš Hrdlička in collaboration with W. H. Holmes, Bailey Willis, F. E. Wright, and C. N. Fenner, "Early Man in South America,"

Bulletin of the Bureau of American Ethnology, Smithsonian Institution 102 (1912): 325. Quoted in Spencer, *Aleš Hrdlička* 344.

PAGE 214 — "Under these circumstances" Aleš Hrdlička, "Skeletal Remains Suggesting or Attributed to Early Man in North America," *Bulletin of the Bureau of American Ethnology, Smithsonian Institution* 33 (1907): 98. Quoted in Spencer, *Aleš Hrdlička,* 312–13.

— "While the scientists" Earnest A. Hooton, *Apes, Men and Morons* (New York: G. Putnam's Sons, 1937), 101–2.

— "Hrdlička had arrived" Information about Hrdlička is from Spencer, *Aleš Hrdlička.*

PAGE 216 — "Hrdlička was consumed" Ibid., 49.

PAGE 217 — "Statistics will be the ruin" M. F. A. Montagu, "Aleš Hrdlička, 1869–1943," *American Anthropologist* 46 (1944): 113–117; 115. Quoted in Spencer, *Aleš Hrdlička,* 90.

PAGE 220 — "The anthropologists" Spencer, *Aleš Hrdlička,,* 420.

— "My conviction that" Ibid., 475.

PAGE 223 — "I know that I have" Ibid., 775.

— "In time, Andrews" The story of the Central Asiatic Expedition is told engagingly in Roy Chapman Andrews, *On the Trail of Ancient Man* (New York: G. Putnam's Sons, 1926).

PAGE 225 — "It came about" Keith, *Antiquity of Man,* 383.

PAGE 226 — "His place in this tree" Ibid., 416–17.

PAGE 227 — "We have not yet found" Ibid., 417.

— "For example, in 1922" Grafton Elliot Smith, "The Rhodesian Skull," *British Medical Journal,* 4 Feb. 1922, 197–8; 197. Quoted in Spencer, *Aleš Hrdlička,* 563.

PAGE 228 — "Born February 4, 1893" Information on Dart taken from R. A. Dart, *Adventures with the Missing Link* (Philadelphia: Human Institutes Press, 1959); and Frances Wheelhouse, *Raymond Arthur Dart: A Pictorial Profile* (Sydney: Transpareon Press, 1983).

— "genius" and "Tall, ruddy-complexioned" Dart, *Adventures,* 26–8.

PAGE 229 — "I was one of those" Keith, 1950. *op. cit.,* p. 480.

— "was dead against" Ibid., 318.

PAGE 230 — "little guessing" Dart, *Adventures,* 5.

PAGE 231 — "the family typified" R. A. Dart, "The Taungs Skull," *Nature* 116 (1925): 462.

— "Professor Dart is not likely" Dart, *Adventures,* 35.

PAGE 232 — "*Speechless with half-human leer*" Ibid., 39.

PAGE 233 — "It is undoubtedly a missing link" Wheelhouse, *Dart,* 49.

— "in adoration" Dart, *Adventures,* 35.

PAGE 234 — "the greatest paleontologist" L. H. Wells, "Johannesburg: The Robert Broom Memorial Lecture," *South African Journal of Science* (Sept. 1967): 365.

— "The most marvellous aspect" Keith, *Antiquity of Man,* 199.

PAGE 235 — "In his recent" Grafton Elliot Smith, "Neanderthal Man as a Distinct Species," *Nature* 121 (1928): 141. Quoted in Spencer, *Aleš Hrdlička,* 589.

PAGE 237 — "At the Société" See Anthony, et al., "Discours," 2–13. In contrast, see Verneau, "Nécrologie," 220–2.

PAGE 238 — "I went to China" B. Bohlin, Personal communication to John Reader, 1978. Quoted in Reader, *Missing Links,* 108.

— "Pei Wenzhong" Much of the account of the excavation and discovery is taken from Jia Lanpo and Huang Weiwen, *The Story of Peking Man,* trans. Yin Zhiqi (Beijing: Foreign Languages Press, and Oxford: Oxford University Press, 1990).

PAGE 238 – "Found skullcap" Ibid., 65.

PAGE 239 – "The supraorbital" and "Dear Old Hrdlička" Spencer, *Aleš Hrdlička,* 596–7.

– "Sir Arthur Keith" Dart, *Adventures,* 59.

PAGE 240 – "an early pleistocene" Arthur Keith, *New Discoveries Relating to the Antiquity of Man* (London: Williams & Norgate, 1931), 254–5.

– "Thus in the fossil" Ibid., 292–3.

PAGE 241 – "certainly very low" Eugène Dubois, "The shape and size of the Brain in Sinanthropus and in Pithecanthropus," *Proceedings of the Section of Sciences of the Koninklijke Akademies van Wetenschappen* 36 (1933): 415–423; 422.

– "*Pithecanthropus* was not a man" Eugène Dubois, "Early Man in Java and Pithecanthropus erectus," in G. G. MacCurdy, ed., *Early Man; as Depicted by Leading Authorities at the International Symposium, the Academy of Natural Sciences, Philadelphia, March, 1937* (Philadelphia: J. B. Lippincott, 1937), 315–22; 317.

PAGE 242 – "He was an idealist" Arthur Keith, "The Creeds of Two Anthropologists," *Rationalist Annual* (London, 1942). Quoted in Reader, *Missing Links,* 54.

PAGE 243 – "But world politics" See Reader, *Missing Links;* Jia and Huang, *Story of Peking Man;* and Harry Shapiro, *Peking Man* (New York: Simon & Schuster, 1974).

PAGE 245 – "gateway of prehistoric migration" Dorothy Garrod, "Near East as a Gateway of Prehistoric Migration," in MacCurdy, *Early Man,* 33–40; 33.

PAGE 248 – "massive little mandible" Theodore D. McCown, "Fossil Men of the Mugharet es-Sukhul, near Ashlit, Palestine, Season of 1932," *Bulletin of the American School for Prehistoric Research* 9 (1933): 9–15; 15.

– "The important contrasts" Theodore D. McCown, "The Oldest Complete Skeletons of Man," *Bulletin of the American School for Prehistoric Research* 10 (1934): 13–19; 14–15.

– "entirely satisfied" and "With a wide experience" Arthur Keith, "Note by Sir Arthur Keith," in McCown, "The Oldest," 18–19.

Chapter 7. Global Thinking for Global Times: 1940–1954

PAGE 254 – "The arrangement of stones" Mary Stiner, "The Faunal Remains from Grotta Guattari: A Taphonomic Perspective," *Current Anthropology* 32, no. 2 (1991): 103–117; 106.

PAGE 255 – "absolute evidence" and "without leaving any doubt" F. M. Bergounioux, "Spiritualité de l'Homme de Néandertal," in G. H. R. von Koenigswald, ed., 1958, *Hundert Jahre Neanderthal.* Utrecht: Kemink en Zoon: 151–166; 151.

PAGE 257 – "It is interesting" A. Blanc, "The Fossil Man of Circeo's Mountain," *Natural History* 45 (1940): 280–7; 283.

PAGE 260 – "Fittingly, there was a Huxley" Much additional information about Julian Huxley is drawn from Clark, *The Huxleys.*

PAGE 261 – "affirms that knowledge" Ibid., 196–7.

– "Huxley was able" Much of this discussion relies heavily on ideas expressed in Ernst Mayr, "Prologue: Some thoughts on the history of the evolutionary synthesis," in Ernst Mayr and William B. Provine, eds., *The Evolutionary Synthesis: Perspectives on the Unification of Biology* (Cambridge, Mass.: Harvard University Press, 1980), 1–50; also see Ernst Mayr, *The Growth of Biological*

Thought; Diversity, Evolution, and Inheritance (Cambridge, Mass.: Belknap Press of Harvard University Press, 1982), 540ff.

PAGE 262 — ". . . [They] were only concerned" Mayr, "Prologue," 40.

— "Indeed, if" The presentation given here of Simpson's role in the synthesis is taken from S. J. Gould, "G. G. Simpson, Paleontology, and the Modern Synthesis," in Mayr and Provine, *Evolutionary Synthesis*, 153–72.

— "The attempted synthesis" G. G. Simpson, *Tempo and Mode in Evolution* (New York: Columbia University Press, 1944), xv–xvi.

PAGE 264 — "paleontologists, morphologists" and "it was almost impossible" Mayr, "Prologue," 42–3.

PAGE 266 — "had little use for" Joseph Birdsell, "Some Reflections on Fifty Years in Biological Anthropology," *Annual Review of Anthropology*, 16 (1987): 4.

— "I hate the word" Ernst Mayr, personal communication to E. T. (1991).

PAGE 268 — " 'sinking' taxa" F. C. Howell, "European and Northwest African Middle Pleistocene Hominids," *Current Anthropology* 1 no. 3 (1960): 195–224.

PAGE 269 — "discredit racial doctrines" and "Anthropologists fell upon this document" W. W. Howells, *Mankind in the Making*. (New York: Alfred A. Knopf, 1959), 262,

PAGE 270 — "If I had a neck" C. Loring Brace, interview with P.S., 21 Jan. 1991.

PAGE 272 — "I believe that all primate forms" Franz Weidenreich, "Facts and Speculations concerning the Origin of *Homo sapiens*," *American Anthropologist* 49 no. 2 (1947): 187–203: 189. Italics in original.

— "Perhaps it would be better" G. G. Simpson, "The Principles of Classification and the Classification of Mammals," *Bulletin of the American Museum of Natural History* 45 (New York: Museum of Natural History, 1945). Quoted in Weidenreich, "Facts and Speculations," 189.

PAGE 273 — "Homo sapiens" Ibid., 192.

PAGE 275 — "A notable exception" Carleton S. Coon, *The Origin of Races* (New York: Alfred A. Knopf, 1962), viii.

— "Judging from the responses" Franz Weidenreich, "Interpretations of the Fossil Material," in W. W. Howells, ed., *Ideas on Human Evolution; Selected Essays, 1949–1961* (New York: Atheneum, 1967), 466–72; 466–7.

PAGE 276 — "I find this work" Ernst Mayr, interview with E. T., 1990.

— "Although it must be retained" W. W. Howells, "Preface," in Howells, *Ideas on Human Evolution*, v–x; x.

PAGE 277 — "consists for the most part" Earnest A. Hooton, *Apes, Men, and Morons*, vii.

— "In order to survive" and "a long and honorable" and "a tendency to" and "a quest for a sort" and "essentially sporting" and "constricted and noncommittal" Ibid., 106–8.

PAGE 280 — "I watched Coon" Earnest A. Hooton, "An Untamed Anthropologist among the Wilder Whites," *Harvard Alumni Bulletin*, 2 Oct. 1930, 41. Quoted in Carleton S. Coon, *Adventures and Discoveries: The Autobiography of Carleton S. Coon.* (Englewood Cliffs, N.J.: Prentice-Hall, 1981), 84–85. Most of the personal information about Coon is drawn from this source or from the authors' personal reminiscences.

— "genteel, Anglo-Saxon" C. Loring Brace, interview with P.S., 21 Jan. 1991.

— "bones (physical anthropology)" Coon, *Adventures*, vii.

PAGE 281 — "a new book" Howells, *Mankind*, 347.

PAGE 283 — "Sherry was always" and "He was deeply" Lita Osmundsen, interview with P.S., 24 Mar. 1992.

PAGE 283   — "Born in 1925" Information about and quotations from F. C. Howell from an interview with P.S., 1991.

PAGE 285   — "Isolation is one" and "One of the most" F. Clark Howell, "Pleistocene Glacial Ecology and the Evolution of 'Classic Neandertal' Man," *Southwestern Journal of Anthropology* 8 (1952): 377–410, 377–8.

PAGE 287   — "incipiently classic Neandertal" F. Clark Howell, "The Evolutionary Significance of Variations and Varieties of 'Neanderthal' Man," *Quarterly Review of Biology* 32 (1957): 330–47; 333.

PAGE 288   — "It is necessary" Howell, "Pleistocene Glacial Ecology," 401.

PAGE 289   — "Proto–Cro-Magnons" F. Clark Howell, "Upper Pleistocene Men of the Southwest Asian Mousterian" in von Koenigswald, *Hundert Jahre Neanderthal,* 191.
           — "Whether the 'classic Neandertals' " Howell, "Pleistocene Glacial Ecology," 404.

PAGE 290   — "NOTICE OF OPERATION" Spencer, *Piltdown Papers,* 176–77.

PAGE 292   — "I remember writing" S. L. Washburn, interview with Roger Lewin, 1984. Quoted in Roger Lewin, *Bones of Contention* (New York: Simon & Schuster, 1987), 75.

PAGE 293   — "I am now convinced" Arthur Keith, "Australopithecinae or Dartians," *Nature* 159 (1947): 377.

PAGE 295   — "Weiner's exposure" Treatment largely taken from Weiner, *Piltdown Forgery.*

PAGE 296   — "From the evidence" J. S. Weiner, K. P. Oakley, and W. E. Le Gros Clark, "The solution to the Piltdown problem," *Bulletin of the British Museum of Natural History (Geology)* 2 (1952): 141–6; 145.
           — "It is a story" Wilfrid E. Le Gros Clark, *Chant of Pleasant Exploration* (Edinburgh: E & S Livingston, 1968), 225–6.

PAGE 297   — "Few of these cases" Spencer, *Piltdown: A Scientific Forgery,* 165.

Chapter 8. Race and Unreason: 1955–1970

PAGE 299   "a veritable passion" Yves Coppens, "Camille Arambourg et Louis Leakey ou un ½ siècle de paléontologie africaine," *Bulletin de la Société Préhistorique Française* 76 (1979) études et Travaux no. 10–12, 293.

PAGE 301   — "On July 26, 1955" William L. Straus, Jr., and A. J. E. Cave, "Pathology and Posture of Neanderthal Man," *Quarterly Review of Biology* 32 no. 4 (1957): 348–63; 350–2.

PAGE 302   — "It is probable" Boule, *Fossil Men,* 232–37.
           — "What contrast with" Boule, "L'Homme Fossile," 227.
           — "It is unnecessary" Straus and Cave, "Pathology," 358–9.

PAGE 303   — "Notwithstanding, if he could" and "must be placed" and "It seems unlikely" Ibid., 359.

PAGE 305   — "Without going into the details" and "the theory of" Henri Vallois, "The Origin of *Homo sapiens.*" Chap. 8 in "La Grotte de Fontéchevade," 2me partie, *Anthropologie.* Reprinted in Howells, *Ideas on Human Evolution,* 473–99; 477.

PAGE 306   — "a few thousand" and "The thesis" Ibid., 480–2.

PAGE 307   — "most seductive" and "is marked by" and "Fontéchevade man" Ibid., 486–7.
           — "In contrast" Henri Vallois, "The Fontéchevade Fossil men," *American Journal of Physical Anthropology* 3 (1949): 339–62; 357. Italics in original.

PAGE 308   — "corpses left on the road" Henri Vallois, "Les nouveaux Pithecanthropes et le problème de l'origine de l'homme," *La Nature* 3123 (1946): 367–70. Quoted in Weidenreich, "Interpretations," 471.

PAGE 308 — "The discovery of Piltdown" Vallois, "Origin of *Homo sapiens,*" 488.

PAGE 310 — "Somewhere in the east" Ibid., 495.

PAGE 311 — "Twiesselmann confesses now" F. Twiesselmann, interview with E.T., 1990.

PAGE 312 — "Left, above, the Polyphyletic" Howells, *Mankind,* 236.

PAGE 313 — "To me, there was something" and "For years" Coon, *Origin of Races,* viii–ix.

PAGE 314 — "My thesis is" Ibid., 657.

— "the Negroes and Pygmies" and "the Bushmen and Hottentots" Ibid., 3–4.

— "Once a race" Ibid., 660–3.

PAGE 316 — "By comparing man" Ibid., 38.

PAGE 317 — "the prime architect" and "The western Neanderthals" and "As the climate" Ibid., 532–4.

PAGE 318 — "Coon had chosen" The following account owes much to Coon, *Adventures.* Various points have been confirmed through interviews with living anthropologists.

PAGE 319 — "ex-chairman of the board" and "I told my fellow" Ibid., 334–5.

— "Soon it was rumored" and "Some, struck by" Lita Osmundsen, interview with P.S., 24 Mar. 1992.

PAGE 320 — "The Executive Board" S. L. Washburn, "The Study of Race," *American Anthropologist* 65 (1963): 521–32; 521.

PAGE 321 — "Those of you" and "Race isn't very" Ibid., 522.

— "I should like to speak" Ibid., 525–6.

PAGE 322 — "You published a review" Quoted in Coon, *Adventures,* 355.

PAGE 324 — "Brace was an iconoclast" Information and quotations taken from C. Loring Brace, interview with P.S., 21 Jan. 1991.

PAGE 326 — "One of his" Coon, *Adventures,* 204.

PAGE 328 — "Second, only one fairly complete" C. Loring Brace, "Refocusing on the Neanderthal Problem," *American Anthropologist* 64 (1962): 729–41; 729.

— "conformity to rigid type" Ibid., 731.

— "If the relationships" Ibid., 736–7.

PAGE 329 — "gentle reproof" C. Loring Brace, "Reply," *Current Anthropology* 5 no. 1 (1964): 32–43; 32.

— "Interpretation of the hominid" C. Loring Brace, "The Fate of the 'Classic' Neanderthals: A Consideration of Hominid Catastrophism," *Current Anthropology* 5 no. 1 (1964): 3–43; 3.

PAGE 330 — " 'noble,' 'handsome,' " Ibid., 5–6.

— "the evidence has undergone" Ibid., 11.

— "which sails on" Ibid., 15.

— "the only one offered" Ibid., 17.

— "The only workable definition" Ibid., 17. Quoting Aleš Hrdlička, *The Skeletal Remains of Early Man,* Smithsonian Miscellaneous Collections, Whole Vol. 83 (Washington, D.C.: Smithsonian Institution, 1930), 328. Italics in Hrdlička.

PAGE 331 — *"Neanderthal man is the man"* Brace, "The Fate," 18. Italics in original.

— "I suggest that" Ibid., 19.

— "A study like Brace's" W. W. Howells, "Comment on 'The Fate of the Neanderthals,' " *Current Anthropology* 5 no. 1 (1964): 26–7; 26.

PAGE 332 — "polemic and tendentious" J. E. Weckler, "Comment on 'The Fate of the Neanderthals,' " *Current Anthropology* 5 no. 1 (1964): 31–2; 31.

PAGE 332   – "aggressive slang" Andor Thoma, "Comment on 'The Fate of the Neander-thals,' " *Current Anthropology* 5 no. 1 (1964): 30.
            – "far-fetched" Santiago Genovès, "Comment on 'The Fate of the Neander-thals,' " *Current Anthropology* 5 no. 1 (1964): 22–5; 22.
            – "I was shocked" François Bordes, "Comment on 'The Fate of the Neander-thals,' " *Current Anthropology* 7 no 2. (1966): 205.
PAGE 333   – "those who, having read" Henri Vallois, "Comment on 'The Fate of the Neanderthals.' " *Current Anthropology* 7 no. 2 (1966): 205–8; 206.
            – "jarring a complacent discipline" C. Loring Brace, "Reply to Comments on . . ." *Current Anthropology* 5 no. 1: 32–43; 32.
            – "I expected fuss" C. Loring Brace, interview with P.S., 1991.
PAGE 334   – "We live in a cultural milieu" C. Loring Brace, interview with P.S., 21 Jan. 1991.
            – "A young archeologist, Ralph Solecki" Information about Solecki taken from Ralph Solecki, interview with P.S., 1990. Accounts of the discoveries and work at Shanidar are in: Ralph Solecki, "Notes on a Brief Archaeological Reconnais-sance of Cave Sites in the Rowanduz District of Iraq," *Sumer* 8 (1952): 37–48; Ralph Solecki, "A Palaeolithic Site in the Zagros Mountains of Northern Iraq. Report on a Sounding at Shanidar Cave," *Sumer* 8 (1952): 127–92, 9 (1953): 60–93; Ralph Solecki, "The Shanidar Cave Sounding. 1953 Season, with Notes concern-ing the Discovery of the First Paleolithic Skeleton in Iraq," *Sumer* 9 (1953): 229–32.
PAGE 336   – "Shanidar 1" Details of the injuries to the Shanidar Neandertals are taken from Erik Trinkaus, *The Shanidar Neandertals* (New York: Academic Press, 1983).
PAGE 340   – "The death had occurred" Ralph Solecki, "Shanidar IV, a Neanderthal Flower Burial in Northern Iraq," *Science* 190 (1975): 880–1; 880.

Chapter 9. Welcome to Hard Times: 1971–1983

PAGE 343   "Milford Wolpoff's is a classic" Information about and quotations from Milford Wolpoff, interview with P.S., 21 Jan. 1991.
PAGE 349   – "The appearance of anatomically" David S. Brose and Milford H. Wolpoff, "Early Upper Paleolithic Man and Late Middle Paleolithic Tools," *American Anthropologist* 73 no. 5 (1971): 1156–94; 1156.
PAGE 350   – "This work seeks" Ibid., 1156.
            – "as would have to be" Ibid., 1158.
            – "Wherever continuous archaeological sequences" Ibid., 1158.
            – "arbitrary cut-off points" Ibid., 1166.
PAGE 351   – "We propose" Ibid., 1167.
PAGE 352   – "Here we are" W. W. Howells, "Neanderthals: Names, Hypotheses, and Scientific Method," *American Anthropologist* 76 no. 1 (1974): 24–38; 34.
PAGE 354   – "The La Naulette mandible" Story recounted by Bernard Vandermeersch, in an interview with E.T., 1991. Vandermeersch believes the remark was made in a nineteenth-century scientific meeting during the discussion session.
            – "Position emission" PET scans involve injecting radioactive dyes into the bloodstream of patients. These dyes bind to areas of the brain where there is high activity and "light up" those areas on a screen that represents the various concentrations of dye as colors. This work is described in S. E. Peterson et al., *Nature* 331: 585–9.

PAGE 356 — "Vandermeersch was born" Information about Vandermeersch from interviews with E.T., Aug. 1990 and May 1991.

PAGE 359 — "Born to a Cockney" Information about and quotations from Christopher Stringer, interview with E.T., 22 Sept. 1990.

PAGE 361 — "Smith spent his" Information about and quotations from F. H. Smith, interview with P.S., 28 Mar. 1991.

PAGE 363 — "Go. Just go." M. H. Wolpoff, interview with P.S., 21 Jan 1991.

PAGE 364 — "There is absolutely no" Fred H. Smith, "The Neandertal Remains from Krapina: A Descriptive and Comparative Study." Report of Investigations Number 15 (Knoxville: University of Tennessee, 1976), 329.

PAGE 365 — "The Krapina data" Ibid., 329–30.

PAGE 369 — "to my surprise" Trinkaus, *Shanidar Neandertals*, xix–xx.

— "because of the good relationship" T. Dale Stewart, "The Neanderthal Skeletal Remains from Shanidar Cave, Iraq: A Summary of Findings to Date," *Proceedings of the American Philosophical Society*, 121, no. 2 (1977): 121–65; 122.

PAGE 371 — "Anne-Marie Tillier" Information about Tillier from an interview with E.T., 1990.

PAGE 372 — "Jean-Jacques Hublin" Information about Hublin taken from an interview with E.T., 1990.

PAGE 373 — "Günter Bräuer" Günter Bräuer, personal communication to E.T., 1991.

PAGE 374 — "But new radiocarbon dates" Radiocarbon dating is a technique that uses the deterioration of a radioactive isotope of carbon, carbon-14, as a "clock" with which to measure the time elapsed since a carbon-bearing object was alive. Thus, it provides an absolute date for a particular bone, shell, or plant, rather than simply a relative age. Radiocarbon dating was developed by Willard F. Libby shortly after World War II; techniques have been refined since then to allow greater accuracy in measurement, which permits physically smaller or older samples to be dated.

PAGE 376 — "A few preliminary" François Lévêque and Bernard Vandermeersch, "Les découvertes de restes humains dans un horizon Châtelperronian de Saint-Césaire (Charente Maritime)," *Bulletin de la Société Préhistorique Française* 77 no. 2 (1980): 35.

PAGE 378 — "the last Neanderthal" A. M. ApSimon, "The Last Neanderthal in France?" *Nature* 287 (1980): 271–3; 271.

— "an individual from" Günter Bräuer, "A Comment on the Controversy 'Allez Neanderthal' between M. H. Wolpoff & A. ApSimon and C. B. Stringer, R. G. Kuszynski & R. M. Jacobi in *Nature* 289 (1981), *Journal of Human Evolution* 11 (1982): 439–40; 439.

Chapter 10. Created in Our Own Image: 1984–1991

PAGE 385 "It was most surprising" Yoel Rak and Baruch Arensburg, "Kebara 2 Neanderthal Pelvis: First Look at a Complete Inlet," *American Journal of Physical Anthropology* 73 (1987): 227–31; 227.

PAGE 386 — "In a pivotal paper" Much of the discussion that follows is drawn from R. L. Cann, W. M. Brown, and A. C. Wilson, "Evolution of Human Mitochondrial DNA: A Preliminary Report," in B. Bonne-Tamir, T. Cohen, and R. M. Goodman, eds., *Human Genetics, Part A: The Unfolding Genome* (New York: Alan R. Liss, 1982), 157–65; R. L. Cann, M. Stoneking, and A. C. Wilson, "Mitochondrial

DNA and Human Evolution," *Nature* 325 (1987): 31–6; and Michael Brown, *The Search for Eve* (New York: Harper & Row, 1990).

PAGE 391   – "the extinction of Neanderthal" Phillip Lieberman, *The Biology and Evolution of Language* (Cambridge, Mass.: Harvard University Press, 1984), 329.

PAGE 392   – "The implications" Information in this discussion taken from: H. Valladas et al., "Thermoluminescence dates for the Neanderthal burial site at Kebara in Israel," *Nature* (1987) 330: 159–60; H. Valladas et al., "Thermoluminescence dating of Mousterian 'Proto–Cro-Magnon' remains from Israel and the origin of modern man," *Nature* (1988) 331: 614–16; H.P. Schwarcz et al., "ESR dates for the hominid burial site of Qafzeh in Israel," *Journal of Human Evolution* (1988) 17: 733–7; C. B. Stringer et al., "ESR dates for the hominid burial site of Es Skhul in Israel," *Nature* (1989) 338: 756–8; and R. Grün & C. B. Stringer, "ESR dating of teeth from Garrod's Tabun cave collection," *Journal of Human Evolution* (1991) 20: 231–48.

PAGE 394   – "Stoneking and Linda Vigilant" Information derived from L. Vigilant et al., "African populations and the evolution of human mitochondrial DNA," *Science* (1991) 253: 1503–7.

           – "In February of 1992" The discussion that follows is taken from A. R. Templeton, "Human origins and analysis of mitochondrial DNA sequences," *Science* (1992) 252: 737; D. R. Maddison, M. Ruvolo, and D. L. Swofford, "Geographic Origins of Human Mitochondrial DNA: Phylogenetic Evidence from Control Region Sequences," *Systematic Biology* (1992) 41: 111–24; and S. B. Hedges et al., "Human origins and analysis of mitochondrial DNA sequences," *Science* (1992) 252: 737–9.

PAGE 395   – "It has been estimated" For simplicity's sake, we use scientific notation here to express an extremely large number. In standard notation, 10^{250} would be written as 10 followed by 250 zeroes.

           – A. R. Templeton, "The 'Eve' Hypothesis: A Genetic Critique and Reanalysis," *American Anthropologist* (in press).

Index

Numerals in italics indicate illustrations.

Text Permissions and Photo Credits

Grateful acknowledgment is made to the following for permission to reprint previously published material:

American Anthropological Association: Excerpt from "Early Upper Paleolithic Man and Late Middle Paleolithic Tools" by David S. Brose and Milford H. Wolpoff. *American Anthropologist* 73:5, Oct., 1971. Reprinted by permission of the American Anthropological Association. ▪ *American Anthropological Association and C. Loring Brace*: Excerpt from "Refocusing on the Neanderthal Program" by C. Loring Brace. *American Anthropologist* 64:4, Aug., 1962. Reprinted by permission of American Anthropological Association and C. Loring Brace. ▪ *American Anthropological Association and S. L. Washburn*: Excerpt from "The Study of Race" by S. L. Washburn. *American Anthropologist* 65:3, Part 1, June, 1963. Reprinted by permission of American Anthropological Association and S. L. Washburn. ▪ *The Estate of Carleton S. Coon*: Excerpts from *The Origin of Races* by Carleton S. Coon (New York; Alfred A. Knopf, Inc., 1962), copyright renewed 1990. Reprinted by permission of Charles A. Coon and Carleton Coon, Jr. ▪ *HarperCollins Publishers Inc.*: Excerpts from *The Story of the Development of a Youth: Letters to His Parents* by Ernst Haeckl, translated by G. Barry Gifford. Translation copyright 1923 by G. Barry Gifford. Excerpts from *The Antiquity of Man*, vol. II, by Arthur Keith (1928). Reprinted by permission. ▪ *Harvard University Press*: Excerpts from *Ideas on Human Evolution: Selected Essays, 1949–1961*, edited by William Howells, Cambridge, Mass.: Harvard University Press. Copyright © 1962 by the President and Fellows of Harvard College. Reprinted by permission of the publishers. ▪ *Journal of Anthropological Research and F. Clark Howell*: Excerpts from "Pleistocene Glacial Ecology . . . " by F. Clark Howell. *Southwestern Journal of Anthropology*, 1952. Reprinted by permission. ▪ *Macmillan Magazines Limited*: Excerpt from "Neanderthal Man as a Distinct Species" by Grafton Elliot Smith. *Nature*, vol. 121, p. 141. Copyright 1928 by Macmillan Magazines Limited. Reprinted by permission. ▪ *Oxford University Press*: Excerpts from *Charles Darwin and T. H. Huxley: Autobiographies*, edited by Gavin de Beer (Oxford University Press, Oxford, 1974). Reprinted by permission. ▪ *The Putnam Publishing Group*: Excerpts from *Apes, Men and Morons* by E. A. Hooten (G. P. Putnam & Sons, NY, 1937). Reprinted by permission. ▪ *Jakov Radovcic, Croatian Natural History Museum*: English translation by Jakov Radovcic of excerpts from *Prehistoric Man from Krapina* by Gorjanovic-Kramberger. Reprinted by permission of Jakov Radovcic. ▪ *The University of Chicago Press*: Excerpts from "The Fate of the Classic Neanderthals" by Brace (*Current Anthropology* 5(1):3–43, 1964); excerpts from "Pathology and Posture of Neanderthal Man" by William L. Straus and A. J. E. Cave (*Quarterly Review of Biology* 32(4):348–363, 1957). Reprinted by permission.

1. Rheinisches Landesmuseum ▪ 2. Musée de l'Homme ▪ 3. Musée de l'Homme ▪ 4. H. Woodward, *The History of the Geological Society of London* (London: Geological Society, 1907), 86. ▪ 5. W. Buckland, *Reliquiae Diluvianae* (London, 1823), 274, plate 21. ▪ 6. Jean-Marie Cordy ▪ 7. Bibliothèque Nationale de Paris ▪ 8. The Natural History Museum (London) ▪ 9. Musée de l'Homme ▪ 10. Rheinisches Landesmuseum ▪ 11. Musée de

l'Homme ▪ 12. The Natural History Museum (London) ▪ 13. The Natural History Museum (London) ▪ 14. The Natural History Museum (London) ▪ 15. Musée de l'Homme ▪ 16. P. Broca, *Deuxième Congrès International d'Anthropologie et d'Archéologie Préhistorique* (1868), 395, figure 84. ▪ 17. Bibliothèque Nationale de Paris ▪ 18. E. Dupont, *Bulletins de l'Académie royale de Belgique,* 2nd ser., 22 (1866): 54, plate 1. ▪ 19. P. Broca, *Deuxième Congrès International d'Anthropologie et d'Archéologie Préhistorique* (1868), 399, figure 86. ▪ 20. W. Bolsche, *Haeckel: His Life and Work* (London: Unwin, 1906), facing 244. ▪ 21. R. Virchow, *Zeitschrift für Ethnologie* 14 (1882): 279. ▪ 22. Musée de l'Homme ▪ 23. Institut royal des Sciences naturelles de Belgique ▪ 24. La Famille Lohest ▪ 25. J. Fraipont, *Revue d'Anthropologie,* 3rd ser., 3 (1888): 152. ▪ 26. A. Hooijer-Ruben ▪ 27. Société d'Anthropologie de Paris ▪ 28. *Zeitschrift für Morphologie und Anthropologie* 16 (1914), frontispiece. ▪ 29. Hrvatski Priodoslovni Muzej ▪ 30. H. F. Osborn, *Men of the Old Stone Age* (New York: Charles Scribner's Sons, 1915), 181, figure 90. ▪ 31. Hrvatski Priodoslovni Muzej ▪ 32. J. M. Mormone and B. Henriette, *La Vallée de Cro-Magnon au Début du Siècle* (Toulouse: Ed. Loubatières, 1987), 55. ▪ 33. J. M. Mormone and B. Henriette, *La Vallée de Cro-Magnon au Début du Siècle* (Toulouse: Ed. Loubatières, 1987), 55. ▪ 34. Musée de l'Homme ▪ 35. Daniel Borzeix ▪ 36. Musée de l'Homme ▪ 37. M. Boule, *Annales de Paléontologie* 7 (1912): 93. ▪ 38. A. Keith, *An Autobiography* (London: Watts, 1950), 312. ▪ 39. The Natural History Museum (London) ▪ 40. C. Dawson and A. S. Woodward, *Quarterly Journal of the Geological Society of London* 69 (1913): 141, figure 9. ▪ 41. Smithsonian Institution Photo No. MNH 31,513 ▪ 42. Natural History Museum (London) ▪ 43. *Nature* 115 (1925): 469, copyright © 1925 Macmillan Magazines Ltd. ▪ 44. *The Illustrated London News* ▪ 45. American Museum of Natural History Neg. No. 318924 ▪ 46. Harvard University ▪ 47. The Natural History Museum (London) ▪ 48. Wenner-Gren Foundation for Anthropological Research, Inc. ▪ 49. Museo Nazionale Preistorico ed Etnographico "L. Pigorini" ▪ 50. Istituto Italiano di Paleontologia Umana ▪ 51. Reproduced by permission of the American Anthropological Association from *American Anthropologist* 49:2, April–June 1947, not for further reproduction. ▪ 52. David Noble ▪ 53. Peabody Museum of Archaeology and Ethnology, Harvard University ▪ 54. F. Clark Howell ▪ 55. University of Chicago Press ▪ 56. Musée de l'Homme ▪ 57. Musée de l'Homme; *American Journal of Physical Anthropology* / H. V. Vallois, copyright © 1949 Wiley-Liss, a division of John Wiley and Sons, Inc. ▪ 58. *Mankind in the Making,* 2nd ed., by W. W. Howells, © W. W. Howells. Used by permission of Doubleday, a division of Bantam Doubleday Dell Publishing Group, Inc. ▪ 59. Museum of Anthropology, University of Michigan ▪ 60. Ralph S. Solecki ▪ 61. Ralph S. Solecki ▪ 62. Ralph S. Solecki ▪ 63. Fred H. Smith ▪ 64. Erik Trinkaus ▪ 65. Paul Richens / The Natural History Museum (London) ▪ 66. Günter Bräuer ▪ 67. Bernard Vandermeersch ▪ 68. Anonymous. *Harper's Weekly* 17 (1873): 617. ▪ 69. André Leguebe ▪ 70. Rheinisches Landesmuseum ▪ 71. M. Boule, *Annales de Paléontologie* 8 (1913): 24, figure 99. ▪ 72. Erik Trinkaus / Musée National de Préhistoire ▪ 73. Carleton S. Coon, *The Races of Europe,* p.24 (New York: Macmillan Co., 1939), copyright renewed 1967. By permission of the Estate of Carleton S. Coon. ▪ 74. United Artists ▪ 75. Zdeuck Burian ▪ 76. Mooney's Modules ▪ 77. Erik Trinkaus / Michael Anderson / Maxwell Museum of Anthropology

A Note About the Authors

Erik Trinkaus, Professor of Anthropology at the University of New Mexico, is one of the world's leading authorities on Neandertals, having written more than one hundred scientific articles on their anatomy and evolution. He received his M.A. and Ph.D. from the University of Pennsylvania. He has also contributed to *Natural History* and *Scientific American*.

Pat Shipman, Associate Professor at the Johns Hopkins University School of Medicine, earned her M.A. and Ph.D. at New York University. Internationally known for her innovative and creative approaches to the fossil record, she has written for *The Sciences, New Scientist,* and *Natural History.* She is currently at work with her husband, Alan Walker, on a book about the mysterious species that links apes to man.